About the Autl

Roland Perry's books include biographies of Sir Donald Bradman (*The Don*) and Shane Warne (*Bold Warnie*).

Perry's non-cricket books include international bestsellers *Programme for a Puppet, Blood is a Stranger, Faces in the Rain* and *Hidden Power*, about the strategy behind the election and presidency of Ronald Reagan. He has written other biographies on people as diverse as Wilfred Burchett (*The Exile*), the espionage agent Lord Rothschild (*The Fifth Man*), and Mel Gibson.

Currently he is working on *Captain Australia*, a book about every Australian Test captain (Random House, November 2000). *Waugh's Way* is Roland Perry's thirteenth book.

Waugh's Way

The Steve Waugh story: learner, legend, leader

ROLAND PERRY

RANDOM HOUSE AUSTRALIA

Random House Australia Pty Ltd
20 Alfred Street, Milsons Point, NSW 2061
http://www.randomhouse.com.au

Sydney   New York   Toronto
London   Auckland   Johannesburg

First published in 2000
This Random House Australia edition first published 2000

National Library of Australia
Cataloguing-in-Publication Entry

Perry, Roland, 1946– .
Waugh's Way

Includes index.
ISBN 1 74051 000 3.

1. Waugh, Steve, 1965– . 2. Cricket captains–Australia–Biography.
2. Cricket players–Australia–Biography. 4. Cricket–Australia. I. Title.

796.358092

Cover photography by John Daniels
Typeset in 11/14.5pt Sabon by Midland Typesetters
Printed and bound by Griffin Press, Netley, South Australia

10 9 8 7 6 5 4 3 2 1

To Fran Clark,
who understands art, but not the art of cricket

CONTENTS

Introduction

IN THE FIELD OF DREAMS

The Waugh approach

In February 1999, Stephen Rodger Waugh was elected fortieth Test cricket captain, the most prestigious and publicised job in Australian sport. The new man had a difficult act to follow after the well-received Mark Taylor leadership of 1994–99. There had been many opposed to Waugh's accession, some of whom had preferred Shane Warne. Waugh began under fire. When Australia struggled in the West Indies in March and April, critics, such as Alan Jones, the Sydney cash-for-comment radio commentator, attacked. Waugh was 'selfish', Jones said, without meaningful elaboration.

It was a tough time as the novice Test leader came to grips with matters on and off the field. Initial team meetings were humourless, rigid affairs as Waugh attempted to impose plans and goals on the team.

According to Ian Healy, 'He didn't give the ranks any ownership of [the plans].'

That was off the field. On it, riots didn't help. Nor did poor policing of grounds where the tourists were in danger from flying bottles.

Australia scraped through the West Indies with a drawn Test and one-day series. In England for the 1999 World Cup, Australia was lacklustre. It looked a beaten unit and almost certain to be eliminated early. At media conferences, Waugh was the only person expressing optimism. Journalists took his hopeful opinions as just the expected skipper hyperbole. The captain seemed uncomfortable and stubborn. He was having trouble keeping his squad focused. His deputy, Warne, was getting beltings on the field and in the media. Warne wanted to give the game away.

Somehow, Waugh held it all together. Just when his own position as one-day leader was on the line, he produced the best pressure innings ever by an Australian in World Cup competition. It did wonders for his team and his own confidence. His demeanour shifted. His body language on the field improved.

It was the making of Steve Waugh. Australia went on to take the Cup and Waugh's short-term career as skipper in both forms of the game was assured. There were problems in a three-Test series in Sri Lanka, but the rain and his own smashed nose in a fielding collision made the nil–one loss seem more like a blip in his leadership run rather than a fundamental flaw.

By the end of the long millennium Antipodean Test summer from November 1999 to April 2000, Waugh had stamped his style on the leadership. It marked a definitive change from his predecessors, Allan Border (captain from 1984 to 1994) and Mark Taylor (1994 to 1999), leaders he had played under for almost their entire reigns. A year after taking control he had led Australia to record-winning sequences in Tests and one-day cricket. He could rightly claim to be the most successful captain of any country in history by the only measure that is definitive—the win ratio, that is, the number of victories attained compared with losses and draws. Of those who have captained Australia fifteen times or more, Waugh (seventeen games as skipper), with a 70.59 per cent win ratio, led a distinguished field of captains, including Don Bradman, 62.5 per cent, Douglas Jardine and Frank Worrell, 60 per cent, and Lindsay Hassett, 58.33 per cent.

Yearnings for Waugh's predecessor, Taylor, voiced during the West

Indies tour, evaporated over the millennium summer. Winning ratios aside, comparisons even favoured the Waugh style. Players, while having no complaints about the Taylor years, appreciated the more personal efforts of Waugh and his support.

Despite his much-appreciated diplomacy, Taylor had not gone out of his way to boost players if they were off the boil or 'down'. Taylor said it was not his style to 'mollycoddle' individuals. Waugh hardly has done that, but if a player was down or out of form, he assisted the individual privately and publicly. He did it with Warne in the World Cup. Then in the 1999–2000 series he in turn supported Langer, Ponting and Mark Waugh. Each individual responded with fine or match-winning responses to their captain's faith in them. Other players such as Brett Lee, Michael Kasprowicz and Gavin Robertson had received the Waugh style of 'pumping-up', a word of encouragement meant to lift self-confidence and self-belief. It continued during the tour of New Zealand. The fringe players particularly received the private word here, the public comment there. When the tour began, Waugh said Martyn was on the verge of Test selection again. This self-fulfilling prophecy saw the batsman perform at his peak in his one-day opportunities, especially under pressure, where a myth had built seven years earlier after he got himself out in the tight finish of a Test versus South Africa at Sydney. Near the end of the one-day series in New Zealand, Martyn was in the Test squad again. He then returned the best average (60.25 from 241 runs) in the following three-Test series.

Ian Harvey, a unique talent with a variety of deliveries and a good temperament, was used in the one-day games at the end of the fifty overs. He did well and soon felt confident at the highest level. Andrew Symonds was used at number three in the batting order and succeeded. When he was belted while bowling, Waugh didn't take him off.

Gilchrist was praised for his opening performances. Waugh said he would be the first to make 200 in a one-day. There was no qualification in the statement. It may be another accurate piece of crystal ball gazing now that the captain has consolidated the thought in the batsman's mind.

The captain dispensed with the idea of the specific 'pinch-hitter'—the late order bat used down the order to pep up the scoring. Several hitters were ready to take on the role.

Waugh goes further to help individuals reach goals—and therefore limit the 'down' periods—by working with team coach John Buchanan in setting short-term aims from day to day in games, and medium aims for future matches and a season. This constant focus on individual and team performances is meant to limit the team's lows—poor sessions, days or complete games.

It worked in helping Australia overcome the 'dead-rubber blues' when, after winning a series, it would lose the final game when it didn't count. This minor weakness was apparent under Border and Taylor. Waugh and Buchanan wanted to win those last games. Australia did so in the three series versus Pakistan, India and New Zealand. In previous seasons under former management, most observers expected Australia to lose the final match. Waugh developed a winning expectation.

As skipper, Steve Waugh also would like to iron out the other weakness—not such a minor one—of failing to make small targets in the fourth innings of a match. This too had been an alarming habit of previous teams. The way Langer and Gilchrist fought back with big hundreds in the Second Test against Pakistan at Hobart in 1999–2000 suggests it might not be a major Australian failing in the future. Australia scored six for 369, the third-highest final innings score in history to win a Test. With this boost, Australia chased medium totals of 174 and 210 in the Second and Third Tests versus New Zealand and won both with ease.

All these matters—team goals, individual aims, player support—have much to do with the psychology of leadership. Border was never one for worrying about where the players' heads were. He had a sink-or-swim mentality—a player either had what it took mentally at the highest level of the game, or he did not. Nothing, it was felt, could be done to change that. Test cricket was tough. If you weren't strong enough, then state and club cricket was for you. That singular fact kept playing at Test level simple.

Taylor, while different in make-up from Border, had a not-dissimilar, uncomplicated approach. Motivation and the hard work needed to do well were natural to them—neither had much trouble in getting themselves up for a game. Taylor was never moody and rarely introverted, even in his long form slump. He needed mental reinforcement just once, right at the depth in the 1997 Ashes tour, but then only from batting partner Justin Langer during an innings against a county. Taylor showed his courage by pulling out of it just before he was to be dumped and making a fine century in the second innings of the First Test of the 1997 Ashes. He played two Tests versus the West Indies early in 1989 before the Ashes tour of England, began wonderfully and usually played in winning teams. Taylor was a very good opening bat when he entered Test cricket and never played anywhere else. He was secure at the top level until his form slump in 1996–97.

Border, like Taylor, walked into Test cricket as a recognised champion, who only needed time to establish himself as a great player, which he did. But Waugh's experience was different. He had stumbled into the Test scene when Australian cricket in 1985 was at rock bottom. The team was criticised, even ridiculed for its ineptitude. Waugh found himself in a squad that was low on self-esteem and self-belief. They were as 'matey' as any other bunch of Aussie Test players, but the experience of being regularly hammered by other nations, continual carping from the media, and some public abuse, took its toll. Waugh wondered what he had wandered into. Because of a lack of talent or competition, he had been thrown into the Test arena without proving himself and maturing at the first-class level. He had struggled to make runs. At any other time, he would have been dropped back to the next rank. But there was no one to take his place. Waugh was young, raw and insecure. None of his leaders or selectors had confidence in him as a batsman. He was designated as a 'potential' all-rounder. This meant any skills he had were unfulfilled.

A turning point for Steve Waugh was an introduction to sports psychology, when he learned in a one-hour lecture more than he had personally gleaned in ten years. This made him aware of how much cricket—or any sport—was played above the neck. Over the years, he worked on his own mental approach. By the England summer of 1989 Australia was pulling out of its worst-ever period, thanks to Border's gritty, uncompromising leadership. Waugh had progressed to a belief that he was capable of being a top Test player. There were bumps in his career to come, but he knew in himself that he was good enough, not as an all-rounder, but as a batsman in his own right. A major part of his eventual success was formulating the correct mental approach. Hence his emphasis on it and helping his fellow players when he took over the leadership.

Another result of coming out of Australia's malaise in the mid-1980s was Steve Waugh's fierce, highly organised, almost clinical desire to win. Never again, certainly under him, would Australia be given an embarrassing drubbing by England or New Zealand, or any other team, if he could help it. Taylor, with his high-spirited goodwill and demeanour, was never quite as single-minded as Waugh or Border. He didn't experience the depressing lows of a team that had been the whipping boy of the world. Waugh's pride, like Border's, was hurt by Australia being seen as an also-ran. The early failures—Border felt them over a longer period—made them both messianically determined to put their country back on top. Border, with a disorganised rabble early in his captaincy, tended to lose his temper. It was most noticeable in New Zealand when he threatened to stand down if the team didn't improve. He didn't wish to lead a 'bunch of losers'. Border lost his cool on several occasions and so earned the sobriquet 'Captain Grumpy'.

But, thanks to Border's determination, the unflappable Mark Taylor had taken on a ready-made professional unit in 1994, well drilled and experienced enough to think they could go beyond these two runs short of a win against the West Indies in 1992–93 that Border had been denied by dumb bad luck rather than anything else.

Bob Simpson's coaching and advice had been important in Border's rebuilding. But Simpson's job was done by early 1995 when Australia, thanks largely to Steve Waugh, finally did beat the West Indies. Taylor needed an assistant, not a dominant figure beside him. He was given Geoff Marsh in 1996. Unlike Border, Taylor didn't take defeat personally. He liked the one-on-one meetings to reiterate each player's responsibility to make Australia the number-one team, and then maintain it. 'Tubby' was no-nonsense and direct.

Taylor had no trouble disciplining a player. He was very much in charge. He knew that the player would realise it wasn't personal. The personable skipper just wasn't like that. Tubby thought nothing of taking a player for a meal for a one-on-one discussion if the captain thought a batsman's technique needed adjusting or he was getting himself out too easily. If a player was doing something a little outrageous on tour that was liable to bring the team into disrepute, Taylor would book a restaurant and take the offender along for a 'chat'. It was Tubby's way and it worked.

Steve Waugh, in contrast to Border and even more than Taylor, inherited a strong, mature side that took the extra step to become the clear leader in Test cricket. He had players under him such as Warne, Langer, Ponting, Slater, Fleming, Mark Waugh and McGrath. They were fine cricketers (Ponting made the Test side in December 1995) in the first half of the 1990s under Border and Taylor, and established champions in the second half.

There had been something natural and easy about 'Tubby' Taylor when he took over the captaincy. He was unruffled and never left a media conference with an air of anger, confrontation or even minor controversy. Border was different again. He had never wanted to be captain, but his outstanding ability and never-say-die willpower enabled him to lead by example without much verbalising. He was disgusted by players who didn't give their all. He had no time for cricketers without 'ticker'. He was a minimalist captain, who may well have instructed his squad, 'Do as I do, not what I say, for there won't be too much of the latter'.

Waugh seemed uneasy when he began as captain. He tended to be defensive. Diplomatic responses did not form part of his vernacular. This was reflected in his body language on the field in the West Indies in early 1999 when he began as skipper. He didn't give the impression of being in total command of himself and his team from the start. Waugh's history as a batsman was instructive to the way he would develop as a leader. He began uncertain of his ability with the blade and worked hard on his mental approach and his technique so that he climbed into the 'over-fifty' club, that tiny group with averages in Tests of more than 50 runs an innings. Only four other Australians who had played twenty games or more graced it at the end of the twentieth century and after 123 years of Test cricket: Allan Border, 50.56; Jack Ryder, 51.63; Greg Chappell, 53.46; and Don Bradman, 99.94.

Waugh had taken seven years in and around Test cricket to grow the way he wanted to and in a manner that assured him of a permanent spot in the national XI. But he would have to develop at a faster pace to maintain the leadership. By the end of 1999 that telltale body language on the field and in media conferences was of an individual in charge of himself and his team. Waugh knew what he was doing and saying. Previous defensive responses were replaced with direct and provocative responses—good copy for journalists. He was articulating what he was thinking and scribes were asking him to comment on everything. Waugh rarely replied, 'I don't think I'll go there', or 'That's a matter for the ACB.'

On the field, he was backing his own hunches with lateral-thinking bowling changes, without gratuitous advice from others. He looked in charge. There was no scowl or pained look when a fielder made a mistake. Waugh had developed an inscrutable face, knowing that commentators, cameras, binoculars, spectators, his own players and the opposition would be searching every muscle twitch. That emotional control was evident in Sri Lanka and Zimbabwe and second nature by the Australian summer of 1999–2000.

The intimidators

Off the field, Waugh was saying things such as, 'I've had a gutful of the sledging issue,' and inviting the media to focus on Australia's good achievements. As his confidence grew, he began using words as part of psychological warfare. He sounded a little strained during the final games of the World Cup in June 1999 when he hinted a second time that the South Africans tended to choke in final games. By December after the First Adelaide Test against India, he suggested 'India would carry scars' into the next Test after its crushing defeat. Now his words seemed to carry hard prophecy.

Where Taylor eschewed confrontation, Waugh liked taking on rivals with verbal jousts on the field. His remark, 'What the fuck are you staring at?' to Curtly Ambrose in the West Indies in 1995 will go down in cricket folklore as brave or foolhardy. He enjoyed his word ping-pong with South Africans such as Hansie Cronje and Daryll Cullinan. It never affected his concentration. Waugh's comment, 'You've just dropped the match, Herschelle,' to Gibbs in the World Cup game (when the fielder dropped Waugh on 56 en route to a match-winning 120 not out) could have backfired by giving the South Africans incentive to make him suffer in defeat. It never quite did. Yet there is a problem here.

Waugh himself would probably never suffer the 'choking' tag, but he seems to have lacked confidence himself during the final throes of a very tight contest. This is a step up in pressure from, say, Waugh's brilliant innings in the 1999 World Cup. He has thrived on such moments. But there is another more telling dimension when your 'sudden-death' actions will decide the outcome of a game. In the Fourth Test of the 1998–99 Ashes at Melbourne Waugh let tailenders take the strike when he should have taken the initiative, farmed the bowling and hit the winning runs. Instead, he let Australia lose a Test. Three months later in the Third Test versus the West Indies at Barbados, he watched his opposite number, Brian Lara, in a worse situation than Waugh at Melbourne, take control, hog the strike and win the game. In a one-day match versus the West Indies on the same tour at Georgetown, Guyana, Waugh and Warne had joined each other, needing 55 to win. They batted with courage and skill to come within 6 runs of a win with one over to go. Waugh swung and couldn't connect with four deliveries. The game ended in a tie because of a pitch invasion. Waugh didn't 'choke'. Yet he struggled like the South Africans under pressure at the death.

Was he unsure of his own capacities when the real heat was on?

Waugh was intelligent in realising his own limitations early in his Test career and working within them. He didn't feel confident about batting in the number three or four 'hot seats' at the top of the order. He went for six and later slotted in at five. He batted within his means and achieved a statistical record that ranked in Australia's top five batsmen ever. But did he feel, in those ultra-testing moments when games would be won or lost by his initiative alone, that he would be performing outside his self-imposed limits? Like batting at number three, did he lack the confidence?

If so, it may indicate that Waugh is revealing his own insecurities when he uses media conferences and other forums for attacking opponents. The thirty-nine captains that preceded him resisted this approach with good reason.

A broader problem is the institutionalising of sledging and intimidation. This was seen in Australia's game-plan assessment of New Zealand players at the beginning of the tour there in February 2000, which inadvertently became public. Waugh presides over a team with three players—Glenn McGrath, Ricky Ponting, and Damien Fleming—who have taken the verbal or physical intimidation too far. Yet the captain encourages this rather than discourages it. Steve Waugh is part of the problem, having been a sledger all his career. It is the one issue that many cricket followers see as a 'weakness' or 'negative', and which time and sporting history will not judge kindly. While never excusable, such behaviour in a weaker team—such as the one Border inherited in late 1984—would be understandable. Verbal attacks coming from a sense of inferiority and frustration are common. But Waugh's players, especially the three main offenders, are all exceptional cricketers, in a team on top of the world. Waugh argues that intimidation is a factor in the winning formula. He has always used it, even in grade games. In one case Waugh gave a young grade debutant batsman such a hard time when he arrived at the wicket that the player was shattered. Waugh had been his hero. The young cricketer went home and tore posters of Waugh off his bedroom wall.

But is bullying really important in Australia's winning ways? It is such an outstanding team it may be counterproductive. Would

McGrath, the world's number-one paceman, perform at less than his best if he behaved like Allan Donald? Would Ponting's development to a point where he can challenge for the world's top batsman spot be retarded if he behaved like the current number one, Sachin Tendulkar, at the crease or in the field? Fleming is another case altogether. He is a relaxed, laid-back, fun-loving individual. Chest puffing and snarling is out of character. But when everyone around was breathing fire and urging him on, he was caught up, out of step with his own natural demeanour. Would attempting to be the tough-guy bully he could never be help his performance?

Waugh's world-beating teams are held in awe around the world. Less of the mouthing-off would give them admiration as well, and a more respected place in the history. The often-heard 'role model' argument is also important. Would it be better for young players to use Keith Miller, Richie Benaud and Alan Davidson as heroic standards? They didn't stamp their feet, verbal or chest opponents when the competition heated up. Yet they were just as tough-minded and desperate to win for their country. In fact, the lines of engagement for those players were clearer. They were effectively amateurs. Everything they did was for national glory.

The form guide

An issue that seems to be afflicting recent captains is form. The last skipper to go out at his own choice of time and near the peak of his form was Greg Chappell in early 1983. A year later he cracked 182 against Pakistan at the SCG in his last Test innings. Kim Hughes fell on his sword in December 1984 against the West Indies after averaging 10.12 runs from 81 runs. Border had slipped a little from his high standard in his last year, and he struggled to make the big scores that had come regularly before that. Border felt he had to go in April 1994, after nine years and four months of unmatched service as leader in a record ninety-three games, to allow the leadership and batting order to rejuvenate. It was an awkward time for all concerned. Taylor's form was an embarrassment for himself and the team from the 1996–97 series versus the West Indies when he averaged 17 from nine innings. This was followed by an average of 16 from five innings in South Africa early in 1997, then 31.7 from ten innings against England in mid-1997. After this kind of stretch over a year, no other player in the last fifty years would have retained his place. But Taylor was a good and popular captain in a winning team. There was little grumbling in the Test squad in that time, although later, when others began struggling, Taylor's retention was used as an excuse by players not wanting to be dropped. More problematic was the effect it had on team stability and morale. For many games Australia was effectively batting with ten men. The team felt it and opposition bowlers thrived on it. A crisis eventuated on tour in England in 1997. This, and his own unsuitability to the short form of the game, led to him losing the one-day captaincy in the home 1997–98 series, when Steve Waugh took over generalship of the shorter game.

Taylor later recovered his Test form, made that 334 not out against Pakistan and went out more or less of his own accord early in 1999. When Waugh took over he was quick to say there would be no passengers in his team. This was meant to be a clear delineation from the Taylor experience and era.

Waugh's Test statistics held firm at around a 50 average for the entire first year of his captaincy, while his one-day form was mixed. Waugh defended himself against critics calling for his sacking from the one-day team, saying he was surprised, given his and the team's record. Team coach John Buchanan said he had to stay, dismissing calls for Waugh to be preserved for Test cricket only, as Taylor and Ian Healy had.

'Steve Waugh's influence on the Australian side is very significant,' Buchanan said, 'not only for the young players but for the more experienced ones. For Australia's wellbeing, the longer he maintains enthusiasm for the job, and therefore maintains the job, then Australian cricket will be well-placed . . . he is certainly the right man for the job.'

Buchanan's words were expected. He was developing a strong, successful link with the captain. But it was overplaying it to suggest he was indispensable. Somehow Shane Warne and his inspired one-day record as skipper had been forgotten (ten wins and one loss). If Waugh did fail or become injured, Warne would again do a more than capable job. With Australia's depth in all departments, Waugh, like Taylor and Border before him, would not be missed as a player in the short version of the game. Yet the Buchanan–Waugh argument was still valid. They had a terrific winning formula developing.

Another factor delineating Waugh from the past was his attitude to one-day cricket. Waugh rates it more highly than Taylor. Where Taylor concentrated on the Tests, Waugh wanted Australia to win everything. Again, during the 1996–97 one-day series in Australia, the home team didn't even make the finals. Once more, Taylor was not concerned because his team kept winning the long version of the game. When Australia went under to England in the three one-dayers before the 1997 Tests, Taylor, as ever, was not worried. He put all his energies into the Tests. But the losses boosted England's morale and they hit the Tests running, winning the First at Edgbaston by nine wickets. Then they hung on in the wet at Lord's to see out an honourable draw. It took Australia until the Third Test at Manchester to regain the initiative.

When Steve Waugh took over the one-day side late in 1997, he changed the attitude of the team to the competition. Australia was expected to win every contest it was in. This ironclad law led to Australia's 1999 World Cup victory after eighteen months build-up under Waugh. The new attitude means that Australia will be expecting to win the World Cup of 2003.

Waugh as his own man

While Waugh would never be as relaxed as Taylor at media conferences, by the end of year one he wasn't uptight either. His confidence and humour were surfacing in the public eye. At the last 1999–2000 media conference at the Sydney Test against India, *Herald Sun* journalist Robert 'Crash' Craddock was about to ask another question when the conference was terminated. Waugh passed him on the way out, smiled and asked, 'What was that question, Crash?'

Waugh too had developed an unusual, sometimes rollercoaster relationship with the ACB. It looked a little warily in his direction for a couple years when he became an activist for players' rights. Despite his seniority over Taylor in terms of Tests played, there was never any doubt that the more diplomatic Taylor would succeed Border as captain. But events, such as Taylor's run of outs after 1996 and his unsuitability (compared to faster run scorers) to play one-day cricket, gave the ACB little choice but to select Steve Waugh as first one-day, then Test skipper when Taylor retired. After Warne's 'naïve and foolish' mistake in taking money from bookmakers for match-day information, his challenge for Test leadership was never serious, especially as his folly became public in the run-up to picking the new leader.

Election to the nation's top sporting job drew Waugh closer to the ACB. He was never going to be quite as flexible as the diplomatic Taylor, who cared little for politics and was unlikely to rock the boat. It appeared that Waugh often did not wait to hear the ACB's views on an issue before making comments himself. Yet this smacked of integrity rather than arrogance.

Success gave him the confidence to contradict his paymasters. Waugh supported Australia's umpires when they made known their grievances about being branded racist. The ACB, by contrast, was unhappy about the umpires speaking up. When Shoaib Akhtar was referred to the ICC over alleged throwing, Waugh thought there was 'nothing much wrong' with Akhtar's action. The ACB would not comment, although it was critical of the way the issue was handled. (Later there seemed to be harmony over this issue between Waugh and the ACB when he criticised the outcome of the ICC's handling of it.)

Waugh was also keen to influence selectors in their choice of players. Whereas Taylor would have made private suggestions to selectors—as was the captain's right—about players he might like in his side, Waugh lobbied subtly in public for Brett Lee: 'He would have to be considered for the squad for Melbourne.' Waugh was following a precedent set by Border. When Australia failed to polish off the West Indies in the First Test of the 1992–93 series at Brisbane, Border had remarked that 'a spinner such as Shane Warne' could have been invaluable on the last, tight afternoon. Border had had his way in the next Test at Melbourne. Warne was the match winner. Border was responsible for 'fast-tracking' Warne.

History and Waugh

Another dimension that separated Waugh from Taylor was Waugh's attitude to the game's history and traditions. Taylor branded, in good humour, Prime Minister John Howard as a 'cricket tragic' for his historical comprehension of the game. Taylor admitted his own knowledge 'began about 1970'. Waugh's study of the game goes back before Dave Gregory, the first Australian Test captain. He has an insatiable desire to understand cricket and consumes books on it. Ask him about Harry Trott or George Giffen and he'll have salient facts in his head. Waugh has devoured tomes on everyone from Trumper and Grace to Bradman and Hassett. He introduced the Joe Darling skullcaps for the Sydney Test against India at the beginning of the twenty-first century. This was no gimmick. Waugh wanted more than a symbolic link with a proud past.

Waugh encourages his players to study the past so that they can better understand the present. It's been said before that 'those who ignore the mistakes of the past are condemned to repeat them'. But Waugh's vision encompasses this and projects a bigger, more positive message. His approach is novel in an age where most young people are happy to remain ignorant of the past and be consumed by instant gratification.

When asked which past Australian captain he would have liked to have met he nominated Lindsay Hassett, the flamboyant, impish life-of-the party who played first-class cricket from 1932–33 to the mid-1950s. Hassett, a private school (Geelong College) man of the 'old school', was a brilliant stylist with the bat and one of the most popular skippers ever to lead Australia. In temperament, approach to captaincy, background, batting and even physique he is a contrast to Waugh. Does Waugh's inner self reach out for the character he admires and cannot be—at least not completely? In an *Age–Sydney Morning Herald* article in January 2000, journalist Peter Roebuck noted that Waugh liked players such as Victor Trumper, Stan McCabe and Doug Walters, 'presumably because they expressed everything he eliminated from his own game, spontaneity, inspiration and a gambler's instinct'.

This is a reasonably accurate description of Waugh the batsman changing from the 1985–1991 prototype who averaged under 38 to a player from 1993 on who lifted his career average to 50. He then worked within his limitations to make his spot in the team, and history, secure. Yet as leader, he has the opportunity to act more like his batting heroes. While being better planned than any skipper before him, he does seem intent on modifying this stolid, cautious image. Waugh has begun to be more spontaneous on the field (bringing on part-timer medium-pacer Greg Blewett to bowl against Indian Saurav Ganguly just before breaks in play in a Test in 1999–2000). Waugh was also more inclined to take calculated risks at the end of his first year by moving Adam Gilchrist up the order because he was the form batsman, and with declarations. He did not 'play safe' in the Boxing Day 1999 Melbourne Test, setting India 376 to get at 3.2 runs an over. Given that the world's best batsman, Sachin Tendulkar, was in the Indian line-up, an Australian win was no certainty. Waugh was prepared to gamble with the skills of his great bowlers.

India had the record for the highest last innings chase for a win— four for 406 versus the West Indies twenty-four years earlier—not such a long time ago that members of the Indian camp would have forgotten it. Waugh turned car salesman. It was like offering a vehicle for $19,990, with no hidden extra costs. If you could get 406 without Tendulkar, why couldn't you get it now with him against Australia? It was heady stuff for the Indians, who began batting like cavaliers intent on victory. If Waugh had offered 430 at 3.8 runs an over, even Tendulkar might have defended for a draw. In the end, India collapsed and was well beaten.

All this may mean Waugh is trying to inculcate some of Hassett's approach and spirit into his own game in order to develop into a more rounded player and leader. Being a confident captain after the successful first year, he has seized the chance to express himself more and better on the field and off it.

Steve will never be the batting stylist that Hassett was or that Mark Waugh is. But his career agenda is different. He wishes to be placed above them in the record books. Steve has entrenched himself with a batting average that places him in the pantheon of the greats of all time, and over a longer period than most. He also has the best captaincy record in Test and limited-overs cricket history.

Future Waugh

Waugh will look forward to more Test cricket to consolidate his amazing first-year gains, in which he maintained Australia at the top of the table in Test and one-day cricket with the most dominating summer ever. After that, who knows? If his troublesome groin and hamstring hold together, along with his form, he could have another few years as captain. Certainly his sights would be on leading Australia in the 2001 Ashes series in England. He would like that. Then he would have led Australia in more than thirty Tests—enough games to be able to judge his true worth as a captain.

And when it's over? Waugh would be the last one to speculate on a post-cricket career when he was attempting to establish history and records while it was on. But his open support for the Labor Party as well as the republic would see him courted by ALP leaders, perhaps as a candidate. Then there is writing and photography. He has published several diary books: Ashes 1993, South Africa 1994, the West Indies 1995, World Cup 1996, Ashes 1997 and No Regrets—A Captain's Diary, published in late 1999. He is keen to develop in this area rather than regarding it as a quick in-and-out chore for extra money. Waugh would be likely to produce more on retirement. His creative photography, an exciting hobby, seen in Images of Waugh, is likely to be pursued with vigour. Television, already stacked with ex-captains, would be wise to consider him because of his experience and exceptional application of intelligence to the game. In 2000, he was being featured as a 'super star' personality in cable television. His managers at Octagon were positioning him for an elevation.

To appreciate why Waugh has come so far and in his own highly individualised way, one may begin with perhaps the most desperate and brilliant performance of his entire cricket career. A hitherto unseen spontaneous, gambling, inspirational Stephen Rodger Waugh emerged for one mighty performance with the bat against South Africa in the '99 World Cup.

PART ONE

LEARNER

1

BANKSTOWN BOYS

Captain Courageous

Steve Waugh took his characteristic Chaplinesque strides onto the Headingley ground with Australia down for the count at three for 48 in the World Cup '99 game against South Africa. With his team still 223 in arrears, he had much on his mind as he swung his shoulders in unison and passed Damien Martyn, who had just been dismissed. Should Australia be defeated, there would be recriminations, postmortems and attempts to relieve him of the one-day captaincy. The knives had been out for Steve Waugh ever since he had ascended to Test and one-day leadership early in 1999. But not just his position was at stake. The whole policy of the Australian selectors—which was to choose specialist one-day and Test sides—was on the line.

Waugh was no slouch in the one-day game. He could hit the ball as hard as anyone and improvise in a way he rarely considered in the longer game. Yet he had scored just one century in 265 previous matches. He needed now to score his second and at a fair clip to overhaul South Africa's 271. No one doubted Waugh's fighting spirit. He was the best player for a tight spot in world cricket, especially in Test matches. If it had been a smaller target and a matter of a determined 50 to pull his country out of a hole, he could manage it. Yet something extra was needed here—a brilliant century at better than a run a ball. Only perhaps his brother Mark, Brian Lara or Sachin Tendulkar were equipped to turn such a position around in a one-day game.

Waugh had been building up to it. His form had steadily improved to this point of the competition. He was peaking in parallel with his team. He began the innings with surprising speed, not waiting to settle in. There was urgency about his play. Waugh had done his calculations. Australia faced a seven-runs-an-over battle when he arrived at the crease. At twenty overs Australia was three for 67, and the rate was still 6.8 runs an over—a figure that caused media observers to suggest the game was as good as over. Just one over of 7 or 8 runs would be considered an achievement against this powerful South African attack. Yet Australia had to do it in about twenty-five of the thirty overs to win, and not lose too many wickets along the way.

Waugh's other immediate task was to settle his partner, Ricky Ponting, who was bogged down, but with good reason. The bowling was accurate and he couldn't afford to be dismissed. It was the type of situation that caused many fine players to tighten up.

'Go for your shots,' Waugh implored him in a mid-wicket chat. 'We can't let them dictate terms. Pick the right ball and go for it.'

Ponting accepted the directive. It was an instruction to loosen up and play his natural game. Both batsmen began to strike out. The game was hardly running away from South Africa, but its captain, Hansie Cronje, thought it time to bring back his champion 'quick', Allan Donald, to slow the rate and puncture a hole in the partnership. Waugh greeted him with two smashing fours, one over the covers. It astounded Donald and brought a deeper frown to Cronje's already dark features. Waugh's fire would be hard to put out.

Waugh crashed his way to 50 in just forty-seven balls. He paused to consider all 'those little [adverse] comments [about his captaincy] and criticisms' that had been festering in the back of his hard-wired brain. There were the attacks from Ian Chappell; the clouts from English journalist Peter Roebuck; the sneers from commentators like

Alan Jones in Sydney; the calls for his head because he didn't appear to have delivered Taylor-like success from his first game at the helm.

Waugh was doing what Bradman had done six decades earlier to silence the knockers. He was leading from the front and taking a game by himself. If Australia won, there would be no argument about his tactics. He had made errors in his first months. He may even have been tactically inept at times, and he did not appear to be a 'natural' leader like Shane Warne or Ian Chappell. Yet he was a quick learner and willing to listen to advice, as long as it sat well with his own instincts.

He and Ponting belted 82 between the twentieth and thirtieth overs—8.2 runs an over, taking the score to three for 149. With an extraordinary effort, the two players had reduced the rate to 6.1 an over for the last twenty overs. The game was still South Africa's, but Australia was putting up a struggle.

When the score was on 152, Waugh, on 57, scooped a ball from Lance Klusener off his pads to Herschelle Gibbs, who moved easily towards square leg to catch it. In his excitement, Gibbs attempted to flick the ball to the heavens, only to see it spill to the ground. Waugh kept his bat grounded, recalling his deputy Warne's pre-match words that Gibbs tended to do this too quickly and could fumble the ball. Umpire Peter Willey turned down Cronje's belated request for a dismissal. Willey didn't bother to call for the video. It was not a catch. The laws of cricket state that for a catch to be taken, a fielder has to 'retain complete control over further disposal of the ball'. Gibbs hung his head.

Waugh, who had been bantering with Gibbs through his innings, tormented him by telling him his mistake had cost his team the game. Waugh, according to Cronje, had taken sledging into a new dimension. It was rare for a batsman to take on fielders in the verbal stakes: he would be out-mouthed eleven to one. Yet such was Waugh's capacity for cool brinkmanship that he would give and take at the crease, without losing concentration. It may have surprised the South Africans. Yet it was nothing new. Waugh even verballed the West Indian speedster Curtly Ambrose, causing him to breathe fire when bowling.

Waugh may have overstated Gibbs' error, but it was a turning point in the game as the batsmen continued with their fast accumulation, especially now against South Africa's 'fifth' bowler. Jacques Kallis, the normal number five, was out injured. In his place were Hansie Cronje bowling medium pace and Nicky Boje delivering left-arm spin. Seventy-nine runs were clobbered off their ten overs.

Ponting skied a catch at 174 and was on his way for 69 off one hundred and ten balls. He had done a fine job. Bevan (27 from thirty-three balls) joined Waugh and they moved along at the same pace, with the skipper dominant. Waugh slog-swept Boje for six, then repeated the shot even more effectively against Elworthy, going down on one knee and ending up on his backside with the force of his smash.

Waugh reached his century in ninety-one balls, but then Bevan chipped a catch to mid-wicket. Tom Moody came out striding like a determined giant. There were less than four overs to go and the job was yet to be completed.

'Don't worry about me,' Steve Waugh told him. 'Do the job yourself. We'll both go for it.'

It was the right directive from the skipper again. Moody was being told not to sit back but to go for his shots. He was a big hitter. That's why he was in the side. Waugh had applied the right psychology to Moody, who had played just sixty one-day internationals in twelve years since October 1987. He was being told he had every right to his chance for glory.

With three overs to go, there were still eighteen runs to secure for victory—a run a ball. Shaun Pollock then bowled a fine forty-eighth over, off which just 3 were scored. That left two overs and 15 to get.

The packed crowd was in full voice, with Australian and South African support evenly matched around the historic Yorkshire ground. Shane Warne was padded up and next man in. He didn't want to have to go out there. He grimaced and muttered, 'Come on Tug ["Tugga" Waugh], come on!'

Waugh and Moody took 7 off the forty-ninth, bowled by Donald. That left 8 to win off the last over, from Pollock. Moody took 2 off the first ball and then played an 'inside-out' shot to the point boundary. Australia needed 1 to tie, which would put them through to the semi-finals. Moody forced a single off the next ball. Waugh ran through and punched the air. The scores were level; Australia had lived to fight another game. Waugh nicked the next ball—the fourth—for a single and Australia had won. Waugh, more demonstrative than usual, held his bat high in triumph. He had scored 120 not out in one hundred and ten balls. It had been the greatest one-day innings ever by an Australian, and the best and most important innings of the '99 World Cup. It saved Waugh's one-day captaincy. He went on to lead a united team to Cup victory against Pakistan on 20 June 1999. It was a peak in his mighty career that had spanned fourteen years in international Test cricket.

Competitive crucible

Steve Waugh's steel was forged in an exceptional crucible of sporting competition in the Sydney suburb of Bankstown. His parents, Rodger and Beverley, who married at nineteen, were accomplished tennis players. They decided to put aside their sporting ambitions and instead have a family. They had four boys—twins, Steve and Mark, and Dean and Danny.

Steve and Mark were both skilled at all sports. No story about either Steve or Mark is complete without mentioning the other. They are not identical twins, but they had similar passions and aims from an early age. Yet their differences were stark. Mark was neat and tidy. Steve was messy. Mark could stand up for himself but disliked fighting. Steve was confrontational. Steve once knocked the teeth out of an opponent and had his own removed on another occasion. Mark didn't like physical contact. Steve enjoyed it, and although soccer is officially not a contact sport, it can get rough and close. He was skilled and didn't mind the attention. He looked disapprovingly on anyone who played dirty, but didn't kick back. Steve couldn't be put off his game as a youngster. Mark's character was low-key to the point that teachers worried about him. Steve was flamboyant. He liked playing up in class.

Both cared little for study, but Mark was more reliable. He did his homework on time.

The twins' parents were more supportive than pushy. Beverley became their taxi driver, adviser and supporter, organising and ferrying them to games. Perhaps even more important in their development was their rivalry in endless, sometimes fierce contests at home, in the street and in the park. In cricket, both wanted to bowl out or smash the other. Had one twin been gifted and the other not, their development would not have been as fast. Where Don Bradman had the brick base of a water tank to hit a golf ball against, the Waugh twins had each other. Yet like all future and would-be champions, they also practised solo. They would steal their mother's stockings—not to cross-dress, but to suspend a tennis ball from a garage roof, which they hit, endlessly.

'I think that was one of the things that helped me improve my cricket,' Steve told Mark Gately in his book on the twins, *Waugh Declared*, 'Just hitting the ball into the roof non-stop made you play straight.'

When they began to play in teams, coaches noted their ability when they were just nine years old. A year later they won a local under-twelve double wicket knock-out competition against twenty other pairs of boys. At age eleven in early 1977, Mark was captain and Steve vice-captain of the New South Wales Primary Schools team that won the national cricket carnival undefeated. The boys were the all-round stars for the team and they combined in one partnership of 150, a rare achievement in that age group.

Both played other sports, particularly tennis and soccer, and they showed the same capabilities. Yet as they grew up cricket became their first choice. At one point their parents wanted to nudge them towards tennis, but the boys chose cricket. Between the ages of thirteen and sixteen years, their commitment and aggressive outlook saw them as dominant players in the Moore, Watson and Green Shield representative teams, in which they played until the age of sixteen. Coaches let them develop more or less by themselves, with only marginal suggestions about general play. No one took either aside and tried to improve their techniques. They would adjust certain aspects of their games as they progressed. If a quick bowler troubled them outside the off stump, they would learn to be more circumspect with cuts early in an innings; if a spinner tied them up, they learned to skip down the wicket to take control. Steve and Mark were so self-confident that any challenger would be soon sorted out. (This mentality stayed with them right through the ranks, although the time taken to meet obstacles, such as the West Indian pace men, would vary.)

In those early teen years, their characters began to come through in their techniques. Mark was more orthodox and stood up straight like Greg Chappell, one of his heroes. He stroked and caressed the ball, and preferred to work his shots through the field. Steve cared little for technique. He liked to belt the ball. He took more risks and was less orthodox. Yet comparisons of their run rates disclosed no discrepancy between the two. They both got on with the business of scoring.

As they advanced in under-age competitions, Steve's leadership talents were more apparent than those of Mark. Steve, while not demonstrative or forceful of personality, was more inclined to take charge. Mark was an individual with clear thoughts on how the game should be played and won. He was no less a thinker on cricket but kept his thoughts to himself unless asked. He was comfortable about being led by someone else, even his twin. Steve became the team captain.

'I tried to let him run the team,' coach Ian Mill said. 'I just advised him. He had the knowledge to set fields and make his own decisions. Steve captained aggressively. He read the game and made changes accordingly. If he were unsure, he would ask me.'

Mill confirmed what others were noticing: the twins' differences in technique were apparent at the age of fifteen or sixteen.

'Steve had a great eye, which made up for his less impressive technique. He was more aggressive. Mark was more textbook. He liked to work and guide the ball. However, they both had all the shots. They exploited the weaknesses in opposition bowlers.'

Their insatiable desire for the game saw them playing with their junior club in the morning and then grade cricket for Bankstown in the afternoon—a long day of eight hours playing time.

At fifteen years in the 1980–81 season, Steve scored more than 1500 runs, including four unbeaten centuries of five in all, by January 1981 in Green Shield and grade cricket. Steve seemed only to have a forward gear, with a desire to go after the bowling from ball one. In a game against Waverley in the Green Shield, he scored 143 in 100 minutes (96 in boundaries), then took five for 45 and seven for 126. The twins were playing fourth grade for Bankstown and Steve averaged 104. He was criticised for his aggression and missed out on the New South Wales Under 15 squad after he had scored most runs in the competition. Mark was selected. The twins' father was annoyed and approached the coach and selector. He was told Steve had scored his runs 'too quickly'. They didn't like his hard-hitting style. Like the young Don Bradman, Steve wasn't copybook early in his career. Yet again, similar to Don, Steve got the job done—scoring copiously and fast enough to win matches—perhaps better than any of his junior peers in the state of New South Wales.

Steve, who had not seen videos of himself, could not understand the selectors' thinking. And if he had been able to see himself in action, it's doubtful that such a creative batsman would comprehend the problem. If he could handle anything bowled at him and win matches, where was the problem? The intransigent thinking of selectors upset him. (Steve Waugh still hasn't forgotten what he saw as a slight.)

Notwithstanding this setback, overall Steve looks back on those formative times as his 'golden years', when he scored runs in the morning and afternoon. The game was enjoyable and without the pressures that would come as he slipped up the grades to the top of club cricket in Sydney. In all, Steve had forty-eight innings in lower grade cricket—seconds, thirds, fourths and fifths—scoring 1463 runs at an average of 40.63. He took forty-one wickets at 15.34. He also had sixteen innings in the Green Shield for an average of 42.15, and took twelve wickets at 19.59. In the Poidevin-Gray Shield he had fourteen innings—average 31.08—and captured seventeen wickets at 15.76. These were encouraging, if not outstanding figures. Few would have seen them as indicators of a great Test career. What couldn't be measured was Steve's tremendous determination and strength of mind. These characteristics, if ever calibrated, would have pointed to bigger things than the statistics could foretell.

Despite being bitter about missing out in the Under 15 state selection, the following year Steve began working on his defensive technique. He was chosen in the New South Wales Under 16 side. His more varied style was vital when facing the higher standard of bowler in this and in grade cricket. At seventeen both twins made the Australian Under 19 side, which played Sri Lanka.

In the early 1983 Adelaide 'Test', Mark hit a century. Steve, batting at number six, made 55. In the Melbourne game, Steve demonstrated the sheer force that was the hallmark of his early career as he smashed 187 off only 216 deliveries. He also took eight wickets and eight catches.

When he was eighteen during the 1983–84 season Steve had several big innings that marked him as a future first-class player. He scored 200 in the Schoolboy Carnival; 170 for New South Wales Combined High Schools against Great Public Schools; and 161 in a sixty-over match in the Australian Carnival.

But it was his performances in Sydney first-grade cricket during the 1983–84 season that forced New South Wales state selectors to take notice of Steve Waugh. Playing for Bankstown, he smashed eight fours and eight sixes in 127 (in 95 minutes of power hitting) versus Sydney University; 110 and five for 50 versus Waverley; 68 and two for 20 versus St George; 92 not out and two for 23 versus Western Suburbs; five for 40 versus Petersham; four for 75 versus Balmain; and 38 and six for 53 versus Sydney.

At about this age, the twins discovered vices. Mark liked a bet, and later, especially when he had big money, became obsessive. He may not have been the gambler when batting, but a contradictory trait in his nature emerged when it came to betting at the trots or the races. Later he would play roulette and blackjack at casinos. Mark would be seen at Randwick or anywhere putting bets on, not only at the track he was at, but at all the tracks around the country on that day. Yet this was the extent of his revelling. He didn't have a girlfriend and he didn't care much for booze, just a beer to two to relax. Mark didn't like to experiment with how he would behave when intoxicated. He liked being in control, which was in keeping with his fastidious, neat side.

Steve could take or leave betting. He didn't care for losing and looked after his money. Yet he loved a drink. And when he first embraced alcohol on those Under 19 tours for state and country, he, like countless teenagers before him, was excessive. There were juvenile stories about 'chundering'—in hotel rooms, even on the cricket field the morning after a binge. Steve was at ease for a time with being somewhat of a 'legend' for experimenting with booze.

During this formative late-teens period, Steve had to make a choice between soccer, which promised a possible future for him, and cricket. It was a tough decision. He loved his football and was talented. Most observers at the time considered he could play for Australia and perhaps professionally in England.

Croatia in Sydney gave him an ultimatum: give up cricket and he could play first grade soccer. Steve gave up soccer. Mark, meanwhile, chose cricket over tennis.

The players against whom the twins were now pitted in cricket were all likely to go on to first grade at least and Test level at best. It was a time when abilities were sorted out. Some players' techniques failed. Others' readiness to face real fast bowling was found wanting.

Steve fine-tuned his style and stroke play. He and Mark were part of an unusually strong group that reached the end of high school in 1983. Among them were opening bat Mark Taylor, paceman Brad McNamara and off-spinner Gavin Robertson. McNamara was alarming. Steve had never faced anyone as quick—a player who could blast him and his brother out with sheer speed.

Both twins sat for the Higher School Certificate but were not interested in anything academic or any profession. They only ever wanted to play sport and earn a living from it. People probed the boys about what they were going to do with their lives. 'Play cricket for Australia' was the reply.

In 1983 Steve fell for Lynette, an attractive brunette with a neat figure, who was also eighteen and attending the local sister school, East Hills Girls. Both the twins were pathologically shy when it came to girls.

They didn't date and were absorbed and obsessed with sport, which usually precluded women. No young woman they knew could play anything as well as they could. They lived in a 'blokey', sporting world that by its nature was womanless, apart from the jokes, the locker-room talk and ogling. It was a major effort for Steve to ring Lynette after being introduced at a school dance. Her reaction didn't help his demeanour.

'Steve who?' she asked. The reticent, handsome lad had had no impact. Lynette, however, appreciated his shyness and the courage it must have taken to call her. They went to a school formal and changed at a friend's house for a party afterwards. Steve lingered, wanting to watch a day–night cricket match. Lynette said she hated cricket and was not impressed.

Soon afterwards Lynette had a cousin and his wife over for dinner and they met Steve. They asked the eighteen-year-old what he was going to do for a living.

'Play cricket for Australia,' he replied in a matter-of-fact manner without a hint of bombast.

The others fell silent and thought he was a dreamer. But Lynette was impressed. She realised that her new boyfriend was different and ambitious. She sensed a certain depth and strength. Later Lynette came to appreciate cricket and why it consumed Steve. And she soon had an impact on him. His dress sense improved and his shyness was less obvious. He opened up to her more than anyone else. She had a settling effect on a young man in a hurry. Lynette, bright and mature for her age, was just right for his ambitions. She would be there with a sensible word of comfort in the down times, and a levelling influence when he touched the heady heights of fame. Not that Waugh ever got carried away. He was too busy concentrating on where he was going to become arrogant or self-centred.

After finishing secondary school, Steve enrolled in a course at Milperra Teachers College, but only lasted a couple of lectures in drama and music, which were not for him. He gave up, despite his mother's and Lynette's protestations. He went on the dole for three months, joining the ranks of the unemployed as Don Bradman did briefly fifty-five years earlier in 1929. The difference was that Bradman had to find a job, whereas Steve Waugh in 1984 could make a living from cricket alone, if he made Test cricket. Steve tried his hand at indoor cricket umpiring but disliked the abuse. He also joined a work gang for the Bankstown Council, but the slack approach of fellow workers irked him.

State start

Steve Waugh's plight was temporarily saved by making the New South Wales state team at nineteen years of age in the 1984–85 season. Steve's first Shield game was against Queensland at the Gabba. He batted at number nine, but with O'Neill retired hurt he entered at six for 284 and added 44 with keeper Greg Dyer for the seventh wicket. He got a bowl first-change with his medium-pacers in Queensland's innings. Steve was used as a brake, rather than someone who would break through. He bowled economically, taking none for 34 off twenty-three overs with twelve maidens. It was enough for him to get the nod for a second Shield game versus Tasmania at Newcastle in early January 1985. He failed with the bat, scoring 4 and 2, but, bowling second change, he snared his first first-class wicket, taking one for 58 for the match.

It wasn't enough to get a third successive match and he was dropped for a game against Victoria at the Melbourne Cricket Ground. He was back in for the next game against Queensland but scored a duck and didn't get a bowl. The selectors thought about dropping him again, but his fielding impressed them so much that he was retained for his fourth match, versus Victoria on the Sydney Cricket Ground from 1–4 March. His temperament matched his aggression and he hit a near-faultless, fluent 94. His adventurous cutting came off and he also drove splendidly on both sides of the wicket. Selectors now had real proof that they were onto a potential champion. Greg Matthews, his partner in a 178-run link, waxed lyrical about his style and ability.

Steve was lucky to be selected for the final versus Queensland, when Geoff Lawson pulled out injured at the last minute. Queensland batted first and scored 374. The New South Wales bowling was dominated by Imran Khan and Dave Gilbert, who took seven wickets between them, but Waugh chipped in with the wicket of keeper Ray Phillips when he was 50 and set. Waugh came to the wicket at number eight— he was being viewed as an all-rounder at this level—and hit a cool, stylish 71 in New South Wales's 318. Queensland collapsed for just 163 in its second innings thanks mainly to Imran Khan taking five wickets. In a thriller, New South Wales was left with a 220-run target to win. It was six for 140 when Waugh arrived at the wicket. He was nervous, but still thrilled to be playing in a Shield final in his first season. He played his 'natural game' and hit 21 in a 33-run partnership with Peter Clifford, who was holding up one end. At 173, Rackemann had Steve caught. A last-wicket stand by Clifford (83 not out) and Gilbert allowed New South Wales to sneak in by one wicket.

It was a terrific experience for Waugh, who played his part in New South Wales's Shield victory with good batting, steady bowling and brilliant fielding, including two catches.

'This boy has what it takes,' Bill O'Reilly declared in his newspaper column after watching the final.

In his initial first-class season Steve had seven innings and scored 223 runs at an average of 31.85 with a top score of 94. It was a fair beginning. Then Kerry Packer stepped in when Waugh was playing in the 1985 season for Essex Second XI and smashing centuries against mediocre opposition. Packer wanted to stop Waugh and four other young players joining the rebel tours to South Africa, where 'mercenaries' were defying international bans and being excluded from playing for their country. Waugh didn't know what was happening. Packer's representative in England explained that any deal with Packer meant he wouldn't be allowed to go to South Africa. Waugh signed a three-year contract eagerly. He hadn't been approached to play there and didn't expect to be. The annual five-figure income alleviated Steve's immediate money worries. He could concentrate on cricket, thanks to Packer's largesse and forward thinking.

Waugh had to pinch himself. It was like being on a lucrative sports scholarship, except that there were no strings attached. All he had to do was collect the cheques. Still in his teens, Waugh could see his dreams coming true. He attended a motivational course at eighteen, which he bought from New South Wales and Australian spinner Murray Bennett. It asked him to set ten life goals. His list included playing for Australia, getting married, building his own house and keeping the many mates he had made, mainly from sport. The course encouraged him to write critically about his cricket. He analysed every game he played. After a year he was to become bored with this exercise, but it was an intellectual awakening of sorts. Steve Waugh was a 'doer'—an action-oriented sportsman—but he was a thinker too. (Less than a decade after setting out his 'life goals', Waugh discovered the list. He had achieved them all.)

Steve's professional stint with Essex's Second XI in 1985 pushed him ahead of Mark, who had opted to play as an amateur for Bolton League club Egerton, which was a rank lower. In one fifty-over game for Essex Under 25 against Sussex, Steve smashed 200 not out from 300 balls. He was more mature in cricketing terms than his brother. Mark was always a more elegant player with style and grace, but early on was not quite sure where he should bat.

Steve was more inwardly and outwardly determined. He had become a tougher character, more organised in his mind about what he was doing and where he was going. Steve knew where he wanted to bat. Even early, if a fast bowler tried intimidation, Steve was vocal in return. He even baited bowlers and fieldsmen when at the crease. He was always a sledger, who didn't care if he received abuse when batting. He could outsledge the opposition and still perform at his best. He learned that intimidation could unsettle opponents, especially younger, sensitive players. Steve's attitude was steadfast. If they couldn't take it at grade or state level then they wouldn't be going anywhere anyway. Why not 'give 'em heaps'? He never comprehended that others played the game without his drive and aims. Steve could only gauge others by his own inner forces. He despised 'weakies'. He figured that you couldn't make it into Test cricket if you were in any way soft, or perceived that way.

2

THE TEST DOOR OPENS

A stuttering start

Australia's destruction by the West Indies in 1984–85 and England in 1985 saw selectors attempt to blood youngsters in a new team that would climb out of the slump. Tasmania's David Boon had been chosen. Western Australia's Geoff Marsh was brought into the Test team for the first of a three-Test series against India in mid-December 1985. Steve, now twenty, was selected for the Second Test. It was at the MCG, commencing on Boxing Day. He felt rushed. Just eleven state games were not an ideal preparation for the big time. At first he was chosen to replace Robbie Kerr, the twelfth man in the First Test. He expected to be the drinks waiter. But a Test-eve injury to Greg Ritchie pushed Waugh into the XI. Father Rodger would have liked to be there to give support to his twenty-year-old son, but he had planned to watch Steve's younger brother Dean play at Hawkesbury near Sydney on the first day of the Test. It was too late to rush down to Melbourne. Rodger and Beverley had to be content with nervously listening on the radio. Rodger booked a flight for early on day two, 27 December.

The circumstances of Steve's debut were not conducive to a first-up success. The side had reached the lowest ebb ever in post-war cricket. The Australian team was going through a malaise. Confidence had all but evaporated. Since 1983–84, which saw the end of the Chappell–Lillee–Marsh era, Australia had been belted in two series by the West Indies at home and abroad, and once by England in 1985. Even New Zealand, advantaged by the formidable bowling of Richard Hadlee, had scuppered it two–one in a humiliating series in Australia just before the Indian Tests. Only Allan Border, the captain and the finest rear-guard fighter Australia ever produced, could feel that his place was safe. He had been a reluctant successor to Kim Hughes, who had resigned during the 1984–85 thrashing by the West Indies in Australia. Border was not happy at presiding over a losing team. He had tasted victory when the side was good. Border never accepted losses well. He was gritty and played to win, or at least not be beaten, and he was disgruntled at having to lead a team that enjoyed few wins. The media didn't help. It wanted to feed the nation news about Australian superiority. It sold papers and lifted ratings. Losers were bad for business. Attendances were falling in proportion to Australia's decline as a cricketing power.

There was a nervous, uninviting atmosphere surrounding the national side. Everyone was looking out for himself. Waugh was thrilled to be selected but scared. He felt inadequate. The unfamiliar feel of the mighty MCG—more of a colosseum than a beautiful cricket ground like Adelaide or Sydney—was intimidating. There were hurried media interviews. This also was new to him. He was uneasy. All he wanted was to play cricket, not answer endless mundane questions.

The new man received no help or guidance, just notification of how to pick up his baggy green cap and get to the team hotel. Border was laconic and undemonstrative, not the type to go out of his way to settle down a first-gamer. There was no encouragement, no taking the new-comer under his wing, no instruction. Border was not a nurturer like Benaud before him or a natural communicator like Taylor after him. He maintained an unapproachable disposition and led by example. Other fellow New South Welshmen in the Test team, Dave Gilbert and

Greg Matthews, were more forthcoming on Christmas Day before the Boxing Day game. They guided him and told him not to worry. But he did. Young Steve was way out of his depth and uncertain how to behave. He was introduced to one-gamer Geoff Marsh, who was feeling nearly as insecure as Waugh after making 5 and 2 not out in the First Test at Adelaide. They were both reticent, unassuming characters.

The agony and the agony

On edge, Waugh waited in the dressing room as Australia batted after Border lost the toss. The tyro was batting at number six. Wayne Phillips and David Boon opened and were both out with the score at 26. The dressing room became unsettled. When Border was out next for 11 at 41, it went dead cold. Not even Greg Matthews was ebullient. Marsh batted at number three. He dropped anchor and let David Hookes do the scoring.

Lunch came and went. Waugh was not hungry. Soon after lunch Ravi Shastri bowled Hookes. Australia was four for 90, not an ideal score for a debutant to enter the biggest stadium in the country, watched by 40,000 spectators and millions more viewers in their living rooms. Waugh's butterflies began. He felt awkward and uncertain as he walked out to face the experienced Shastri, who was bowling, and batsmen Gavaskar and Vengsarkar in the field. Between them they had played for thirty years at this level. Waugh felt he had no right to be competing with them. His inadequacy weighed on him. He had scored just two first-class centuries and they had come recently—107 versus Tasmania at Hobart in late October and 119 not out against South Australia at Sydney in mid-December. These two scores had influenced the selectors and got him a Test spot, more on a hope and a prayer that he could run this sort of form into Test cricket than on proven substance. Waugh, being a realist, knew he had not earned a place at the Test table. The thrill of being selected had blown away. It wasn't a pleasant moment.

The wicket was turning. He pushed and probed, scratching together 13, while looking the novice.

Sivaramakrishnan put him out of his misery and had him caught by Kapil Dev. Waugh returned to the pavilion with mixed feelings. He would have liked to reach 30 or 40. At least the ordeal was over. Australia scraped together 262, thanks to a fighting century by Matthews.

India batted steadily and passed Australia's score with six wickets in hand. Border saw the young Waugh as a useful change or surprise bowler. He had experienced his occasional burst of pluck—a well-directed bouncer—in the nets. The skipper tossed the ball to him when all the front liners had failed to break a partnership. Waugh felt far more at ease bowling. He delivered no half-trackers or embarrassments. On the contrary, his fierce drive and confidence surfaced. He bowled accurately without penetration. Yet there was zip in his quicker ball and guile in his slower one. He beat Shastri on 49 with a swinging delivery and had him caught behind by Phillips. The team embraced and congratulated him. For a moment he felt wanted. He made Border smile. Perhaps he was okay at this level after all. That feeling returned, fleetingly, when he also had the wicketkeeper Kirmani caught behind. India made 445 and Waugh took two for 36 from eleven overs with five maidens. It was an encouraging first-up effort. Only paceman Bruce Reid, with four for 100, did better.

In Australia's second innings, Waugh saw up close for the first time a great cricketer in his element. Border, in a stubborn, backs-to-the-wall knock, scored 163 out of a total 308, saving the team from a humiliating innings defeat, a rare event for the home team in a century of cricket on the MCG. Waugh could see the resolve and iron in Border before he went out to bat, and briefly at the wicket with him when he contributed just 5 before Shastri bowled him. Border was an authentic Aussie hero, someone you would like in the trenches with you. He was never beaten—a battler with whom the spectators related. He could be relied on. Australia was never defeated while Border was alive at the crease.

Border's mental approach became a yardstick for young Waugh.

Even though he could not get close to Border, he related to his attitude. They both hated coming second. Other players might be happy-go-lucky and roll with the punches. These two wanted Australia and themselves to be on top—all the time.

Waugh was not going to be dropped. Australian selectors had no options, such was the lack of talent in the mid-1980s. There would be no immediate pressure on his spot in the team, which was both good and bad. On the good side, it meant he could settle in to Test cricket without competitive threats. The downside was a fact he realised himself. In a perfect build-up to his career, he should have had another two, even three seasons playing Shield cricket to solidify his development and confidence. Steve Waugh wasn't really ready for Test cricket, and he knew it.

His second Test at Sydney a few days after his first confirmed this. He scored 8 and 0, and took no wickets for 33 off seven overs in a game where India climbed all over the Australians without winning the match. The visitors had been on top throughout the game with superior batting, bowling and fielding.

Waugh did better in one-day cricket, but in the mid-1980s this competition was regarded as a giggle and hit sideline designed for television. Test cricket still reigned supreme, although more enlightened administrators knew that the short version was the game's financial saviour. Yet the crowds loved the one-day game, even if not all the players did. Top Test cricketers still made disdainful remarks about it. Waugh handled the different pressures of the short game well, and this helped his Test reselection.

Vital signs

Waugh accompanied Border's team to New Zealand in February and March 1986 for a three-Test series and a one-day competition. In the First Test at Wellington, batting at number seven behind Greg Matthews, he flopped for the fifth successive innings, scoring 11. He was only given four overs when New Zealand batted. The game was curtailed by rain and fizzled to a draw that didn't see two innings completed. Waugh had scored 37 runs from five knocks. His average would have embarrassed a tailender. In any other era, the twenty-year-old would have been sent back to his state for a period of consolidation.

In the Second Test at Christchurch Waugh padded up again, once more at number seven, a sure sign that the selectors had dwindling confidence in his batting capacities. Hadlee was in fine touch, and had ripped out four of the first five batsmen, bringing Waugh to the wicket to join his skipper. The score was five for 74. If Waugh failed this time, he would be out the door.

While Border kept the scoreboard ticking over, Waugh worked his defences and stayed there, inspired by Border's single-minded, fierce focus. They engaged in a century stand. Waugh reached a half-century, his first major milestone in Test cricket. He was not on top of the bowling, yet as he passed 70 he had thoughts about reaching a hundred. Hadlee came back and ruined that flirtation by trapping him lbw when he was on 74. He and Border had put together 177 well-grafted runs. Border went on to 140 and Australia 364. Waugh felt relief. He had broken through a barrier of self-belief. For the first time, he had earned his place as a batsman, both in his score and in a game-saving partnership with his leader. Waugh was not about to break open the champagne, but it was a step forward.

His confidence was up and it showed in his expression and step. Border rewarded his performance at the batting crease by tossing him the ball earlier—first change after a few overs—and for longer bursts. Waugh tore in with renewed vigour and broke through early, having John Reid caught behind by new keeper Tim Zoehrer. Waugh was used as a partnership breaker when he had New Zealand skipper Jeremy Coney caught by Reid for 98. He helped himself to two more wickets in the tail and finished with the excellent figures of four for 56 off twenty-three overs with six maidens—the best effort of the Australian bowlers. Waugh wasn't yet up to regular Test standard with either bat or ball, but his returns in these games gave the selectors arguments for retaining him. Border (114 not out) once more saved a stumbling batting effort. Waugh (1) failed again in another draw.

At Auckland nine days later, Steve Waugh found himself coming in at number eight—behind Tim Zoehrer—when the score was six for 293. He managed just 1 before being caught. It wouldn't have mattered much if he had batted on. The tail collapsed and Australia reached 314 (Marsh breaking through with 118). New Zealand replied with 258, Waugh chipping in for one wicket late in the innings. Off-spinner John Bracewell ran through the Australians in the second innings, taking six for 32 out of a miserable total of 103. Among his victims was Waugh (0), who seemed inept at handling the spinning ball. New Zealand grabbed its chance and went on to win by eight wickets.

Border was disgusted with his team's overall performance in the series. He threatened to resign unless Australia won the one-day series that followed. 'I've said everything I can to that bunch,' Border blurted out after the Test. 'If they don't know how I feel, they never will. The guys should be hurting pretty bad, because Test careers are on the line.'

He didn't specify who, but none of the other ten players, including Waugh, had a secure Test spot. It was a new, struggling squad, but Border was upset. New Zealand had always been the easy-beats across the Tasman—a team at times barely up to Test standard. Now the Australians were even lower than the Kiwis. Border hated leading a side that was being branded as losers.

'You can stick with blokes for so long,' Border added. 'I'm basically leaving it to the players. They are going to show whether they really want to play for Australia and whether they really want to play under me. It's reached a point where if we continue to lose, you've got to let someone else come in and see if they can do something different ... The fellas are not responding to me. The enjoyment level has gone out of it.'

Australia only managed to draw the one-day series two all. But Border withdrew his resignation threat.

This was the lowest point for Australia in more than a century of international cricket. And Steve Waugh was right in the middle of the horrors and bad atmosphere. It was a feeling he would never forget.

Second tour

Steve Waugh was selected to tour India for three Tests in September 1986, with a batting average of 12.50 from nine innings in five Tests. It was the poorest batting record of anyone ever selected to tour with an Australian squad. His 1985–86 first-class figures—twelve innings for an average of 37.8 with two centuries—were not of much assistance. Nor was his bowling. Most Australians taken on tour for their batting would normally have solid averages around fifty in first-class cricket. Yet no one among the newcomers was doing any better. The selectors had little choice but to send the best they had, and hope.

Waugh was little more than a passenger in the three Tests played. In the First at Madras he scored 12 not out and 2 not out and looked on in awe and admiration as Dean Jones scored 210 in oppressive 40-degree heat that could have killed him, while Boon notched 122 and Border 106. Waugh took one for 44 and none for 16 in the game, which became the second tied Test ever. Waugh at least had been part of history. This was one of the most exciting Tests ever played. Team manager Bob Simpson said it was even more dramatic than the Brisbane tie against the West Indies at Brisbane in December 1960, in which he had played.

Waugh scored 39 not out and took one for 29 in the drawn Second Test at Delhi, a game ruined by the weather. In the Third Test, also drawn, he took none for 41 and was bowled for 6, giving him a quaint average of 59 for the series.

Australia left India with the consolation of not being disgraced, which was an advance on the past five series. It had also shown some real fight, another improvement. Border was now not alone in the capacity to show guts. Boon was dour and determined. Jones literally put his life on the line for his country. These three and Marsh were seen as being a solid foundation. And Steve Waugh? Selectors and the public had seen little to suggest he would develop beyond being a 'useful' batting all-rounder, who was fortunate to have a place in the side. Nevertheless, his first-class figures continued to improve. He didn't score a century on tour but averaged 56.75 from seven innings with a top score of 82. Waugh also took ten wickets at 36.70. He had not earned his place in the Test side, but had justified his spot on the tour. What's more, Border liked his fire. Selectors were informed as much in the tour report.

Ashes, no fire

A month later, Waugh made the team for the First Test of the 1986–87 Ashes battle at Brisbane in mid-November. England had its strongest batting line-up since the 1960s, featuring a top order of Broad, Athey, Gatting, Lamb, Gower and Botham, which remained settled throughout the five Tests. Mike Gatting won the toss and the Botham bogy of the 1981 Ashes, which had been buried in two series since, returned. He clobbered a power-laden century. Border brought Waugh on and he removed him, caught by Hughes for 138. Waugh picked up two more wickets to end with the best figures of three for 76 off twenty-one overs with three maidens, a good effort considering England amassed 456. This ensured that it would not matter if he failed with the bat, which he did, scoring 0 and 28. England went on to a comfortable seven-wicket win.

It began with more of the same at Perth nine days later, when England scored eight for 592 over most of the first two days. Waugh failed with the ball as a stock bowler, sending down 24 overs with four maidens while taking none for 90. Yet he couldn't be kept out of the game as he took three good catches. Border's growing confidence in his quietly determined young charge saw him go in as nightwatch-man at one for 4. Waugh concentrated well into the next day before spinner Emburey duped him into a catch to Botham at slip when he was 71. This effort and Border's 125 just helped Australia to 401 and avoidance of a follow-on.

Border judged that Waugh was feeling more secure about his Test spot. Going on the hunch that he would be inspired in the field, Border tossed him the ball early again. Waugh proceeded to make the formidable batting order look brittle, taking five for 69, his best first-class bowling yet. His scalps included Broad, Gatting and Gower. England was checked at eight for 197 declared. The game fell away to a draw. Waugh's tail was up. He had given a man-of-the-match performance. He had really earned that Test spot now.

Australia was in first at the Third Test at Adelaide, and everyone managed runs as Australia reached five for 368. It was an unusually luxurious way for Waugh to enter the beautiful oval with Sir Donald Bradman tucked away in his favourite spot in the members' pavilion watching the game. Waugh was at last in a situation to dream about: England struggling in the field and a big score on the board. He capitalised and went on to 79 not out in an unbeaten 146 partnership with the indefatigable Matthews (73 not out). Waugh was on his way to a century when Border called a halt at five for 514. The skipper was mindful that Australia had to win one to keep its Ashes hopes alive.

Broad (116, following 162 at the WACA) and Gatting (100) set the challenger's aspirations back as England reached 455. Waugh kept his reputation as a surprise partnership breaker by sending back Broad caught by Marsh. He took one for 56. The two big innings scores didn't allow Australia a chance to win. Nevertheless, Waugh salvaged something important out of the Test. He had done well now in successive contests against tough opposition. His innate strength and deep-down supreme self-confidence welled in him. For the first time, he felt some comfort at this level. He thought he might belong in Test company after all.

Down and ... up, at last

Australia's inability to force a win in Adelaide made the Fourth Test at Melbourne beginning on Boxing Day a crucial encounter. If Australia drew or lost it, the Ashes would stay with England. Gatting won the toss and sent the Australians in. Waugh was in at four for 108 but was out caught off Gladstone Small for just 10. The team collapsed to be all out 141, with Small taking five for 48. Only Jones, with 59, resisted. England was one for 95 at stumps and the next day forged on to 349 (Broad, again, this time 112)—208 ahead, which shut Australia out of the game. Waugh could extract nothing from a flat track and returned none for 16 from eight with four maidens, Border using him to slow the run rate with his nagging-length medium pacers.

Apart from a solid 60 from Marsh, Australia fell apart again, and Waugh was left with a long tail. He fought but was eventually bowled by Edmonds for 49. Australia made 194 in its second innings and was left with a defeat by an innings and 14 runs. After showing promise in the last two Tests, the team had been thrashed. The media attacked. It questioned their courage, commitment and ability. It was always the worst series to lose. To do it without a whimper brought back the team depression that had dogged it through five series before the Indian tour. Australia now wallowed again in a feeling of inferiority. Scorn was poured on the team.

The dead-rubber Fifth Test in Sydney began on 10 January 1987 with Border winning the toss and batting. Waugh this time joined an in-form Jones at four for 184 but was caught behind off a Small away swinger for a duck. Australia struggled to 343, Jones staying undefeated on 184. Waugh didn't get much of a look in at the bowling crease as the spinners Peter Sleep and Peter Taylor (six for 78) were used in preference to him on a typical Sydney pitch. England reached 275. Australia's lead was just 68 and it was imperative now that it did not collapse. Waugh was in this time at four for 110. He applied himself to the task of batting Australia into a prominent position. He hit straight, and early on refused to play his favourite back-cut slash. But he sprinkled his innings with his natural instinct for attack, making a top score of 73, and steering his country to a winning position. Australia's 251 gave it a lead of 319. The spinners did the trick again, with Sleep snaring five for 72. Waugh contributed an important breakthrough when Border brought him on to bowl to the dangerous Gatting, in the nineties. The theory was that the Gatt would think Waugh was an easy route to a century, and therefore lapse in concentration. He did just that and sent back a caught and bowled at 96. England reached 264, 55 runs short. Australia had salvaged something. Waugh was elated. He had at last played in a winning Test team. It had taken thirteen attempts. His batting in the series—310 runs at an average of 44.29—had turned respectable. His bowling figures—ten for 336 at 33.6 runs a wicket—were also fair. It had been a struggle over thirteen months and thirteen Tests, but Waugh had now earned his place over a complete series. Yet he had a precarious hold. His batting was still not quite potent enough and he would never be selected for his bowling alone.

Waugh was hungry for more top competition, yet had to wait eleven months before he played in another Test. He would have to be content with Shield games at the end of the 1986–87 season, the one-day World Cup in India and Pakistan, county cricket and then more Shield matches. His 1986–87 season ended with easily his highest aggregate—741—from twenty-one innings at an average of 39. His highest score was just 89, and he was consistent with six fifties. But again, in another era, he would have struggled to hold his place in a New South Wales XI.

3

GLIMMERS OF GREATNESS

World Cup wonders

Australia arrived in India for the 1987 World Cup as one of the long shots of the tournament. Bookmakers had them from fifteen to one out to twenty to one to win it. Border and his men, who numbered a few gamblers such as Dean Jones, were aware of their underdog status, and were comfortable with it. They did not have the stress of hot favourites and this allowed them to play with less pressure. Journalists, judging the Australians on the last few years, wrote them off. Former Pakistan batting star Zaheer Abbas suggested that local schoolboys could give them a run for their money. Another scribe argued that they were the worst team in the competition. These comments and others were passed around the Australian squad. Border was annoyed with these assessments, but also motivated by them.

The Australians began well, crushing the opposition in two trial games. The odds closed to ten to one, but they were still outsiders. They played their first game against India at Madras. Geoff Marsh dropped anchor for 110, which helped Australia reach 270. India scored steadily but also lost wickets as they pushed up over 250.

47

Border tossed Waugh the ball for overs at the tight finish. The skipper had observed him now at Test and state level for a couple of years and judged him a cool character, who could bowl accurately in a pressure-cooker finish. Not only that—he could swing the ball. His slower delivery—bowled out of the back of the hand—was deceptive. Waugh also had a useful shorter ball that he could lift into a batsman's ribcage from a short run-up. But he would be unlikely to deliver it in a one-day contest.

A big Indian crowd howled for a home-team win. Waugh was not intimidated. He bowled the tailender Maninder Singh with the second-last ball and it gave Australia victory by a solitary run. The team partied, in keeping with their image of battlers not expected to win anything. But image and reality were different. The same individuals who could enjoy themselves celebrating were likely to give 100 per cent in any contests. They proved it in a tough and tight match against New Zealand at Indore in which Boon starred by clobbering 87. Waugh's performance at Madras saw Border honouring him with the last over of the game, which had been reduced to thirty overs each. This time New Zealand had seven runs to get to win. Its top bat, Martin Crowe, was 58 not out. He tried to go over the top off Waugh's first ball and was caught. Next man in was keeper Ian Smith. Waugh kept the next ball well up and straight. Smith was bowled. New Zealand had one wicket left and still seven to make. Tailenders Martin Snedden and Willie Watson scrambled three runs. Waugh then ran out Watson, thus dismissing three batsmen in his final over. Australia had won another close one, this time by three runs.

Before playing New Zealand, Australia beat Zimbabwe by 96 runs, lost the return to India by 56 runs, won the second match versus New Zealand by 17 runs and the second match against Zimbabwe by 70 runs. This took Australia into the semi-finals where it accounted for Pakistan by 18 runs. Every member of the top order had had a solid innings.

Australia thus fought its way into the final in front of 70,000 fans at Calcutta against England, which was far and away the favourite. The English and local press again wrote the Australians off. But Boon and Marsh got them off to a fine start with 52 in the first ten overs. After Boon was dismissed for 75, Border and Veletta added 73 in ten overs. England's last six overs cost 65 runs, including 11 from the last, which lifted the Australian tally to 253.

England began like winners, scoring two for 131 off thirty-one overs, and the Australian fielders seemed to be flagging in the heat. Gatting then tried a reverse sweep, which was caught by keeper Dyer. Waugh was in fine touch in the field. He ran out Athey with a brilliant throw. But England was still on top, especially with Allan Lamb in touch. But then Waugh bowled him in the forty-seventh over. In the forty-ninth, he removed Phillip DeFreitas, who had crashed 17, and conceded only 2 runs. England did not have a batsman left who could take the game at the finish. It had 18 to make to win in the last over, but only got 10 off McDermott. It reached eight for 246.

The seven-run win gave Australia its first World Cup victory. The key players were openers Boon (446 runs in eight matches at 55.75) and Marsh (428 at 61.14). Mike Veletta was also important, hitting three scores of more than 40, including 45 in the final. The victory was the biggest lift for Australian cricket since the Packer split a decade earlier.

Waugh said that he enjoyed being given the responsibility of bowling in close contests. He suggested it was tougher for the batsmen than the bowlers. 'If you keep your head,' he said, 'it is going to be very hard for a batsman to hit boundaries. I've always fancied myself in that situation.'

He considered bowling the final overs as the biggest challenge in one-day cricket.

Waugh was another important performer in the tournament, especially in those pressure moments. His efforts boosted his confidence, and his credentials as an all-rounder with an excellent temperament were enhanced.

County clashes

Steve Waugh's 1987 first-class season in England was limited by the one-foreign-player-per-county championship match rule. He played just four county matches for Somerset.

Waugh showed his true mettle in one game against Surrey at The Oval and West Indian 'quick' Sylvester Clarke, regarded in England as the most ferocious paceman in the world. It was Waugh's first experience of West Indian fast bowling delivered with speed and menace he had never before encountered. The pitch was a green-top and lightning fast. If Brad McNamara had unsettled him in his under-age years, this was another level again.

In its second innings Somerset was six for 114 and in trouble. Clarke didn't charge in. He strolled, but his last-second thrust of powerful shoulders propelled the ball quicker than any other West Indian in the 1980s.

'The ball was a blur when it whipped past,' Waugh recalled. 'Even sharper than I expected.'

Waugh knew that he would not be able to counterattack in a heroic fashion. Just surviving and not getting struck would be a considerable achievement. He had to adjust to the bounce and pace generated. Runs were at a premium early in the innings, but Waugh concentrated more than ever before. The runs began to come. He even managed the odd drive and cut to the fence. This brought cold stares from Clarke, but like most of the West Indian pacemen, he didn't say much. He preferred to bang in a short ball at the batsman's throat. Wickets fell but Waugh, without being spectacular, took control and hit 111 not out to save the match.

It was his first county century and the innings lifted his level of self-confidence another notch. 'I proved to myself that I wasn't going to be blown away when Australia played the West Indies,' Waugh said.

Waugh played a similar innings against Gloucestershire at Bristol and another fast West Indian, Courtney Walsh. At one point Somerset was eight for 138, with Waugh in and batting well. He was joined by tailender Neil Mallender. Waugh took charge, counterattacked and slammed 137 not out. This brought Somerset within 30 runs of overtaking Gloucester's score, when Peter Roebuck declared in order to challenge the opposition and make a real contest of the encounter. Waugh's petulance, never far from the surface, was usually kept in check and never manifested as more than a scowl or a mutter under his breath. But this time he couldn't contain himself. He was ropable. He threw his bat down, opened his arms to the pavilion and wanted to know why. In the dressing room, he demanded to know what the skipper was doing. Roebuck explained. Waugh remained unconvinced. The game was opened up when Gloucester lost early wickets. Roebuck claimed that Somerset would have won but for Waugh dropping an easy catch in slips.

In six county innings in 1987 he scored 340 runs at 113.33 with those two outstanding centuries. He also took eleven wickets at 31.63. County officials searching for a future star foreign representative who could be picked up cheaply noted his performances. Waugh turned 22 during the England season and his self-confidence was building as he prepared for his fourth first-class season in Australia.

Kiwi fruit

The Australian squad for the three-Test series against New Zealand in 1987–88 was the best line up since the retirements of Lillee, Marsh and Greg Chappell in 1984. The bowling available was strong with Bruce Reid and Craig McDermott developing well. There was support for these pacemen from Merv Hughes, Mike Whitney and Tony Dodemaide. In the spin department, there were Taylor, Sleep and Tim May to call on. The batting was settling down, with the steady Marsh and Boon being tried in Tests now as an opening combination. Border was at the peak of his form and Jones was promising big things after his success in India. Then there was Steve Waugh. He was solid without being spectacular in the middle order, and a handy bowler for Border to toss into the mix for a surprise, to retard rampant batting or to break a threatening partnership.

At Brisbane in the First Test in early December 1987, Waugh (one for 35) was handy in the field, taking two catches and trapping Jeff Crowe (16) lbw in New Zealand's first innings of 186. Border was not prepared to push him up the batting order, leaving him at six despite the introduction of Mike Veletta, who came in at number five. Hadlee was in his usual rampant form against the Australians, backed by Danny Morrison. Only Boon (run out for 143) could keep them out as the side struggled up to 305. Waugh contributed 21. Australia rolled New Zealand in its second innings for 212 (Waugh one for 2) and mopped up the 90-odd runs required to win by nine wickets. Border and his men celebrated.

They flew to Adelaide for the Second Test, which began just four days later. Tim May, the South Australian off-spinning accountant, was chosen to play his first Test on his home ground. He remembered Steve Waugh's greeting. 'He was terrific,' May said. 'I never felt like an outsider, even though I was on the "outer" in terms of a permanent spot in the side. He embraced me into the Test fold. He has always done that with younger players.'

May felt Waugh was captain material even then. 'He was always optimistic. He had the attitude that we were never beaten. He expected always to snatch victory from the jaws of defeat. That optimism rubs off on the other blokes. It's infectious. The game is played 70 per cent from the eyes up. That's why Steve is so successful. He is the type that backs up his mates. In my time he was the least selfish player in the team. He was supportive and would express confidence in you.'

In May's debut game, New Zealand batted first and were boosted by a 213-run third-wicket partnership between Andrew Jones (run out 150) and Martin Crowe (137). Waugh (none for 71 off thirty-one overs) was not quite the surprise for the New Zealanders now. They had faced him in Tests and one-dayers. They were on the lookout for his slower ball and refused to underestimate him any more. The tourists pushed up the total to an unbeatable nine declared for 485. Memories of the Kiwis' recent victories over weak Aussie sides came back to haunt the home team. But Border, at his most tenacious, was not about to let his improving combination slip back to the dark days. He hit 205 and figured in a 116-run partnership with a determined Waugh (61). Sleep and keeper Greg Dyer also managed 60s and Australia slipped past New Zealand to be all out for 496. These big scores took the game into the final day and it ended in a draw with New Zealand on seven for 182.

May had had an impressive first-up display taking three for 68 in the second innings. His fellow South Australian spinner, Peter Sleep, took three for 61. Waugh, who knew the Adelaide pitch less well, was still effective as an opening bowler in partnership with McDermott and in place of the injured Reid, taking none for 17 off ten overs with four maidens.

Australia had to draw or win in Melbourne over the Boxing Day Test to claim a series victory. New Zealand batted first for the third successive time. It was held to 317 thanks to McDermott (five for 97) and Whitney (four for 92), leaving other bowlers, including Waugh (none for 44 off ten overs) as support. Australia stumbled to three for 31, then four for 78 when Waugh arrived at the crease. He began a strong recovery getting 55, boosted by Sleep (90) and Dodemaide (50). Australia reached 357, giving it a slim lead of 40.

Having to bat last, it didn't seem enough. New Zealand was stopped from reaching a match-winning score by Dodemaide (six for 58). It ended with 286, a lead of 246. One big Australian innings was needed. While six of the top seven batsmen reached double figures (Waugh 10), no one could withstand an onslaught by Hadlee (five for 67). At one point on the last day in the middle session, Australia stood a fair chance to win, but then the side crashed to nine for 227, still 20 short. McDermott and Whitney hung on until stumps for a nail-biting draw with Australia on nine for 230.

Australia won the series. Victory, even over New Zealand, was cause for jubilation. For the moment, the team was on the winning list and Waugh's prestige mounted. He had a modest series with four knocks for 147 at an average of 36.75, and the thrill and historic honour of playing in the Bicentenary Test against England at Sydney early in 1988. He bowled well, taking three for 51 off 22.5 overs. He dismissed Broad (who played on, and then smashed down his stumps as he left the wicket) for 139, and Gatting for 16. England mounted 425, putting the game out of Australia's reach with a miserably slow two for 221 on the first day. Australia responded with a mediocre 214 (Waugh 27), which seemed to put the New Zealand series in perspective. Then Boon (184 not out) gave the best batting display of the game and led Australia out of trouble to three for 328—a lead of 117 with seven wickets in hand. It restored some team faith that they might be emerging from their bleakest period ever.

This was confirmed in a strong performance in a first-ever Test against Sri Lanka in Australia at Perth in February. Australia scored 455 (Jones 102, Border 88). Waugh's contribution was another modest 20. Yet he got into the game when bowling. The Sri Lankans had no answers to his change of pace and swing. He had the best figures—four for 33 off twenty overs with seven maidens—including the wickets of Aravinda De Silva and Arjuna Ranatunga. Sri Lanka scored 194 and followed on with 153 (Hughes five for 67).

Waugh was reasonably pleased with his figures for the 1987–88 first-class season. He scored 517 at 36.92 in fifteen innings, with three fifties and one big 170 against Victoria at Sydney. His bowling figures—twenty-three wickets at 21.69 runs a wicket—were flattering. The record gave him confidence for the 1988 season in England.

Somerset summer

Steve Waugh stepped up his connection with Somerset when Viv Richards and Joel Garner left that county in dispute, along with Ian Botham, who walked out in sympathy with his good mate Richards. New Zealand's Martin Crowe would have taken Richards' place, but he had a back injury. The way was open for Waugh. He grabbed the opportunity and performed far beyond any Somerset member's expectations, slamming eight centuries (two in one-dayers and six in championship matches) in thirty innings. In twenty-four championship innings he notched 1314 runs at an average of 73 with a top score of 161. This was as good as anything Richards and Crowe had ever done for the county.

More important than the weight of runs was how and when Waugh got them. (The strong bowling line-up for the county saw his chances with the ball limited to just twenty-three overs. He took three wickets for 60.) His batting figures were a big improvement on any previous season, except for his limited 1987 county statistics. His average had doubled since the season in Australia. It had much to do with English wickets, which were slower with less bounce. Waugh could employ his backfoot cuts and drives into the off side, knowing that he would get away with them. In Australia his style of opening the face of the bat and slashing had often caused his downfall. Even in England, he could slip into dangerous habits. But if he played straight from the beginning of a knock, he was almost assured of a score. The slash was a flaw in his technique. His advancement, particularly in Australia, would depend on whether or not he paid attention to it.

Waugh was equally effective in the one-dayers. He was not just a run accumulator like South African opener Jimmy Cook, who had played for Somerset before him. Waugh was a match winner. He would take on the speed bowlers early in a Somerset innings, or stay with the tailenders in several brilliant performances. He was an unselfish player, who was driven to win games, not merely garner glory for himself.

Somerset's skipper, Peter Roebuck, said that, apart from his fine batting displays, Waugh was popular and mature for his age (he turned twenty-three during the season). He assumed a role as a natural leader among his peers and the younger players. He was a reliable teammate, who liked to drink with the boys and enjoy the after-match festivities. Roebuck also noted Waugh's laconic style. He was a young man of few words. But when he spoke, especially concerning tactics regarding opposition players, everyone, including Roebuck, listened. He valued his judgment.

Waugh's county performances prompted *Wisden* in April 1989 to name him one of the Five Cricketers of the Year for 1988.

Waugh left England in late August 1988 with his confidence high and ready to resume Test cricket—this time in a three-Test series in Pakistan. It was a tour that had tested visiting squads from all nations in more ways than one for the past thirty years.

Pakistan pain, Windies woes

Australia chose Ian Healy for his first tour ahead of Dyer, Zoehrer and Dimattina. Healy was best at keeping to spin, which was expected to play a big part in the Pakistan series. The atmosphere was tense when the players arrived, and not because of the cricket. Pakistan was on the brink of civil war following the death in a plane crash of General Zia ul-Haq, the president. There was much ethnic violence and this caused two one-day matches to be cancelled. As if that were not enough, floods caused one of the one-day internationals to be called off.

The atmosphere on the field was also tense. The Australians had heard all the stories during the Bicentenary Test from Gatting and his team about the standard of umpiring in Pakistan. Gatting had clashed with an umpire on the field after many decisions had gone against the English. On one occasion, Gatting wagged his finger in the umpire's face and was heard to remark, 'One rule for one and another rule for others!'

Pakistan batted first in the First Test at Karachi, beginning on 15 September, and Bruce Reid broke through to put back both openers with just 21 on the board. Shoaib Mohammad and Pakistan's captain Javed Miandad then combined for a big partnership. Its compilation and Mahboob Shah's umpiring set the pattern for the series. The Australians appealed often for lbw decisions—especially against Miandad—but they were turned down. Border brought on Waugh. He managed to bowl Mohammad for 94. Miandad went on to 211 and Pakistan was able to declare on day three at nine for 469. May had the best figures, with four for 97 on a wicket that was more responsive to spin than speed. Waugh battled hard but was less economical than normal, taking one for 94 off twenty-six overs.

Australia floundered on a worn pitch against the spin of Iqbal Qasim and Abdul Qadir. Jones (3), then Waugh (0) received poor lbw decisions as Australia slumped to all out for 165. In the follow-on innings Marsh and Graeme Wood received more doubtful lbw rulings as Australia collapsed for 116 (Waugh was dismissed by Qasim, this time stumped for 13), thus giving Pakistan a win by an innings and 188 runs. Qasim and Qadir took fourteen wickets between them and were most responsible for the home team's success.

The Australians were angry, especially with Mahboob Shah. The team wanted to abort the tour. Former Test umpire and now team manager, Col Egar, managed to smooth matters for the moment. Complaints were made through appropriate channels, particularly about Mahboob. Pakistan authorities ignored demands for him to be replaced. He was chosen to stand at the Second Test at Faisalabad a few days later.

Waugh had a match he would rather forget, taking none for 36 and one for 44 (to get rid of opener Rameez Raja), and scoring just 1 and 19. Again the spinners troubled him. He and his teammates, except for Border, looked all at sea on the turning pitches. Border showed everyone how it was done in a typically resolute knock of 113 not out in Australia's first innings. It was enough to help force a draw. Once more, the tourists were frustrated by the umpires in their lbw judgments in favour of Miandad, who scored 43 and 107. The bowlers reckoned that six appeals were out and several more doubtful. Mahboob kept shaking his head. But he was quick to nod his agreement to appeals against Jones (16), who seemed hardly done by again when adjudged lbw to Qadir.

The feeling throughout the team was still not good, and most players were wishing the tour was over. Yet there was still one Test to play at Lahore and a win would lift spirits. Border won the toss and batted. Boon (64), Marsh (43) and Border (75) contributed well to a solid top order effort, while Waugh (59) found his form and kept the tail wagging. Australia reached 340. Pakistan replied with 233, with Reid, Dodemaide and May each taking three wickets. Waugh was economic, while not penetrating, taking none for 34 off eighteen overs with four maidens. Australia then went in search of quick runs and declared early on the last day at three for 161 (Marsh 84 not out), leaving Pakistan a very fair target—269 in 300 minutes. The home team, content with its one–nil lead, refused the challenge and put up the shutters. But this dithering was almost Pakistan's undoing when Peter Taylor took three wickets in fourteen balls to leave it seven for 131 with sixteen overs remaining. The off spinner took another wicket, but Pakistan hung on to be eight for 153 at stumps. A draw was the result.

Bruce Reid was the success of the tour, taking twenty wickets at 20.35. A fracture in his back prevented him from bowling on the last day. Waugh, like most of the other team members, had had a series he would rather forget. His final innings of 59 saved face, but it was still a poor period for him, which was reflected in his batting figures: 92 runs at 18.40. Statistically and in terms of his personal morale, Waugh had reached a low ebb.

During the tour, 'Sixty Minutes' reporter Mike Munro did a hatchet job on Border and his team, making them appear like a bunch of whingers and losers. The only positive to come from the tour was pressure on the ICC to appoint neutral umpires for international series.

Waugh was astonished on his return to find the extent of the bad press and misreporting to which he and the squad had been subjected. Girlfriend Lynette kept a file of press items. Reading it made Waugh really angry, for the first time in Lynette's experience. From then on he was more wary of media reporting and its innate fickleness. There would also be scores to settle with Pakistan.

Reality time

The team had to put those sour matters behind them and prepare for a strong West Indian team led by Viv Richards. The fast-bowling line-up was one of the most fierce ever to play the game: Ambrose, Walsh, Marshall, Bishop and Patterson.

All except Bishop played in the First Test at Brisbane on 18 November

1988, and once more an unfavourable pattern for the Australians was set in the first innings of the series. Australia was blasted out for 167, Waugh falling lbw to Marshall for 4. The Windies quicks lifted many balls up into the ribcage. They also insisted on strolling back to their bowling marks—each man taking around six minutes to deliver an over. It was boring for spectators at the ground and it also made for poor television viewing. Yet the West Indies approach was bound to continue. It had put it on top of the world cricket table for a decade and it never looked like being toppled while it had such a powerful bowling combination.

McDermott and the nervous third-gamer Chris Matthews failed to dislodge one of the great Windies opening team—Greenidge and Haynes. Finally May broke through to remove Greenidge (80) at 136 and then Waugh eased into the game, causing Haynes (40) to nick one to Healy. Waugh took Hooper's wicket before he got going and surprised Viv Richards with a bouncer. One lifted off a good length and whistled past his ear. Viv raised his eyebrows and smiled down the pitch at Waugh, who glared. Two more bouncers had the West Indian taking evasive action and scowling. He was not used to such cheek, especially from a medium-pacer. Waugh's challenge would not be forgotten when Richards's speed quartet attacked him in the second innings.

Waugh ended with two for 61 off eighteen overs. The Windies reached 394—a lead of 227. Courtney Walsh took a hat trick, a wicket off his last ball of the first innings and two more in the next two deliveries he sent down in the second innings.

Waugh sweated over his second knock. He batted at four. The fourth wicket fell at 65 and Border joined him. On his mind was his mastery of Courtney Walsh and Sylvester Clarke in England county games eighteen months earlier. He had been struck then too, but he had counterattacked and won those battles. That experience gave Waugh a life raft—something to cling to. He started nervously as usual, and pushed with late urgency at deliveries that beat him.

'He thinks he's tough, this one,' Richards said to Ambrose. 'Thinks he can bowl a bouncer. Let's see how he takes it.'

Ambrose gave him a testing short one. Waugh swayed out of the way.

With Border's encouragement, Waugh settled in. They put on 92 until Ambrose removed Border (41) caught by Haynes at 157. Healy and Waugh then put on another 42 before Marshall removed Healy (28) and ended any real chance of a fight back. The score was six for 199. Waugh was left to prop up the tail. He reached 90—by far the highest score for the team. He then drove the hardest shot he had played all innings—straight to Desmond Haynes at cover, ending his most important performance so far for his country. Waugh surprised his critics, who had written him off as a determined pretender. It was an innings marked by sound defence and counterattack. Waugh was attacked by short-pitchers. His unique 'jumping' technique to get over a delivery encouraged the quicks to bounce him more. But this unorthodoxy was misleading. Waugh was not frightened. His technique worked.

However, Australia only reached 289 (McDermott 32 not out), and the Windies won easily—mopping up the 60-odd needed for the loss of one wicket. They marched on to Perth for the Second Test on 2 December. Border won the toss and sent the West Indies in. Richards led the way on the bouncy WACA pitch with 146 out of a score of 449. Waugh took a catch but was ineffective with the ball this time, taking none for 90. Hughes took five for 130, including the last two wickets.

Australia's response to the bounce of the Windies speed quartet demonstrated increased backbone as Boon (80) steadied the team early. Graeme Wood was joined by Waugh with the score at four for 167. Waugh was in a defiant mood, fresh from his fine effort at the Gabba. His innings was close in style and construction to the previous knock. He and left-hander Wood, on his home pitch and loving the pace and bounce, put on a fine 200-run partnership. Ambrose made the break at 367, having Wood (111) caught in slip and then, at 374, Waugh (91) caught behind.

A century would have been terrific for Waugh's morale. Yet, as he said after the game, he would have settled for 91 against 'that mob' any day. Border declared at eight for 395, trying to make a game of the contest. The Windies ground out nine for 349 (Haynes 100). Waugh took none for 70. He found himself being used as a stock bowler in support of Hughes. Merv was in the best form of his short career, taking a wicket with his first ball (Greenidge lbw for 0), thus giving him a hat trick over two innings, which was almost the way Walsh did it in the First Test. Hughes's figures of eight for 87 gave him thirteen for 217 for the match.

This Test was proving a milestone for both Hughes and Waugh, as they demonstrated that former strong performances were not flukes. Big Merv, with his unathletic girth and fearsome moustache, seemed more than a bullyboy pretender for a paceman's spot. Waugh, with consecutive nineties against the best attack in the world, seemed like a very strong number six. In 1987 Waugh had countered West Indians Clarke and Walsh with determination. Now he had done well against the team itself and its lethal pace line-up. Waugh's unorthodox technique of jumping to get over a ball had drawn criticism, usually from those who had never faced such a fast battery. Waugh's style was not based on fear. In fact, it took more courage to attempt to 'ride' the delivery. The batsman who tried to evade the ball by ducking under it or turning his back created more of a possibility of being struck on the bat or glove, and thus giving a catch. Waugh's aim most times was to drop the wrists and bat under the ball or to get on top of it.

His success in this series confirmed in his own mind that he could overcome the world's best and most dangerous fast bowlers.

Australia was left 404 to win. Marshall, Ambrose, Patterson and Walsh were all in form and Australia's bats struggled early, losing both openers by the time the score was 14. It never recovered despite promising starts from Wood (42), Border (26), Waugh (26) and Healy (52). The final score of 234 meant a second comprehensive defeat, this time by 169 runs.

Patrick Patterson's boxing test

The combatants had a break from Test cricket for part of the one-day tournament and then regrouped in Melbourne for the Boxing Day Test. The Windies batted first and struggled from the beginning of the innings. Waugh supported Terry Alderman (four for 68), back from suspension after touring South Africa, and McDermott (three for 62), when he had Richards caught by Border for just 12. He also removed Jeff Dujon and Marshall to end with three for 77 from twenty-one overs. The Windies tally of 288 was its only mediocre effort so far. In reply, several Australian bats got going but could not sustain a big innings. Waugh, coming in at four for 117, found himself batting with the tail. He top-scored with 42, as Australia failed again, making 242. Ambrose and Patrick Patterson with four wickets each did the damage on an awkward pitch.

Waugh bowled at his best in Test cricket, given the opposition, taking five for 92 from twenty-four overs with five maidens. His haul included Richardson (122), Richards again (lbw for 63), Gus Logie and Marshall, as the tourists reached nine for 361. Australia was left 400 to win. Not even the most optimistic Aussie fan expected the home team could reach that considering the Windies quicks and the wicket, which was causing the ball to jump into arms and body. The Australians didn't help their cause by riling big Patrick Patterson while he was batting. He was furious and was threatening to do damage. He was true to his angry words, hitting several batsmen. He wasn't alone. Marshall, Ambrose and Walsh also pummelled the hapless home team. While Patterson did most of the roaring and bruising, the others took five of the first seven wickets.

Waugh fell to Ambrose early for just 3. Australia disintegrated in front of a small crowd, reaching 114. They had lost by 285 runs.

Australia had fallen to the depths of despair in the mid-1980s, but after some up blips in recent years, this was the lowest point of all. 'It was no fun out there,' Border said after the game. And no one was laughing. Not the players, the administrators or the spectators, who were staying away in droves, and not just because of the West Indian dominance. The way the West Indians flouted the slow over rate rule—90 in a day—had disillusioned patient fans. They were docked $22,000 from their earnings. But Richards dismissed this as a mere trifling compared to winning.

The fall-off in gate takings worried the Australian Cricket Board. The long retired Sir Donald Bradman then expressed concern about the style of play, which was not entertaining. Bradman feared the game could be killed off as a spectator sport. He realised that nothing could be done to stop the Windies picking four quicks. But he hoped that Australian administrators and coaches would avoid trying to copy the West Indies and opt for a balance of pace and spin. But few spinners—especially leggies—had been encouraged in the last decade. Australia's hammering at Melbourne caused the lowest ebb in morale in recent times. Border's team had made progress since 1985, but the way to the top seemed permanently blocked by a superior, brutal opposition. Waugh noted Border's anguish, yet also observed that his captain would never throw in the towel. He marvelled at and endorsed Border's steadfast belief, even at this depressing time, that Australia would eventually, somehow prevail. The captain's dedication had an enormous impact on Waugh, who displayed a similar nationalistic fervour. His only regret was that Border didn't communicate his faith more to the team and to individual members, one-on-one. Border's way was to grumble and look set-upon, but still put the horrors of the defeat behind him, even on the day of inflicted defeat, and always after 'a few beers'. The greatest Aussie battler of them all had the capacity to move on and fight another day, without the baggage of the previous encounter.

No way to go but up

The first three weeks of 1989 saw a reversion to the one-day competition, which the West Indies won against Pakistan and Australia.

The issue that concerned Bradman was temporarily swept away in the Fourth Test in Sydney, which was typically a slow, turning, grass-less pitch. Trevor Hohns, a capable leggie, was at last given a chance. He joined Peter Taylor. New South Wales opening left-hander Mark Taylor (no relation) was chosen for his first Test.

The West Indies batted first. Hughes and Alderman were both soon off and replaced by spin. Border, always reluctant to bring himself on to bowl his left-arm orthodox tweakers, liked what he saw as both Peter Taylor and Trevor Hohns took early wickets. The skipper came on and ran through the tourists, taking seven for 46 from twenty-six overs with ten maidens. The West Indies fell for 224, its lowest total of the series. Australia responded well with Boon (149) and Border (75) in a 170-run stand that took the score to four for 284. Waugh was once more left to prop up the tail. He remained 55 not out in his fourth good performance of the series. Australia reached 401.

Haynes (143) held the West Indies' second innings together in which just 256 were mustered—113 by the rest of the team including six sundries. Border with four for 50 was again among the wickets, making his match analysis eleven for 96. Waugh (none for 18 and none for 10) and the other faster men were pushed out of the picture, but they were happy just as long as the West Indies was beaten. Australia went on to an easy seven-wicket win, and some pride was restored.

The team's collective confidence was up when it reached Adelaide for the Fifth Test. Australia batted on a typical flat, true wicket, and Jones found form. Waugh (12) failed to capitalise on an opportunity when he came in at four for 289, but Jones was rewarded with a late-order partner in Hughes (72 not out), who joined him in a ninth-wicket stand of 114. It saw Jones through to his second double century in Tests. He was run out for 216. Australia reached 515, and an unas-sailable position. Whitney was the star with the ball when the tourists batted, taking seven for 89, from a total of 369 (Richardson 106). Border declared at four for 224 (Marsh 79), in which Waugh was run out for 8 trying to push it along. The West Indies held firm at four for 233, and the game fell away to a draw, giving the tourists a three–one series win.

After the series, Bradman again called for the introduction of a third umpire, armed with camera and video, to adjudicate on tough catching, run-out and stumping decisions. He had first made the call three years earlier and repeated it now after several poor umpiring decisions had caused controversy.

Bradman's worry that Test play was turning away crowds was supported by the aggregates for the summer. Twenty-four days of Test cricket had attracted 325,000 at an average of 13,541 a day. Fifteen days of one-day cricket saw nearly 500,000 turn up to watch—an average of 33,300 a day.

Steve Waugh was one player who could not be blamed. His batting pulled the crowds in and kept viewers watching, and he never dallied when bowling, preferring to keep at the batsman. His batting statistics for the series—331 at 41.73—were more than respectable considering the opposition. His bowling figures—ten at 47.20—belied his effectiveness in breaking partnerships and removing those who had conquered everyone else. But while he lifted himself for the higher battle against the West Indies, his first-class batting results were less impressive—711 runs at 30.91 with a top score of 118 against Queensland. His bowling figures were better—thirty-six wickets at 30.94.

Inspired by Border's exceptional determination, Waugh and the rest of the Australians resolved to build into a unit that would live to challenge the West Indies again. To do that it would need to develop into a cohesive force against England, which had thrashed Australia in the last two Ashes contests. The coming 1989 Ashes tour would be a test to see if Australia had made serious advances under Border's astute leadership.

4

ASHES AND EMBERS

The making of Waugh

Waugh's record was easily good enough for him to make the squad to tour England for the Ashes in 1989. He was eager to capitalise on his previous years there, which made the trip seem like a return to his second home. Brother Mark, known at this point in the press as 'Afghanistan'—the forgotten Waugh (war)—went along too, but to play for Essex. Mark may have been overshadowed by Steve but was it a case of the tortoise and the hare? Mark had out-batted his brother in the last two first-class Australian seasons in aggregates, averages and centuries (six to two).

Steve Waugh joined a strong squad led by Allan Border, which included Marsh, Mark Taylor, Jones, Hohns, Geoff Lawson, Hughes, Alderman, Greg Campbell, Healy, Veletta, Tom Moody, May, Carl Rackemann, Zoehrer and Boon. They formed an experienced and talented group. Most members had been battle-hardened in losing campaigns, apart from the New Zealand win 1987–88 and the drawn series in India, for half a decade. If ever they were going to transform into bona fide winners it had to be on this Ashes tour.

Border was on a grim mission. He had suffered Ashes defeats in 1981 and 1985 in England, not to mention the drubbing in 1986–87 in Australia. He hated coming second to the ancient adversary. He would stand for no nonsense on tour, and imposed discipline, including a cut-down on social engagements. Players were allowed to drink, but the days of getting legless at any time, other than at a Test-win celebration, were history. He was even less friendly to the opposition. There would be less fraternising with English players such as skipper David Gower and Botham during the Tests. Border said they were the enemy and should be treated as such until after the Ashes had been won. Training routines beyond cricket practice, such as running and exercise, were stepped up.

Border had a varied bunch, from the flamboyant Hughes to the laconic Waugh and Boon, but they were dedicated and all took their captain's directives seriously.

Waugh delivered no outstanding performances in the lead up to the Tests. The English media saw Border, Jones, Boon and Marsh as Australia's key bats (while, as ever, rating the squad as the poorest ever to tour England). Yet Waugh's form was promising. He saved the team against Sussex at Hove with a strong 86. Against Worcester at New Road he recovered from a golden duck in the first innings to record a solid 63 in the second. Waugh missed two successive games that he would have liked to play—against Somerset at Taunton, and then Middlesex at Lord's. His progress was held up further in a one-day game against Yorkshire (13) but he bowled well, taking three for 41. In the one-day internationals (England and Australia won one each and another was drawn), Waugh scored 35 and took two for 45; run out 43 and one for 47; and 35 and none for 70. When the county games resumed, he was again missing against Warwickshire at Edgbaston, but back in the side versus Derbyshire at Derby, where he failed (14 and 9), as did all the other batsmen in a game the tourists were lucky to win by 11 runs. He out-bowled Tom Moody, his immediate rival for the all-rounder number six spot, taking two for 25 as opposed to Moody's none for 18.

Waugh's limited opportunities and unspectacular form still saw him selected for the First Test at Headingley on 8 June, just pipping Moody, who put in a strong claim with 144 not out against Warwickshire.

Border lost the toss. Mark Taylor, who was in poor form in the lead-up games, set a pattern for the Test by scoring a fine 136, while Border hit 66. Australia moved from three for 207 on day one to four for 273 on the second morning, when Waugh arrived at the wicket. It was his forty-second Test innings. His average was a modest 30.52 and he had yet to score a century.

This did not look like a time for a breakthrough. Waugh was nervous. He pushed at the first ball from Neil Foster, who was in good form, and edged it just short of first slip. Waugh played and missed in the first few overs, until a slashing cut to the fence and then another strong shot through midwicket settled him down. He moved easily to 50 and thought, 'This could be it, at last.' The attack, led by Foster, was steady without being threatening. He increased his concentration and only cut at deliveries he thought were far enough away from his body not to risk a catch behind. His partner was Dean Jones, with whom Waugh enjoyed batting. Jones was always confident and supportive with compliments for good shots. He also looked for every run.

'Let's nail them,' Jones said. 'Let's bury them. It's our day.'

They put on 138 before Jones (79) was caught. Waugh lost Healy (16) and the score was six for 441 when Hughes joined him. Waugh sailed into the nineties and had to fight hard not to panic. Underneath that cool exterior was a very nervous character.

'I had no saliva,' Waugh said later. 'And I thought, "If I don't get a hundred now, I'll collapse."'

His saliva may have dried up, but the runs did not. He continued at the same rate in the nineties and reached the coveted 100 in just 124 balls. Waugh spat out his chewing gum and tried to hit it, but missed. But that was all he missed for the rest of this astonishing innings. He went on to 177 not out from 242 balls with 24 fours—many of them from square cuts and drives. It was one of the best innings of the 1980s. Hughes (71) helped him lift the score to seven for 601 on the third morning of the match, when Border declared.

England replied with 430 (Allan Lamb scored 125). Australia was forced to bat again and declared this time at three for 230, leaving England a 402 target to win. Alderman (five for 44 following five for 107 in the first innings) ran through the batsmen and the home team was dismissed for 191, giving Australia a win by 210.

Waugh felt a foot taller after the game. He had broken the century barrier and in a most emphatic way. He had silenced the critics and the many people who wished to give him gratuitous advice on how to make it to three figures. The worries over his constipation and failure in the 90s evaporated. He was now set to wipe the memory of previous struggles with the bat by the best way he knew: making more hundreds.

The team collectively was given a monumental lift by this clear-cut big win and flying start to the Ashes. Border, particularly, seemed to have a less furrowed brow in the days that followed the long celebration into the night at the team hotel. He had suffered defeat in successive Ashes campaigns. The losses in England in 1981 and 1985 were still seared into his mind and he had wanted retribution.

Waugh slipped back to his pre-Test form in the next two county games scoring 42, 13 and 2 (although he bowled well, taking two for 28, one for 13, two for 40 and three for 10). It didn't matter. He had shown a capacity to lift for a big contest.

England batted first in the Second Test at Lord's and scored 286, which was restricted by Waugh's dismissal of Graham Gooch—caught behind for 60. Waugh came to the wicket at four for 221 and a far more challenging situation than at Headingley. Australia was still 65 behind. He proceeded to bat with authority, but he was more subdued in this innings, running into a fired-up Foster and accurate Graham Dilley. He had to work harder for his runs. A fine first-up Test century at Lord's—'a dream come true'—was his reward. He remained unconquered on 152 not out from 307 (Geoff Lawson scored 74) runs made while he was at the wicket. Australia reached 528.

A beautiful 106 from Gower and a power-laden 96 from Robin Smith lifted England to 359. Australia was left with 118 to win. Memories of Australia's woeful capitulation in two similar low-score chases in 1981 haunted Allan Border, especially when he was out for one, and Australia was four for 67.

Border shut himself in the shower, unable to watch as Waugh (21 not out) and Boon (58 not out), both steady in the mini-crisis, harvested the remaining 50-odd to win the Second Test by six wickets.

Urning the Ashes

Waugh had now accumulated 350 runs in two Tests without being dismissed. London newspapers were quick to designate him 'the new Bradman'. The Australian press, while glowing, were more circumspect. A lot of reincarnated Bradmans of different hues had been announced since the original retired in 1948. None had come anywhere near the Don when their careers unfolded. The Third Test at Edgbaston saw Waugh dismissed for 43, which gave him an average of 393. Rain spread Australia's first innings over three days, during which it reached 424, mainly because of Jones's 157. England replied with 242, just enough to force the Australians to bat again on the last day. The game fizzled to a draw.

Waugh hit 112 against Hampshire prior to fronting up for the Fourth Test in the Ashes series, at Old Trafford. England won the toss and thanks to a hard-hitting Robin Smith (143) reached 260 in their first innings. Waugh came to the wicket at four for 274 and was distracted twice, once by an ample female streaker and again, on 92, by an Angus Fraser bouncer, at which he had a go and was caught. His aggregate was now 485, and his average 242. Australia was all out for 447, an even performance, with Waugh top score and contributions from Taylor (85), Marsh (47), Border (80) and Jones (69). England's second innings of 264 was propped up by a fighting 128 not out from keeper Jack Russell. But it wasn't enough to avoid defeat—this time by nine wickets—which gave Australia a three–nil lead, and the Ashes.

The Australians celebrated their return after six years and two series defeats by England. Beer and champagne flowed in the Old Trafford dressing room, later at the team hotel, then in various other

Manchester nightspots. The team mood was one of ecstasy on top of palpable relief. Border, who had turned thirty-four on 27 July, the first day of the Test, now allowed himself to wallow in celebration. Yet two days after the win he reminded the team of its responsibility to travel on to Trent Bridge for the Fifth Test and go just as hard as in the first four matches. Border wanted to do better than Bradman's Invincibles and win five–nil, which would equal the feat of Warwick Armstrong's 1921 side. Australia won the toss and batted. The first day saw the tourists score none for 301, with Marsh on 125 not out and Taylor on 141 not out. The next day Marsh was out to spinner Nicholas Cook for 138 with the score at 329. Two hours later Taylor was out, stumped off Cook for 219. In the last session of the second day, Waugh came to the wicket at four for 543. He was bowled by the fearsome but erratic Devon Malcolm for a duck, thus reducing his average to more human proportions—161.66.

England (255) collapsed to the swing of Alderman (five for 69) with only Smith (101) counterattacking. The enforced follow-on saw a demoralised England capitulate for 167 and a fourth loss, this time by a whopping innings and 180 runs.

Waugh scored just 1 against Kent. He scored one more in the next county game against Essex, where brother Mark was playing. Australia declared at seven for 387. Mark then styled a fine unbeaten 100 as Essex reached six declared for 290. That was too much for Steve, who was galvanised into an equally impressive performance—also exactly 100 not out—from Australia's two declared for 258. It was as if the twins had tuned in to each other, so that no one could claim that one was better than the other. Yet it did get press tongues wagging and pens scribbling: how long would it be before this other talented Waugh was in the Australian team? Mark had now scored nine first-class centuries and was paying the sort of dues that would have better prepared Steve in other circumstances.

As if to confirm his credentials, Mark scored another 57 and again top score in Essex's second innings of 205. The tourists were winners by 150.

This match highlighted the layered relationship between the twins.

As brothers, they wished each other well always. No one could say a bad word about one to the other without receiving a swift rebuke. They did not mix together apart from at family reunions, and certainly didn't room together on tour, mainly because, as Mark said, they had 'roomed' together for years as kids and that was enough. They were not identical twins like the English Bedser brothers, Alec and Eric, who were two peas in a pod and never out of it. The Waughs tended to have different habits, vices and friends, with some notable exceptions, like Shane Warne. They were rivals to the extent that neither liked the stereotyped supposed differences between them. For instance, Mark resented being seen as the cameo performer without the guts for a tight game. He would later prove he could show as much courage and concentration as his brother in many big knocks, especially against the West Indies and South Africa. Likewise Steve didn't like being viewed as the stodgy one, incapable of tearing an attack apart, especially as he had been seen as the aggressive one in their teen years. When pushed, he could go shot for shot with the more technically correct Mark. Mark, in turn, would later not accept that his brother's superior Test average suggested Steve was somehow a better, or more effective cricketer. He pointed to the fact that Steve went in later in the order when the best bowlers had been thwarted and there was a chance for a not out. (This would become a point of contention near the end of their careers when Steve's average hovered around 50, and Mark's was closer to 40.)

The Australians were keen to go home after a long and demanding tour, but they still had the Sixth Test to play at The Oval. Border (76), with Jones (122) and Taylor (71) still run-hungry, kept his team inspired and it reached 468. England replied with 285 (Alderman five for 66). Border declared Australia's second innings at four for 219 (Jones 50, Border 51 not out, Waugh 7 not out), a lead of 402. Bad light came to England's rescue at five for 143 as it headed towards probable defeat. Alderman finished with two for 30, and a series haul of 41 wickets at 17.37, just one short of his 1981 record.

Waugh topped the Test averages of both teams with eight innings and 506 runs at 126.50. His excellent strike-rate of around 63 runs per 100 balls was about the same as Bradman's in 1930, when the Don had amassed 974 runs at 139.14. Mark Taylor had three more innings and scored 839 runs at 83.9. Waugh's tour record of twenty-four innings for 1033 runs at 64.37 (four centuries and three fifties) was second only to Dean Jones, who in just twenty innings scored 1510 runs at 88.82 (five centuries and eight fifties).

Waugh put his form down to his confidence and shot selection. He eschewed the more risky options and defended well. He also didn't attempt to analyse why it all fell together for him. Waugh had perhaps thought too much about what was going wrong when he was out of form. Part of the success was put down to the tour group's harmony. Everyone got on and there were no arguments or petty jealousies. It led to better team cooperation, which translated into good performances in the field.

Waugh only had fifty-seven overs in the six Tests and took just two for 208 (compared with his first-class figures of twenty-three wickets at 24.83). The series was a watershed. Waugh would no longer be seen as an all-rounder. He had stepped up to be a world-class batsman and 'spare-parts' bowler.

Waugh would have none of the 'new Bradman' tag that the British media placed on him during and after the series. He was happy to have taken a big step up from battler to respected bat. Off the field it would mean more income as a contracted player and lead to endorsements. After the years of struggle and unemployment in the 1980s, he looked forward to a Test career and the ability to provide for a future family. He was prepared for ups and downs. But he now had a core belief in his own ability and powers of concentration. This mattered more than any words from the fondest critic.

Waugh's flaws

This advance was held up over the 1989–90 summer in which he played in the first and last Tests against New Zealand (in Australia and New Zealand), two Tests against Sri Lanka and three against

Pakistan. His scores in these seven Tests (in which Australia only lost the last to New Zealand) were 17 versus New Zealand; 60, 57, 16 and 134 not out against Sri Lanka; 20, 3, 17 and 4 against Pakistan; and 25 and 25 against New Zealand at Wellington. He had ten innings for 361 runs at 40.11. While not as spectacular as his Test performances in England, it was still good, especially for a number six. Yet flaws were evident during the summer. His technique—especially in facing away swing—was found wanting against Wasim Akram, Waqar Younis, Imran Khan and Richard Hadlee. They presented a different level of opposition to the English bowlers, and on wickets with more pace and bounce. It was reflected in his overall first-class figures of nineteen innings for 704 at an average of 44, some twenty short of his England summer average. Waugh was aware of his shortcomings, but reluctant to curtail his favourite shots through backward point. Despite this retreat, Waugh's highest score—196 versus Tasmania at Hobart— indicated his gradual greater capacity for the big score, directly related to his concentration level, over five years. A graph would indicate that his first double century would be scored soon. He was in the New South Wales Shield win of 345 runs in March 1990, versus Queensland.

Waugh spent the 1990 winter preparing for an Ashes series in Australia over 1990–91. On a more important personal front, he and Lynette decided to marry in the off season the following year. Before that there would be ten Tests against England and the West Indies.

Tortoise triumphant

Graham Gooch brought the thirty-seventh England Ashes team to Australia. England struggled early on the tour, mainly because the skipper had an infected finger. Gooch missed the First Test, which England lost by ten wickets. Waugh made 1 run and took a wicket (for 7) when he trapped Jack Russell in England's second innings. Steve's form may not have been an issue a few years earlier, but Tom Moody and Mark Waugh were scoring so heavily in state games and matches against the tourists that his place was in jeopardy.

Steve realised his brother had to be a chance for a Test spot when they combined against Western Australia on 20 and 21 December. Western Australian skipper Geoff Marsh sent New South Wales in. He had Bruce Reid, Terry Alderman, Chris Matthews and Ken Macleay to exploit the fast, bouncy WACA wicket. Steve joined Mark, who had been in for 38 minutes, when the score was four for 137 (Reid already had three for 25). Mark's confidence and rating lifted with his brother at the wicket. These two played cautiously at first then moved into top gear, playing all their shots. Mark was 128 not out and Steve 112 not out in a 238-runs link in 244 minutes. The stumps score was four for 375. The runs kept coming the next day and the twins turned the country's best bowling attack into a rabble. Marsh even asked keeper Tim Zoehrer to remove his pads and bowl five overs of leg spin. They batted for 407 minutes in all, amassing a world first-class cricket record for the fifth wicket of 464 runs. It was the highest-ever partnership in Australia.

New South Wales skipper Geoff Lawson declared at four for 601, with Mark on 229 not out (35 fours and one huge six off MacLeay)—his third first-class double—in 446 minutes off 343 balls and Steve 216 not out (24 fours)—his maiden double—in 407 minutes off 339 balls.

But it wasn't just accumulation of runs. It was the way the twins got them. Rod Marsh even ranked their innings above Barry Richards' 325 not out in a day for South Australia versus Western Austalia in November 1970. Steve, for one, was not happy when Lawson declared. He was aware of the world record partnership of 577 by India's Vijay Hazare (288) and Gul Mahomed (319) for the fourth wicket for Baroda versus Holkar at Baroda in 1946–47.

'We could have put on 600,' a disappointed Steve told Lawson.

During the English summer of 1990, Mark had scored eight centuries for Essex (including two doubles) and had come of age. His Perth double was his twenty-fourth first-class century. Steve's double was his nineteenth century. Mark the tortoise was gaining on Steve the hare. The twins were twenty-five years old and both now seasoned cricketers, but Steve had played forty Tests against Mark's none.

A few days after the Waugh triumph in Perth, Steve arrived in Melbourne for the Boxing Day Test feeling an urgent need to make runs. Yet he made only 19 (and didn't take a wicket) in Australia's eight-wicket win. The form of Bruce Reid, Terry Alderman and Merv Hughes meant that Steve couldn't fall back on his bowling. On top of that, Greg Matthews was at the peak of his career as an all-rounder, batting at number seven and making more runs than Waugh. Matthews would not be dropped.

Waugh felt the pressure in Sydney early in the New Year of 1991. Australia won the toss and batted. He came to the wicket at four for 226 and batted his best for the summer until he was 48. Malcolm beat him for pace and induced an edge to slip. Waugh knew it wasn't quite enough. He had to make a good score in his second innings—a sixty at least—to show that he was back in form. But he was out caught behind off spinner Eddie Hemmings for just 14. He could feel the cold steel of the guillotine on his neck, but wondered who might also get the chop. The form of Taylor, Marsh and Jones had not been scintillating either.

After the Test, which was drawn, Waugh was informed that he had been dumped, but all the other batsmen had held their places. He was told that his brother would replace him.

Waugh went to his mother's home and congratulated Mark.

'Who was dropped?' Mark asked.

'Me,' he replied, as laconic as ever. He was disappointed but was quickly over the hurt. In fact, he was relieved. He had been feeling the pressure and was glad it was over. He now faced going back to the New South Wales team to find form. Steve had reached the heights with his batting in England in 1989 and this made it easier for him to resolve to fight his way back. Had he never made those brilliant innings, he might not have had the confidence in his own ability. It was a matter of working on his technique and climbing back up by a different route.

The inclusion–exclusion was difficult for the Waugh family and their friends. On the one hand they wanted to congratulate Mark. On the other, Steve would suffer with every phone call, handshake and pat on the back for happy Mark. Steve wished his brother well. But he would have preferred not to witness all the congratulations. He was, however, surprised and lifted by the support from so many teammates who rang to commiserate and wish him well.

Mark, who had earned his spot, made a brilliant first Test innings of 138 at Adelaide in another drawn Test. Steve also missed the Fifth and final Test, won by Australia by nine wickets, which gave it a three–nil series win.

Soon afterwards, Steve was relieved to find that he had been selected in the squad—along with his brother—for a tour of the West Indies beginning in February 1991. This would test the newly discovered winning style of the Australians. He was hardly over his disappointment at being dropped when this fresh opportunity presented itself.

Wilderness years

Steve Waugh sat out the first two Tests of an acrimonious Caribbean tour, and was recalled for the Third Test in Trinidad in early April 1991, where he made 26 (caught behind off Walsh) in a drawn game. It was the first ever Test match in which twins had played together. Steve retained his tenuous position for the Fourth Test, but made just 2 (caught behind off Patterson) and 4 not out in a game Australia lost by 343 runs. He was still having trouble with pace and swing outside his off stump. The Caribbean did not provide the conditions to work on his technique. He was dropped again from the Fifth Test, which Australia won, due to Mark Waugh's brilliant 139 in the first innings and Mark Taylor's dogged 144 in the second.

Mark's form meant he would retain his place, along with Taylor, Marsh, Boon, Border and Jones, who had consolidated the top six. Barring injuries and retirement or a sudden drop off in form from any of these batsmen, Steve faced more time in the cricket wilderness.

Steve took time to achieve one of his life goals, as set down nearly a decade earlier, when he married his teenage sweetheart, Lynette, on

16 August 1991. Waugh was now twenty-six and at a major crossroad in his life. By marrying he was embarking on a path that would be even more important to him than cricket. Yet the occasion was also a spur to regain his Test place. It was the route to good income, at least in the short term. It still seemed the only way for him. He had no tertiary qualification or profession. The way chosen over the last eight years since leaving school had left him with few, if any, options. With this in mind, he looked forward with hope to the coming home season.

He was not selected in any of the five Tests against India in Australia over 1991–92. Yet Steve was still in the team for the 1992 World Cup, to be played in February and March in Australia and New Zealand. He had an undistinguished time in a team that came nowhere near its potential. In a game against Pakistan he took three wickets; against Zimbabwe he hit 55 from 43 balls (as opposed to Mark's 66 from 39 balls) in a partnership of 113 in just forty-eight minutes. Steve also took two for 28. Pakistan beat England in the final to win the Cup.

Steve's 1991–92 first-class figures during the domestic season—472 runs from eleven innings at 42.91, with two centuries and two fifties—did little to inspire selectors to recall him for the three-Test series in Sri Lanka in August–September 1992, and he missed out again. Yet their decision to dump Geoff Marsh for the last of the 1991–92 Tests against India paved the way for Steve's return. The selectors couldn't find another opener. They tried the Victorian Wayne Phillips and Tom Moody, who didn't succeed. Instead of experimenting with a third opener, they slipped Boon into the position for the beginning of the 1992–93 season against the West Indies, which was without Viv Richards, their highest wicket taker Malcolm Marshall, Jeffrey Dujon and opener Gordon Greenidge. The selectors brought Steve back, toying with him in the tough position of number three—first wicket down. They also dropped Moody and Jones, allowing the highly thought of Damien Martyn in at the Gabba for his first Test.

A battle, not the war

Waugh would have preferred number five or six in the batting order at Brisbane. In a sense he was the sacrificial lamb, scoring just 10 and 20 before falling both times to Ambrose, caught behind. Mark did well scoring 39 and 60, while Martyn did enough (36 and 15) to warrant another opportunity. Australia had every chance to win the match. But it did not have the bowling power—particularly a spinner—to win on the final day when it had the West Indies on its knees at eight for 128 and still more than a hundred short. Greg Matthews didn't deliver and was dropped for the next Test.

The successful move in the Brisbane Test was Boon opening. He scored 48 and 111 and looked unfazed and solid against the West Indies. His minimalist style of batting, sound defence and courage was an inspiration at the top of the order.

Border had his wish for a leg spinner granted against the West Indies when Shane Warne was brought back into the side for the Boxing Day Test at Melbourne. Steve Waugh's place was still shaky. His 38 and 1 were not convincing when compared to his brother (112) and Border (110) in the first innings, and Martyn (67) in the second. Warne fulfilled Border's hope and belief in him by winning the game with seven for 52 on the last day. He had destroyed the West Indies' second innings. Australia went one up in the series with a 139-run win.

Steve retained his place for the Third Test at Sydney early in the new year, and was given his last chance at the number three hot spot. Coming in at one for 42, he peeled off a dashing 100 to save himself from the chop again and help push Australia to an unbeatable position. Every batsman except for Martyn (0) contributed as Australia reached nine for 503 declared. But Waugh's fine knock was soon overshadowed—as was everything else in the match—by the scintillating form of the young left-hander Brian Lara, who stroked his way to a sensational 277. Lara looked set to break Gary Sobers's record of 365 not out when he was run out. The West Indies were all out for 606 (Richardson 109) and the match drifted to a draw.

Steve Waugh's knock allowed him to breathe more easily. He was selected for the Fourth Test at Adelaide late in January of 1993. The West Indies batted first and Steve (one for 37) was brought on when the openers—Haynes and Simmons—proved difficult for McDermott and Hughes to remove. He soon had Simmons (46) caught. Tim May removed Haynes (45) and this start saw the West Indies contained to just 252, thanks mainly to Hughes, who took five for 64. Australia ran into a rampant Ambrose. Only Steve Waugh (42) and Hughes (43) could stay long enough to look threatening. The great paceman had Steve caught behind and went on to take six for 74. It was a big performance when his team needed it most. Tim May then brought his country right back into the contest with a dazzling display of off spinning, taking five for 9 off 6.5 overs. Australia had to make 186 to win. Karate-trained Justin Langer in his first Test had looked sound in his first innings, scoring 20. Now he needed all the mind concentration demanded by martial arts to fend off the West Indies, whose speed quartet—Ambrose, Walsh, Benjamin and Bishop—threw themselves at the home team. Langer kept his head still and his shot selection simple. He looked like a left-handed Boon. At 54 he was caught behind off Bishop. Australia was providing the biggest challenge yet to the West Indies' long reign as the world's number one Test team. Nevertheless, the Caribbean squad, even though weakened by the loss of four champions, was not going to hand over the crown without a bruising fight.

Ambrose again was Steve Waugh's nemesis, forcing a catch from him when he was just 4 and desperate to win the match—and the series—for Australia. The home side went into a tailspin to reach nine for 144—still 42 from victory. The last men in were May and McDermott. They would have been excused for capitulating and saving their bodies and hands from injury in order to fight another day, but they shuffled behind every ball. Both were hit often. There was no let up from the barrage. Yet these two defied the odds and sneaked closer and closer. They reached 184—one run short of the West Indies— when McDermott was given out caught behind.

The home team had been beaten by that solitary run. Two more runs would have given them a win, and the series two–nil, with just one Test left to play in Perth.

The Australians, particularly Allan Border, were shattered. He had suffered at the hands of the West Indians for more than a decade in five series. Now he had been teased by a nerve-tingling afternoon and the possibility of revenge, an emotion that had been usurped yet again by the agony of defeat. So very near but so far. Border had been striving towards this moment for the better part of a decade. First he had had to haul Australia out of the cricketing doldrums. Then he had set his sights on the West Indies' crown. Border took little comfort at that moment from the remarkable fact that he had lifted Australia to a position where it could challenge the world champs.

Steve Waugh there and then realised where all his and his team's energy should be channelled: towards a series victory over the West Indies. He had a long memory and his passions for the game ran deep. He would mentally file his own and Border's anguish and use it at the appropriate moment. For now, he had to survive and consolidate.

Australia's fear that the hard Perth wicket in the Fifth Test would play into the West Indians' hands proved well founded. Mark Taylor and Tim May were casualties before a ball was bowled. Taylor was dropped. May's fingers were so badly battered that he wouldn't be playing cricket for several weeks.

The carnage continued on the field from day one of the Test, when Ambrose rocked Australia, taking seven for 25 in the first innings, which netted just 119 runs. Only Boon was a rock this time, making 44. The West Indies managed 322 and then Bishop (six for 40) rolled Australia in its second dig for 178 (Boon scored 52), giving the tourists a win by an innings and 25 runs, and the series two–one. Border's leadership had seen Australia capable of beating everyone except the West Indies. But this series was closer than it had been for eight years. A change at the top of world cricket was coming.

Steve Waugh was dismissed by Bishop both times in the final Test for 13 and 0. Putting him at number three had not worked. He averaged 25.33 from nine innings with an aggregate of 228. Yet apart from Boon there had been no consistent batting successes against these talented pacemen.

Revival in Apteryx Land

The Australians hardly had time to lick their wounds before they were on tour in New Zealand for a three-Test series. Border tinkered with the batting order for the First Test at Christchurch. Mark Waugh was to be tried at number four, Steve at five and Border at six, with Langer in the troubled number-three position.

It worked, but against an attack that was nowhere near as potent as the West Indies. Hadlee, the great bowler who had destroyed Australian batting in the 1980s, had retired. The batsmen celebrated the fact with a consistent effort, reaching 485. Taylor, back in the line-up after being shell-shocked by the West Indies, batted with confidence for 82, and Langer (63) seemed to have settled well into number three. Steve Waugh came in at three for 170 and made an impressive 62. He was much freer and relieved not to be forced to jump and weave away from pace. Steve could employ his back-foot slash with impunity. Border (88) too found batting a holiday, although Danny Morrison could not be taken lightly.

Australia then dismissed New Zealand for 182 and 243 to win by an innings and 60 runs. Australia's bowling line-up of McDermott, Hughes and Paul Reiffel was given another dimension by Warne (three for 23 and four for 63), who was settling in as a reliable spinner. Not even Lara had taken liberties with him in the recent series. Border now seemed ready to step up his presence.

In the Second Test at Wellington, Steve gained a boost in confidence with his top-score performance of 75 from Australia's 298 in reply to New Zealand's 329. He was being called on to bowl less because of Warne's capacity as almost a strike bowler. This may have worked in Waugh's favour. He liked his role as a surprise change bowler and Border would always have that option. But the strengthened bowling line-up meant Waugh could concentrate more on his batting. His main aim would be to eliminate risk and concentrate on not giving his wicket away through a rash shot. The wild cut backward of point was reduced to action against the loose ball outside off. The hook and pull, never Waugh strengths, were dumped altogether. His revised approach was going to make or break the rest of his career.

Mark Waugh's run of scores since his century in Melbourne—16, 57, 0, 26, 9, 21, 13 and 12—saw him axed from the team for the Third Test at Auckland. Damien Martyn took his place. Australia batted first and was soon in trouble. Steve arrived at the wicket with the score at three for 39. Martyn went for 1 and then Morrison, bowling at his best, removed Border (0), and Healy (0), leaving Australia a lamentable six for 48. Steve had demonstrated an ability for capitalising on a good team start, but his capacities when the team was down had yet to be defined. Border had been the player to bat for the team's life since the late 1970s. Boon was as solid as any player who ever played for Australia. Was Steve Waugh made of the same material? There were positive signs as he defended stoutly in a mini fight-back with Hughes (33). Waugh top-scored again with 41 from 139 all out. Steve then did his team an important service by having Martin Crowe (31) caught by Taylor at slip. This allowed Warne to tie up the middle order while taking four for 8 off fifteen overs with an astonishing twelve maidens. New Zealand made 224. Australia responded with 285 (Martyn 74, Border 71, Steve Waugh 0). It wasn't enough as New Zealand battled to a five-wicket win, drawing the series one all.

Waugh's consistent batting encouraged him to think he could retain his place in the Test line-up for his second tour of England in 1993. Waugh's aim was to bat well enough to hold on to his number-six spot. All things being equal, he hoped he would be selected because of his extra dimension as a bowler. But there were no guarantees.

Border would favour Waugh unless another fringe player did something spectacular early. The captain was just as ruthless in his approach as in 1989. He wanted the ledger of recent Ashes defeats in England— 1981 and 1985—squared. The players who applied themselves early would receive his support at the selection table.

PART TWO

LEGEND

5

IN DEFENCE OF BURNT BAILS

Reinvention for a higher average

Steve Waugh was still in competition with brother Mark and Martyn for two Test places. By the time of the First Test of the 1993 Ashes series, Slater, Taylor, Boon and Border (at number 5) had taken four of the six places. The Waugh twins' form in the run-up was good enough for them to keep Martyn out.

The game at Old Trafford began well for Australia, with an opening stand of 128 before Slater, in his first Test, was out for 58. Taylor (124) continued on but the rest of the team collapsed to the off spin of Peter Such (six for 67). He bowled Waugh for 3 and had Border (17) stumped after removing Boon (21). Australia was all out for 289.

Border then pulled his bottle-blond rabbit from the hat in the form of Warne, who had been shielded before the series. When he did bowl against the counties he limited his deliveries to stock leg breaks. Now his captain had given him licence to let loose his full repertoire of five or six modes of delivery. He began in sensational style by bowling Gatting with his first ball of an Ashes Test. This incredible delivery drifted in the air from middle stump to well outside leg and into

Gatting's blind spot. It then hit the pitch and spun almost a metre past the bat to take the off stump. The ball bewildered Gatting, a seasoned campaigner and a fine player of spin, to such an extent that Warne and Australia had a psychological hold on England for the rest of the series. The leg spinner took four for 51, and England was dismissed for 210.

In the second innings Waugh came in at a familiar time in Ashes Tests, with the score four for well over 200. He later played second fiddle to a dashing Healy, who clipped an unbeaten 102, in an unfinished 180-run partnership. Border declared at five for 432 (Waugh 78 not out), giving Australia a lead of more than 500 and shutting England out of the game. Only Graham Gooch, in top form and happy that Australia didn't have Terry Alderman to torment him, resisted as Warne early then Hughes later collected four wickets each. He was out, 'handled the ball', one of the more bizarre methods of dismissal, when he flicked a free hand at a ball from Hughes that looked as if it might rebound off his bat onto the stumps. England crumbled for 332, giving Australia a win by 179 runs.

Steve's form was now judged as 'consistent' rather than 'Bradman-like' as he had been viewed in 1989. His recent run of Test scores read 62, 75, 41, 0, 3 and 78 not out, which suggested he was due for a big hundred soon. It wasn't allowed in the Second Test at Lord's in mid-June. Waugh came to the wicket at four for 591—following Taylor (111), Slater (a brilliant 152), Boon (164 not out) and Mark Waugh (99). Having contributed 77, Border declared at four for 631 with Steve Waugh on 13 not out.

England, demoralised again by having to climb over such a huge score, could only manage 205 (Warne and Hughes again taking four wickets apiece), and then 365 (this time Warne and May took four wickets apiece). Australia won by an innings and 62 runs.

England revived in the Third Test at Trent Bridge and looked as if it could win on the last day. It scored 321 and six declared for 422 (Graham Thorpe 114 not out and Gooch 120). Australia made 373 (Boon 101) and was left 371 to win from seventy-seven overs. Gooch seemed to have been overcautious, but at four for 81, Australia was in danger of defeat. Steve Waugh came to the wicket. By scoring 47 not out, he again proved that he had the sort of backs-to-the-wall will that had so distinguished Border and Boon. Where Mark had put his stamp on the number four spot—an early-order run-chaser—Steve found himself happy at number six. He didn't have to take the brunt of speed bowling and he could strengthen the middle order and bolster the tail. The spot also allowed Steve to demonstrate his tough fighting qualities if a battle were required. He would never open, and preferred not to come in at number three, where he had never had confidence or consistent success. Mark suited number four and Border liked number five. Six was Steve's and he was satisfied with it. He could perform within his limitations without the pressures up the order. His aim was to build scores from that less-demanding vantage point. It would allow him to fulfil other ambitions. Number six wasn't set in concrete for him forever. But it would do at this point in his career.

Brendon Julian stayed with him in this Third Test, against-the-odds battle, scoring a hard-hitting 56 not out as Australia held on to be six for 202 at the end of the match. The tourists were two–nil up with three Tests to play. England had to win three successive Tests to take the series and regain the Ashes.

As you were

Rain interrupted much play in the county games in the sixteen days before the Fourth Test at Headingley. Despite Australia's two–nil lead, Border remained concerned. He started the tour as Captain Grumpy, with a rebuke for McDermott after his bowling was wayward in a county game, and he had maintained a stern demeanour with total concentration on the job at hand. Waugh took note of Border's approach. Would he be the same if ever elected skipper? Yes and no. Waugh would focus on the job like Border. Their batting was styled similarly. They sold their wickets dearly, a fine trait in a captain. Yet Waugh thought Border could more often communicate directly to individual team members. It was one thing Waugh vowed to do if he were ever made captain. And while Border had given no sign that he wanted to give up the leadership, there was a likelihood that the captain would be replaced in a year or two.

Border would be turning thirty-eight a couple of weeks later on 27 July, a day after the Fourth Test. Next year would mark his tenth as captain. Only Don Bradman had been skipper over a greater span of time, from 1936 to 1948, but with a six-year war in between. This meant Border had been Australia's longest-serving skipper. But he was keen to hang on if he could. He had unfinished business, which was beating the West Indies in a series. Border had reluctantly taken the reins in early December 1984, when Australia was down as low as it could go, after hidings from England and the West Indies. Now he was rectifying the ledger in regard to Ashes conquests. He also wanted to retire as the captain who brought back the Frank Worrell Trophy. Yet the next trip to the Caribbean was scheduled for 1995 when Border would be forty. Mark Taylor, who had been skipper of New South Wales for two years, was tipped to succeed him.

Waugh noted in his tour diary, *Steve Waugh's Ashes Diary*, that Border was at his inspirational best during this rain-induced lull before the Fourth Test. Border took the opportunity to refocus the team and avoid the mid-tour doldrums, which had been deepened by the grey, wet weather. One soggy afternoon they were all in and around the dressing room during a county game when the BBC replayed part of the 1981 Headingley Ashes Test. Botham with the bat and Bob Willis with the ball had humiliated Border and his teammates to turn around the game and defeat Australia.

'Whenever a Pom says to you, "Remember Headingley '81?" as they're saying now,' Border told the players as they watched, 'I want you to be able to say, "Do you remember Headingley '89 and '93?"'

He couldn't erase the memory of that 1981 comeback win for England, one of the finest in Ashes history, but Border wanted to help bury it under layers of Australian wins. Eventually, he hoped, the cry 'Remember Headingley '81' would sound hollow. He wanted that event to seem like a historical fluke.

Waugh loved this approach. He couldn't quite engender the kind of deep passion against England that Border felt. He hadn't suffered as Border had. But he liked the idea of keeping the old enemy down and quiet for as long as he played for Australia.

At the start of the Fourth Test Border won the toss and elected to bat on the ever-enigmatic Headingley strip. Australia reached two for 307 on day one. Boon made an unconquered century after Slater (67) and Mark Waugh (52) batted with certitude.

Boon was out for 107, bringing Steve Waugh to the wicket at four for 321. Everything was set for him to make a big hundred. The weather was fine, the attack controllable and Border, the embodiment of cool concentration, was at the other end. Steve could feel his captain's sense of mission. Like a good digger, he wanted to be beside him, wherever he was going. Steve began with less discomfort than normal, pushing at the right ball, and daring to cut on the true, even-bouncing wicket. Border was 40-odd ahead of Waugh when their part-nership began and this differential remained through a long stay at the wicket. Their shot selection was excellent. They cut, drove, pulled and nudged their way to the end of the second day to be four for 613. On form this was 200 more than was needed. Border was 175 not out and Steve 144 not out. Their stand then was worth 292. The media expected Border to declare before play. But he did not. He had too many scars from being in the reverse situation.

Border announced that Australia would bat on for thirty or forty minutes, 'to cause further mental and physical disintegration of the opposition'.

It was overkill to the media and the British public, but not Border. It was a display of his style of competitiveness. It would kill the game as a contest and for spectators, but ensure Australia did not lose. He and Steve wandered on into day three and the record books in an unbroken 332 link. It ranked eighth in Australia's best-ever partner-ships. Border remained 200 not out and Waugh 157 not out, his third 150-plus score against England in England.

Border declared at four for 653, shutting England out of any chance of winning. It ensured that Australia retained the Ashes, even if the home team squared the series with wins in the last two Tests.

England, once more faced with an impossible task, was vulnerable, especially to Paul Reiffel (five for 65 and three for 87) in his first Test for the tour. He swung the ball and was often unplayable in England's first innings of 200. In its follow-on knock of 305, he was well supported by May (four for 65). Australia ran out winners by an innings and 148. It was three–nil up with two to play. Australia had won the series and retained the Ashes.

Border and his merry men let go for the first time and partied hard into 27 July, his birthday.

'It's the nicest present I've received since '89,' Border said.

Yet still he wouldn't give up the campaign. Border now wanted to try again to match the five–nil Test record of Warwick Armstrong's 1921 side. The 1993 team began well in its Fifth Test at Edgbaston early in August, rolling England for a mediocre 276. Reiffel, with six for 71, was proving a huge bonus in the second half of the series. Australia struggled to four for 80 when Steve joined Mark. The brothers, who rarely enjoyed each other's company on tour, were flung together with a mission to turn the game around. They said the minimum to each other, hardly ever acknowledging a good shot. Yet their appreciation for each other was tacit. There was a nod from Steve when Mark reached 50, but fifties were not impressive to them any more. Only centuries would satisfy either of them, now that they were 28-year-old professionals. They batted freely and there was no trouble identifying which twin was which. Mark was all style and flow. When he miscued, which was rare, he threw his head back in disgust, annoyed for transgressing his polished orthodoxy. Mark batted as if at one with the bowler, who delivered smoothly to him so that (or so it seemed) he could stroke the ball to the fence in sweet harmony. Sometimes the eye played tricks with Mark's shots. He seemed to be into them even before the bowler had completed his action. He was rarely hurried or ruffled, unless tied down. Then an ungainly urgency would creep into his shots, and he would get himself out. Fastidious, brilliant stroke-maker Mark, like David Gower before him, hated to lose his aesthetic rhythm and free-scoring authenticity. A way to dismiss him was to starve him of runs to the point where he did something rash.

Steve, by contrast, made you gasp at his late flurry in stroke making. He seemed to hold back the decision so late that there was no harmony with the ball delivered. Early on in his innings, he would play and miss. Then, within a dozen runs, his timing would arrive. Steve didn't seem to move his feet with the deftness of his brother. He appeared more aggressive. Where Mark caressed the ball, Steve belted it. Fielders chased Mark's strokes; they gave up when Steve clobbered a delivery past them.

Mark finessed, where Steve wound up and walloped in one action that invariably struck the ball in the middle of the bat, indicating an exceptional 'eye' and lightning reflexes. Mark seemed to have so much time that you never expected anything to get through him. Not so with Steve. You would think a ball was through him and then realise it was on its way to the fence, exquisitely struck. Unlike Mark, he would be more patient if tied down. He sold his wicket more dearly.

The Birmingham crowd that second afternoon of the Test had hoped for further England breakthroughs. When resigned to a Waugh partnership, they settled down to watch a rare phenomenon: twins of different method and style batting brilliantly. Mark was due. He had so far scored 6, 64, 99, 70, 1 and 52. This time he went on to 137. The partnership was worth 153, and when he was out the score was five for 233. Steve was caught behind for 59, leaving Healy (80) to take Australia to 408 and a lead of 132. England was contained and tamed again by Warne and May (five wickets apiece) and all out for 251.

Australia went on to mop up the 120 needed for the loss of two wickets, with Mark Waugh in continuing fine touch scoring 62 not out. Australia was ahead four–nil with one to play. Border, looking drained but relaxed, spoke of 'not slackening off' and the desire to make it five–nil. But he wasn't convincing. There was very little to play for. The squad's collective mind was already on holidays with girlfriends or back in Australia with families.

England under new skipper Mike Atherton saved some face in the final Test at The Oval with a win by 161 runs. Steve got two starts (20 and 26) and two very good deliveries—one from Fraser, that bowled him, and one from the demonic Devon Malcolm, who had him jumping and struggling before trapping him lbw.

The series ended with Australia ahead four–one. Steve was well satisfied with his series—he had made 416 runs at 83.20 to again top the averages of both sides in an Ashes series in England. But there was a subtle difference this time in Waugh's approach, if not in his execution. He guarded his wicket with more purpose than even during the 1989 Ashes. The hook was gone from his stroke play. The slash/cut was pretty well dormant.

Mark, with 550 at 61.11, was equally effective for the team. Both twins had established themselves as regular Test players. Barring a fall-off in form, they were assured positions for some time to come and would no longer be rivals for a spot in the batting line-up. With Shane Warne proving himself a great leg spinner in this series, the team had a balanced, skilful look—the right blend of experience and appearance to take on the South Africans for the first time in a quarter of a century.

Waugh against fruit and flowers

Less than three months later in Perth, the Australian team was immersed in a Test against New Zealand, which was playing above itself. Steve came to the wicket in Australia's first innings at four for 129, and steadied the team with a competent 44 before being caught off spinner Patel. Healy saved the home side with a forceful 113 not out as Australia restored itself to 398.

The home team's 'new look' bowling line-up, with Warne, McDermott back and McGrath in his first Test, was expected to account for the Kiwis with ease. But Andrew Jones (143) and Chris Cairns (78) showed little respect for Australia's much-vaunted attack. New Zealand reached 419 and a lead of 21.

Australia declared at one for 323 in its second knock (Taylor 142 not out, Slater 99), but New Zealand (four for 166) was equal to the task of forcing a draw. The lack of a result when a big home-team win had been expected was a wake-up call for the Australians, who applied themselves better in the Second Test at Hobart, beginning on 26 November. They ran up six for 544 (Slater 168, Boon 106, Mark Waugh 111 and Border 60), and Steve Waugh, coming in at four for 485, scored 25 not out. He had several 'not outs' now dangling at the end of big innings, which helped his average. The Kiwis were then dismissed (an apt description) for 161 twice, giving Australia a massive win by an innings and 222 runs. Warne (nine wickets) and May (seven wickets) did the damage. The sides were not well matched. It was not the best preparation for an expected tough series against the Proteas. The lack of competition continued in the Third Test at Brisbane early in December 1993. New Zealand made 233 in the first innings. Australia replied in a manner that had become common against weaker opposition, by running up a big score. Steve Waugh came in at four for 277 after Taylor, Boon and Mark Waugh had managed half-turies. He began well in a 159-run link with Border (105) and then just 29 with Healy (15), before being joined by Warne at six for 465. The spinner had a good batting technique, but had rarely shown the discipline for scores in Test cricket. This time he was able to combine defence with flogging and stay at the wicket to make 74 not out. Waugh remained 147 not out in another big knock in which he moved well into 'the zone', that state of mind that some batsmen could reach by exceptional concentration and application. It allowed them to make runs without risk and methodically build a big score, no matter what the interruptions and tactics used against them. Waugh had the mental capacity for reaching this special mental state. He loved it more than anything else in sport.

Border declared at six for 607 and Australia then rolled New Zealand for 278, giving the home team a win by an innings and 96 runs. This poor series saw attendances drop and caused cricket inistrators more concern. One-day cricket revenue, television rights and sponsorship were propping up the game in Australia. Test cricket in the early 1990s was still suffering from the dominance and unattractive cricket of the West Indies in the 1980s. Officials hoped that the visiting South Africans would be more appealing.

Steve Waugh had a leg injury and missed the drawn Boxing Day

Test versus South Africa, which was ruined by the weather, and the thrilling Sydney Test, which the tourists won by five runs. It's unlikely Waugh would have failed twice, particularly in the second innings, when the Australians choked in a small run chase of 117 runs. He returned to the team for the Third Test at Adelaide in late January 1994 and picked up where he had left off in his 147 not out against New Zealand at Brisbane eight weeks earlier. Steve came to the wicket at four for 183 and joined Border (84) in a 208-run partnership. Waugh could have renamed his 'zone' the 'Waugh zone'. He entered it again after his century, knuckling down to reach 164 and doing most to push Australia to seven for 469 declared.

The home team was frustrated by the Proteas' uninspired yet dogged persistence when batting and Border was forced to try Waugh. He soon got rid of the stubborn opener Andrew Hudson (90), then ripped through the middle order, taking four for 26 off eighteen overs with seven maidens. His other wickets were Jonty Rhodes (5), Daryll Cullinan (10) and Brian McMillan (2). The tourists could only put together 273, but it was enough to avoid a follow-on. Australia declared at six for 124 in the second innings and then crashed through the opposition for 129, thus squaring the series and saving face at home. Steve's dual effort with bat and ball won him the Man of the Match award.

Waugh's reputation after this Test and the previous one against New Zealand was now restored to what it had been during the 1989 Ashes. It had taken him nearly five years, but he was now a permanent member of the team in the manner Border and Boon had been over the years.

Fracas in South Africa

The Australians were challenged by the first official trip to South Africa (from 5 February until 9 April 1994) since 1969–70, when Bill Lawry's team was thrashed four–nil. The tight series in Australia assured that it would be a struggle as both teams, who liked to play it hard, fought for early supremacy. Steve Waugh found some form early in the tour games with 102 against Orange Free State in a 332-run partnership with Mark (154). They were upstaged by Hansie Cronje, who scored 44 and 251, despite his team losing by 60 runs.

The one-day games were split into two blocks of four day contests before the Tests and four day–night games after them. The Proteas bolted in the early one-dayers, with Cronje smashing 112 in the first, which South Africa won by 5 runs in a thriller. Steve took none for 54 and made 46 not out. Cronje continued his thunderous form in the second game before he was run out for 97. Steve (86) led a fightback but no one could stay with him long enough to threaten the home team, which won easily by 56 runs. In the third game Australia batted first and set up a winning tally of 281—if Cronje could be contained. Border, standing and delivering like a baseball batter, belted 40 in seventeen balls. Mark Waugh (60) batted magnificently.

Steve this time stopped Cronje at 45, forcing a catch to McDermott. South Africa was always pushed on the run rate, and could not handle Warne, who took four for 36. Australia collapsed in the fourth game for 154 and was beaten by seven wickets. Thus South Africa led three–one in the best of eight.

Before the one-day winner could be decided, the Tests began at New Wanderers, Johannesburg, on 4 March. South Africa batted first and made a moderate 251. Australia was at one point three for 70. After lunch on day two Mark Waugh (42) was run out due to bad calling. It brought Steve to the wicket at four for 136. Soon after he called badly and ran out Border (34). Two top batsmen had been out in wasteful ways after being set. Waugh was disappointed to have run out his skipper but, unlike most, he didn't let the error cause his own downfall. Instead of fretting, he knuckled down for a dogged display, scoring a solid 45 not out as the tail crumbled around him in the first innings of 248. This unspectacular innings allowed him to display his determination not to lose his wicket.

South Africa took advantage of the moment, led by Cronje, who was in a dominant mood as he compiled a balanced 122. The score of 450 put the game out of reach of the Australians. Steve Waugh came in at four for 164 but edged one behind off Craig Matthews to be on his way for a duck. His removal was the white flag for Australia, and the rest of the side fell for 92, to be all out for 256, 197 short of South Africa.

Warne on the field and Merv Hughes coming off it were involved in nasty incidents, for which they were penalised. Warne had abused batsman Andrew Hudson after dismissing him, and Hughes had wielded his bat at a spitting, abusive spectator as he moved through the players' race to the dressing rooms.

The Australians applied themselves better in the Second Test at Cape Town nine days later, despite South Africa's capable batting in the first innings when it accumulated 361 (Hudson run out 102). Steve came to the wicket at four for 244 (Boon 96) and hit a four first ball. It set him on the right path. He attacked while Border held up the other end in a useful 66 link. Waugh went on to 86 before Craig Matthews skidded one under his bat and bowled him. Australia reached 435 and a lead of 74.

When South Africa batted again it was nearly out of trouble at one for 69 when Steve Waugh took a terrific caught and bowled to put back Cronje, who the Australians knew had to be removed before they could take control. South African skipper Kepler Wessels (9) was run out by his partner Hudson. Hearing Wessels's unkind words to his partner on the way to the dressing room, Steve sensed Hudson was unsettled. He tried him with his specialty, the slower ball, which few Proteas had seen. It worked, trapping the opener lbw for 49. South Africa never recovered and was all out for 164, with Steve producing a match-winning five for 28 off 22.3 overs with nine maidens. Australia knocked off the 90-odd without trouble and won by nine wickets. The series was squared with one game to play. Once more the two sides had wrestled each other to a stalemate. Would it remain that way after the Third Test at Durban?

Australia began poorly, losing five for 123. Steve Waugh and Healy were both runless at that point but managed a strong 92-run recovery before Healy (55) played on. Steve got to 50 on the last ball of the day and the next morning was unsettled by the quick fall of wickets. He was caught off Matthews again, this time for 64, the side's top score out of a mediocre 269. It was made to look even more ordinary by South Africa, who relied on seven batsmen in an even performance that reached 422. Steve Waugh bowled tidily again, taking three for 40 off 27.2 overs with twelve maidens. Only Warne, with four wickets, did better. Much depended now on Australia's early batsmen in their second innings, and Mark Waugh came through with a well-compiled 113 not out. He was supported by a defiant Border, who scored 42 not out in his last ever Test innings. Australia was in a safe position once these two took control and reached four for 297. The game ended in a draw.

Steve made 195 in the three Tests at 65.00 and he took ten wickets at 13.00. His tour aggregate was 400 for 66.66, which was second only to Mark Waugh's 573 at 71.62. Steve's additional form with the ball (eleven wickets at 14.27) generated the best bowling analysis, and helped see him win the award for Player of the Series. It was his second such award. He was Player of the Series in Australia versus South Africa, earlier in the summer, despite playing only one match. He now felt more secure in Test cricket than ever before.

The one-all Test series was followed by the four remaining one-day matches. All were day–nighters. Waugh was dominant in number five, top-scoring with 67 not out in Australia's seven-wicket win. South Africa won the sixth, giving it a four–two lead in the eight games. In the seventh, Australia won by 31 runs, thanks to Mark Waugh's 71. Match eight was a tight affair, with Australia winning by 1 run. This squared the series four all and reminded South Africa yet again that the Australians were never beaten. They had come from behind in two Test series and the one-dayers to make the two teams level.

Waugh hit 47 in the final game, giving him an aggregate of 291 at 48.50. It was enough, with his bowling and fielding, to give him the player-of-the-series in this contest too. No wonder he was keen to write a book about the experience, which he did—*Steve Waugh's South*

African Tour Diary. He dedicated it 'to all those responsible for the end of Apartheid and the renewal of official sporting links with South Africa'. Waugh's codedication was to Allan Border, 'for the great legacy he has left Australian cricket'.

After the South African tour, Border, as expected, resigned the captaincy and retired from Test cricket amid some acrimony concerning the ACB. Border was not happy with the timing of the announcement. The ACB was keen to regenerate the leadership with Mark Taylor, who was a decade younger. Border would be thirty-nine in July 1994. He had played a record 156 Tests, ninety-three of them as captain. He had been a big part of the sporting consciousness of Australia from the late 1970s to the early 1990s, and had played in exactly three times as many Tests as Don Bradman. Border had hit twenty-seven Test centuries and had scored a world record 11,174 runs at an average of 50.56—always a sign of true cricketing greatness. His legacy would be the revival of Australia as a top cricketing nation. It was now up to the new skipper, Mark Taylor, and the secure stars in his side, including the Waugh twins, Ian Healy and Shane Warne, to take the team one step further to the top of world cricket in both Tests and one-day cricket.

6

TO THE TOP

Tubby time

Steve Waugh felt comfortable with his good mate Mark 'Tubby' Taylor becoming Australian captain. He had long recognised the opener from Wagga Wagga's outstanding character. They were about the same age (twenty-nine) and had shared cricket experiences in state representative sides for more than a decade. Taylor was a regular bloke whom everyone liked and respected, yet someone who could make the hard decisions. He would be a good man in a crisis either for the team or personally. Waugh also liked his vigorous sense of fair play, which he thought was similar to his own. Taylor wouldn't grumble if things went against the team, but would put it behind him and move on to the next encounter. Taylor, like Waugh, would be generous about the opposition when it was warranted but never bow to a foe, superior, alleged or otherwise. In that respect, these two dissimilar characters were as one. With Healy, another seasoned campaigner, they formed the best group of leaders Australia had had since the early 1950s, when Lindsay Hassett, Arthur Morris, Neil Harvey, Keith Miller and Ray Lindwall—all capable of strong leadership—were in the same side.

It augured well for Australia's objective of becoming the clear number-one cricketing nation. Nevertheless, like all skippers before him, even though he had inherited a strong team, Taylor would have to crawl before he walked. His first challenge was to lead the team for a series of one-dayers and three Tests in Pakistan.

Steve Waugh failed with the bat in the first one-dayer against Pakistan at the SSC ground in Colombo, Sri Lanka, but took a match-winning three for 16, in helping Warne (three for 29) win the game for Australia. It was a contest that would later come under scrutiny when it was alleged that certain Pakistani players had been bribed into throwing the game, which had been the subject of a big betting plunge. But at the time, the Australians knew nothing about this: had they been aware of such a situation they would not have played the game. There would be no point—they wanted to play and win for Australia, not be subject to the whims of bookies in India.

Australia lost the second game against India at the Premadasa International Stadium in Colombo, thanks to a smashing 110 by Sachin Tendulkar. The Australians had not seen Tendulkar for a few years since the 1992 World Cup. Waugh thought he had matured in his stroke-play, but he didn't yet rank him as highly as Brian Lara as a threat to Australia.

The next game was against Sri Lanka at Colombo. Australia went under again, but Taylor was not perturbed. He didn't put as much store in winning the one-dayers as he did the Tests, which were due to begin at Karachi at the end of September.

In the First Test against Pakistan Australia batted first. Taylor felt irritated when he made a duck: it wasn't the auspicious debut as captain he would have liked. Australia slumped to four for 95, but a strong partnership emerged between Steve Waugh and Michael Bevan, a left–right combination that threw the line of Pakistan's speedsters, Wasim and Waqar, and spinner Mushtaq Ahmed. They took the score to 216 before Mushtaq removed Bevan (82). Waugh (73) was later bowled by Waqar with the score at 281, and the team managed a respectable 337 (Healy 57) after the poor start. Once more Waugh had pulled the side out of a slump and held the middle order together.

Pakistan (256) succumbed to a combination of pace by Glenn McGrath and Jo Angel, who removed half the side, and the spin of Warne and May, who removed the other five wickets.

Taylor completed his pair when he was out for a duck in the second innings. It seemed that Boon (114 not out) and Mark Waugh (61) could make the game safe when the score reached two for 171. But then Bevan (caught) and Steve Waugh (lbw) received first-ball ducks courtesy of Wasim, which rocked the side and saw it collapse for 232. This left Pakistan to get 314 to win in a day and a half. It was three for 157 at the end of the fourth day's play. With seven wickets left and halfway to the target, the odds were even.

But the betting odds were far from it. Asian bookies had put a huge amount on Pakistan to win. Salim Malik that night tried to bribe Warne and May with $250,000 to bowl badly and lose the game. The Australians laughed it off and told the Pakistani to go forth and multiply.

The next day, thanks mainly to Warne (five for 89), Pakistan was reduced to nine for 258. Amid some strident appeals for lbw and one for a blatant catch behind, the last two men in, Inzamam-ul-Haq and Mushtaq, scrambled the score up to 311. Warne came on at the 'death'. He bowled a quicker ball to Inzamam, who moved out of his crease a few paces, swung and missed. Inzamam was stranded metres out of his ground. The ball raced through Healy's legs and sped to the fence for 4 byes. Pakistan had won by one wicket.

Malik chided Warne for not taking the bribe, which developed ill-feeling between the teams and caused the Australians to be even more determined to win. They shaped in the Second Test at Rawalpindi beginning on 5 October as if they were going to win. Taylor (69) found form and with Slater (110) led the way with an opening stand of 176. Then Mark Waugh (68) and Bevan (70) took the score to 323, when Steve Waugh, one of the most talented batsmen ever to walk onto a Test field as a number six, was in. He did what he did best at this stage in his career: ground the opposition down before taking control of the attack to put the Australians into an unbeatable position. He and Healy (58) put on the third big partnership (109) of the innings until Steve Waugh was stopped two short of his century. Throughout his career, he had converted more innings into centuries than not from that position. Rationalising his demise just short of the magic three figures, Waugh said afterwards that he would take 98 at any time if he were offered it. After all, it was close to Don Bradman's 99.94 average. Waugh's near-hundred placed his team in a good position. It reached 521.

If natural justice were to prevail, Australia would blast out the bad boy of Pakistan, Salim Malik, who was known to the tourists as 'the rat', not for his alleged nefarious activities but, in cruel Aussie school-yard fashion, for his looks. McDermott was the judge, bowling Malik for 33. Pakistan made 260.

Should Taylor bat again or make the opposition follow on? One argument was to drive home the advantage straight away. But Taylor's bowlers had toiled hard. Shouldn't they be rested? In the end he opted to take a chance and send Pakistan in again. This time natural justice deserted them. Malik was dropped twice, but went on and on to a big, match-saving 237 out of Pakistan's 537. It was a great innings. Despite anything said about Malik, no one could fault him as a batsman and fighter. He was a cool, quiet customer, who played spin as well as anyone in the game. His reply put the game out of reach. It was a draw.

The tourists overcame their disappointment by applying themselves to another one-day series, which resumed after the Second Test for the rest of October. In Sri Lanka in September, Pakistan, India, Sri Lanka and Australia played in the Singer World Series. Now, in Pakistan in October, Pakistan, South Africa and Australia played in the Wills Triangular Tournament.

Steve Waugh (56) stamped his name on the first encounter with South Africa at Lahore, which Australia won by just six runs, despite 98 from Cronje. Waugh (59 not out) was prominent in the next game—a thriller—against Pakistan at Multan, as Australia won again. Then the tourists rolled South Africa a second time, lost to Pakistan and made it a clean sweep against South Africa with a third victory. Australia went on to win the final against Pakistan at Lahore on 30

October with ease. Taylor held his first cup high and breathed a sigh of relief. His winning ways had begun.

Steve Waugh's hamstring and groin problems, which had flared in late 1993 and would continue to plague him, returned and he missed the Third Test, which was drawn. The Australians went home losers in the Tests, the score one–nil to Pakistan, but they were satisfied that they had made a fair start in the new Taylor era. Now the team looked forward to an Ashes series against a rejuvenated—or so it was claimed by the English media—England XI.

Ashes dashers

On paper, England's First Test line-up did look outstanding: Atherton, Stewart, Hick, Thorpe, Gooch, Gatting, McCague, Rhodes, Gough and Tufnell. If anything it was a champion bowler or all-rounder short. Otherwise, it seemed a worthy challenger. However, England's form was unconvincing going into the First Test at Brisbane in late November 1994. It needed to win the toss, but lost and had to bowl to a rampant Slater (176) and Mark Waugh (140, his highest Test score so far). Steve came to the wicket at number seven (Warne was in before him as nightwatchman) at five for 352. Steve made just 19 and Australia was all out for 426. England replied with a disappointing 167, mowed down by McDermott (six for 53). Taylor, smarting from the draw in Pakistan when he had enforced a follow on, batted again and declared at eight for 248. (Steve again failed, making just 7.) In so doing he indulged in overkill, leaving England a target of 508 to win. England (Hick 80, Thorpe 67) fought hard but ran into a forceful Warne (eight for 71) on a spinning pitch. Warne restricted the innings to 323 and Australia won by 184 runs.

The series then went into recess for a month while the World Series Cricket one-day games were played. Waugh didn't get much of a look in because of the form at the top order (Slater, Taylor and Boon) in the preliminary games of the series between Australia, England and Zimbabwe.

The Test sides reassembled at the MCG for the 1994 Boxing Day Test (begun on Christmas Eve, with no play on Christmas Day). Atherton won the toss and sent Australia in because of rain the night before and forecast bad weather. It looked a good move by the time Steve came to the wicket at four for 100. He joined Mark in a mini-partnership of 71 before Mark (71) was removed. Steve hung on with the tail and remained 94 not out from Australia's mediocre 279. He didn't attempt to farm the strike—it had never been his policy with tailenders. This time it cost him a hundred. It was a bad habit to get into. What would he do if Australia was chasing a win and he was in with the tail? Would he leave it to 'bunnies' in a pressure finish?

England was encouraged by the low target, but tormented by Warne (six for 64) as he continued his Brisbane form. The tourists' 212 was just not enough. Australia's second innings of seven for 320 declared (Boon 131, Steve Waugh 26 not out) gave it a lead of 387. England lost four for 79 by the end of the fourth day, leaving it 308 in arrears with six wickets in hand. Warne wrapped the game up with a hat trick and England reached just 92, making it the loser by 295 runs.

Steve had his worst Test yet in Sydney early in the new year, being bowled by Darren Gough for 1, and caught off Fraser for a duck. Australia struggled to a draw, after a second innings opening stand by Taylor and Slater of 208 looked like stealing the game.

England's improvement continued and it won both its final one-day games in early January 1995 against Zimbabwe and Australia, although it wasn't enough to get it into the finals. That was left to Australia versus Australia A. The senior team won two–nil in the best of three finals. Steve Waugh was equal top score (56 not out) with Slater in the second game.

England's progress culminated in a more competitive effort at Adelaide at the end of January in the Fourth Test, when Steve Waugh had another disappointing Test, scoring 19 and 0. Australia was set 263 to win on the last day and collapsed for 156, giving England a win by 106 runs. The Ashes would stay with Australia but the tourists could still square the series two all if they won at Perth in the Fifth and final Test.

Steve Waugh was batting at number five after Bevan had been dropped from the Fourth Test. He had been at six for most of his Test career, apart from the interlude in 1992–93 versus the West Indies when he was tried at three without much success (the century at Sydney in the Third Test aside). Neither he nor the selectors thought he was suited to that hot seat. Traditionally, since Bradman through Harvey, Ian Chappell and Boon, it had been the place for the team's most accomplished bat. Waugh didn't seem to have the confidence to fill it. Like Border, he preferred to come in at five. It would preserve his career and his average. Waugh would love to play 150 Tests and hold an average over 50. He came to the wicket at three for 238 and was still there with Blewett at stumps on day one with the score at four for 283. At lunch on day two the home team had lumbered on to seven for 345. After the break, Waugh, who as usual hung on with the tail, was left stranded on 99 not out when the last three men—apparently still in one-day mode—were run out. The last man out was Mark Waugh, running for McDermott. Thus, Mark had unfortunately caused his brother to miss a century. But once more, he worked within the range of his own abilities. Again, did he lack that bit of confidence to take control and go for his century? Was he content with a healthy not out that would help his average once more? Since the beginning of his second 'life' in Test cricket he seemed to have shut out all risk taking for the sake of his survival and a prospering average. It was calculated but successful for Waugh and Australia. For the same reason he avoided batting up the order at three or four, Waugh was not prepared to take a chance, even if it meant missing a century. His argument that he liked to let the tailenders have their head if they wished it was not convincing. Few tailenders would admit they couldn't cope with the bowling. It was human nature to say, 'Sure, I can stick around. I can get a few.' And some of them could, for a while. But unlike batsmen, sooner rather than later they would be dismissed.

Waugh's attitude was questionable. Many believed that instead of letting things happen, he should have taken control.

Australia reached 402. England's response was 295 (Thorpe 123). Australia was two for 87 at stumps on day three with a handy lead of 194. The next day the home team stumbled, losing three quick wickets to be on five for 123 with a lead of 230 and more than five sessions of play left. There was tension in the Australian dressing room as Steve Waugh and Blewett set out restoring the position. At lunch on day four the score was five for 186, Blewett 37 not out and Steve on 22 not out. Blewett went on to his second century in his first two Tests with 115 off just 158 balls. Waugh remained steady. After he was out at 80 (caught off Lewis), Taylor let the innings continue until declaring at eight for 345. The lead was 452. McDermott (six for 38) stopped any thought of batting heroics and England, five for 23 at stumps, was all out for 123 the next day, giving Australia a win by 329 runs and the series three–one. Warne, with twenty-seven wickets at 20.33, shared bowling honours with the consistent McDermott (thirty-two at 21.09) and Gough (twenty at 21.25).

Steve Waugh (345 runs at an average of 49.29) could be pleased with his series. Alongside Blewett, Thorpe, Taylor and Mark Waugh he was a strong performer behind Michael Slater, the outstanding bat of the series with 623 runs at 62.30.

The team then had a 'busman's holiday' in February in New Zealand in a one-day series. It was a relaxed tune-up for the West Indies tour beginning early in March 1995. Steve Waugh saw it as the biggest challenge of his career to that point. If Australia could win the four-Test series it could lay a fair claim to being the best Test side in the world. No side had beaten the West Indies in fifteen years and twenty-eight series on end. It was having the greatest run ever at the top of world cricket.

7

CARIBBEAN CLASS

Waugh's hot warm up

Taylor's leadership, along with the resort-like conditions conducive to beach and poolside relaxation, created a team buoyancy from the beginning of the tour on 3 March 1995. Australia looked forward to playing good, *winning* cricket and knocking the West Indies off its perch. It had been twenty-two years—1972–73—since an Australian team had beaten the West Indies at home.

However, the tourists' confidence was dealt a big blow when the West Indies dominated the one-day series that preceded the Test, winning it four–one. Steve Waugh's consistent form was one of the very few positives to come out of the one-dayers for the tourists. His 26, 58 and 44 meant he was in good early form in the non-preferred style of game. Waugh was having a good look at the Windies speed force. He felt Ambrose was 'foxing' and not bowling at full tilt. But apart from him, Walsh, Benjamin and the other West Indian bowlers held no potential terrors.

The Australians had lost McDermott and Fleming, injured and out of the series before the Tests even began. They were replaced by Julian and Reiffel. Richie Richardson, the West Indies skipper, won the toss and batted in the First Test at Barbados. Fifteen minutes in, for Aussie supporters at the ground and in a million living rooms at home, patriotism turned to unexpected jingoistic fervour. Julian, bowling with great pace and surprising bounce, sent back Williams (1) and Richardson (0) while Reiffel removed Campbell (0). Healy took two catches and Taylor one. The Windies were reeling at three for 6. Lara held up the Aussie breakthrough until he cut at Julian. Steve Waugh took a tough, juggling catch in the gully. Everyone on the field with a view of it, including Lara and both umpires, thought Waugh had taken the ball and that it had not touched the ground. The crowd and the media contingent were stunned. Lara was travelling so well that a big hundred seemed likely. Now he was on his way for an ordinary—for him—65. The shock would later translate into mischief making when a video replay was interpreted by some journalists and commentators as suggesting that the ball *may* have touched the turf. Given that almost any ball caught close to the ground could, if recorded from a certain angle and viewed on video replay, be construed to have *possibly* touched the ground, the beat-up by the media after the first day was ludicrous. Waugh, who had displayed sportsmanship in such matters throughout his career, was being vilified. The bleating of ex-players became the howls of the mob.

On the field, meanwhile, Australia strove on. Glenn McGrath, fulfilling Border's belief in him as an on-field tough guy despite his pencil-thin appearance, attacked the Windies tail of fast bowlers with a venom that no Caribbean tail had experienced even in the days of that talented, bruising *femme fatale*, Lillee 'n' Thomson. McGrath's blast and Warne's guile ended the Windies innings at 195. Australia's reply was solid and slow, as the Windies bowled without the expected brutality and enthusiasm. Taylor was not timing the ball, but he hung on to his wicket to be 42 not out at stumps. He would sleep well, having taken four catches and with his wicket intact. Slater (18) and Boon (20) fell in compiling two for 91 at stumps. The tourists' talk at dinner bordered on bombast. Taylor reminded them that they were still 100 short of the Windies. He fought to calm down the euphoria of a strong start to the series.

Steve Waugh had to contend with the undue opprobrium building over the Lara catch. Subdued, he told his diary that night he would put it behind him. He had a job to do on day two.

In the morning, coach Bob Simpson was about to take some catching practice when he asked the team physio, Errol Alcott, to look at a swollen leg. Simpson was sent straight to a doctor. The swelling had been caused by a blood clot in Simpson's upper left calf. He was rushed to intensive care at a local hospital.

Meanwhile, unaware of the seriousness of the coach's problem, the Australians resumed their innings. Taylor, wanting a team 350 to 400 and a big hundred from someone, battled on to 55 before Kenny Benjamin induced an edge to slip. That brought Steve Waugh to join his brother and they added 45 until Mark (40) was facing Ambrose. Steve had a premonition that Mark would be caught behind next ball. He was. Steve had had six such 'visions'. (When he told Mark later, Junior was not amused and suggested that Steve inform him next time.)

Waugh knuckled down in his frugal manner, while Blewett, the big spender, came out blasting in an effort to notch his third hundred in his first three Tests. There was nothing wrong with his approach except that he ran into a pumped-up Ambrose and was caught behind at 14.

All the Windies' speedmen tilted at Steve Waugh. He made his characteristic jump to make sure he was over the ball each time and didn't give a chance in compiling a good 44 not out, which left Australia on five for 197 at lunch. Australia was 2 runs ahead with the last true batsman, Healy, at the wicket.

Waugh, on 65, looked sound. He was thinking of a big hundred when Kenny Benjamin bowled a short one. Waugh fended at it when he could have left it and Murray behind the stumps took the catch off the outside edge. Australia ended up 346, a lead of 151. The next day, Warne was on early to put pressure on Lara. He had Campbell (6) caught by Steve Waugh trying to slash his way out of a runs trough. McGrath then found a faint edge from Lara (9), putting the Windies at three for 31. The back of the world's best bat so early was a delightful sight for the Aussies.

Taylor kept the pressure on, rotating his bowlers, with Warne and McGrath being used most. In the over before lunch, Richardson drove at the accurate Reiffel who removed his off stump. With the Windies tottering on four for 91, the ebullient Australians gathered in the break and went through tactics to finish off the opposition.

Adams and Murray fought until Warne out-thought the keeper (23). Warne looped a ball. It tempted Murray into a big hit over midwicket, which was unpatrolled territory. The batsman connected but not the way he would have wished. Steve Waugh at short midwicket turned and dashed towards the boundary. He looked up into the sun and could just make out a golden dot high overhead. Waugh seemed to stretch out as the ball descended. He clutched at it as it came over his right shoulder. It stuck as he tumbled over. A roar went up from the Australian supporters, while the locals sat stunned. In the media area, some reporters jumped from their seats and clapped. Waugh hurled the ball high with the widest grin ever from him. Players ran to him. Waugh regarded it as the most important catch he had ever taken. It had been a match-winning grab. The Windies were five for 136 and still fifteen short of making Australia bat again.

McGrath returned to the bowling crease with more brimstone for the tail, and they found it repugnant. In between making them jump about like unhappy flamenco dancers, he trapped Winston Benjamin (26), had an uncomfortable Ambrose caught for 6, and bowled a jittery Walsh (4). It was an inspired spell, taking his figures to five for 68 off twenty-two overs. Warne bowled Kenny Benjamin (5) to finish the innings at 189. Slater and Taylor crashed the 39 to win in just 6.5 overs, and then grabbed the stumps as souvenirs, only to see all but one of them wrestled away by an overenthusiastic crowd.

Viv Richards tried in the press to stir up the Australians when they landed in Antigua for the Second Test beginning on 8 April by saying Lara was 'robbed' of a century because of Waugh's poor sportsmanship. This was hypocrisy considering Richards's failure to call back Dean Jones after he was 'bowled' on a no-ball and then 'run out' in

1991. But Richards was on his home island of Antigua and here he was *the man*. He planned, he said, to confront Waugh during the Test and tell him what he thought of him. This was bluff. His frothing was designed to build ill-feeling towards the Australians and unsettle their camp.

Richards's intervention only had an impact on the media and was soon forgotten on the first day of the Test at the Recreation Ground, St John's. Taylor lost the toss and was asked to bat by an uncertain Richardson. Australia began well against some uninspired bowling, except from Walsh, who looked dangerous. It lost Taylor (37) hooking on lunch with the score at 82. After lunch Slater (41) and Mark Waugh (4) were back in the pavilion before the others could digest their meals. Steve Waugh came to the wicket at three for 89 but didn't stay long. He was bowled by Kenny Benjamin for 15. There was a steady decline for the rest of the day until Australia was all out for 216. Many had starts but did nothing with them as Walsh scythed his way through the team, taking six for 54.

The Windies were on top with Lara and Hooper together and the score three for 186. Taylor threw Steve Waugh the ball. Waugh had been restricted by hamstring and groin problems in recent years, but felt fit enough to bowl now. The pitch was keeping low. He liked the idea of delivering to Hooper, whom he regarded as his 'bunny', that is, someone he could get out any time he put his mind to it. Lara was a different challenge. But he had a plan to bottle him up with accurate bowling until he forced an error. Waugh bowled tightly for two overs, tying up an impatient Lara on 88. Waugh placed Boon next to the batsman at the bowler's end, on the on-side edge of the pitch. Lara drove the next ball towards mid-on, as if challenging this unconventional field placing. Boon leapt for the catch and took a 'blinder'. One run later, Waugh had Hooper (11) caught by Julian and ended with two for 20 off six overs.

Waugh was underestimated when it came to bowling. He seemed military medium, but his cunning, intelligence and combative nature unsettled opponents. More often than not he made the necessary breakthrough.

The West Indies made 260. Australia replied and received a barrage of bumpers. Waugh came to the wicket with Australia not yet out of the woods on three for 149, just 105 in front.

He was attacked with the now expected 'throat ticklers' from the speedmen. It was wasted effort, and seemed to galvanise the batsman.

At 162, Mark Waugh (61) was bowled middle stump by a Winston Benjamin yorker. Blewett (6) edged Hooper to slipper Williams right on lunch with the score at five for 196. The lead was 152. After the long break, Healy (26), Julian (6) and Steve Waugh, entrenched and defiant, took the Australians beyond danger to seven for 273, a lead of 229.

Day five disappointed, with more rain, and play could not resume until the middle session. Taylor declared at seven for 300 with Waugh unbeaten on 65 and a lead of 256. The Windies had 37 overs to get them at an impossible seven runs an over. It managed two for 80 off thirty overs and the game was drawn. All the Australians, except Blewett, who failed twice with the bat, contributed in a strong team effort, with Steve Waugh being the main Aussie influence with bat and ball and in the field. He was travelling well. There was something more focused than ever before about his demeanour. In his mind this series represented a 'now or never' situation. Fifteen years of defeat at the hands of the West Indians had created an air of invincibility, even when they were down. Waugh, more than any other player, was intent on breaking the hold the champions had on world cricket.

Beaten, by the toss

The Australians inspected the wicket on the first day of the Third Test at Port-of-Spain, 21 April, and realised it was so bad that the toss could well decide the game. The wicket was grassy and excess moisture had made it far below Test standard. Taylor again called wrongly and rued it in less than half an hour as Australian wickets tumbled. The noise of kettle drums and conches was deafening as the Windies crowd urged on the speedsters to do physical damage to the visitors on the problematic pitch. The ball was flying at various heights.

At three for 14, Ambrose had removed Taylor (2) and Mark Waugh (2), while a Walsh lifter had sent back Slater (0). Steve Waugh was greeted by booing as he walked to the wicket to join Boon. Both defended with grit in between breaks caused by rain. Ambrose was boosted by the ball darting off the seam. His previous lethargy had gone. He was all fire, glares and stares. The lanky bowler hurled a steepling bouncer at Waugh, who watched it whiz overhead. Ambrose continued his run down the wicket and stopped, hands on hips, a few metres from Waugh. He lingered, trying to intimidate the batsman. Waugh met his gaze.

'What the fuck are you looking at?' Waugh demanded.

Ambrose was stunned. He was not used to batsmen taking him on. The bowler took a pace nearer Waugh. No other cricketer had the temerity, or crassness, to rile the tall fast bowler with backchat. It was a pivotal moment in the series. It sent a message to everyone that the Australians were prepared to do almost anything to win this series. The visitors would not be intimidated or put off their game.

'Don't cuss me man!' Ambrose said, leaning close to Waugh.

He was furious, and looked as if he was about to take it further when Richardson intervened, grabbing Ambrose by the arm and edging him away.

Ambrose tried to bounce Waugh again, but failed to dislodge him. Australia missed an hour's batting due to rain before lunch when the score was three for 31. Boon (18) didn't last long after the break as Ambrose continued his more controlled rampage. Only Steve Waugh resisted en route to 50. Rain stopped play at seven for 112 and Waugh was booed all the way from the wicket to the pavilion. The mob's response was ugly and it upset Waugh. His only solace was that it had been engendered by his defiance. It had been the hardest 50 of his career, and he had welts and bruises on his right arm and body to remind him of his courage.

At the after-play conference, the media focused on the confrontation with Ambrose, which had caused match referee, Pakistani Majid

Khan, to demand that both sides cool it. His even-handedness was a little misplaced: it hadn't been Waugh who had hurried over to Ambrose to 'eye-ball' him. Yet perhaps the batsman should have looked the other way, as most professionals would do to bullyboy bowlers. The perfect response was great batting, which Waugh had produced. The next day, not even the sight of Allan Border in the commentary box could hold up the Windies assault, as Australia capitulated at 128. Waugh remained not out 63, almost half the score. Ambrose returned five for 45 and Walsh three for 50.

McGrath, lifted by the pitch and what he had seen from Ambrose, delivered with fire and speed. McGrath crashed through the bats after Reiffel had bored in with the first wicket of Williams (0) caught by Taylor at slip with the score at 1. McGrath first sent back Richardson (2) caught behind. He then broke a promising partnership between Lara and Adams by having Lara (24) caught by Taylor. Adams went on to 42, but after Steve Waugh again dismissed Hooper (21) cheaply the Windies' tail fell apart to be all out for 136. McGrath had taken the final step to match winner with six for 47.

Australia was none for 20 at stumps—12 runs ahead—and full of hope and a real feeling the game could be won. It needed 200 to make it tough for the Windies, and 250 to make it nigh impossible. The Australians were travelling with promise at one point on three for 85 with the Waughs together. A few minutes later there was chaos. Australia slid to eight for 87 and any hope of pulling off a miracle went when second-top scorer Steve Waugh was out for 21, caught by Hooper off Kenny Benjamin. Five wickets fell for just two runs as players came and went in a nervous, hurried progression. It left the dressing room in more turmoil than any member of the team could recall. And with the collapse went the Australians' chances of wrapping up the series. The tourists were all out for 105. The West Indies reached the 90 needed for the loss of just one wicket to square the series one all, with one to play.

The mood in the Australian dressing room was depressed. It wasn't helped when Steve Waugh was booed when mentioned as a candidate for man of the match. It again touched him. The champion cricketer had been pushed to the limit. No one was sure which way his reaction would manifest. His demeanour was smoothed just a fraction by learning that his 63 not out was judged by the cricket ratings agency Coopers & Lybrand as equivalent to a double century in degree of difficulty. It placed Waugh as the number two bat in the world behind the West Indies' Jimmy Adams. This consolation would be worn, like his bruises, into the next encounter.

High noon in Jamaica

Taylor lost the toss yet again at the beginning of the deciding Test at Sabina Park, Kingston, Jamaica, on 29 April 1995. The West Indies batted first. Lara looked promising with 65, but Warne out-thought him and had him caught by Healy. Richardson scored a dashing 100 before Reiffel had him lbw. Steve Waugh took the new ball after Warne had dismissed Browne caught by Boon for 1, and he enjoyed shaking up the tail with the odd bouncer. He knew what to expect when he batted and thought it nice to slip in some 'chin music', as he called it, before the Windies attempted to dent his helmet. His accuracy put a brake on the more adventurous West Indians, none of whom could cope with being pinned down for long. They had not come to terms with his swing and change of pace. He took two for 14 off eleven overs with five maidens, while Reiffel, Julian, Warne and McGrath shared the rest of the wickets to hold the West Indies to 265.

Australia's start on day two was not encouraging as first Taylor (8) fell to a freakish catch by Adams at short leg, then Boon (17) was given out caught behind when the ball brushed his helmet, not his bat. At 73, the over-adventurous Slater was removed by Lara, who took a flying catch at deep backward square leg. It was fifteen minutes to lunch when the Waugh brothers came together. This was the most critical moment of the series. If one of the Waughs departed early Australia would probably end up behind on the first innings. This would most likely mean that the game and the series were lost.

Steve Waugh felt fine despite having no sleep after waking up to a prowler in his hotel room. Waugh chased him out. Was the prowler intent on sabotage to disrupt the tourists? It seemed so. Despite the intrusion, Waugh's confidence was high. And Mark Waugh? Well, he was his cool, calm, even languid self. The brothers saw it through to lunch. Both remarked that the pitch was like a WACA wicket to bat on—hard and bouncy—just what these two shot makers loved. This may have been the Waughs' modest way of saying they could be in for a big partnership. The WACA was where they put together that masterly 464 in a Shield game for New South Wales against Western Australia.

Ambrose, Walsh and the Benjamins came out firing after the break and threw everything at the twins. About four balls each over shot above shoulder height. The other few balls were often misdirected as all bowlers lost their way. The Windies' approach from the beginning was to try to bounce the Waughs. Perhaps the captain and his bowlers lacked collective nous. It was the major strategic error of the series. Steve Waugh had been the best Australian batsman of the series and the bouncing tactic had helped him settle in almost every innings. He seemed galvanised, sharpened and challenged by the bouncers as he side-stepped, weaved and ducked. If Ambrose and the other West Indian pacemen had concentrated on the away swinger pitched just outside Waugh's off stump he might just have been removed. But as Steve's confidence built and the runs accumulated, he looked in complete control.

WACA Waughs revisited

The tourists had watched a television drama of Mike Tyson's life the night before, but perhaps Muhammad Ali's story would have been a more apt choice. Ali's 'rope-a-dope' tactics in conning George Foreman in a title fight in 1975 were what the Waughs seemed to be copying. In that historic contest, Ali let Foreman throw everything at him for several rounds before he retaliated and knocked out his opponent. The Waughs were dodging or absorbing the bouncers while giving their equivalent little jabs of retaliation in the form of short, sharp singles to keep the scoreboard moving.

The Windies became frustrated with the Australian tactics. As the brothers both crept into the twenties and thirties, Kenny Benjamin twice threw four overthrows, which lifted the tally by 10 in a couple of balls. The fielders' heads dropped. The Waughs had a mid-pitch conference, which, according to them, went this way:

'They're getting a bit loose,' Mark remarked.

'Yeah, let's keep working hard.'

'Ambrose is slowing up.'

'We're getting on top.'

And they were. Steve, on 42, played the only undisciplined shot of the mid-session, a wafty drive at Kenny Benjamin, which was dropped by keeper Courtney Browne, who had replaced the injured Murray. Australia went to tea at three for 192. It was 72 in arrears and back in the match.

After the break, a Waugh mid-wicket mix-up occurred when Steve called for a dangerous single. But such was the state of Steve's mind, the incident was turned into a positive in another mid-pitch chat.

'Sorry,' Steve mumbled.

'Let's not blow it,' Mark replied.

'I think it's our day.'

'Yeah, right.'

'Mark showed a steely resolve not to get out,' Steve noted later in his published diary of the tour. '[He] weathered the short stuff and punished anything remotely off line. It was a superb all-round display of batsmanship.'

Hooper came on and soon managed some alarming turn. The score reached 265, with Mark on 107 and Steve on 83. Steve crept into the nineties and then also reached his eighth Test century. A pitch invasion held up play but not the scoring. Shortly afterwards at 304 and with the lead at just 39, Mark (126) popped up a gloved catch to Adams at short leg. The partnership of 231 had come in 233 minutes. At that moment the Australians were on top. Blewett hung in with Waugh until stumps at four for 321, a lead of 56, with six wickets in hand

and three days to play. The tourists were sensing a big chance for a win, and they had earned it. The Windies were renowned front-runners and not experienced at fighting back from a long way down.

Coopers & Lybrand delight

Back in Australia, a million viewers went to bed feeling tired but inspired. The Windies came out firing with the new ball, knowing that a breakthrough was imperative to lurch them back into the match. Failure to do so would see the game slip away. The telling moment came when Blewett, in a punchy mood, pulled a searing Ambrose bouncer off his nose and straight to the midwicket boundary. The lanky speed merchant trudged back to his mark, head down. He looked defeated, something that the tall man had rarely shown or experienced in a decade at the top.

Blewett (69) delivered a memorable knock then lost his wicket when he mishit an Arthurton off-break and was caught by Winston Benjamin at midwicket. This second strong partnership was a demoralising blow to the fielding team. The score was then five for 417 and the lead 152. Waugh was struggling and fatigued but made it through to lunch on 141 not out. He remained disciplined throughout the mid-session and went to tea on 177. Wickets fell until Reiffel (23) proved a useful partner in a link of 73 runs before he was bowled by Kenny Benjamin. Shane Warne came to the wicket and realised that the grille on his helmet had been twisted, probably because the prowler who had been disturbed in Waugh's hotel room had been more successful in Warne's, two nights earlier. Warne couldn't see properly through the grille and he blamed his dismissal—caught Lara off Kenny Benjamin for a duck—on this possible sabotage.

It left Australia on nine for 522, and Waugh on 195 with Glenn McGrath at the wicket with him. McGrath seemed determined to see Waugh—his net batting coach—through to a double century, as he took a ball on the shoulder rather than surrender his wicket.

On 196, Waugh moved into a quick full toss from Hooper that

shot away towards deep backward square. Waugh saw his chance. Instead of settling for three he pushed his tired legs for a four, all run, taking him to 200, his first in Test cricket.

At the ground, in Australia and around the world a huge audience applauded as Waugh raised his bat in acknowledgment of what many saw as his most important knock. It ranked with Dean Jones's fighting double century in India in 1986 as one of the best performances by an Australian batsman since the war. Given the circumstances of the series and the Windies' dominance for so long, it was arguably one of the best 'big' innings (200 or more) in the history of Test cricket.

The pitch invasion that followed included former Australian batsman Greg Ritchie, who in a spontaneous display of appreciation had leapt onto the oval and dashed to the middle to hug Waugh.

Four balls later, Waugh received a throat-lasered bouncer, which he could not keep down. It was caught off his glove by Lara. The bowler was Kenny Benjamin, who was the only West Indian to take Steve Waugh's wicket in the series. The double century had taken 555 minutes, or nearly five sessions at the wicket, in which he had faced 425 balls. About a third—140—had been bouncers. He looked likely now to be judged as the world's best batsman, displacing Jimmy Adams in the Coopers & Lybrand ratings. Waugh had reached a peak in his career after climbing from the depths of the mid-1980s, his fortunes and decade-long development inextricably bound to Australia's rise to the top of world competition. Right at the moment that it was needed to help dethrone the West Indies, he had played his finest-ever Test innings.

Australia had reached 531—a lead of 266. With more than two days to go it could not now lose the game, and had every chance to win it.

Reiffel penetration

Reiffel, the quiet achiever who had risen to the occasion before in big games, bowled Williams (20) at 37, just when the Windies looked as if they would sneak through to stumps without loss. Lara came in looking as if the weight of the Windies, if not the cricketing world, was on his trim shoulders. Reiffel bowled one that kept low. The pocket dynamo was judged (with some doubt, even by the bowler) lbw for a duck. The Australians were ecstatic.

Reiffel was not done yet. He induced a caught and bowled from Richardson (14) with a slower ball. The Windies were three for 63 at stumps and reeling. The only thing that could stop Australia now was the weather.

Right on cue, it poured the next day, but as Aussie luck would have it, it was the rest day, 2 May. Day four saw nightwatchman Winston Benjamin stay until lunch and in the first session the Windies only lost Adams (18), caught by Steve Waugh in the gully off McGrath. Soon after the break, Winston Benjamin (51) was cornered by an in-swinger from the irrepressible Reiffel. Hooper (13) then lost his wicket to an unnecessary second run to Julian at fine leg. The lanky West Australian threw down the wicket, sending the Windies to six for 140, still 116 short of making the visitors bat again.

Arthurton came in blazing against Warne, who, despite an injured thumb, was hungry for wickets that would finish the match. The batsman connected with a huge six into the newly constructed stand. Warne, unfazed and even encouraged by the batsman's desire to take him on, tossed one into the rough. The left-hander went back on his stumps, half-lifting his bat in a 'leave'. The ball struck him dead in front, giving the umpire an easy lbw decision.

Ambrose came in and demonstrated from his first ball that he didn't place any value on his wicket. Perhaps he was just a realist. He had no desire to suffer any bruising of body and ego by McGrath, so he wafted at most and missed as many. It wasn't long before he was stumped by Healy off Warne for 5. The tall man left, smacking his lips and looking darker in spirit than normal. His roommate was in for a very quiet night.

Walsh joined Browne, who was resisting well with a mix of defence and good shots. Walsh was relieved to have Warne and not McGrath and he lived, if that could be the word for his hilarious hitting, dangerously, collecting 14 before holing out to Blewett off Warne. The spinner now had three wickets as he wrapped up the innings. He tied the bow of victory with a terrific leg-break to Kenny Benjamin, who edged it to Taylor at slip.

The Australian skipper would not let the ball go until it was in the hands of a recovering Bob Simpson, who had presided over his nation's gradual rise to the very top of world cricket over a tough decade.

Browne remained a stoic 31 not out as the Windies in the end only mustered 213, giving Australia a whopping win by an innings and 53 runs.

Warne ended with four for 70, giving him a creditable fifteen wickets at 27.07, which was not his usual performance of five or six wickets a Test. Yet he was vital in the chemistry mix of a series victory, as was Reiffel, who took four for 74, giving him fifteen wickets at 17.53 for the series. McGrath took one for 28, leaving him with seventeen wickets at 21.71 in the four Tests.

But it was Steve Waugh's series. While he had taken five wickets at 12.40, more than useful for a part-timer who loved to deliver a bouncer, it was his batting that made the difference between the two teams. Waugh had hit 429 runs at 107.25, eclipsing Lara, who had made 308 at 44. Waugh was named Man of the Match in the final game and Player of the Series.

Australia had taken the series two–one and had become the first team to beat the Windies in twenty-nine attempts by all the world's leading cricket nations. With Border, Dean Jones, Geoff Lawson, Greg Ritchie and David Hookes joining in the celebrations of this historic sporting achievement, there was extra verve and emotion in a stirring rendition of the victory chant of 'Under the Southern Cross I Stand', led by David Boon.

Several hours after the game, the team was told to leave by fed-up Sabina Park ground staff. Steve Waugh, still in his creams, spikes and baggy green cap, looked around tipsily for his cricket bag. It had been packed by Warne, who could see that his mate was not in any state to accomplish such a task. Warne's selfless act was typical of the team, from Langer, who hadn't made the Test side, and May as twelfth man, to Taylor, the ever-solicitous, inspiring skipper. Added together, this all for one, one for all spirit on and off the field of combat had transformed these often incorrigible revellers into the fittest, most united and driven team to represent Australia since Bradman's Invincibles had toured England in 1948.

That Anzac feeling was alive and well.

Waugh had been playing Test cricket for the last decade and this was the most satisfying win of his career so far. Ever since he had walked into the team he had heard stories about the Caribbean bogymen. Every batsman had his horror stories, every side its bad-luck claims. Waugh had done well in his first encounter in 1988–89 but had flopped in 1991 and 1992–93. Each time the team he was in had been beaten soundly, except for 1992–93, which was line ball.

It was a case of fourth time successful. He had been the standout player of both sides by a long way in an otherwise even set of performances where everyone contributed. Waugh had the highest aggregate, average and score. He also had the best bowling analysis, although McGrath, Reiffel and Warne contributed more with the ball. He was even brilliant in the field, taking the best catch of the series to dismiss Murray in the First Test. It turned the game Australia's way.

His rope-a-dope strategy against the West Indies of dogged defence then, when the bowlers were fatigued, counterattack, had worked. The jumping-in-the-air tactic had convinced the West Indies to bang the ball in short, playing into Waugh's hands. His series effort was the single most important factor in the defeat of the Caribbean champions and Australia's hard-earned elevation to the world's number-one Test team.

8

THROWING, BRIBES AND BAD VIBES

Twin superstars

The half-year break from Test cricket had done little to diminish Steve Waugh's form when he batted at Brisbane early in November 1995 against Pakistan. It was the first day of a three-Test series. He was looking solid at 24 not out with Australia on four for 262 at stumps. Yet Waugh was uncomfortable the next day against the speed and swing of Wasim and Waqar. He also offered two chances off Aamir Sohail's left-arm spin when in the eighties. But he hung on in what he later described as an 'ugly' innings. It wasn't a smooth knock yet he held the side together, reaching his ninth Test century and leading the score up to a strong 463. Waugh's 112 not out took a day's batting. Pakistan, one batsman short because Salim Malik had injured his hand while fielding, replied with a miserable 97, with Warne the destroyer taking seven for 23. Taylor felt safe enforcing the follow-on against Pakistan this time and Malik, coming in at number eight, provided the only interest in the game. Malik, his hand strapped, lasted four balls before Warne had him caught. The bowler saw it as sweet justice. Pakistan was all out for 240, giving Australia a win by an innings and 126 runs.

In the Second Test at Hobart, spinner Mushtaq Ahmed had Waugh caught behind for 7 when Australia batted first. But it was unusual now for both Waughs to fail in the same innings. This time Mark made a fluent 88 in his fiftieth Test. It helped Australia to an ordinary score of 267. Pakistan made only 198 in reply. Slater (73) and Taylor (123) did best in Australia's second innings of nine for 396—Warne being unable to bat because of a broken toe sustained by a Waqar yorker in the first innings. The lead was 375. Pakistan could only muster 220 in the chase, thus losing the Test by 155.

After two Test losses and a beating by Victoria, Pakistan rallied in the Third Test at Sydney, beginning 30 November, to score 299 (Ijaz Ahmed 137). Australia was in trouble at three for 91. Steve joined Mark and they fought back, taking the score to 3 for 151 at stumps with Mark on 54 not out and Steve 26 not out. Mushtaq struck the next morning, having Steve stumped for 38. Mark went on to a conscientious 116, drawing him level with his brother on nine centuries in Tests. Australia made just 257. Pakistan could only reach 204 in its second innings, leaving Australia with a target of 247. Steve Waugh's groin was injured and he didn't come to the wicket when Australia was three down. Healy took his place and Australia was three for 117 at stumps, just 130 short. Soon the Australians were five for 146 with Steve Waugh in with a runner and struggling. He couldn't stretch to Mushtaq and it was no surprise to see him out—played on—for just 14. Australia collapsed for 172 and was beaten by 74 runs. It was a disappointment to drop a Test, even if it was a dead rubber. Australia had been making a habit of this in the 1990s. The loss also revived uncertainties about the team's capacity to chase small or moderate totals in a final innings.

Waugh's injury kept him out of the First Test against Sri Lanka in Perth a few days later, which Australia won easily, scoring five for 617 (Slater a dashing 219, Mark Waugh a smooth, majestic 111, Taylor a solid 96 and Ricky Ponting, in his first-ever Test, a fine 96) as opposed to Sri Lanka's 251 and 330. The game would not be remembered for the home team's victory but the alleged ball tampering by the tourists.

Steve Waugh returned to the side for the Boxing Day Test. Arjuna

Ranatunga won the toss and sent Australia in. It was one for 63 at lunch in a boring start, but proceedings were livened up in the second session, not by any player, but by an umpire—Australia's Darrell Hair. Hair no-balled off-spinner Muttiah Muralitharan, whose elbow seemed crooked on delivery. The way the Sri Lankan bowler curled the ball out appeared suspect to some. His quicker delivery brought gasps from the crowd. Excuses were later made for Muralitharan's alleged arm deformity, but cricket's law 24, note (a) said that the arm could not straighten during delivery. Hair's ruling left Sri Lanka a bowler short.

Mark Waugh (61) boosted Australia's rating and Steve (2 not out overnight) took over the next day after Boon's stodgy 110 (in 408 minutes). Steve was joined by Ponting, who was poised and positive in scoring 71 from 94 balls in a stay of just over two hours. Healy (41) then became linked with Waugh for a 93-run partnership. Waugh remained 131 not out in Australia's six declared for 500. It was his tenth Test hundred, drawing him level with his twin again. He hit 11 fours and a five. Sri Lanka was all out for 233 on day three—267 short. Taylor, showing he was flexible, again called for the follow-on and the tourists were all out for 307 (Gurusinha 143). Australia only needed 41 and went on to win by ten wickets.

There was a break from Test cricket with a triangular one-day World Series competition between Australia, Sri Lanka and the West Indies. Steve Waugh missed most of the games through injury but came back to hit 102 not out against Sri Lanka in Melbourne. It was his first century in 187 one-day internationals. Australia won the finals two–nil against Sri Lanka amid more controversy. An overweight Arjuna Ranatunga asked for drinks every few overs and called for a runner in a run chase in the second game at Sydney. Ian Healy challenged this. Ranatunga's gamesmanship generated more feeling between the teams, and Sri Lanka's players refused to shake hands with the victorious Australians after the game.

Steve Waugh thought this a 'disgrace'. He didn't enjoy the contest against the Sri Lankans. Nevertheless, there was still one more Test to play—at Adelaide, beginning 25 January 1996. Australia won the toss and batted. Waugh was in this time at three for 96 and he joined his brother in a face-saving partnership of 85 before Mark (71) was dismissed. Australia at stumps had recovered to be five for 239, with Steve unbeaten on 71 and looking in the form he had shown in Melbourne. He reached his eleventh century, then he and Healy (70) took the score to 326 in the second morning. The good batting wicket gave Reiffel (56) a chance to show some prowess with the bat and he assisted Waugh in a 117-run combination. Waugh was eventually out—bowled for 170. Not long afterwards Taylor declared at nine for 502, Australia's third 500 score of the series.

Sri Lanka replied with 317 and avoided the follow on. On day four the home team cruised to six for 215 after tea, a lead of 400. Steve Waugh batted with his now expected assurance and application for 61 not out, bringing his tally for the series to 362 for once out.

His part in the game was not over. Sri Lanka was one for 69 at stumps with the exciting Sanath Jayasuriya on 50 not out. He continued on his way the next day and reached a century after lunch. Not long afterwards, Taylor tossed the ball to Waugh, who was relaxed after his terrific summer. The skipper wanted that cool confidence harnessed at the bowling crease for one last tilt at Sri Lanka. Waugh's groin had prevented him from bowling more than a handful of overs for the season. Now he had the responsibility of winning a Test. Waugh elicited surprising movement off the pitch with his seamers and soon dismissed Jayasuriya, caught behind for 112. In the same over Waugh sent back the dangerous Kaluwitharana, bowled for a duck.

Sri Lanka went to tea at six for 208. After the break, Waugh removed Dharmasena (2), and then the defiant Sanjeeva Ranatunga (65). Sri Lanka was all out at 252, giving Australia a win by 148 and the series three–nil. Waugh ended with four for 34. He finished the season with Man of the Match, Man of the Series and International Cricketer of the Year (1995) awards.

Waugh had kept up the remarkable standard he set in the West Indies by scoring 562 runs at 112.4 (three centuries) in the five Tests he played in the 1995–96 season. Brother Mark was not far behind with 555 runs (two centuries) at 61.67. Steve took five wickets and two catches; Mark four wickets and six catches.

The twins, now thirty years of age, were entrenched as superstars of Australia's line-up, along with Warne, McGrath and Healy.

Awards were coming fast enough for Waugh to get used to them. Yet he never took his continuing good form or his secure position in the Test team for granted. He still shuddered at the thought of those two years in the wilderness and the frustration of that extended 'time out'. Now he refused to retreat from his flair-free, risk-free minimalist batting, which since 1993 and phase two of his career had seen his average climb steadily through the 40s to hover around the 50 mark. Only a handful of Australian players who had played twenty Tests or more—Don Bradman (99.94), Greg Chappell (53.86), Jack Ryder (51.62), and Allan Border (50.56)—were in this elite bracket. Waugh's aim would be to maintain that 50-plus average for the rest of his career. If he could do that, he probably would never be dropped again.

World Cup wonders

Australia opted out of playing in Sri Lanka in the 1996 World Cup after a bomb attack there not long before they were due to arrive. On top of that there were death threats against Warne, McDermott and Simpson. This meant the Australians would only play in India and Pakistan and the team had twelve days' break before their first game on 23 February. Steve Waugh was the only member of the squad who had competed in India and Pakistan in the winning Australian side in 1987. His reputation as a cool man in a crisis had taken off there. The last decade confirmed that he was an exceptional performer with the ball in tight situations.

The Waugh twins (or 'Wog' twins, as they were known in India) began at Visakhapatnam on India's east coast in style with a 207-run partnership, which set up an easy win versus Kenya. Mark hit 130 from 128 balls and Steve 82 from eighty-eight balls, despite stomach problems. Steve passed 4000 runs in his 190th one-day international.

It was then on to Mumbai (Bombay) for a game against India in front of a capacity crowd of more than 41,000. Mark Waugh won the game for his country by scoring 126 in 135 balls and then dismissing Tendulkar for 90 (off 84 balls). Australia made it three in a row against Zimbabwe and Mark Waugh starred again with 76 not out. He might well have reached his third successive hundred if he hadn't been chasing just 155.

The West Indies stopped Australia in the 'pink city' of Jaipur. The Caribbean squad came out firing after a shock loss to Kenya, and attempted to blast Australia out. But the West Indies nemesis Steve Waugh (57) and a new challenger in Ponting (102) added 110 for the third wicket in 114 deliveries, which lifted the total to 229. However, the West Indies, with Lara (60) leading the way, got the runs.

Despite the defeat and the forfeit of the first game, Australia finished second in Group A and met New Zealand in the quarter-final at Chennai (Madras), in front of 45,000 people. New Zealand made a very good 286. Mark Waugh attacked from the first ball. He and Steve later put on 87 runs for the fourth wicket before Mark—seemingly exhausted—was out for 110 in 112 balls. Steve (59 not out) carried on. Despite twisting both ankles he saw his team home for an impressive victory.

Miracles and shocks

Now it was tough. Next up was the West Indies in Chandigarh in India's north. An opening salvo from Bishop and Walsh had Australia on the ropes at four for 15 inside ten overs. But Bevan (69) and Law (72 run out), batting as if in a Test, restored the Australians' position. At the end of the fifty overs the score was eight for 207. Steve Waugh, having a terrific series, bowled Lara (45), but the West Indies reached two for 165. It had just 43 to make with eight wickets in hand and 54 balls with which to get them.

Warne came on at four for 173. The batting side had 41 balls to get 35 runs. He bowled a dazzling spell in which he took three for 6 and swung the game, ending with four for 36 off nine overs. Fleming was left with the last over to bowl and two wickets to fall or, for the West Indies, 10 runs to win. Richardson belted a four off the first ball, which reduced the target to 6 with five balls to get them in. Next delivery Ambrose was run out. That left four balls and 6 runs to win. Fleming then bowled Walsh. The Australians embraced. They had pulled off the miracle of Chandigarh.

Australia had to play Sri Lanka in the final at Gaddafi Stadium in Lahore, Pakistan. Ranatunga began the propaganda war before a ball was bowled, saying that Warne was overrated. It was a thoughtless remark, given he was the best spinner in the world. The Sri Lankan skipper also said that the Waugh twins had been given 'far too much good press of late'.

Ranatunga was attempting to balance this 'good press' by giving them, and himself, bad press.

Fifty thousand screaming fans rooted for Sri Lanka, the underdog. Mark Waugh (12) and Steve (13) both failed—a rare event, especially in a big game—and only Taylor (74), Ponting (45) and Bevan (36 not out) were in touch as Australia reached seven for 241. Australia had not counted on the late evening and night dew on the grass making the ball slippery for Warne. It restricted him and weakened Australia's challenge. Aravinda De Silva batted magnificently for 107 not out and, along with Gurusinha (65) and Ranatunga (47 not out), polished off the runs with seven wickets to spare.

Sri Lanka, the Cinderella of the competition, had won the World Cup.

Steve Waugh noted in his diary that he and his teammates wanted to turn the clock back. They felt they should have won it, and the cricket world expected them to.

'At times like these,' Waugh wrote, 'words are of little or no comfort. It's best to let the players work their regrets out of their system.'

Change of guard, same enemy

There was nearly nine months break between the last Test and the next in India, beginning on 10 October 1996, and the team had a different look. David Boon had retired after 107 Tests and 7422 runs at 43.66. His gutsy, heady-steady style at number three had given Australia stability and some resistance in facing the West Indies. Boon and Border had been right for the defensive needs of the 1980s and early 1990s. But a style and method modification was under way with Ponting tried out at number three, Mark Waugh settled at four, and Steve at five. There was more attack in the pack, although the stability that Boon and Border had brought was yet to be seen. The talented Craig McDermott, who had led the bowling for a decade, was not coming back after a series of injuries. McGrath was a suitable replacement. Warne was temporarily out after finger surgery. Geoff Marsh, who promised to form a good partnership with Mark Taylor, had replaced coach Bob Simpson, who had been an important figure in Australia's revival since the dark days of the mid-1980s. Marsh and Taylor had set records as openers together. Now they plotted something even more grand.

There had been significant change, too, in Steve Waugh's personal life with the birth in August 1996 of his daughter, Rosalie. Steve was thirty-one and his expanded family gave him a glimpse of life beyond cricket. Waugh would play on if he could until his late thirties. But then or earlier he would have different responsibilities and aims in life. Seeing more of, and looking after, his family were precious luxuries to him. It would come, some day, with a 'normal' existence with a work place and a home to go to every day, and family life in general. He yearned for it and felt the loss of not seeing his daughter's smile every day. It was the price he paid for a sporting career of fame, and was something that could never be replaced. That's why he enjoyed the ever-reducing off-seasons so much, when he retreated to a private life with a minimal number of intrusions from outside, particularly the media.

The inaugural Border–Gavaskar Trophy Test match at Delhi began badly for the Australians who batted first and were dismissed on an awful pitch for 182. Waugh made a duck. India, captained for the first time by Sachin Tendulkar, replied with 361 (wicket keeper Nayan Mongia scored 152). Waugh came to the wicket at three for 72 in the second innings. He was in a defiant mood. He had left his good luck charm—a red handkerchief—at home, and in a weak moment he blamed his first innings duck on that. But Steve Waugh allowed himself fewer jelly moments than ninety-nine per cent of players who had represented Australia. This time he was determined to play tough, limited Test cricket. He was not selling his wicket at any price. It was perhaps the only way to survive on such a rotten strip against bowlers like 'quick' leg spinner Anil Kumble. Defence was the area Waugh had thought about for fifteen years since he was left out of the New South Wales Under 15 team for being 'too aggressive'. He had mainly run-scoring gears then, without the fluency of his more elegant-looking twin. When he had reached Test level, Steve Waugh had no choice but to modify his technique or be left to wallow in Shield and club cricket. Further calibration of his shots was needed once it was established that he was not a number three or four at the highest level. Steve Waugh was a natural five or six, a player who could kill off an opposition after a big start by the first four batsmen, or someone who could work with the later order and hold an innings together with a subtle mix of defence and attack.

This battling knock in India was vintage defensive Waugh. He concentrated on every ball without executing a false shot. He turned over the strike so that no bowler could corner and dismiss him. The end result was 67 not out from 221 balls. He had not presented pretty cricket for spectators wanting to be entertained with attack. This was one for the connoisseurs.

Australia reached 234 with Waugh the only batsman to score a fifty for the tourists in either innings. India polished off the fifty-odd needed with seven wickets to spare.

Steve Waugh put that loss behind him and prepared for a full series in 1996–97 at home against the West Indies. It seemed like just last month that he was scoring 200 at Sabina Park. Waugh and his team-mates were galvanised for a short-pitch blitzkrieg. The West Indies was back with six speedsters—Walsh, Ambrose, Ken Benjamin, Nixon McLean, Ian Bishop and Patterson Thompson—in its squad.

The first clash at the Gabba demonstrated that the West Indies had not changed its game plan. Ambrose blasted out first-gamer Matthew Elliott, but he and his fellow speedsters were stunned by a Ponting counterattack for 88. Australia was three for 146 midway through the second session when Waugh dug in for the duration in much the same way as in Delhi, except now he was facing serious speed and swing, not spin. The bowlers showed that they still thought they could bump him out, but it didn't work. He was 48 not out at stumps along with Healy (47 not out). Australia was five for 282. Waugh (caught by Lara at slip off Bishop for 66) didn't last long the next morning but when he left the score was six for 338. He and Healy had put on 142. Healy (161 not out) took charge for the most accomplished innings by an Australian keeper to that point. The team reached 479.

The West Indies were soon three for 77 but a strong partnership of 172 between Hooper and Chanderpaul looked like threatening Australia until Taylor threw the ball to Waugh. Steve bent his back and removed Hooper (102), his 'rabbit', caught at leg slip by Ponting. But the effort caused Waugh to damage his troublesome groin. He was lame for the rest of the game as the Windies fell for 277. Taylor declared Australia's second innings closed at six for 217, setting the tourists 420 to win from 120 overs. It reached 296 on the final day (Sherwin Campbell 113), giving the Australians victory by 123 runs.

Waugh's injury kept him out of the Second Test at Sydney beginning three days later on 29 November, which Australia won by 124 runs in an even performance from batsmen and bowlers. The lowlight was a collision mid-pitch between batsmen Elliott and Mark Waugh. Elliott, approaching his first Test century (78 not out), injured his knee and put himself out for the season.

Steve Waugh returned for the Boxing Day Third Test at the MCG and ran into a rampant Ambrose, who had so far taken three for 279 for the series. Waugh came in at three for 26 and at four for 27 joined

Blewett (62) in a restorative link of 102 runs. Bishop got through Waugh again to have him caught behind for 58. Australia reached 219 (Ambrose five for 55). The West Indies responded with 255 (McGrath five for 50). Australia's second innings saw another early collapse to serious pace from Ambrose (four for 17) bringing Waugh to the wicket at much the same stage as in the first—with the score at three for 28. He couldn't find a partner until Warne stayed with him to wriggle the score up to 107. Benjamin then bowled Waugh for a top score of 37. No one else reached 20 as Australia fell for a pitiful 122. The Windies stumbled in, picking up the 80-odd and winning by six wickets.

The series was now alive, but had to be postponed for the end of the CUB one-day series. Australia lost five games in a row and missed the finals, which were contested by the Windies and Pakistan and won by Pakistan two–nil. This flop after the World Cup defeat caused Australian selectors to rethink their strategy. Mark Taylor, who had not scored 30 in eight starts, was rumoured to be for the chop.

The resumption of the Tests at Adelaide on 25 January 1997 promised a titanic struggle, but it fizzled because of the tourists' incapacity against spin. Once Warne out-thought Lara and had him caught for 9, the Windies slumped to all out for 130. Bevan took four for 31 and Warne three for 42. Australia then went for the kill. An even performance by four contributors (Hayden 125, Mark Waugh 82, Blewett 99 and Bevan 85 not out) saw Australia reach 517. The Windies failed again, Lara once more beaten by Warne (caught behind for 78), and reached just 204, giving Australia a win by an innings and 183 runs. Bevan took six for 82, giving him ten wickets for the match.

The series was now safely with the home team at three–one. Waugh had a quiet Test and was caught in the covers off a terrible ball by Chanderpaul for 26. But it didn't matter. For once, the team looked strong without his input.

Steve had a shocker in the Fifth Test at Perth early in February. Ambrose had him caught behind for one in the first innings, while Walsh had him caught for a duck in the second. Australia was thrashed in the dead rubber by ten wickets. Once more the team had crumbled in an inconsequential game. It was a team weakness, but not significant.

Waugh returned his lowest aggregate and average for four years with 188 in four Tests at 31.33, while Mark managed 370 in five Tests at 41.11. Both failed to score a century, but were part of an even team led this time by the bowlers—McGrath, Warne and Bevan.

Despite beating the Windies for the second successive time, the only points ratings system—devised by *Wisden Cricket Monthly*—placed South Africa just ahead of Australia on the Test table. It made the three-Test series in South Africa over February and March 1997 another world championship contest.

South African salvos

A fit Australian unit lined up for the First Test on 28 February at the Wanderers Stadium, Johannesburg, after winning its four warm-up games. Elliott was back from injury and replaced Reiffel. Hansie Cronje won the toss and South Africa batted its way to a fair 302 thanks to a tenacious 72 not out by keeper Richardson. Australia replied with a blazing 85 from Elliott before Waugh came to the wicket at three for 169. Blewett joined him at four for 174, and Australia was in trouble, still 128 short. It was four for 191 when rain stopped play for the rest of day two. The partnership began slowly the next morning, before the batsmen began to despatch bad balls. Waugh worked quietly on his partner, telling him to restrain himself when he was bogged down.

'The wicket is good,' he told Blewett. 'You can get a big score if you keep your head down.'

By telling this to his younger, more trigger-happy partner, Waugh was also cautioning himself against any headstrong action. There was no need. This was Test cricket where a batsman could sail on from session to session.

Blewett's confidence grew. He built his innings into a superb display of shot making without taking undue risks. It took someone of his talent to play some of the strokes—the hook for instance—without trouble. Waugh, meanwhile, rolled with his brighter partner. They both scored centuries. Late in the afternoon of day three the link reached 300 runs. At stumps the score was four for 479, Blewett on 156 not out and Waugh on 130 not out. The partnership had added 305.

Steve Waugh was first to go the next morning, caught behind off Kallis for 160. The score was five for 559. Blewett and Waugh had added 80 in the morning and the link had been worth 385. Blewett, who had celebrated overnight, went on to his best ever innings of 214, and Taylor had the luxury of declaring at eight for 628. Bevan and Warne (four wickets each) then ran through South Africa for 130. Australia was the winner by an innings and 196 runs.

The Second Test at Port Elizabeth beginning on 14 March was a see-sawing thriller, which looked lost by Australia twice. Taylor won the toss and sent the opposition in on an underprepared grass-top, which had been set-up for South Africa's speedsters led by Donald and Pollock. Australia's move seemed to have paid off when the home side was dismissed for 209. But Australia's reply of 108 (Steve Waugh 8) was a near disaster. South Africa managed to reach none for 83 at stumps at the end of day two, a lead of 184 with all wickets intact. Australia needed a Houdini act to get out of this one. Rookie Gillespie provided it the next morning. His express bowling soon had South Africa four for 100—a lead of 201 with six wickets in hand. The home team struggled on but could only reach 168, a lead of 269. Australia had 270 to get. Even its most ardent fans were nervous. It had not been the best chaser in recent times and this was a big score on this particular wicket. The odds favoured the home team.

Australia was three for 113 when Waugh strode in with the Test on a knife edge. He (11 not out) and Mark (54 not out) took the score to three for 145 at stumps. Australia was just over halfway there with seven wickets left and a day to play. Twenty-three minutes into the morning Kallis had Steve (18) caught. It was a shock. Australian hearts sank. If Australia were to win, you would have picked Steve Waugh as the player who would do most to secure it. Yet his other half, Mark, the most graceful batsman of the 1990s, was still in and looking sound. Today Mark was displaying that incredible grace under the biggest pressure that Test cricket could provide.

Steve was fourth man out at 167. Australia was 103 short of victory with just six wickets left. The scales had tipped to South Africa. At 192, the frog-in-a-blender-style spinner Adams bowled Blewett. Bevan dug in with Mark for a vital link of 66. Then Kallis bowled Mark Waugh for 116. He had done the job—almost. There were still a dozen runs to get with four wickets in hand. Soon afterwards Cronje removed Bevan (24). Australia was seven for 258. At 265, Warne was trapped lbw by Kallis. There were five runs to get and two wickets left. Gillespie came in and survived the remainder of Kallis's over. That left Healy to face Cronje. The Australian keeper hoisted his third ball over square leg for six. Australia was home by two wickets. They had won the series.

The tourists had just stopped celebrating four days later when they had to appear at Centurion Park, Pretoria, for the dead rubber Third Test. Cronje won the toss and sent the Australians in. Waugh arrived at the wicket with the score at three for 72. He and Blewett improved matters again, but much more modestly than in the First Test, taking the score from 110 to 190. Waugh received a poor decision when caught down leg side for 67. It was top score. No other batsman reached 40 as Australia rolled over for a timid 227.

South Africa then rammed home the advantage, scoring 384 in an even team effort. Australia made a worse start than in the first innings, and Waugh found himself marching to the wicket at three for 28. He remained 60 not out as Australia crumbled for 185, with several more poor umpiring decisions that even South African commentators found embarrassing. The home side went on to win by eight wickets. Healy received the worst decision, when given out caught behind down the leg side. He stomped off and threw his bat up the dressing room steps. Television cameras picked it up and Healy was suspended for two one-day matches. Worse, the act of frustration threatened his Test vice-captaincy. It seemed Australia could not shake its unprofessional habit of dropping a dead rubber.

Waugh took the Man of the Series award and the averages, 313 runs at 78.25. He was adjudged Player of the Series for the third time in a row against South Africa. Gillespie took fourteen wickets at 20.50; McGrath thirteen at 22.23. But they weren't done yet. There were still seven one-day games to play. South Africa now was determined to win this anticlimactic competition. Australia lost the first game, but the Waugh twins (Steve 50 off 52 balls) and Mark (115 from 125 balls) swung the second to the tourists. Mark Taylor, whose poor form through the Australian summer against the West Indies had continued in South Africa, dropped himself from the third game. Healy came back from suspension as captain, but Australia lost. Healy's main rival, Adam Gilchrist, made 77 from 78 balls in the fourth game, which led to a second Australian win. It was two all with three to play.

The tourists lifted their rating in the fifth game and another newcomer, Michael Di Venuto, cracked a quick 89. It was enough to help his team scrape in again. It was three–two to the tourists with two to play. In game six South Africa hit a strong 284—its highest-ever score against Australia. Steve Waugh (80 off 100 balls) and Bevan (103 off ninety-five) put on 189 runs for the fourth wicket, and this led to a five-wicket win with an over to spare. Australia was first to four wins—and the series. Did the tourists slacken off in the final game, whether consciously or not, as they had done during the Tests? They lost, but Waugh again performed as if it counted, after hitting 91, doing his best in a losing team in his first one-day game as skipper.

Steve Waugh retained his ranking as number-one batsman in the world with all the ratings agencies in the analysis after the tour of South Africa. Mark took the number-two spot. The twins were in good form for the upcoming Ashes battle in England. But they needed a good break. All they had was a few weeks. Was it enough to fire up for the longest, most demanding tour of all?

Steve Waugh was promoted to vice-captain in place of Ian Healy, who was demoted after his bat throwing in South Africa. Waugh was close to thirty-two years old and his appointment had come at a critical time. Mark Taylor was in a prolonged form slump that had run for two seasons. If not for the patronage of the ACB and his position as captain, he would have been dropped a year earlier. Now his performances were demoralising the side, which was guaranteed to get off to a poor start. If this continued much longer, he would have to go. Steve Waugh would be captain. As it was, Waugh would take over sooner or later, providing his fitness and form could be maintained. Steve had stolen a march on his brother Mark and Shane Warne.

But the choice of Steve for captain wasn't unanimous. Former Australian skipper Ian Chappell preferred Mark Waugh to Taylor and Steve. 'He has got a good cricket brain,' Chappell commented, 'but the best thing is he's a gambler. In the field you can see he's always thinking about getting a wicket. That's how he used to bowl. And he's a magnificent batsman ... Mark could lead from the front. If he told the team to go out and attack, you know he'd do it himself. Steve's not that sort of player, nor is Taylor.'

Despite Chappell's comments, Steve Waugh was the front-runner to succeed Taylor.

9

THE EMPIRE STRIKES OUT

Rust and restoration

Australia was rusty in England during the Texaco Trophy one-day competition and the home team beat it three–nil. Steve Waugh managed starts with scores of 19, 24 and 17, but couldn't go on. Bevan hit a century and Mark Waugh scored 95, but the other bats were down, with Taylor scoring 7 and 11 run out. The loss was further evidence for selectors that they had to give the limited-overs side a different, more specialist look if Australia were to challenge for the World Cup in 1999, which was now just two years away. Taylor, who was still struggling, stood down from the final one-day game, and Waugh was captain. England's win made it an inauspicious debut.

The British press's response to the home team's win bordered on hysteria. Even the more sober, thoughtful papers were jingoistic. Sensing the unease in the Australian camp over Taylor's form, articles centred on the problem of leadership. The skipper told Geoff Marsh and Steve Waugh that he would give himself two county games and the First Test to find form. If he didn't, he would stand down. It was a tough time for Waugh too. He would prefer not to have to take control in a situation where Taylor had fallen on his sword. Taylor scored 0 and 30 versus Gloucestershire.

Waugh, who had been in fine form with 92 in his only knock, had to face the press conference. It was all about Taylor. Waugh fielded questions with his typical directness. He defended his good mate and leader. The press was not given an inch.

Taylor made 5 in the first innings versus Derbyshire and the screws tightened. Dropped early in his second innings by Australia's Dean Jones (Derby's skipper) in slips, Taylor went on to 63, but he was unconvincing. Taylor was selected for the First Test at Edgbaston on 5 June on faith and hope. His batting was all but shot. He won the toss and was out for 7. It set a low standard for the innings and Australia was soon three for 26. It was a scene Taylor-made for Waugh, but even he failed as the malaise set in, and Caddick had him caught behind for 12. Only Warne with an up-and-under innings of 47 gave the score some respectability. No one else had managed 20. England replied with nine for 478, including a brilliant 207 from Nasser Hussain.

Taylor came to the wicket in the second innings knowing that this was it. If he failed, his Test career would be over. He felt he had nothing to lose by striking out. He managed some good shots early and soon reached 50 in sixty-nine deliveries. He and Elliott (66) opened with a stand of 133. Then the skipper partnered Blewett (125) for a link of 194, before Taylor fell, caught and bowled to off spinner Croft for 129.

At last he had shown some form. It was a relief for him and for the rest of the touring squad. The team could relax a bit now that its leader was among the runs after a drought. Waugh came to the wicket at four for 393, but on 33 was trapped lbw by Gough. Australia crumbled after that to be all out 477. A winning opportunity had been squandered.

England, hungry for an early-series victory, smashed the 120 runs or so needed in quick time to take the game by nine wickets. The media went over the top in its praise for England and scorn for the vanquished.

The tourists licked their wounds, drew with Nottinghamshire, beat Leicestershire easily and plotted the Lord's Test, which was scheduled to start on 19 June. The Test didn't get under way because of the weather until day two. Taylor won the toss and sent England in, who were mesmerised by the pace and swing of an accurate McGrath. The score was soon three for 13. At three for 38 the rain returned and no more play was possible. On day three, McGrath routed England for 77, taking eight for 38. Australia chased runs hard, knowing it had to win and time was short. It was seven for 213 at stumps on day four after another day or so had been lost to rain (Steve Waugh was lbw to Caddick for a duck), Elliott having belted a terrific 112—his first Test century. Taylor declared at seven for 213 on the final morning with the lead at 136.

England then cruised to four for 266 and the match was drawn. Australia's collective confidence was returning. It lifted its performance another notch five days later and thrashed Hampshire. Mark Waugh stroked a brilliant 173 and Taylor made 109.

At the double

Steve had little sleep the night before the Old Trafford Third Test beginning on 3 July. Baby daughter Rosalie woke up three times. Lynette offered to move into another room but Waugh wouldn't hear of it. He was happy to have his family with him on tour and they came first. He recalled the time he had been woken in the middle of the night by an intruder just before the Fourth and deciding Test in Jamaica in April 1995. He'd made 200, his best-ever effort in a Test, which did most to win the match and the series. He took the disturbance this time as a positive omen for the following day.

But if he was half-hoping for a day in the field and the chance for more rest the next night before he batted, it wasn't to be. Taylor won the toss and made the most courageous decision of his captaincy. The wicket was moist and grassy. The sky was overcast. He would have been excused for letting McGrath, Gillespie and Reiffel loose on it first.

But he decided to bat. His logic was simple. Australia had to do everything to win the Test to level the series after three games. There was no point in drawing a Test and giving England a one–nil lead with three to play.

Taylor was first to go for 2 with the score at 9. Waugh came to the wicket at three for 42. He and Elliott (40) dug in against swing and seam until Elliott received a bad decision and was given out caught behind at 85. Waugh took belts on the arms and hand. He managed the discomfort and batted on in a tenacious display. He found a partner in Reiffel at seven for 160. Rain delayed play for two hours but Waugh was still able to reach his century in the last over before stumps with the score at seven for 224.

Gough bowled Waugh the next morning for 108 and Australia was all out for 235. Warne lifted in England's reply of 162, taking six for 48. Waugh came to the wicket at three for 39 in Australia's second innings, with one hand swollen to twice its normal size, and again batted on, holding the innings together once more. He found a solid partner in Healy (47), then Warne, who was 33 not out at stumps. The score was six for 262 and Waugh, in a heroic effort, was 82 not out. The next day he batted on to 90 and then crawled to 99 virtually batting with one hand. He stroked one through midwicket to reach his second century for the game. It was a match-winning double that would rank with the great performances in Test history. He had come to the wicket under extreme pressure in both innings. The batting conditions were hazardous and he was injured. To score one century in such circumstances was brilliant. Only perhaps Lara, Tendulkar and Mark Waugh among contemporary cricketers could have combined such courage with the level of skill required to survive. To do it twice in a match put him in a class of his own.

Taylor had the luxury of declaring midway through day four at eight for 395. The target was 469 with 141 overs to secure them. McGrath (four for 46), Gillespie (three for 31) and Warne (three for 63) dismissed England for 200. The win was by 268 runs. Thanks to Man of the Match Steve Waugh, the series was one–one, with three to play.

Waugh's injury kept him out of four of the mid-tour games in July before the Fourth Test. He had a 103-run partnership with Mark (142) while scoring 57 against Middlesex at Lord's before heading for Head-ingley for the Test beginning 24 July. Taylor showed his flexibility by winning the toss and sending England in. Gillespie took seven for 37, demonstrating what a find he was. His problem was his lean frame, which made him injury prone. If he could be kept on the field, he and McGrath would be a formidable opening attack. England reached just 172.

Taylor again failed early. His scores for the series were 7, 129, 1, 2, 1 and 0. Was it enough to justify his place? It didn't matter. He would remain in the team for the rest of the series. But his duck in this innings unsettled the side. Steve Waugh came to the wicket at three for 43, but this time he fell to Headley caught at bat-pad for 4. However, Elliott (a fine 199), Ponting (127) and Reiffel (54 not out) did most to allow Taylor to declare at nine for 501. England was all out for 268 (Hussain 105, Reiffel five for 49), giving Australia a win by an innings and 61 runs, and a two–one lead in the series.

The tourists had recovered from the low at the start when it lost the one-dayers and the First Test, and the English media began to turn its critical eyes to the home side. Yet an incident at Taunton in a three-day game against Somerset allowed another round of Aussie-bashing. Warne had come in for much heavy and foul abuse while bowling. The small ground allowed every word to be heard clearly. Lines such as 'Warne takes it up the arse', 'Warne is a poofter', 'We own your country, we own your arse' reverberated. Waugh, who was captain while Taylor rested for the match, complained to the umpires. Security men escorted two ringleaders of the abuse from the ground.

Later Steve Waugh had to face a press conference. A journalist pointed out that abuse went on all round the world. Waugh countered by asking if the journalists would bring their wives and children to a game where this was going on. No one responded at the conference. But the next morning Waugh had his reply from some, who suggested the tourists couldn't take it.

Despite this, Waugh's handling of the matter enhanced his

credentials for one day taking on the Test captaincy. He had never lobbied for it, but would accept it if it were offered. For the second time on tour—the first was when Taylor received offensive and poor media treatment during his slump—Waugh had shown strong leadership qualities off the field. ACB chairman and tour manager Alan Crompton had been present both times. Waugh's efforts were noted.

Steve maintained his good form in this game, scoring 62 before Caddick had him caught. The bowler's effort (five for 54) ensured he would be picked for the home team to play in the Trent Bridge Fifth Test beginning three days later on 7 August.

Taylor's golden touch with the toss continued and he at least got among the runs again (76), as did Elliott (69), Blewett (50) and Mark Waugh (68). Steve Waugh came to the wicket at a more comfortable three for 225 and was involved in a mini-partnership of 86 with his brother en route to 75, when express bowler Malcolm got on target and bowled him. Australia reached 427. England fought harder to reach 313, but another even performance by the Australian batsmen from Taylor (45) through to Reiffel (22) at number nine saw the tourists all out for 336. Caddick again removed Waugh, caught for 14. Australian bowlers Warne, McGrath and Gillespie took three wickets each to hold England to 186 and a defeat by 264 runs. The victory gave Australia the series three–one and the Ashes.

Waugh made a strong 154 in the final county game against Kent before the dead-rubber Sixth Test at The Oval. England won the toss, batted and fell to the accuracy and late swing of McGrath (seven for 76). It reached just 180. But Australia's reply, on what looked a spinner's wicket as the days rolled by, was just 220. Steve scored 22, while no batsman managed to reach 50 or could handle the leg-spin of Tufnell (seven for 66). England crumbled again for just 163. This time Kasprowicz took seven for 36. Australia was left with a target of 124 and choked in the chase, reaching just 104. Caddick (five for 42, including Waugh's wicket once more for just 6) and Tufnell (four for 27) did the damage. This time Australia once more completed the ignominious double by losing a dead rubber and failing to reach a small target.

The series ended three–two to Australia.

Waugh's Test figures of 390 at 39 were modest by his standards and compared with his overall Test average of around 50. His first-class tour returned better results: 924 runs at 54.35. Elliott was Australia's Test star with the bat with 556 at 55.6, while Reiffel, who hadn't been selected at the start of the tour, made 179 at 59.67 in the Tests. But the form of Mark Waugh (averaging 20.9) and Taylor (31.7) was worrying for selectors.

McGrath (36 wickets at 19.47) and Warne (24 wickets at 24.04) were the bowling mainstays.

Australia's retention of the Ashes meant Taylor would hold his tenuous Test spot for the moment. Waugh hoped that his eventual transition to the leadership would happen naturally and not in a crisis, which nearly occurred in England. It all depended on Taylor's form.

Under new management, partly

The Australian selectors took a brave, even radical step by selecting Steve Waugh to captain Australia's one-day team, while leaving a disgruntled Mark Taylor hanging on to the leadership of the Test side. They also dropped Taylor and Ian Healy from the one-day team. Adam Gilchrist, one of the best hitters in Australia, took Healy's place as a keeper–batsman. Taylor told selectors, 'If you are going to leave me out of the one-dayers, you should leave me out of all cricket.'

The selectors told Taylor they wanted him to remain leader of the Test side, but that they had 'doubts' about him as a one-day player. It left Taylor bitter. He maintained that there should be just one skipper for both teams. Otherwise, he suggested, it would be divisive. The selectors held firm.

The media was mainly opposed to the move. It made a better story than supporting the selectors and the ACB. Waugh came in for criticism. Ian Chappell and others didn't think he was the best choice.

Waugh and Taylor, long-time friends and teammates, didn't take matters personally. Waugh had not lobbied for the job, although he was happy to accept it. On the contrary, in Taylor's time of struggle, he had given strong support to his captain, telling the British media to back off.

Taylor was so disappointed in the new two-captain policy that he drafted a letter of resignation from the captaincy. But his wife Judi and close friends talked him out of it. It didn't happen. He played on in the Tests.

This change in the one-day leadership was for a time overshadowed by a dispute between the ACB and the ACA—the Australian Cricketers' Association—over pay and conditions. Steve Waugh had become the secretary of the ACA in 1997 and was in the thick of negotiations. He was a political individual, intent on improving the lot of players. Steve could easily have left matters to others, but he chose to be prominent in opposing his ACB paymasters. Waugh was aware of his power—next to Taylor, he was the most powerful current player. He was happy to flex his muscle in what he saw as an important player cause. There was even talk of strike action.

Waugh was in touch at the start of the season, scoring 202 not out for New South Wales against a Victoria that included Warne. This was his fourth double hundred and forty-sixth century. He and Mark (72) put on 156 in 130 minutes.

Waugh faced a media conference when on 113 not out, saying it was good to see so many reporters at Shield cricket. They were there to question him about the ACA–ACB dispute. Would he strike the next day?

'I'll be back,' Waugh replied. 'One hundred and thirteen not out on a small ground on a good batting wicket—I'd be silly not to.'

At another conference after he had made 202 not out, questions concentrated again on the possibilities of a strike.

'Thanks for asking about the double hundred,' Steve Waugh said.

There was no strike, but the dispute took up the first half of the 1997–98 season. The ACA, led by president Tim May and Steve Waugh (the key current player), and aided by former ACB CEO,

Graham Halbish and entrepreneur James Erskine, primarily wanted a better pay structure for all first-class cricketers in Australia, not just Test players. Steve Waugh, Shane Warne and other top players were unselfishly looking for a bigger money 'pot' to be spread among all first-class players, and not just pay increases for themselves.

Waugh said he was happy with what he was paid (more than $400,000 a year), but that he was carrying on the fight for underprivileged Shield players. He remembered only too well the struggle and concerns in the early and mid-1980s over how he would make a living. Waugh had lucky breaks when Packer put him on a retainer for three years to stop him ever becoming a rebel in South Africa, and when he was prematurely selected for Test cricket, allowing him to survive. He believed that there should be a reasonable base pay in Shield cricket that would allow a budding cricketer time to develop rather than be forced out of the game because he had to make a living elsewhere.

Many older cricketers opposed this, arguing that it would 'soften' first-class cricket, as it had in England, where second-rate 'trundlers' held on to their county places far too long when it was clear they would never become Test cricketers. (In Australia it would be a state matter. States would have the right to contract an old player or replace him with a younger person.) Waugh and the ACA argued that professionalism had to be the course to take to remove uncertainty and allow budding players time to develop and to create careers. In the end, Ken Piesse, editor of *Australian Cricketer* magazine, pinpointed the most basic and important factor. If the money was in the ACB coffers, and distribution didn't affect payments to the states, it should be passed on to the players. Piesse pointed out that multi-gifted teenagers had to be attracted to cricket rather than football, soccer, basketball, baseball and other growing sports in Australia.

The ACA also wanted more and better consultation with the ACB over the way the game was run, the number of overseas tours, better tour itineraries and a tiered contract system.

In 1997–98, players were paid match payments only and a top state player could earn between $25,000 and $27,000. The outcome of the dispute saw player contracts linked to a share of Australian cricket revenue. They were certain to earn much more from the deal over the next few years. (By 1999–2000, the base contract for a Pura Milk Cup player was $12,500, with the possibility of another $30,000 for match payments, meaning the lowliest player in first-class cricket could earn around $40,000 a year. Each state had to contract twelve players. The maximum allowable retainer for a state-contracted player was $50,000, with the chance to pick up another $30,000 from match payments, making around $80,000 in all. The top twenty-five players for 2000–01—ranked 1 to 25—contracted by the ACB began with a base contract of $80,000 for number 25 and worked up to payment for number 1—Glenn McGrath—of $315,000. With match payments McGrath and Steve Waugh, who also had a captain's allowance, could earn more than $600,000 for the season.)

While all this was being resolved, the Test side in 1997–98 got down to business in the First Test versus New Zealand on 7 November 1997 at the Gabba. Kiwi skipper Stephen Fleming won the toss and sent the home side in. Waugh (2) was part of an early collapse—not an uncommon occurrence for the Australians at the start of a competition. Series were coming so quickly on top of each other that batsmen, particularly, were finding it hard to crank up. At one point the team was four for 53, but Taylor, rediscovering form that had deserted him for so long, dropped anchor and reached 112. This hard-fought knock facilitated an Australian recovery. At stumps it was six for 269. The next day it reached 373, thanks to Healy's 68 and a dashing 77 from Reiffel in 113 balls.

New Zealand was dismissed for 349 (Fleming 91). Steve Waugh was again removed cheaply in another poor innings beginning. Australia was four for 105 before Blewett (91) and Ponting (73 not out) pulled the innings around, allowing Taylor to declare at six for 294. McGrath (five for 32) did most to cause New Zealand to crash to all out 132. Australia was the victor by 186 runs.

After this game Mark Waugh was criticised for his long run of failures and low scores for an Australian number four since the Test versus South Africa at Port Elizabeth eight months earlier. Then he had scored 116. Since that Test he had hit 5, 42, 5, 1, 33, 12, 55, 8, 68, 7, 19, 1, 3, and 17—276 runs in all at just 19.71.

Mark had a credible defender in his brother. Steve didn't think anyone could be consistent over a year, let alone two years. He cited matters such as family and business problems that impinged on a player's game. Steve thought Mark was going through a stage experienced by all modern-day professionals—receiving unfortunate umpiring decisions on top of poor form and unlucky dismissals. The confluence of all this had caused a drop in confidence. 'He's just got to believe in himself now,' Steve Waugh commented. 'Because with eleven hundreds he has the ability. It's got to come from within.'

That self-belief came back in Perth nine days later in the Second Test, but not, at first, with the bat or ball. Mark took a screamer of a catch in New Zealand's first innings of 217 when he launched himself sideways and horizontal at midwicket.

Steve Waugh came to the wicket at three for 71 and joined his brother in one of their all-too-rare big partnerships (153). Mark hit an aggressive 86 and silenced his critics for the moment, while Steve went on the next morning to be out bowled by O'Connor for 96—his eighth stoppage in the nineties—with the score at 262. It was enough to earn him Man of the Match. He also became the seventh Australian to reach 6000 runs in Tests.

Healy (85) and Reiffel (54 in 48 balls) helped the score up to 461 and a lead of 244. New Zealand crumbled again for 172 (Simon Cook, a stand in for the injured McGrath, took five for 39), giving Australia a win by an innings and 72 runs, and the series two–nil. There was still a Third Test to play at Hobart. Taylor won the toss, batted on 27 November and reached five for 273 at stumps on day two after most of day one was washed out. Waugh (7) failed as Australia rattled up 400 (Mark Waugh notching a majestic 81), but he came back with the ball and took the bowling honours, with three for 20 off nine overs in New Zealand's score of six declared for 229 (Horne 133) on day four. Fleming's gesture was sporting and sensible. There was no point in going home nil–two when he could steal one. Taylor took up the challenge and declared at two for 138, leaving New Zealand 288 to score to win in sixty overs—at less than five an over. With limited-overs experience this was not an outrageous target, although the wicket was wearing and the fielding side had the luxury of placing fieldsmen where it wished.

New Zealand made an expected chase early but collapsed to be nine for 222. The last men in—Doull and O'Connor—stayed thirty-eight minutes and faced sixty-four balls to deny Australia a clean sweep of Test wins.

After the series, Waugh was replaced as the world's number-one batsman in the Coopers & Lybrand ratings by Inzamam-ul-Haq. This was after a record thirty months from May 1995 to October 1997 as the world's best. Mark, who was returning to somewhere near his classy best, had slipped from number two in May 1995 to out of the top ten.

In December, the summer swung into one-day mode with its new look under Steve Waugh and with Shane Warne vice-captain. The difference from the Test team was marked. Out went Taylor, Healy, Elliott and Blewett. Gilchrist, Andy Bichel, Kasprowicz, Reiffel, Paul Wilson, Moody, Ian Harvey, Adam Dale and Gavin Robertson formed the pool from which choices would be made to add to the Waughs, McGrath, Darren Lehmann, Bevan and Warne. In the December games, Australia was beaten twice by South Africa, and it beat New Zealand twice. The media began to grumble, saying that the split team experiment was a failure. Steve Waugh, it was said, did not look inspired in the field, and Mark Taylor again complained about the new two-captains policy.

Grudge matches

Before the one-day series could resume and the wisdom or otherwise of the changes could be determined, Australia had to play two Tests against South Africa. It was 'as you were' in the look of the home side. The games against New Zealand had been just the preliminary bout before the main contest with the heavyweights from South Africa, who were still bristling from their encounter early in 1997. The first contest was the MCG Boxing Day Test in front of 73,000 fans, who had been denied a full Test versus South Africa in 1993. After winning the toss, Australia started poorly, losing three for 44, a familiar scoreline that signalled the emergence of Steve Waugh from the pavilion. It was his ninety-ninth Test. He and Ponting revived the home side's fortunes with a strong link that took the score to four for 206 at stumps. Waugh went on to 96 before being caught off Donald. Australia wriggled up to a mediocre 309. South Africa folded for 186 in reply.

The home team followed up in its usual fashion, losing quick wickets early. Waugh this time came to the wicket at three for 12 and temporarily stopped some serious embarrassment. But when on 17 at 44 Pollock dismissed him. The slump continued until Reiffel came to the wicket at seven for 128 and blasted 79 not out, which lifted the score to 257, a lead of 380. The talented all-rounder Jacques Kallis hit his maiden century and held off an Australian victory by doing most to hold on until stumps on the last day at seven for 273—107 behind.

The teams had two days' break before facing each other again on 2 January 1998 in the Second Test at Sydney. Steve was congratulated in the pre-game ceremony in front of a home crowd for playing in his one hundredth Test.

Cronje won the toss and batted. The Proteas crawled to five for 197 at stumps. The next morning Warne, who was having a fine summer, took five for 29 in the pre-lunch session, and South Africa were all out for 287.

Waugh came to the wicket at three for 103 and joined Mark. At stumps Mark was on a fine 74 not out, showing that he had returned to his true cameo form. Steve was on 18 not out. The score was three for 174. On day three, Steve awoke determined to reach a century in his one hundredth Test, but Mark upstaged him as they worked in tandem against the full force of Donald at his top pace. Mark reached his century and was out to Pollock with the score at 219. The Waugh brothers had put on 116 in 131 minutes. It was only the fourth time the brothers had been linked for a hundred or more in a Test, and the big Sydney crowd loved it. Ponting and Steve then added 98, which took Australia into the lead. At 317, Donald came back to spoil Waugh's celebration by bowling him for 85. He was disappointed to be dismissed just 15 short of an historic moment. He remarked with his usual resigned dryness that it was better than getting out in the nineties. Yet again, he was playing down an excellent effort for his country. An 80 or more against Donald and the other South African bowlers would be a credit to the ability of any of the game's finest batsmen from Bradman to Lara. Thanks to the Waughs and some wagging of the tail, Australia made it to 421 early on day four. The lead was 134.

Warne (six for 34) then turned on one of his sensational bowling spells, taking his 300th Test wicket en route to obliterating South Africa for 113. Australia was the victor by an innings and 21 runs. But it would have to wait several weeks for the final Test at Adelaide as the limited-overs series continued.

Steve's route to revenge

South Africa accounted for Australia for the third successive time in the one-day competition. Waugh, who had failed in each game with 1, 7, 0, 0, was under pressure. He and the team seemed to be failing. Yet he was as positive as ever with his 'It'll be all right on the night' attitude, implying that Australia would win the series. No one in the media accepted his words. Journalists began editorialising about the selectors' 'failed experiment' of two teams. But they were engaging in premature denunciation. The vultures were circling too early. Waugh was frustrated further by a hip injury that forced him to hand over the reins for one game to deputy Warne. The spin bowler led the side like a football skipper, with body language and verballing. It was Warne's style and it was successful. In newspaper and magazine articles, the Chappell brothers weighed in for Warne as the next Australian Test skipper to follow Mark Taylor. But the selectors remained silent. Cool-headed, laconic Waugh, with his magnificent record, was still the ACB's choice as Taylor's successor.

Meanwhile the pattern on the field continued with the Australians easily accounting for New Zealand but losing a fourth time to South Africa. It led to an Australia versus South Africa best-of-three final series. Waugh's scores until this moment resembled the stretch that had characterised Mark Taylor's several seasons in the horrors. His scores were 1, 7, 0, 0, 45 not out versus New Zealand in a lost preliminary game. And then, as ever, he stepped up a notch in the first final at the MCG, scoring 53, and was involved in a 101-run fourth-wicket link with Bevan (57). But an insipid finish with some irresponsible late order batting handed the game to the tourists. Australia fell six runs short on the second-last ball. It was the fifth successive loss to South Africa.

The home team was written off for the finals. Ian Chappell wrote a most damning article in *The Bulletin*. It appeared before the end of the series and anticipated an Australian obliteration. No doubt Steve Waugh would frame it if he were to pull off an upset.

In the second final at Sydney, South Africa batted first and scored six for 228. Waugh, in a daring but much-called-for move, promoted Gilchrist to open with Mark Waugh. It came off. Gilchrist smashed a century in 102 balls as Australia coasted to a crushing win in 41.5 overs.

Waugh took the moment at a media conference to point out that South Africa did well in preliminary matches, but tended to break down under pressure in the matches that mattered. He cited the 1996 World Cup. There were also examples in two series (1994 and 1997) when they couldn't finish off Australia, which came back to level one series and win another.

In colloquial terms, which headline writers used, Waugh was saying that the Proteas were 'chokers'. On the face of it, this cheeky, confrontational approach by Waugh, which had never been adopted publicly before in a century of Australian cricket, would either leave him looking like a flannelled fool or else a mind-game master after the last match, which would decide the series.

The South Africans were incensed. It intensified the atmosphere when the third game began in Sydney—a day–nighter. Waugh won the toss and batted in order not to have to chase under lights. He appeared at the wicket with the score at three for 79 and exhibited his iceman, low-temperature style by hitting 71, second-top score to Ponting's 76. The skipper had not 'choked' himself, which was a relief for his many fans. Australia reached seven for 247. It was a gettable target, in normal conditions. But now the pressure was on the Proteas. The always underestimated Reiffel lifted for a big performance, which was his wont. He removed the openers. Warne came on and swung the game by having Cronje stumped for five. Steve Waugh couldn't be kept out of the game. He took a sensational running catch over his shoulder at midwicket to dismiss the dangerous Klusener for 46.

The Australians kept the pressure on until South Africa was nine for 204. The home side received a little fright from last man Adams, but the tourists fell 14 short when Waugh swooped on an Adams shot into the covers and ran out McMillan. The Australians had won the series two–one. Waugh had triumphed—with the bat, in the field, as a tactician, a propagandist and a daredevil psychologist. Had the Proteas really choked? It was unlikely. They had peaked too early. When Australia cranked up it performed better.

The selectors stopped sweating. Their two-team adventure had come alive a year earlier than expected and with the 1999 World Cup just sixteen months away.

More Waugh dramas

Two days after the one-day final Hansie Cronje and his team headed for Adelaide for the Third Test. A Test win would level the series and restore some prestige to the tourists. South Africa batted determinedly in compiling 517. At least one bat had to stay for a big one if Australia were to stave off defeat and for once the task didn't fall to one of the Waugh twins. Mark (63) delivered a cameo but Waugh, in at three for 197, made just 6, caught behind off Pollock. This time skipper Mark Taylor brought up his seventeenth Test century and carried his bat to 169 not out in a total of 350. This outstanding effort took Taylor back a decade to his best days.

South Africa declared at six for 193, leaving Australia 361 to chase for a win. At stumps on day four the home team was two for 32, with Mark Waugh 11 not out. Everything pointed to a victory for South Africa. Steve Waugh came to the wicket in another crisis at three for 54. He was in fine form and judging from his aggressive approach it seemed he thought the target was achievable. But on 34 with the score at 112 he was caught behind off Klusener. Mark Waugh was playing with the same head-down style he exhibited in Port Elizabeth less than a year earlier when he had scored 116 in a cliffhanger. He had luck, being dropped three times, yet it was still a more durable kind of innings than Mark usually liked to deliver. His natural style was flamboyant. Tie Mark down and he was yours. But his game had reached a new level of maturity. He could play like Steve when he really wanted to.

Mark reached his century, but still the job needed to be done with an hour to play. Australia was six for 212. Andy Bichel was at the wicket and Mark on 107 when Pollock hurled down a bouncer. It hit Mark on the shoulder. He had finished his shot and was walking in pain towards square leg when his hurt arm flicked involuntarily. He knocked down his stumps with his bat. Umpire Randell called for a video. The third umpire correctly ruled not out. The key in the decision was the fact that, by any definition, Waugh had finished his shot by several seconds before he hit his stumps. Cronje would not accept the decision. He tried to argue that a player who was hit on the head and toppled onto his stumps would be given out. But this was out only if it were judged that the player was in the act of finishing his shot when he fell on his stumps. Mark Waugh was into a completely different action—walking away towards square leg.

Hansie Cronje was furious. In a pathetic display he remonstrated with the umpires. After a few minutes the game went on. Mark, unsettled and in pain, was dropped on 109. Bichel (7) was lbw to Klusener. Warne joined Mark and they had to negotiate six overs. Both played out of character and saw out the overs, Waugh on 115 not out and Warne 4 not out. Australia was seven for 227. South Africa was shattered. Cronje took a stump and speared it into the door to the umpires' room, demonstrating very poor sportsmanship.

The home team achieved an amazing draw and so won the series one–nil. Since returning to the Test arena in the early 1990s, South Africa was yet to win a Test or limited-overs series against Australia.

Warne took twenty wickets at 20.85 for the series and won the Man of the Series award. Mark Waugh topped the averages with 279 runs at 69.75 and there were no more cries for his dumping. Steve had a standard season for him, scoring 238 at 47.60, which was an improvement on his New Zealand Tests, when he hit 130 at 32.50.

10

INDIA BOUND, PAKISTAN AND ENGLAND DOWNED

Tendulkar tussles

After a long, hard summer in Australia the squad went to India from February to April 1998 for a three-Test series in India and two one-day series in India and the United Arab Emirates at Sharjah. Taylor lost the toss in the First Test at Chennai and Mohammad Azharuddin decided to bat. Indian openers Nayan Mongia and Navjot Sidhu put together 122 but then India crumbled for 257. Warne dismissed Tendulkar early for just 4. It was now Australia's turn to face India's answer to Warne, Anil Kumble, who bowled fast leg breaks and wrong'uns like Bill O'Reilly, Australia's star leggie of the 1930s. Steve Waugh (12) was an early victim, trapped lbw when he shouldered arms and watched a wrong'un slam into his stumps. Thanks to Healy (90) and debutant off spinner Gavin Robertson (57), Australia reached 328 and a lead of 71. In India's second innings, Tendulkar took control, scoring 155 not out in a magnificent performance over 286 minutes, in which he faced 191 balls. India declared at four for 418. Australia was a miserable three for 31 at stumps. Mark Waugh was in with nightwatchman Paul Reiffel during yet another crisis after an early-order batting slump. Kumble had precipitated it.

The next morning was marked by a series of poor umpiring decisions. Mark Waugh (18) was given out caught at bat-pad when the ball missed his bat by several centimetres. Reiffel (1) was given out, caught off his boot. Steve Waugh steadied the innings and was travelling well on 27 just before lunch. He was given out caught at bat-pad, when videos showed he had also missed the ball. Australia was six for 96 at lunch and it folded after the break for an ignominious 168, giving India a win by 179 runs.

The Second Test at Eden Gardens in Calcutta, packed with 50,000 cheering fans, began disastrously for Australia even by its poor standard. It lost two (Slater and Blewett) with the score at one. Srinath took his third wicket (Mark Waugh) and Australia was three for 15 when Steve Waugh arrived at the crease. Taylor (3) was dismissed at 29. Waugh then found a partner in Ponting and they took the score to four for 67 at lunch. They continued after the break to 141, when Ponting (60) was bowled by Kumble. At tea Australia was seven for 175 with Waugh on a dogged 79 not out. He had been cut down by a groin injury and had to use a runner. After tea there was a mix-up and Waugh was run out for 80. Australia was all out for 233.

India then put a clamp on the series by amassing five for 633 declared. Skipper Azharuddin was the star with a brilliant 163 not out. Australia was one for 38 at the end of the third day. Steve Waugh, not risking a runner, though still injured, came to the wicket at five for 97. After lunch he and Healy battled on until Healy received a bad lbw decision, leaving Australia six for 133. Waugh batted on courageously, scoring 33 in nearly three hours of defiance. But Australia was all out for 181 and beaten by an innings and 219 runs, its fourth-heaviest defeat ever. India had won the series two–nil.

During the game Steve Waugh had received a fax from Shamlu Dudeja, an Indian social worker, inviting him to visit the Udayan home for children of leprosy sufferers in Barrackpore. Australia's defeat in four days meant Waugh had a day off. He decided to take up the offer, and spent hours playing cricket with the children. He signed autographs and showed compassion for the plight of these unfortunate kids and their parents, all of whom were regarded as outcasts. The Udayan home had a wing for 250 boys. Waugh, the father of a baby girl, committed himself to raising money for a girls' wing.

It showed another side to the tough, ruthless Waugh who never gave an inch on a cricket field to any opponent. His sensitivity was something that surprised some, but not those close to him, who knew of Steve's feelings away from the sporting spotlight. Of all Australian cricketers in recent decades, he was the most interested in exploring a nation's underbelly, especially on the subcontinent, where poverty is rife. He used his camera to capture life as it was away from the rarefied atmosphere of the sporting superstars, who lived and ate in plush hotels insulated from the social problems of a host nation. This self-exposure, often alone, opened Steve's mind and kept him in touch with reality, so often lost to players always in the limelight. In this way, Waugh was never likely to become carried away with his own astonishing success as a sportsman. Instead, he began to understand what his superstardom could do for some of the vast mass of humanity who could never aspire to his heights by virtue of where and when they were born. Australia seemed a land of plenty and privilege compared with the deprivations he witnessed in India.

After what he had seen in Barrackpore, the groin injury that kept him out of the Third Test at Bangalore didn't seem quite the problem it might otherwise have seemed. In any case, he wasn't needed. Australia won despite a blistering 177 by Tendulkar in India's first innings. The Indian batsman scored just 31 in the second innings (to give him an aggregate of 446 at an average of 111.25 for series). With his twin missing and out of the action, Mark Waugh countered the Indian master with a 153 not out, despite being ill in Australia's first innings, and 33 not out in the second, when Australia cruised to an eight-wicket win. Taylor, who had failed in five successive innings, salvaged something with 102 not out, and kept his Test captaincy.

However, when Taylor returned to Australia to make way for the

one-day players, he continued to complain about the split captaincy.
Again the selectors stood firm.

Back in India, Steve Waugh spoke out in defence of the new strategy. 'It's the start of a new era,' he said. 'It was never going to be an
easy transition ... I don't think we have given it a fair go as yet. [The
two team approach] has been going for only half a season. I'd like to
have a look at it after one full year ...'

This conflict put some strain on the relationship. Taylor would not
let go of his 'lost' position. Waugh was settling in as a one-day leader
and didn't need hassles from the former skipper.

Regardless of the debate, Steve Waugh was the leader of the one-
day squad, which competed in a series against India and Zimbabwe in
April. India beat Australia on 1 April at Cochin. Waugh hit 49 against
Zimbabwe in an even Australian batting effort in Ahmedabad, where
the temperature reached 43 degrees Celsius.

Australia's second encounter against India—at Kanpur on 7 April—
ended with another host victory, thanks to a century in 88 balls by
Tendulkar. Australia then beat Zimbabwe at Delhi on 11 April to
make the final against India. The tourists were in the same position as
they had been against South Africa in Australia. Then Australia had
not won a pre-final game against South Africa. Now it had not been
able to defeat India before the final at Delhi on April 14.

Damien Fleming had an uncertain Tendulkar caught brilliantly
by keeper Gilchrist for just 15. India didn't recover and was all out
for 227.

Waugh came to the wicket at four for 111, after sending Warne in
for a pinch-hitting 14 in fourteen balls. The Australian captain and
Bevan took the score to 167—61 short of victory with ten overs to go.
Waugh then launched himself into an over from the youngster Hrishi-
kesh Kanitkar, which cost India 18 runs. Australia now had 43 runs
to make in nine overs. Waugh was bowled by Kumble for 57 with the
score at 218—just ten short. Soon afterwards Bevan (75 not out) hit
the winning runs and Australia had won by five wickets, against the
odds once more.

For the second successive series, Waugh had led his team from nowhere to a remarkable victory. It seemed that his leadership style was settling in. Despite the misgivings about the two-team policy, Australia was still winning.

The team then travelled on to Sharjah, United Arab Emirates, for a one-day series with India and New Zealand. Australia met India and began well with nine for 264. It didn't seem enough when Tendulkar crashing his way to 80 in 66 balls. But once he was out at 161, Waugh thought the team could win it. He bowled himself and took a match-winning four for 40 to wrap up India's innings at 206. New Zealand beat India and then was defeated by Australia. Tendulkar hammered another whirlwind hundred against the Australians in a game that put India into the final on run rate, despite losing.

The final, on 24 April, was dominated by Tendulkar, who slammed 134 off 131 balls. His success gave India a six-wicket win, chasing Australia's nine for 272.

A weary Steve Waugh met the media when he and his side returned to Australia. Still shell-shocked from several Tendulkar blitzes, Waugh said, 'Take Bradman away, and [Tendulkar] is next up, I reckon.'

Apart from this last game defeat, Australia under Waugh had acquitted itself well. He was satisfied with his own progress and now had one eye on the 1999 World Cup, just a year away. Waugh knew that the team would have to step up a notch to win it. The Indians and West Indians had all had stronger one-day performances during 1998 so far. South Africa was always a threat.

Steve Waugh made good his promise to the children of leprosy sufferers in Barrackpore by explaining their plight to his sponsors, Channel Nine and the public. The television program 'A Current Affair' followed him back to Calcutta to publicise the issue. Waugh brought with him pledges of $10,000 from Carlton and United Breweries, and another $5000 from the Canterbury–Bankstown Leagues Club. Steve saw the great possibilities for doing further good works for this and other worthy causes.

It is not too much of a stretch to suggest that Waugh's success on the field was helped by this kind of activity. It kept the game he played in perspective and allowed him to focus better. No matter what happened to him playing cricket at any level, it would never mean as much to him as helping those children whose lives were so deprived. Sport was just that, and insignificant beside the greater game of life, with all its inequities. This kind of experience would make his cricket world seem smaller. It could be conquered with less difficulty.

At the games

The ACB at first wanted to send a one-day second XI to the Commonwealth Games in Kuala Lumpur, Malaysia, in September 1998, but Waugh talked the board into sending a full-strength team. He and his squad were keen to be part of the 300-plus Australian contingent.

It wasn't enough to win the cricket team a gold medal. In a competition that the ICC didn't recognise as 'official', Australia easily accounted for Canada, Antigua and India (Waugh hitting 100 not out and Tom Moody 76 not out) but was beaten in the final by a half-strength South African side. Waugh gave the best batting performance of the match scoring 90 not out of his side's 183 (Pollock four for 19). South Africa won by four wickets. He and his team had to be content with the silver medal, and a marginal psychological advantage conceded to the Proteas, especially Jacques Kallis, Herschelle Gibbs, Shaun Pollock and Mark Boucher, who would encounter Waugh's team in the 1999 World Cup in less than nine months. They and South Africa as a whole were ecstatic over the Commonwealth Games win. The Proteas were yet to win a major contest against Australia anywhere since its return to international cricket in the early 1990s. The South African media billed the victory as a turning point. The World Cup would now be the target for an official conquering of Australia.

But even though Australia missed out on gold, Steve felt that the two-week experience was as good as any he had had in sport.

As he wrote in his book *No Regrets*, 'To see the dedication and application these athletes put into gaining that extra split-second advantage over their rivals was inspirational.'

Thirty-nine steps

After this 'fun' interlude, Australia arrived late September 1998 in Pakistan—a country where it hadn't won a Test in thirty-nine years. Taylor was on a mission, after losing there in 1994 in his first series as captain. He didn't have Shane Warne, who was recovering from shoulder surgery, but Warne's stand-in, Stuart MacGill, was already a Test player of proven ability with a combative temperament that was right for this level. Pakistan, led by Aamir Sohail, was expected to present tough opposition. It had beaten the West Indies three–nil in its last home series.

Australia kicked off with a 333-run win over Karachi City Cricket Association in Karachi, Slater smashing 221 and Waugh finding early tour form with 92. In the second innings, Langer hit 101 not out. Only Taylor missed out in his two knocks.

Pakistan won the toss in the First Test and batted. Opener Saeed Anwar (145) was the only player to handle spinner MacGill with any confidence, although the leggie eventually bowled him. MacGill took five for 66 in Pakistan's 269—the innings finishing on the second morning. Waugh was prepared to be at the wicket early, which was the case more often than not. The score was three for 28 when he strode out to join Slater, whose form in the opening game was holding. Slater (108) reached his century first and he and Waugh put on 198 for the fourth wicket. Steve reached his century just before stumps and was 104 not out at stumps with Australia on four for 237. Waugh went on 'into the zone' until caught off Sohail for 157 at five for 352. He had been in for 392 minutes and had faced 325 balls. Australia was all out for 513 with Lehmann (98) unlucky not to reach his first Test century and Healy in form reaching 82.

Pakistan was routed for 145 in its second innings, with MacGill taking four for 47, making it nine for the match. Australia was the winner by an innings and 99 runs. There had been a long wait for a victory. The team celebrated and moved on to Peshawar for the Second Test. Taylor won the toss and batted on a perfect wicket. Waugh was put in a most unusual position by Taylor (112 not out) and Langer (97 not out), who took the score to one for 224 at stumps. He remained padded up until the middle of day two, when the score was three for 418. The new young speedster Shoaib Akhtar caused him to edge a ball to keeper Moin Khan and he was on his way for just 1 run. Such was life and cricket. In a Test where everyone else scored runs and there was little challenge for Waugh, he was out cheaply. He was the type who needed to be motivated to make runs, although he also had a history, especially early in his career, of crushing the opposition when the innings had been set up by batsmen before him.

Waugh had dominated the First Test, but the Second was Taylor's match, as he ploughed on to be 334 not out at stumps with the score at four for 599. He was level with Don Bradman's 334 against England in 1930—the highest score ever by an Australian. Taylor had not meant to be not out on the score. He had tried to make another run to edge ahead of the Don in the last over of the day. People urged him to go on to take the Australian record and also Brian Lara's world record of 375.

Back at the hotel room, Steve Waugh asked Taylor what he was going to do, declare or go on.

'To be perfectly bloody honest,' the captain replied, 'I don't know.'

They considered all the options. Waugh's remarks demonstrated his sense of sporting history and personal positioning.

'If you declare now, on Bradman's score,' Waugh told him, 'you know that's something that will be remembered for a long time. If you bat on and get the record, on your own, that will be remembered too.'

These comments showed that Waugh—and others in the team—would not have begrudged Taylor going on, although coach Geoff Marsh thought that it was the moment to declare.

Taylor considered the mechanics of going on to take the world record.

'It would take another hour at least to get 42' (to be 376), Taylor told Waugh. 'It might take more. They would take the third new ball and probably slow the run rate.'

Waugh realised that his selfless mate Tubby felt uncomfortable with the idea of being out there on day three with his score stuck on about 360. He didn't want the extra dilemma then of either declaring or going on to the world record. But Waugh felt Taylor could be excused for continuing on day three. He'd had a terrible time in patches over the last few years where he couldn't buy a run. Now he had an opportunity that came along a handful of times in a century of cricket: to make the highest score ever. That 376 would make Mark Taylor a talking point and the owner of a brilliant statistic for some time—at least until another player came along and scored more.

Taylor went to his own room and pondered the decision alone until the early hours. If it had been the final Test and Australia was up one-nil, he might have continued. But the object of being out there was to win for Australia. This had been the Bradman philosophy. In all his monumental Test innings—the twelve double hundreds and two triples—he had batted with a main aim in mind: a win for his country. The Don wanted to break records, particularly the highest Test score, which he did in 1930 aged 21, but only in the context of setting up a win. He scored at such a pace (309 not out in a day) that he could achieve both a win for Australia and the record. Yet scoring for scoring's sake was never his or the game's major aim. Winning had to be paramount.

With this in mind, Taylor declared. He now would forever be bracketed on 334 with Bradman, and would be recalled as an unselfish leader who maintained the highest ideals of sportsmanship.

Pakistan now had a chance on this marvellous wicket to respond with nine for 580 (Saeed Anwar 126, Ijaz Ahmed 155, Inzamam-ul-Haq 97). Australia was five for 289 at stumps on the last day, Taylor hitting 92. Waugh made second top score—49 not out. The game fizzled to a draw, leaving the last Test at Karachi beginning on 22 October as Pakistan's chance to level the series.

Taylor won the toss and batted, but this time Australia reached a mediocre 280, with only Slater (96) scoring a half century. Waugh was given lbw for a duck off Shahid Afridi in his Test debut. Aamir Sohail (133) once more was the glue for a shaky home team, which struggled to 252 (McGrath five for 66). Steve Waugh came to the wicket at a more reasonable three for 152 for a mini-link of 56 with brother Mark, but was caught behind off Shakeel Ahmed for 28. Mark went on to a typically polished 117, this time a little more than a cameo, demonstrating again that he was expanding his capacities. He lasted 334 minutes—about twice as long as his flair-filled 'sprints' to 60, 70 or 80. Australia was all out for 390. Pakistan replied in its second innings with five for 262, leaving it 156 short in a tame draw.

The Australians were content with their one–nil victory, Mark Taylor sharing the Man of the Series award with Ijaz Ahmed.

Mercifully for Steve Waugh and the others who were in both the Test and limited-overs games, there were only three one-dayers in Pakistan to play. Australia won all three but lost a game on 28 October in a 'World Championship' in Bangladesh. Waugh was not under pressure to perform as the job was done by Lehmann (103 in 101 balls) in game one at Karachi, Bevan (83, 57 not out) in the first two games, and Gilchrist (103) and Ponting (124) in game three.

This clean sweep meant Australia had gone through the tour of Pakistan undefeated. Waugh put the success down to a change of attitude to touring the subcontinent. In the past there had been a negative mindset. He recalled the disaster of the 1988 tour when the squad were apprehensive about every aspect of Pakistan, from the umpires and the crowds to the food and hotel deficiencies, based on horror stories from previous tours. The England team particularly had made jokes about Pakistan being a 'cricket hell on earth'. Ian Botham had thought it was a good place to 'send the mother-in-law'.

But on this tour, Waugh led the way in exploring the local culture, especially with his trusty camera. He and the team did their best to learn about the country and enjoy themselves. They left their hotels (now a better standard) and visited the Khyber Pass, cultural shows, and Murree, in the stunning mountain range surrounding Rawalpindi.

The more open-minded approach meant that Australian teams

would never again fear the tour of Pakistan. Taylor's diplomatic style and Waugh's approach to comprehending a different culture would mean such ventures in the future would be looked forward to.

England's challenge

After such an uplifting tour it was back to cricket business that had dominated Australian cricket since the mid-nineteenth century. England arrived in Australia in October 1998 for an Ashes challenge after five successive failed attempts, and once more the touring squad appeared impressive. The bowling, led by Gough, Mullally and Cork, looked good, while the batting line-up had an apparent fair mix of flair and solidity with Butcher, Atherton, Hussain, Stewart, Thorpe and Mark Ramprakash. But as ever in the last decade, the question of how effective it would be on the field in the tension surrounding Tests depended on team cohesion. Were they united fighters under Stewart, or would they tend to be a rabble when the going got tough?

The First Test at the Gabba began well on 20 November for Australia after Taylor won the toss and batted. Waugh arrived at the wicket in the middle of the second session with the score at three for 106. He was 26 not out and settled at tea. In an extended final session held up by rain, he should have been run out on 29 by Mullally, whose hand had broken the bails before he took a throw from Stewart. Unperturbed, Waugh moved his score to 50 in 80 balls and then 68, when he was dropped by Hussain at second slip off Gough. England could not afford to give Waugh one chance let alone two. He was 69 not out at stumps with Healy on 46 not out and Australia at a sound five for 246.

This was a typical Steve Waugh Test innings based on sound defence and peppered with backfoot cuts, drives, and pushes through midwicket. He went on to 112 in 330 minutes scored off 232 balls. Healy, 46 not out overnight, made 134. Even Damien Fleming, who never made claim to being other than a tailender, got into the act once all the groundwork had been laid. He smashed 71 not out in 107 balls and Australia reached 485.

A century by Butcher (116) and even contributions from England's line up saw it reach 375 in reply. Slater (113 in 139 balls) led the way in Australia's rush to set up a tough chase with plenty of time to spare. Taylor declared at three for 237, leaving England 348 to win in about 100 overs. Thunderstorms on the last afternoon saved the tourists at six for 179. The game was drawn, with honours in Australia's favour.

Taylor kept a grip on the opposition four days later in Perth in the Second Test by winning the toss and sending England in on a bouncy WACA pitch. The speed men (Fleming five for 46, McGrath three for 37) shot the tourists out for 112 by the middle of the second session. Australia was nicely ahead at stumps on three for 150, with Mark Waugh on 19 not out and nightwatchman Gillespie on 5 not out. Waugh came in at four for 165 and went on to a score of 33 in a 78-minute stay. Only Taylor (61) reached a half century. All the top eight batsmen got to double figures but none could build a big innings with the English fast men (Gough three for 43 and Alex Tudor four for 89) making good use of the wicket's pace and lift. Australia was all out for 240.

England crumbled again to speed (Gillespie five for 88, Fleming four for 45), making just 191 in its second innings. Only Hick (68), going for his shots, stopped England losing by an innings. Australia had just 64 to make to win. It won by seven wickets before tea on the third day. The tourists were not proving to be a rabble, but their batting was letting them down.

On 9 December a scandal broke that would deflect the course of the future Australian captaincy. Media commentator and former Test player David Hookes disclosed on Melbourne radio station 3AW that Mark Waugh and Shane Warne, two noted gamblers in the Australian team, had taken money ($US4000 and $US5000 respectively) from an illegal Indian bookmaker for passing on match-day information during one-day games and Tests in 1994. Both claimed that they had only given weather and pitch reports and that they had not given any information that could have affected a game's outcome. They said they were not match fixers. It transpired that they had 'confessed' to the ACB during an internal inquiry early in 1995, just before the tour of the Caribbean. The ACB fined the players the amount they had taken from the bookie and did not disclose the incident to the media.

In the next four years the bigger, all-encompassing bribery and corruption scandal surrounding cricketers of many nations emerged, making the Waugh–Warne revelation and cover up a big news story. Some people—like former champion batsman Neil Harvey—wanted them banned for two years. Others wanted them thrown out of the game. Several journalists suggested Warne should never be captain of Australia. The upshot from Steve Waugh's point-of-view was that he now had no serious rival for the Test captaincy, which could be open after this Ashes series if Taylor decided to resign.

On a personal level, Steve felt sorry for his brother, who was upset by the negative media attention that the story brought. He understood, however, how Mark, who was a serious gambler, could have 'fallen among thieves' in gambling circles in Asia, without realising that he and Warne were being set up for bigger involvement and blackmail.

Steve never doubted that they would not have taken bribes to fix a game. After all, it had been Mark and Shane Warne who had claimed publicly early in 1995 that Pakistan's Salim Malik had offered them and Tim May $US250,000 to play poorly and lose a Test in Pakistan in 1994. It's unlikely they would have come forward had their involvement gone beyond taking small money for weather reports.

The story was pushed aside for the moment by the ACB organising Mark Waugh and Warne to say publicly that they had been 'naïve and stupid' in accepting money from a bookie.

Taylor won the toss again in the Third Test at Adelaide beginning on 11 December, and Waugh found himself rolling his arms on the way to bat with the score at three for 156. He was more aggressive than in the first two Tests as he went for slashing drives and cuts. At 59 he pushed one to Hick at slip off Gough. The score was four for 264 and just before stumps. Langer had reached his century. He went on to his finest Test innings (179 not out) until this point and Australia reached 391. England had trouble with spinner MacGill (four for 53) who was back after omission from the WACA game and proving an adequate replacement for Warne. It could only make 227 (Hussain 89 not out, Ramprakash 61). Australia declared at five for 278 (Slater a more 'responsible' 103), in its second knock, setting a target of 443. England at no point looked like mounting a serious challenge and it was rolled for 237 (McGrath four for 50).

The only consolations in a 205-run loss for England were the consistent form of Ramprakash, who made 57 in the second innings, and the return to form of Stewart (63 not out). The English skipper was finding his three roles as keeper, batsman and captain too much. He and his co-selectors on tour decided to move him into the opening position and hand over the keeper's gloves to Warren Hegg for the Fourth Test beginning on December 27 after a washed out Boxing Day. The move worked. Stewart hit a dashing 107 in England's 270. Australia was quickly two for 26 late on day two and Steve Waugh had visions of being in at his well-accustomed three for 30-odd. But Langer and Mark Waugh were there at stumps with the score at two for 59. Steve Waugh was given time to digest his breakfast on day three and was in mid-morning at three for 98. The biggish crowd of 43,353 watched a tight battle. Waugh counterattacked as wickets fell. At tea he was 77 not out and Australia was eight for 252—still 18 runs behind.

So far Waugh had played a percentage innings, being shrewd and careful in his shot selection. He found a most unlikely partner in MacGill after tea. The number nine played straight. His technique was ordinary but he had a good eye and gumption. Waugh made no effort to farm the strike as he pushed to his seventeenth Test century. When the score was 340, he was 122 not out and the partnership was worth 88 for the ninth wicket. At that score Mullally dismissed both MacGill (43 in sixty-three balls) and McGrath (0) in three balls. The lead was 70.

England was restricted to 244 in its second innings, thus leaving Australia a target of 175 for victory. It began with intent, but was soon two for 41. Then Langer and Mark Waugh steadied the innings and cruised to 103 when Langer (30) was dismissed. This brought Steve in to join Mark. They were moving easily towards a win with the score at three for 130 when Mark was caught brilliantly by Ramprakash at square leg. Lengthening MCG shadows over the pitch made it possible for Waugh to come off, but he decided to bat on to win the match that night. He judged that England was flagging in the field. It was a fair decision, given that Gough and the other English bowlers would be fresh for a burst on the final morning. Waugh's decision could not be called an error. But his not farming the strike as wickets fell was a mistake. First Lehmann (4) was caught behind off Headley, who two balls later had Healy (0) caught in slips. Headley next over trapped Fleming (0) lbw in an inspired spell. Australia was suddenly seven for 140, still 35 runs shy of the target. England was in the box seat. Waugh was content to let things happen. Instead of telling the tailenders to let him take as much of the strike as possible, he watched the steady procession of batsmen to and from the pavilion. Australia's penchant for making heavy weather of smallish targets was apparent once more.

First-gamer Nicholson found himself in a fairytale or nightmare situation. He didn't panic. Nor did he turn over the strike to his accomplished batting partner, who had not been troubled by any bowler. Nicholson may have given Waugh a false sense of security. He faced 28 balls to Waugh's 20 while at the crease. But with every delivery he faced, the chances that the inspired Headley and Gough would break through rose. It was Headley who delivered the twenty-ninth ball to Nicholson and trapped him lbw. It was the fifth ball of the over. Australia was now eight for 162 and just thirteen runs away from a win.

MacGill saw out the sixth ball from Headley. Then Waugh faced Gough. The Yorkshireman, a gritty and talented character, let Waugh have a single at the beginning of his over. The run should not have been taken, but when it was, Gough saw his chance. If he could remove MacGill, then McGrath, a true bunny, would be the last man in. Gough lifted and bowled MacGill for a duck on the second ball of the

over. This brought McGrath to the crease with four balls to face.
Gough trapped him lbw on the fourth ball. England had created a
stunning and surprising victory by just 12 runs.

Steve Waugh was left dangling at the other end on 30 not out. He
had been in impregnable form and should have guided Australia home.
His decision not to take most of the strike from the moment Fleming
was at the crease cost Australia a Test. Some expressed the view that
Waugh was more concerned with a not out than a win. In other words,
that he was selfish. This seemed harsh. It was more likely to be an
error of judgment. He had always been happy to let a game unfold
with tailenders rather than take complete control and hog the strike.
That was fine under normal conditions. But when a Test was at stake
it was a different matter.

Would Waugh do something different under similar circumstances
in the future? Such a situation was bound to arise again before his
career was over. The question arose: did Waugh lack the confidence
to take control? His career was replete with gutsy fightbacks and rear-
guard actions. But a close finish in a Test was another level of pressure
again. All the greats had struggled in such situations over the decades.
He lacked the confidence to bat at three or four, when the best players
were always placed there. Did the lack of confidence apply to batting
at the death in a Test as well? It was one thing to build an innings
under tough conditions. Then, Waugh could work hard within the
limitations he judged for himself—as, for instance, he did with great
courage when scoring centuries twice in the Test versus England at Old
Trafford in the 1997 Ashes. But when wickets were tumbling and a
Test was slipping away, it took another, or different level of self-belief
to control the strike and put the destiny of a game in his own hands.

His good mate Mark Taylor said that Waugh had changed since
his return to Test cricket into a batsman who would never give his
wicket away. The situation in the Melbourne Test meant Waugh had
to risk losing his wicket by hogging the strike and going for a win.

Tim May, the Australian Cricketers' Association president, saw
Waugh's actions in Melbourne differently from Taylor. 'I don't think
it was a matter of selfishness,' he said, 'because Steve is not a selfish

person. I don't think he is that concerned with figures and stats. Winning for his country is paramount. He is incredibly single-minded and determined, and this may have caused some to misjudge him.'

Did he miscalculate in not farming the strike?

'He may have,' May said. 'His attitude was to ask the incoming tailender if he was feeling okay to face the bowling. If the player said he was comfortable, then Waugh would not try to take singles off the fifth or last ball.'

May conceded that Waugh might have been better off in that situation taking control.

'But he's only human,' his former teammate remarked. 'He's allowed to make mistakes.'

England's shock victory changed the complexion of the series and brought it alive. Australia led two–one but Stewart's band of battlers could now make it two all at Sydney in the Fifth Test. This, plus the return of Shane Warne, kept ticket sales high for the game, which began on 2 January 1999.

Taylor won the toss for the fifth successive time and batted. Steve Waugh was not surprised to join brother Mark at three for 52. They settled in for a classic link. Steve was in striking form and seemed to be intent on answering his critics, who had been tough on him in Melbourne for guarding his wicket too much. He crashed the ball through mid-off off either foot with that characteristic one-action punch. Meanwhile, Mark was batting with his habitual smoothness and grace. Steve managed to out-score his brother in a powerful partnership of 190 runs off 171 balls in front of an adoring home crowd. Steve, on 96, drove over one from spinner Peter Such and was bowled. It was his ninth score in the nineties, with two not outs. With a fraction more luck here and there he could have had not 17 centuries but 23 or 24. Statistically it meant that Waugh would reach a century two out of every three times he got to ninety. It was better than one out of three or none.

The twins had scored their fifth century stand in eight years. It didn't seem enough, not so much for Australia's benefit, for they were not always at the crease together and one or other of them normally scored well in every innings for their country. The regret was that cricket fans around the world had not seen them together more often. There were contrasts between them in styles, temperament and staying power. They formed a lethal, complementary combination capable of destroying any attack on offer in the 1990s.

Mark, once more showing the restraint that turned sprints into centuries, went on to 121 from 205 balls. Gough managed to collect a hat trick of tailenders and Australia was all out for 322.

England responded with 220, with MacGill (five for 57) the destroyer. It was a disappointing effort by the tourists, yet they were kept in the game by Such (five for 81) in dismissing Australia for just 184 in its second innings. Slater made a sensational 123 off 189 balls, more than two-thirds of the entire Australian score.

The tourists were left with a target of 287 and an opportunity for a glorious recovery that would rank with England's efforts at home in 1981. It began with a surety that signalled something special might be about to happen. Taylor brought on Warne, who had Butcher (27) stumped. The score was one for 57. England had 230 to make with nine wickets in hand. At 77, Stewart (42 off fifty-five balls), who had made perhaps a too-ambitious dash for glory, was stumped off MacGill. It wasn't as if England was short of time. It had all the fifth day. But it was Stewart's way. He preferred to die by the sword rather than defend. He didn't seem to have reverse gears. Defence or a middle way didn't seem to be options. It was a weakness in Test cricket.

England went to stumps on two for 104—just 183 short of victory with eight wickets in hand. Most observers thought it was anyone's game. Shane Warne was not going to be as penetrating as before because of his shoulder. That left it all to Stuart MacGill (seven for 50). He grabbed his chance on a spinner's paradise and never allowed the opposition a serious sniff of victory on the final morning. England was seven for 157 at lunch and all out for 188 in the second session. Australia won by 98 runs and took the series three–one.

Steve Waugh, with an aggregate of 498, topped the averages at 83, with Mark second (393 at 56.14). The brilliant MacGill (twenty-seven

Don't cuss me man!
Steve Waugh confronts Curtly Ambrose during the 1995 series in the Caribbean.
Waugh's defiance signalled to the West Indies that it was facing the biggest threat to its
fifteen-year reign as the world's best Test team.

Chin music.
Waugh drops his wrists and jumps in a typical response to the West Indies short
bowling—during the 1992–93 series in Australia.

Waugh appeals.
Waugh was regarded as a batting all-rounder when he first arrived on the Test scene. He was given plenty of bowling and was successful.

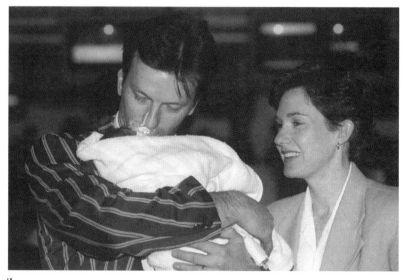

Family man.
Waugh with his 18-day-old daughter Rosalie and wife Lynette just before flying to Sri Lanka in 1996.

Waugh's duck.
Waugh ducks under a short one from Darren Gough in the Fourth Ashes Test at the MCG in 1998.

Waugh attacks.
Waugh drives through the covers during the Ashes Tests 1998-99.

No flies on him.
Steve Waugh and a constant summer companion wear the baggy green with pride and distinction.

Mobile power.
Steve Waugh at VCA House in February 1999, receiving congratulations after being named Australian captain.

Waugh room.
Waugh looks relaxed at his first media conference as captain early in 1999.

Portrait of a champion (civvies).
A relaxed and happy Stephen Rodger Waugh early in 1999 soon after being named
Australia's fortieth Test captain.

A rare grin.
Waugh is thrilled after scoring 120 not out v South Africa at Headingley during the 1999 World Cup. It was the greatest one-day international innings ever had by an Australian cricketer.

One-day wonders.
Waugh and Shane Warne holding the 1999 World Cup trophy during a ticker tape parade in Melbourne.

The brains trust.
Waugh with vice-captain Shane Warne and coach John Buchanan. Waugh and Buchanan plotted both the winning records for Tests and one-day internationals in 1999 and 2000.

Full face of a champion.
Waugh batting during the 1999 Boxing Day Test v India.

The capping of history (skull cap—black).
Waugh, in the first Test of the twenty-first century, wears the skull cap donned by Joe
Darling and his team in the first Test of the twentieth century. It will become a tradition
every century.

The cutting edge.
Waugh executes one of his favourite shots through point.

wickets at 17.7) proved a more than adequate replacement for Warne, while McGrath (twenty-four at 20.5) kept up his usual penetrative standard.

Steve Waugh withdrew from the first few games of the limited-overs CUB series against England and Sri Lanka because of a hamstring injury. It recurred during his second game mid-series and he pulled out again. Shane Warne led the Australians to a two–nil finals win against England.

On 2 February 1999 Mark Taylor retired from Test cricket after a distinguished five years as captain and a decade as a Test opener. He had played 104 Tests, scored 7525 runs and nineteen centuries and averaged 43.49. Whoever was chosen to replace him had a hard act to follow. Taylor had taken Australia away—in image at least—from the sledging, confrontational era under Border, which had been brought about by Australia's failure and frustration. Border had restored the team to a high pedestal near the top and Taylor had put it on top—in Test cricket. His unruffled, pleasant demeanour and reputation as an unblemished sportsman of the highest character, accentuated by his 334 decision, was not something that could be easily reproduced.

Shane Warne was a candidate but his image had been tarnished by the bribes scandal. There was never a serious chance that the ACB would consider letting him leapfrog Waugh for the job, despite support from some in the Channel Nine commentary team, especially Ian Chappell, who lobbied for Warne.

In early February 1999, the ACB delayed its decision. This built speculation that there might be a battle going on.

Waugh's detractors, including Ian Chappell, thought him too selfish and negative to be captain of the Test team. But as Waugh's only rival was Shane Warne, he was odds on to take over. In the week before the ACB was to make known its decision on the new leader, the influential Fairfax newspapers made clear they did not want Warne as leader. The group had been quick to dump him as a columnist after it was revealed he had taken money from an Indian bookie. Now they set out to destroy his credibility. Two papers in the Fairfax stable, Melbourne's *The Sunday Age* and Sydney's *Sun Herald*, bought extracts from the biography of Warne—*Bold Warnie*—and selected editorial (2000 words from several sections of the book out of 200,000 words) that were unfavourable to him. The two papers went further by selecting unflattering photos mainly from their own photo libaries to surround the extracts. The layout was designed to make Warne look foolish, ugly and unworthy. This slant would have had an impact on any member of the ACB looking at it. Those who were undecided may well have been influenced against Warne.

In any case, Waugh always appeared to have the numbers and was the favourite. He was quietly confident he would get the nod. Warne, in typical, refreshing style, was open about his desire for the position, even though he knew he was the challenger and unlikely to win. An important factor for Australia was that both would accept the other being captain. Each would play on without rancour under the other man.

PART THREE

LEADER

11

CAPTAIN AUSTRALIA

A doer, not a talker

Waugh was in a Melbourne hotel answering phone calls early on 12 February 1999. 'Sesame Street' was on the television. At 8.42 pm the ACB rang to tell him he had Australia's most coveted job. Stephen Rodger Waugh was officially the fortieth captain of Australia's Test team. His deputy would be Shane Warne.

Steve Waugh was a different character altogether from Taylor. He would have to carve out his own style and niche as a leader. His less open mien made him appear somewhat austere by comparison. But he would not compromise his own personality to suit the whims of others. His 'no-nonsense' demeanour would not, and probably could not, change.

By his own admission, Waugh was 'not into talk', which was in contrast to Taylor, who was a chatty, friendly type.

'Once I make friends they will always be friends,' Waugh wrote in *No Regrets: A Captain's Diary*. 'I do not open up myself to people until I trust them and really know them. Perhaps some observers see that as arrogance and consequently find it hard to write good things about me, which I can accept.'

Waugh covered for his lack, in comparison to Taylor, of communication skills by falling back on his 'leading from the front' approach.

'The only way to prove something is to go out and do it,' he noted emphatically.

Waugh also admitted that even at thirty-three years he would be learning on the job. He promised to take Australia into a new, unspecified era that would see no passengers in the national sides.

The matter of ascendancy settled, Steve Waugh prepared for his time as skipper. The Caribbean would be the place for his first Test at the helm.

MacGill's early form

Steve Waugh led his squad to St John's, Antigua, in early February 1999 with two major concerns on his mind. One was Shane Warne and the other Brian Lara. Waugh thought the Warne problem—whether to play him alone or with Stuart MacGill—would sort itself out as the tour progressed. More pressing was the question of Lara. The Australian captain found that the West Indian was being put under enough pressure from his own people. There was a chance that Lara would be unsettled after the furore surrounding his captaincy against the Proteas. The dismal failure of the West Indies—they lost nil–five—in South Africa, plus Lara's alleged slack leadership, put his captaincy at stake. The problem was, there was no one to replace him, at least not anybody of Test standard who could lead the Windies long after Ambrose and Walsh eventually retired.

In the end Lara was put on 'probation' for two Tests, although no one could explain what this meant. If Lara batted poorly and the Windies won two Tests, or Lara made two centuries and the Windies lost both games, what then? It didn't make much sense, yet it pleased Steve Waugh. He could see the pressure mounting on his opposite number and the West Indies team from day one.

This showed in the two games before the First Test in Trinidad. In the first game against a West Indies Board XI, the Australians collapsed on a damp wicket for 156, then Adam Dale took seven for 24 in dismissing the Board XI for 55. Australia replied with four for 209—Ponting (61 not out) and Blewett (58 following 52 in the first innings) fighting neck and neck for the number six spot in the batting order. The Board was four for 121 off fifty-nine overs, after being set 311 to win from seventy overs, when the game was called off. The second match—against a West Indian Board President's XI at Guaracara Park, Trinidad—was all MacGill, as he ran through the opposition (177), taking six for 45 and pressing for selection in the First Test. Warne took just one wicket. McGrath, also showing early form, took three for 33. Mark Waugh (106), Steve Waugh (57) and Slater (49) led the way in Australia's reply of 368. Then MacGill went one better in the President's XI second innings (185), taking seven for 29, giving him an astounding thirteen for 74 for the match and Australia a win by an innings and 6 runs. Warne took the other three wickets, giving the spinners all ten wickets and seventeen out of the twenty for the match. The New South Welshman's form was the better. He deserved to be the first leg spinner chosen. He was gaining prodigious turn with his stock leg break, and his wrong 'uns. Warne's wrong 'un had never been strong and he was bowling more top spinners in order to provide contrast to the big turn of MacGill.

Waugh ended speculation and said MacGill would play in the First Test, along with Warne, even if the wicket were a green-top as expected.

No pain at Port of Spain

Waugh won the toss at Port of Spain on 5 March at the commencement of the First Test and decided to bat on a pitch that had been covered for the last three days because of rain. Even if the pitch was to prove low scoring, he had faith in his line-up of Slater, Elliott, Langer, he and his brother, Blewett, Healy, Warne, MacGill, Gillespie and McGrath.

It was a struggle for the batsmen. It was one of those pitches where they never felt 'in'. The ball held up or kept low, making driving difficult. And if the batsmen did get onto a shot, the thick grass held the ball up short of the boundary. Australia batted slowly.

Waugh came to the wicket at three for 53 and found it tough to score. He was in for an hour, facing forty-three balls in accumulating just 14 before Merv Dillon had him caught behind.

Elliott was watchful, using his height to thrust well forward. He hit 44 off 208 deliveries to be out to a rough lbw decision by umpire Peter Willey. Walsh bowled an in-swinger to the left-hander, who shouldered arms and was given out. The ball looked to be missing off stump. Perhaps the umpire was punishing the Australian for pushing his luck by so blatantly playing the 'leave' perfected by Elliott's predecessor, Mark Taylor. Or maybe Willey was carried away by Walsh, who needed a decision in his favour to give him his 400th wicket. He and Ambrose bowled with superb control and even a little menace on the docile yet difficult pitch. They seemed to have lost little since the last time they played Australia. The question was, how long could their ageing bodies stand the strain? The second-stringers looked sound with Pedro Collins on debut and Dillon bowling steadily. But they were not in the same class as the opening attack.

By close of play Australia had stumbled to six for 174. The next morning, the two last men in, Gillespie and McGrath, got in behind each ball and put on a more than useful 66 in partnership to streak Australia's score up to 269. McGrath (39) and Gillespie (27 not out) batted at their best in Tests. Walsh took three for 60 and joined the small '400 Club' that had just two other members—Kapil Dev (434) and Hadlee (431).

The West Indies response was held up by McGrath, who dismissed Campbell cheaply, and the run-out of opener Suruj Ragoonath (9). Then Lara (run out for 62) and another first-gamer, Dave Joseph (lbw to McGrath, 50), put together an attacking 88. Lara had slammed both spinners and looked in fine touch, using his feet and playing a range of shots that until 1996 had ranked him just ahead of Tendulkar. (Since then, the Indian had moved ahead—just).

At the end of the day, the Windies had crumbled to nine for 167. They were all out at the same score in the first over of day three. McGrath took five for 50, and MacGill three for 41, bringing up fifty Test wickets in this, his ninth Test. His average per wicket of under 22 was also outstanding.

Australia, dominated by Slater (106), rattled up seven for 227 by the end of day three. Once more, Slater, on a tough wicket of uneven, slow bounce, held the side together in a knock of power and concentration. Langer (24), Mark Waugh (33), Blewett (28) and Warne (18 not out) did their bit and compensated for three ducks by Elliott, Steve Waugh and Healy. But it was Slater all the way in his fifth century in his last nine Tests, which included another two scores in the nineties. His figures were standing up after forty-six Tests with an average of 46.12 against those of Ponsford (48.23), Lawry (47.15), Bob Simpson (46.82), Arthur Morris (46.49), Bill Woodfull (46) and Mark Taylor (43.49). Not only that, he was attacking, and an entertainer who would continue to pull in the crowds. Only two other Australian openers in a century were as entertaining—Syd Gregory, early in the twentieth century and Keith Stackpole in the 1960s.

Walsh took four for 72 and showed there was life in the old dog yet. He was bowling on great memory and experience, but hardly getting a bouncer up. The years were catching him and Ambrose. The difference from the younger McGrath and Gillespie was noticeable. They could be menacing as they scythed their way through the Windies' second innings to dismiss them for just 51—the first time the team had scored under a hundred in Tests at home. McGrath took five for 28, giving him his first ten-wicket haul in a Test and match figures of ten for 78. Gillespie, a star every time his body allowed him onto the field, took four for 18. He also dismissed Lara caught at slip for 3 after the dynamic and compact left-hander had faced just two balls.

Australia won by 312 runs and went one up in a series of four Tests. Waugh may not have been thrilled with his own form, but he couldn't have been happier with the first up win as skipper against the West Indies in the Caribbean.

Less spark at Sabina Park

The teams travelled to Kingston, Jamaica, Courtney Walsh's home, and ran into a barrage of anti-Lara sentiment. The proximity of the Tests didn't allow enough time for the home side to settle down and regroup. Yet when the Second Test at Sabina Park began on 13 March, the Windies were quickly on top and appeared the team with the momentum. Walsh removed Elliott for his second successive duck and then fellow left-hander Langer for eight, both caught behind the wicket edging at deliveries moving away outside off stump.

Steve Waugh was in at three for 46. He joined Mark. Sabina Park was the scene of their triumph four years earlier, and for a while they relived it. Then, more than halfway through the middle session, and with the partnership at 112, off spinner Nehemiah Perry, on debut, bowled Mark (67) with a ball that grubbed along the ground. Steve motored on and felt that this was one of his best innings. He played his shots, especially the cut, with certitude. He was involved in a mini-partnership with Warne after tea that briskly restored Australia from six for 184 to seven for 227. Waugh went on to 100 (in 165 balls), his eighteenth Test century. He was last man out chasing runs.

Australia was all out for 256, with Walsh the star with the ball, taking four for 55, and Pedro Collins three for 79. The latter was a good foil to Ambrose and Walsh. He was fitting in as if Test cricket had always been his scene.

The Windies had sixteen overs to face before stumps. They were four for 37 when bad light stopped play. McGrath (three wickets) and Gillespie (one) continued where they left off at Port of Spain. The next morning, after some anxious moments against Warne, Lara's confidence returned and he moved quickly from 40 to 100, being lucky to survive a run-out. The third umpire's view was obscured on the video replay and he had to give Lara not out. The Windies skipper was relieved as he acknowledged the cheers for his tenth Test century and his first in fifteen Tests. He had to crack it sooner or later, such was the class of this left-hander. Lara was in a mood to go on and he went after Australia's bowlers, but he seemed to falter after 150. A bit of bolstering by partner Jimmy Adams and some self-discipline caused him to put his head down for the last half hour. He careered on to a fine double century and was mobbed. He raced from the ground to the sanctity of the pavilion. He was wary of the local crowd, many of whom were hostile to him. Lara returned to be 212 not out and Adams unconquered on 88. Lara had been at the wicket for 340 minutes. He hit 28 fours and 3 sixes. The Windies were four for 377 and 121 ahead.

Early on day three, Lara was out caught behind off McGrath for 213. Adams, who had been the anchor, was out caught at close extra cover by Elliott, also off McGrath, for 94. The Windies were all out for 431 just after lunch—175 ahead of Australia.

McGrath, with five for 93, again took the honours with his third five-wicket haul in the series. Australia's second innings was a woeful display against a fired-up Ambrose and Walsh, and the surprise packet of Nehemiah Perry. Perry had been overawed in the first innings but now settled in with distinction. Walsh began the rot by forcing the impetuous Slater (0) to cut too close and play on. Langer (24) and Elliott (16) pottered for a while before Perry struck. He had Langer caught behind and Elliott out leaving his arm ball, which clipped the top of his pad. The delivery was straight enough to be judged lbw. Perry then collected the prize scalp of Steve Waugh. He was caught behind for 9 as the keeper dived and just appeared to get his gloves under the ball.

Waugh was unhappy with the decision. Soon after he returned to the pavilion he jumped into the third umpire's box, presumably checking on his dismissal. Mark Waugh (21) was caught indulging in some happy hooking to Ambrose, who was only too delighted to feed this dangerous tendency. When Blewett (30 from 80 balls) pushed a Perry arm-ball to Lara at slip, the score read eight for 157 at stumps. Australia could not recover.

It added 20 the next morning, with Walsh dismissing Gillespie to take his figures to three for 52. Perry took MacGill caught at leg slip and ended with the figures of the match at five for 70. It had been a fine debut and he seemed just as proud of his fighting 15 not out in the West Indies' first innings.

McGrath was left on 11 not out, which included a fine skip down the wicket for a drive through mid-off. His determination pleased the Aussie dressing room. With half the Tests played he was challenging his batting coach, Steve Waugh, for top spot in the averages. Australia was all out for 177. The Windies polished off the 3 runs needed to win, making it one all in the series.

Steve Waugh had his problems as the squad flew to St John's, Antigua, to play the West Indies 'A' team before the Third Test in Bridgetown. Langer's form didn't warrant another opportunity and Ponting's chances for a recall looked good. More problematic for Waugh and his fellow selectors was the Bridgetown wicket. It had never been a spinner's paradise. In 1991, in the Barbados Test, neither Australia nor the Windies had played a specialist spinner. In 1995, the Windies hadn't had anyone who could turn the ball, apart from batsman Carl Hooper, and Australia had Warne in the side. (He bowled well without help from the pitch, taking two for 57 and three for 64.) In 1999, could Australia afford the luxury of two leggies, especially as this had failed against left-handers Lara and Adams in their big, match-winning stand? MacGill had had a poor Second Test and Warne's wrong 'un and flipper weren't on show. The tourists needed variety, from either Adam Dale or Colin Miller. But would Waugh swap Warne for one of them?

Lara, super-confident now after his return to form, used Australian tactics by trying to unsettle the tourists' camp. He had dominated MacGill and now he rubbed it in by saying that Australia had 'three very good bowlers—McGrath, Gillespie and Warne'. This was a calculated snub to MacGill.

Pressure mounted on the selectors as it seemed likely that the Windies would include five left-handers in its line-up: Lara, Adams, Chanderpaul, Jacobs and Ambrose.

In the end, Steve Waugh had the final say in selection for the Third Test at Barbados and opted for MacGill and Warne ahead of Miller, and Dale, who had been sensational on tour. The only change was

Ponting for Blewett, who had injured his thumb. The Windies brought in Hooper as expected, but Chanderpaul's shoulder was not fit enough for him to play.

Australia won the toss at Barbados on 26 March, batted and was promptly—within the hour—three for 36. In marched skipper Steve Waugh, having seen his brother just bowled (played on) by Ambrose for a duck. It was the right situation for this steel-minded star. Along with Allan Border, Waugh ranked as the best big-occasion performer for Australia in decades. He thrived on the tough moment. Just to show that the captaincy had strengthened his resolve, he was at his most wilful, often tucking the ball to leg, and driving straight or through midwicket. Every run seemed important to him, scampering for ones and twos as if in a one-dayer. By stumps he had hit a magnificent 141 not out from 241 deliveries in 323 minutes at the crease. It was Test hundred number nineteen. Langer (51) and Ponting (65 not out) supported him. Australia reached four for 322 on day one.

Waugh went on, as did Ponting, who was boosted by the concentration of his skipper at the other end. Their partnership (281—a fourth-wicket record between these teams) only ended when Ponting (104) lost focus and was caught sweeping Perry. Waugh reached 199 before going lbw, again to a good off-spinner from Perry. Australia reached 490 and soon reduced the Windies to four for 80.

On day three, Campbell reached 105 and Jacobs 68, as the home team cruised to 329—39 beyond the follow on. It would not have troubled Steve Waugh too much as he most likely would have batted again. Gillespie was the pick of the bowlers with three for 48, while McGrath kept up his standard by taking four for 128.

Waugh was worried by his early order's batting form. But his concern would be nothing to the feelings of Matthew Elliott, who made his third duck of the series. Langer was frowning, too, after going lbw for 1. The old combination of Ambrose and Walsh grabbed a wicket each. Australia stumbled to two for 18 at stumps, Gillespie in as nightwatchman and Slater, due for a substantial knock, on 14 not out. Australia's lead of 189 with eight wickets in hand put them in a strong position.

Slater was run out on the morning of the fourth day for 26 and it precipitated a collapse to all out for 146, only briefly arrested by top-scorer Warne (32 in 48 balls) and Ponting (22 in 77 balls). Steve Waugh could manage just 11 before Collins bowled him.

The West Indies was left with a target of 308 to win—in 123 overs. Sensible batting would give them a big chance. It only had to score at 2.5 runs an over. Yet anything over 300 in the last innings was tough. Griffith and Campbell started with a 72 opening partnership. After McGrath trapped Campbell (33) lbw, MacGill pierced Joseph's defences with a top spinner that trapped him in front. McGrath (moving up to twenty-one wickets for the series) then made it the third lbw in a row when he beat nightwatchman Collins, leaving the West Indies on three for 85. Lara was not out 2 and looking solid, with Adrian Griffith, the relaxed left-hander, not out on 35 and acting as a sheet anchor.

With Lara still in, the game was on a knife edge going into the final day. The West Indies had 223 to make with seven wickets in hand. If Lara were out early, Australia would win. If he stayed, the West Indies could take it.

Gillespie removed Griffith (35) at 91, then had Hooper (6) caught behind wafting at a late swinger with the score on 105. With just five wickets to remove, the game was moving Australia's way, but for one fact: Lara was still in. Adams joined him. They set about turning the game around in much the way they had done in the Second Test.

Waugh brought on his spinners, not together but one after the other, with speed at one end. The problems of the previous encounter returned. The wicket was not especially helpful, providing turn on the last day, but it was slow. MacGill seemed more dangerous after his first over, from which Lara carved 14, and Warne tried hard to fulfil his captain's faith in him. The sameness of the two bowlers delivered little variety. The two left-handers parried most balls with ease, and kept the score moving up.

Lara's innings built momentum as he cranked up to his unmatchable top form. He reached a century. McGrath hit him on the helmet with a bouncer. It felled him. Lara jumped to his feet and ran for a single. Upset, he stepped after McGrath, making body contact and verbally attacking the bowler. McGrath half-turned to face him, but wisely did not go on with it. Despite the media wanting to support Lara, his response was questionable. McGrath had bounced him. Perhaps Lara wanted an apology. It would not be coming from the part-time pig farmer. It was not the way of modern speedsters, who had taken on Merv Hughes's tactics of upsetting batsmen. Australian bowlers had rarely apologised, except when a ball 'slipped out'.

Lara was in danger of becoming a sucker. The steady Adams calmed him down. It was a vital moment. If Lara lost concentration, he would hand the game to the Australians. He heeded his partner's advice and batted on, lifting his tempo.

In the next hour, Waugh did what his two captains before him had done in the last seven years: he put his faith in Warne to deliver a killer blow. Warne bowled tightly but could not penetrate the left-handers' defences. There was one tough caught and bowled chance that tipped the top of Warne's fingers en route to the boundary. Eighteen months ago, Warne's luck would have been in and his confidence up. It would have stuck. Not this time. Meanwhile MacGill cooled his heels in the deep, waiting for a chance to bowl. It didn't come.

It took a McGrath special, an unplayable ball on left-hander Adams's blindspot, which uprooted his off stump, to turn the game again. Adams had made 38 in ten minutes short of three hours as sheet anchor. The score read six for 238. The Windies had 70 to get with four wickets in hand. Then McGrath trapped Jacobs and Perry lbw in successive balls with the score at 248. Now there were 60 to get with two wickets in hand, Ambrose and Walsh, both certified bunnies. The Australians were confident they would win with their champion bowler turning on a match-winning effort.

Lara farmed the strike and refused to take singles until near the end of overs. He struck out against all the bowlers and reduced the target. Soon there were 50, 40, 30, 20 and then just ten to win. Waugh seemed at a loss to know how to dismiss or even impede Lara, who was taking the initiative and going all out for a win. Waugh would not have had time to reflect on it at that moment, but Lara was doing what Waugh should have done in Melbourne, when Australia was in the same position at the end of the Fourth Test versus England a few months earlier.

Waugh turned to pace at the finish as the runs dwindled. Gillespie was back in the attack. He tempted a tired and desperate Lara to cut at a lifter and he sliced it to Healy's right. The keeper's sore calf muscles weren't allowing him to position himself with his usual confidence. He got a left glove to the ball and dropped what he would have taken every other time. Poor Healy! The same thing had happened when he missed stumping Imzamam-ul-Haq in 1994 at the death. Arguably Australia's greatest keeper ever would suffer for eternity for such misses. Easily forgotten by some would be his exemplary work behind the stumps for a decade. It was his first dropped catch in three years.

Lara then pushed another ball just wide of Warne at slip. Moments later, with the score at eight for 302, Ambrose (12 from thirty-nine balls) spooned a ball from Gillespie to Elliott. The Australians embraced. They could still win it. Walsh came in to face four balls. He took five deliveries as Gillespie delivered a no ball. The Windies had five runs to win. Lara brought the scores level with two shots for two runs off McGrath. Then he cover-drove into a tidal wave of Bajan fans for four and victory by one wicket. He remained unconquered on 153.

It had been a magnificent innings, not because it was faultless. Lara had been beaten many times, especially by the pace bowlers, who were unlucky not to take the edge on at least ten occasions. The brilliance was in the battle that produced such an innings. He had faced 258 balls in five minutes under a complete day's batting. Such sustained courage and stroke-play in a pressure situation that would swing a series put Lara back up at the top of the world batting tree with Tendulkar and Steve Waugh. Lara was up against the best Australian speed combination since Lillee and Thomson a quarter of a century earlier. McGrath (five for 92) had removed half the opposition yet again, taking his wicket tally to 24, three clear of Walsh. Gillespie, hampered by a strained back, had taken three for 62.

Australia was left to ponder the what ifs: should Adam Dale have replaced Warne? Should the injured Healy have kept wickets? What if Blewett had played, even with his injured hand? Could Steve Waugh have been more daring and tossed the ball to MacGill when Warne had shown he was not penetrating? Waugh would have none of this. He spoke well at the press conference with Tubby-like statesmanship. 'I'd like to think this could be remembered as just a great Test match, not that one side played badly or well. We gave it our best shot. Somebody had to lose.'

It was the right sentiment for public consumption. But you wondered whether Waugh, behind the mask of positive rhetoric, had any doubts. Were there regrets about leaving MacGill out of the contest? And deep down, did Lara's approach have any impact on the Australian captain beyond his admiration for a fight well fought?

The media was not going to let him get away with it. Some wanted to blame his lack of imagination in the field, the way he used his bowlers and the fact that he didn't try something different. He was also criticised for not using MacGill more in the final hour.

When the pain of defeat and going one–two down in a series sank in, the skipper would have to face cold realities. Should Warne be dumped? He had taken two for 268 in the West Indian Tests (and four for 378 since his return from injury) against MacGill's seven wickets at 32 runs each in the Caribbean. Both had been disappointing and the expected advantage of them bowling in tandem had not brought success. Commentators and former players were lining up now to give their opinions, which were divided. Richie Benaud wanted him to stay. Neil Harvey, often wheeled out for a 'drop him' comment over the years, thought he should go. If he were dropped, Miller would take his place, given that Dale would probably take over from Gillespie.

Waugh apologised to MacGill for not bowling him more in the final hour or so, which seemed to demonstrate that the skipper had reflected on his own performances and regretted moves not taken. MacGill took it well. The skipper, he realised, had been loyal to Warne. This was the Australian way. It had put the team on top for most of the 1990s. And the precedent, right or wrong, had been set with Mark Taylor, who had been carried for a long time, especially because the team kept winning. Yet now it was in danger of losing the Frank Worrell trophy.

The media quizzed Waugh about Warne and his position. He discounted Warne's batting and vice-captaincy as being enough to keep him in the team.

'He's batting well,' Waugh said. '... but he's got to be picked on his bowling, not his batting.'

Waugh dismissed the vice-captaincy position as 'just a title'. He said he saw Healy, Warne and Mark Waugh as co–vice-captains, with Healy the player whose advice he valued most. This indicated that Waugh had indeed reflected on his failure to use MacGill. Warne was likely to suffer for the hard decisions not taken on the field. But even if Waugh had used MacGill and Australia had won, facts had to be faced. Shane Warne was not delivering. The West Indies' line up was stacked with left-handers that he couldn't dismiss. His confidence in his shoulder and therefore his own ability to spin the ball hard had yet to return.

The day before the final Test at Antigua, Waugh decided to drop Warne, along with Elliott. Warne took it hard. It was a shock. His great career flashed in front of him and he went through several emotions, most of them negative. The stress caused him to take up smoking again.

Healy was in the end declared fit, but Gillespie's injured back didn't come up. In came Adam Dale, Blewett and Miller.

Waugh won the toss and batted in the Fourth Test at Antigua. He was in at three for 96 and ended up 52 not out as Australia struggled to five for 221 by close of play on day one. Wickets fell quickly on day two, but then Colin Miller came in and, with encouragement from Waugh, smacked as many shots as he could, baseball-style. He collected 43 from thirty-eight balls, including two big sixes off Ambrose. Waugh remained 72 not out and his tactic of letting the tailenders do their own thing, and not protecting them, remained contentious. Yet in this situation, where a Test was not at stake, it was a reasonable approach, especially when it worked. But there was a case for Waugh getting into the habit of attempting to take more of the strike. This would not deter a tailender building some sort of innings.

Australia reached 303. Ambrose took five for 94, and would have been happy with the effort. He was still a great bowler, but the sustained spells were not quite coming as they did a few years earlier.

The West Indies answered with hurricane Lara. Dropped at 14 by Miller at mid-on, he went after MacGill as he had all series and hit 34 off three overs. Lara also crashed 22 from one Adam Dale over. This set the tone as he raced to a hundred in eighty-four balls and 101 minutes. It was the third-fastest by a West Indian, behind Viv Richards (fifty-six balls) and Roy Fredericks (seventy-one balls). He was third man out at 136, and his team didn't ever recover as it struggled up to 222. McGrath led the bowling with three for 64, and the others—Dale, Miller and MacGill—took two each.

Australia responded with two for 209 at stumps with Langer on 84 not out and Mark Waugh unconquered on 60. Ambrose was tight the next morning, and he forced Mark into an unnecessary shot. He was caught behind for 65 and the score was three for 223. Steve Waugh pottered for half an hour while facing 27 balls and was caught behind off Ambrose for four. After this, Australian wickets tumbled, but Langer batted well to reach his third Test century and his first against the West Indies. He went on to 127 from the team's total of 306. Walsh mopped up the tail and took four for 78.

The West Indies came out firing, but lost Griffith, retired hurt, hit on the elbow by Dale. After some big hitting against Dale by Joseph, the bowler had his revenge when the ball was lobbed to Miller at mid-off. Then McGrath had Campbell caught behind. Lara came in and looked comfortable. Waugh brought McGrath back into the attack after a spell. He soon had Lara lbw for 7. Stung by criticism that he had not been inventive enough in the Third Test, Waugh put Blewett on. Blewett had taken just nine wickets in Tests but was a most effective surprise and change bowler in Shield cricket. He did the job, nailing Hooper lbw before he was settled. At stumps the Windies were four for 105, with Griffith, back after elbow treatment, and the resolute Adams still there. Australia led by 272 with six wickets to remove and a day to play. The Frank Worrell trophy was likely to remain for the third successive series in Australian hands.

'Funky' Miller had Adams stumped before any addition to the score the next morning. Forty runs later, Blewett struck again, removing Jacobs lbw. Waugh then demonstrated he was prepared to take his innovative thinking to new heights by throwing MacGill the new ball. 'MacGilla' did the rest, taking three wickets—Perry, Ambrose and the stubborn Griffith (56). The West Indies were all out for 211, giving Australia a win by 176 runs that was full of relief for the team and its captain.

Langer won Man of the Match and Lara, Man of the Series. However, the man of the tour from Australia's perspective was Glenn McGrath. He had taken three for 50, giving him thirty wickets in four Tests at 16.93. This branded him as Australia's most potent fast-bowling weapon since Dennis Lillee, and, before him, Ray Lindwall. McGrath was number two in world ratings behind Allan Donald. That was on paper. In reality, he had left Donald and all other speed merchants in his wake. In this series he headed Walsh (twenty-six wickets at 20.88) and Ambrose (nineteen at 22.26).

Steve Waugh had an exceptional series with an aggregate of 409 and an average of 58.43. Only Lara with 546 at 91 did better.

Waugh's decision to ditch Warne, as hard as it had appeared for the skipper, seemed justified. The new bowling team balance seemed right for Antigua. Miller justified his place, as did Adam Dale and MacGill. Waugh was able to mix and match with more versatility.

The captain would not be drawn about Australia's next tours of Sri Lanka and Zimbabwe in September concerning the choice of MacGill or Warne.

'It's too far away,' he remarked and then added jokingly, 'I'll give Stuart and Shane ten balls each, and whoever hits the stumps the most, we'll pick.'

It was said in jest but would not have brought much of a smile to the faces of the two bowlers, who were conscious of their precarious positions.

Report card, series one

After the West Indies series, skipper Steve Waugh gave a frank assessment of his own performance in his usual open and direct style. 'You're always learning as captain. I felt today was probably the best I've captained. I went more with my gut instincts on the field placings, and giving Stuart (MacGill) the new ball. It's not out of the manual, but I thought that was what I had to do.

'I'm the first to admit I'm going to learn as captain. I've only done it for four [Test] games for Australia and ten first-class games. I'm not going to pull all the right strings in the first couple of Test matches. That's probably a bit much to expect. I expect myself to improve every game, and think I did a good job in this game.'

Waugh added that above all he was beginning to trust his intuition. 'If your instincts tell you the ball's going to go to a place, I'll put a man there rather than holding back and saying that's not quite the right position.'

The Windies series seemed to have straightened out a few problems that emerged during the Ashes series in Australia. Slater slid through the Caribbean with a 'pass', scoring 277 at 34.63. He would remain an opener in Tests. Langer had been the best of those battling to secure a batting position, making 291 at 36.38. He had scored two fifties, including a run-out, and a century when it really mattered in the last Test (with Lara the only other player to reach three figures). Langer could be left at number three. Ponting at number six seemed more secure (168 at 56). This would mean that for the Sri Lankan series in September the batting order would be Blewett, Slater, Langer, Mark Waugh, Steve Waugh and Ponting. Elliott was the batting disappointment, yet he was too skilful to be neglected and it would seem a misjudgment that he was to lose his ACB contract. Healy would retain his place while he kept wickets as he did in the final Test—brilliantly. But his batting had fallen away. If he could not improve, Gilchrist would take his place.

The bowling line-up was less predictable. Fitness would be a huge factor. All things being equal, McGrath and Gillespie were the first two choices, leaving two places to be filled by Dale, Fleming, Reiffel, MacGill, Miller and Warne.

Face-saving in the one-dayers

Steve Waugh was not over the draining effect of the Tests when Australia began its seven-game one-day series versus the West Indies. But he felt he had to skipper the first game at the island of St Vincent. Dale contracted pneumonia and had to leave the one-day squad.

Waugh won the toss and bowled, preferring to chase. The home team managed just 209, with Campbell hitting 62 before Lee bowled him. Australia's batting response was feeble as it collected just 165. Only Julian with 35 from forty-two balls was resistant.

Over the weekend before the game on 11 April, a media storm brewed over a dead issue, the Australian captaincy. Alan Jones, the influential Sydney radio broadcaster, suggested Waugh was 'selfish'.

Not surprisingly Waugh was upset by the remark and he took umbrage at the use of the word 'selfish', saying he had given a tremendous amount for his country.

This attack was the worst Steve Waugh had so far endured. Did it affect his game? Probably not, but he scored a duck in the second one-dayer at St George's, Grenada, on 14 April. He looked on as Lehmann smote a sensational 110 in ninety-two balls in an unbeaten fifth-wicket 172-run record stand with Bevan (72), between the teams in this form of the game. Australia scored four for 288, the highest ever against the Windies.

The home team's reply began in front of 12,000 fervid Grenadians packed into the idyllic ground situated next to St George's harbour at the foot of mountains. The locals were set back by Fleming, who dismissed Chanderpaul for a duck in his comeback international, and then bowled Lara for 9. The Windies were never allowed to recover as Warne found form for the second game in a row. Adams was set to worry the Australians when Warne bowled him with one that bit back a long way from outside the left-hander's off stump. The Windies fell 46 short at 242, leaving the series at one-all with five to play.

Waugh had improved his tactics in the field after the first game disappointment. He had used eight bowlers, including himself, in short bursts through the West Indian innings, deploying seven of them in the first twenty-three overs. He wanted to energise his team and keep everyone in the game. It was experimental and would not be advised in an important final. But the object was to keep the side fresh and interested. A win had been the result, so it could not be called folly. His other inspired tactic was to move his fieldsmen around like chess pieces, placing them in and out of their usual positions. Mark Waugh started at cover, and Shane Lee at gully, where he took a tough one-hander diving to his left. Steve Waugh put himself between short and deep cover and stayed out of the gully. He had been criticised for not standing more in line with the stumps, and for not being close to his bowlers for inspiration, a rather thoughtless attack considering that Mark Taylor was rooted at slip for most of his career in both forms of the game. However, there was some merit in Waugh being more in line with the stumps. Was he fielding in the covers on his eventual way round to mid-on or off? Only future games could tell. In the meantime, Julian, often Waugh's replacement in the gully, shared the position with Lee. How did the players respond? That Aussie speech tic among sportsmen and kids—'Yeah, good,'—was the most common response when players were asked later.

The squad moved on to Port of Spain, Trinidad, for the third match on Saturday, 17 April. Australia was held up by Perry (three for 45) and his off spinners and struggled to seven for 242, with Mark Waugh run out on 74 from 100 balls. It was a welcome show of top form from this batsman, who had to be firing if Australia were to win this series and the World Cup. Gilchrist too was in touch, striking 43 from sixty-five balls. The problem was Steve Waugh, who failed for the third time, making just 2. Somehow you felt this was a minor aberration. Waugh would steel himself at the right moment.

Australia received a blow when it bowled. After one over, McGrath went over on his ankle while fielding and had to leave the arena, perhaps for the rest of the series. The tourists never recovered as Adams, coming in at number three, hit 82, Campbell 64, and Hooper 56. The West Indies reached the target in the forty-ninth over with five wickets to spare.

The back-to-back game at Port of Spain on Sunday, 18 April, was now important to Australia. If it lost it would be down one–three with three to play, a tough assignment at the end of a gruelling tour. The game looked all over early as Australia slumped to eight for 104. Then Bevan 'the Unbelievable' combined with Warne for a sensible, superb turnaround, lifting the score to 181 before Warne was run out for 29 from fifty-six balls. Bevan maintained his extraordinary average of around 57 in one-dayers by scoring 59 not out from 103 balls. He was slower than normal, but the situation demanded a sound approach.

Warne carried his batting mood onto the bowling track with a sustained spell after two run-outs sent back Jacobs and Adams. Warne's first victim was the big one—Lara (6). He swept at the ball, played over it and was bowled. Because the 190 target was smallish, Waugh was forced to use Warne—his key strike bowler—long before the death. Within weeks of his Test dumping, the skipper's faith was back in the spinner. The move worked. Warne took two more wickets and ended with three for 35. The West Indies were all out at 169, just 20 runs short. The result levelled the series two all, with three to play.

Warne was awarded the Man of the Match award for his bowling and his role in the recovery partnership with Bevan.

Steve Waugh had been given a poor lbw decision after scoring 16 runs from seventeen balls. A Dillon off-cutter had struck him on a bent knee outside the off stump. Waugh was concentrating on a better performance. He blamed his batting 'slump' on 'burn out' after the strain of the Tests. Waugh spoke frankly about his form after the fourth failure. 'Mentally, four Tests really do drain you. Brian [Lara] was under a lot of pressure, and I was in my first series as captain, so I guess I was under a lot of pressure as well.'

Waugh admitted that once the Tests were over there was a big let down. It had been hard to pump himself up for the one-dayers.

'Today,' he added, 'I felt really motivated for the game. I've been trying my best to fire up for the games, but obviously I've been lacking that five per cent, which I think I had today.'

He surprised the media by indicating that his position in the one-day team was under review.

'It's up to the selectors,' he said. 'No one's guaranteed a spot. I'm going to prove that I'm good enough to be in the side. Things can go against you in one-day cricket. Bevo [Bevan] is on a roll one way, and I'm on a bit of a roll the other way. But I'm going to turn it around.'

The Bevan analogy wasn't appropriate. He had never been off his good-form 'roll' in one-day cricket, whereas Waugh had not been a consistent big performer in this form of the game. Waugh had also struggled in the one-day series against South Africa in 1997–98, but had the mental toughness, luck and skill to perform when it counted in the finals. He would need to improve for the last three one-dayers at Georgetown, Guyana, and the final double-header at Bridgetown, Barbados, which would decide the series.

The pressure was off the Australians to a degree with the news on 20 April that Lara's wrist was causing him problems. He would miss the last three games, but hoped to be fit for the World Cup. Now the two most influential and best players of the Test series—McGrath and Lara—were out of the one-dayers. They cancelled each other out.

The one-day circus moved on to Georgetown, Guyana, for the fifth game. It was reduced by rain to thirty overs each. The Windies won the toss, batted and raced to 83 in the first fifteen overs. First Lee then Warne struck twice, reducing the home side to four for 101. In the slather and whack finish to its innings, Lee managed a third wicket to give him three for 39 off six as the Windies reached five for 173.

Australia looked in good shape when Gilchrist streaked out of the blocks for a slash and burn innings before being run out for 44 in forty-three balls. Simmons bowled Bevan (10) for a rare failure and then Lee (0) in one over. Moments later Tom Moody (2), in need of a match-winning innings to restore the selectors' faith in him, lobbed an easy catch into the outfield, leaving Australia stranded on seven for 119. Shane Warne joined captain Steve Waugh when Australia needed

54 to win off forty-two balls. The two went about their task sensibly with Waugh taking most of the strike, which was in contrast to his approach to the same situation in a Test. His return to the runs was timely as he took up the against-the-odds challenge.

Waugh hit 16 off one over from Hooper and Australia reached the end of the twenty-ninth over with 6 to make to win. There was a pitch invasion that took several minutes to clear. The local police had been huddled in front of the ladies' stand, hardly the place to stop the village idiots who ran onto the arena and tried to steal the stumps.

With 6 runs to get off six balls and three wickets in hand, the odds were in Australia's favour, despite the gathering gloom and thousands of spectators ready again to invade. Waugh took two off the first ball from Keith Arthurton, who was bowling his slow 'spinners'. Then, in a nightmare for the Australian skipper, he swung but couldn't connect properly with the next four deliveries. No runs were scored. From near-certain victory, there was four to win off just one delivery. Waugh lobbed the ball to mid-on and the batsmen ran for two. By the time they had crossed for the second hundreds of people were around them, impeding the play. Warne (remaining 19 not out) completed his second run and kept his bat in the crease and Arthurton removed the bails. Then Waugh came through for the third run. Arthurton looked for stumps to remove from the ground (a requirement once bails were dislodged), but they had been grabbed by spectators. The Australians technically completed the third run, which tied the scores on 173 each. The final seconds were chaotic as the batsmen were jostled and pushed. It was like watching an unofficial match in a schoolyard. The big difference was the potential danger of tanked-up spectators running wild.

Had the invasion not occurred the Windies would have won, but the match referee Raman Subba Row had no choice under the rules but to call it a tie.

After the game Waugh (who scored 72 not out) complained about the invasion, warning that someone could be injured or knifed. He cited the attack on United States tennis player Monica Seles. Yet he couldn't complain about the result. His inability to strike a winning hit was saved by the stupidity of the Guyanese fans. Australia walked away with a lucky result that left a double-header as the decider at Barbados on 24 and 25 April. Now one team had to win both games to take the series.

Australia was hoping for another special Anzac effort.

Jimmy Adams won the toss and batted first on a good batting strip at Bridgetown, Barbados, in front of a sell-out crowd. The West Indies took a tight hold on the game with Ridley Jacobs and Sherwin Campbell blazing away to reach 100 in the first fifteen overs. The bowlers took a belting. Shane Warne came on with the score at none for 59 after just eight overs. Waugh used him once more as a strike bowler and it worked. He took wickets and slowed the run rate.

The West Indies lost eight for 160 (with Adams playing a captain's knock of 46 and Chanderpaul finding some form, 44) to be eight for 249 in all—a total that Australia viewed as gettable. Gilchrist was superb at the start again, making 64. He was supported by an even Australian effort by Mark Waugh (25), Julian (put up the order as a pinch-hitter, 31), Ponting (43) and Bevan (35 not out).

One negative in the batting was Steve Waugh, not because he was caught close in for 5, but because of his behaviour. Instead of walking off, he glared at the umpire. It may have been a poor decision, but Waugh had to set a better example. In the previous game he had 'chatted' the umpire when an obvious catch was given not out off his own bowling. No doubt there were more pressures on him as captain and with his own mixed form, but he was not presenting a good image. This came on top of the sight of him hopping into an umpire's box during a Test to see why he had been given out caught by a third umpire when he wasn't sure himself that the catch had been taken. It was just a check, but the picture portrayed was that of a dissenter and a whinger.

Australia reached six for 253 in the forty-ninth over and took a three–two lead in the series.

A troubled end

Steve Waugh won the toss and batted in the final game, also at the Kensington ground in Barbados. Gilchrist got up and under a square cut for six over point in the second over but was out caught trying a repeat. It was a carefree start that turned sloppy against some good fast bowling. Dillon then removed Ponting caught at slip. Ambrose, in the side because of the sudden overnight retirement of Carl Hooper, dismissed Mark Waugh. Lehmann came in and played one smash through midwicket that would have to be the power shot of the Caribbean season. But he too was out cheaply. Steve Waugh made a forceful 30 before King had him caught behind. Australia found itself five for 80 and floundering, although the run rate of 5 after sixteen overs was good, considering the collapse. Moody played a solid knock for 50 not out, Lee, 47, Bevan 34, and Warne—again batting responsibly—was run out for 20 off seventeen balls. Bevan's run-out was controversial. He was blocked and jostled when going for a run.

Australia reached a respectable nine for 252.

The West Indies was away quickly with Jacobs again dominant and Campbell solid. Fleming and Moody were attacked, and Waugh had to call on Warne again to stem the run flow. Waugh was forced to use himself and Bevan. After Warne, there were no bowlers who could control the West Indians.

At one for 138, Julian bowled to Chanderpaul. He placed a ball on the on side and set off for a quick single. Julian ran across to gather and stopped when he saw Bevan dashing to field the ball. Campbell ran into a propped Julian and fell over. Bevan rushed in and removed the bails. Campbell, lying on the ground, protested, but the umpires were adamant that he was out. As Campbell left the field, the 15,000 sell-out crowd responded murderously. Beer bottles and debris were hurled from stands. Waugh wanted to recall Campbell, but the umpires refused. The bottles kept coming. Waugh, fearing for his team's safety, led them from the field. More missiles were hurled, forcing players to take evasive action. It was pure luck that one didn't hit a player as they left the arena. A bottle was thrown at Steve Waugh from high in a stand and narrowly missed his head. The crowd seemed set to riot.

The police advised that the Australian players would be in serious danger if the match were abandoned, not just at the ground, but anywhere in Barbados. Officials met in a flurry of activity and match referee Raman Subba Row brokered an agreement—put up by Waugh for the second time—that Campbell be allowed to return to the crease to continue his innings. It was a generous, sensible gesture by Waugh. The alternative was to risk life and limb, literally. The seriousness of the situation was again evident when Barbadian legend, Sir Garfield Sobers, walked onto the ground and made the announcement of Campbell's reinstatement in an effort to placate irate fans. Mob rule had won the day, overriding umpires, players and the referee. It had happened in two of the last three matches. Ugly fans, their brains dulled by alcohol, had decided the outcome twice. The scenes were broadcast around the world and sure to incite idiots everywhere. There was little difference in Australia, except that Australian yobbos could only throw plastic cups, not glass beer bottles. It was a calamitous moment for cricket, and a severe test for Steve Waugh—an examination that no captain deserved to go through.

The game now had to be reduced to forty overs batting by the West Indies. Its target was now 194—another 66 from sixty balls. Ten minutes later Campbell returned with Chanderpaul, but was soon out caught behind off Bevan for 62. However, Bevan, Julian and Moody bowled loosely and Australian hearts were not in the contest. The West Indies coasted to two for 197 and an easy win. The series was drawn three all with one tie.

At the after-game ceremony and later media conference Steve Waugh again said that something had to be done about crowd behaviour in the Caribbean. He was flat with the series coming to such a nasty anticlimax, and unhappy that Australia had not managed an expected win. He made it clear that his men hadn't bothered making an effort after the enforced break in the match.

'The spirit had gone out of the game,' Waugh said. 'The players were thinking about safety, and worrying. The result didn't mean anything.'

Waugh said it wasn't worth playing the game if players' safety, indeed their lives, were threatened.

Back in Australia there was some huff and puff from the ACB. It would not send teams to certain Caribbean venues on the next tour in 2003 unless local authorities could provide solid guarantees about player safety.

Waugh summed up the disaster by saying. 'Cricket was the loser.'

Fortunately, Waugh was not a loser on the tour overall, although the two drawn series were not expected. The Australians believed they were a better side and should have won both the Tests and one-dayers. Waugh naturally talked up the toughness of such a tour, and no one doubted it had created special demands with flying around the islands, variable food, rough crowds, lack of practice facilities and sometimes poor grounds. But after winning the last two Test series, a draw was a disappointment, although the Frank Worrell trophy remained with the tourists.

The media were unforgiving. Waugh was given poor to average marks for his efforts first up, although, once more, no one could fault his batting performances, especially in the Tests. He had played at his best and had led from the front.

The team's struggle in the one-dayers did not augur well for the next challenge in the 1999 World Cup in England. The Australian short-game side didn't seem to have progressed over the previous twelve months—at least not enough to make a serious challenge for the Cup. South Africa was the short-odds favourite to win, with India a big chance and England expected to do well at home. The world media, even the Australian journalists, wrote Australia off as a very long shot. Much of this was put down to Waugh's leadership, which was not regarded as effective. He was unimaginative and lacked spontaneity, critics such as Peter Roebuck wrote.

But Waugh had done enough in the Tests for the ACB and selectors to hold their faith in him, and he would be captain through 1999–2000, but for unforeseen circumstances. Leaders in five-day Tests needed time to develop. Teams had to settle properly under a new captaincy style.

The one-day game was a more urgent proposition. Waugh was experienced enough now, having been the skipper for eighteen months. If he didn't have success in England—that is, at least make the semi-finals—he was in danger of being stripped of the leadership.

12

WAUGH OF THE
WORLD CUP

Many a slip . . .

Steve Waugh and his one-day squad arrived at Gatwick airport early
in May to be met by a media pack hungry for his reaction to the
stunning end to the West Indian tour. Waugh and an Australian journalist travelling with the tour party had been slapped with a writ issued
by the Barbados Police Commissioner, Grantley Watson, late on
Friday, 30 April 1999, as the team prepared to leave the island. Watson
had alleged that Waugh's post-match comments relating to the security
of the Australian players after the Kensington Oval bottle-throwing
fiasco were defamatory. Watson claimed that he himself had not been
present at the ground when the fans nearly rioted. In a general sense,
the writ demonstrated the dangers of anyone, especially captains,
opening their mouths in public.

The Australians took off from Gatwick for Cardiff, where they
would be based for the two weeks leading up to their opening World
Cup match against Scotland at Worcester. There were three
warm-up one-dayers against Glamorgan (8 May), Worcestershire

(10 May) and Somerset (12 May), all of which were interrupted by the wet weather.

The World Cup began under dark skies across England on 14 May at Lord's. England easily beat Sri Lanka. The next day at Hove, the favourites, South Africa, accounted for India. The Proteas' three all-rounders, Kallis, Pollock and Klusener, looked in form. Over the tournament they would be instrumental in pushing the Proteas far, perhaps to the Cup itself.

Australia, without one all-rounder in the South Africans' class, entered the fray against Scotland at Worcester on 16 May. Waugh won the toss and sent the Scots in. The Australian bowling was wayward and the fielding dreadful. Extras at 39 were top score as the Scots ploughed their way to a dour seven for 179. Warne was the best of the bowlers, taking three for 39, including two wickets with his last two balls.

Fleming also bowled well, taking one for 19, but the rest were poor, dishing up wides and no balls. The only consolation the Australians could take was to consider that such a performance was better out of the way against the Scots in the first game.

The Australian bats plodded to four for 182 for a six-wicket win. Mark Waugh was made Man of the Match for his 67. Lehmann (0) and Ponting (33), Australia's suspect links, didn't do enough while Steve Waugh (49 in sixty-nine balls) steered Australia to a win in 45.1 overs.

After the game the skipper described Australia's out-cricket as 'atrocious'. He gave his team 4 out of 10 for its effort. 'The batting needed a run,' he said, and was thinking about lots of runs.

Waugh complained again about controlling crowd behaviour and seemed to have taken it on as a cause. He had to be careful that he didn't appear to be seen as a perennial carper. The cricket world media knew that he was always good for a quote. He was honest and pulled few punches. When Cronje used an earplug to take advice and instruction from his coach Bob Woolmer on the sidelines, Waugh thought it was a 'put-down', demeaning for Cronje as captain. When a drunken spectator ran onto the ground at Hove and grabbed Indian skipper Mohammad Azharuddin, Waugh was asked for a view and he reiterated his attitude.

Off the field, he was grappling with the team's unease with his drink ban, which he had instituted at the start of the tour. They were professionals, unlikely to end up in the condition of the spectator at Hove (except on rare occasions). Tom Moody passed on a little rumbling in the camp to the skipper. In response, Steve took booze restrictions off and went back to a sensible 'drinks with meals' policy. Waugh had been influenced by Allan Border's prohibition during the successful 1987 campaign. The current captain was keen to recreate the winning conditions, but the high proportion of players in this team that enjoyed a drink meant he had to trim the discipline accordingly. Since the nineteenth century alcohol had been a part of the touring culture of Australian teams (which often split between drinkers and non-drinkers). It was not going to be stopped now, despite the side's ever-increasing fitness consciousness. The players had to relax and enjoy themselves on arduous trips away from home.

Meanwhile, back on the field, Pakistan beat the West Indies. Shoaib Akhtar, the young speed demon, and Wasim Akram were in form. New Zealand then accounted for Bangladesh, and England for Kenya. Zimbabwe just beat India—penalised for a slow over rate and without Tendulkar, who had rushed home to attend the funeral of his father. South Africa defeated Sri Lanka on 19 May, coming back after an ordinary batting effort had been saved by Klusener, and then running through the Sri Lankans to win easily. At this early point South Africa was the frontrunner on form and confidence. Its all-rounders were proving hard to keep out of any contest and they went on to beat England with ease.

On 20 May, New Zealand played Australia at Cardiff. Waugh won the toss and batted. Only Lehmann (76) and Ponting (47) performed, as Australia struggled to eight for 213. Geoff Allott took four for 37. The Kiwis sank to four for 49 and looked beaten, but Roger Twose (80 not out) and Chris Cairns (60) combined in a 148-runs partnership to help their country win easily in the forty-sixth over. Twose was most pleased. He had always felt bullied by Australian teams and was delighted to retaliate in the best way possible.

The loss didn't dim the Aussie team spirit. At a favourite Cardiff Italian café they ended up in a singing competition with a group of priests at another table, which was all part of the celebration for the birth of Shane Warne's son, Jackson. Steve enjoyed these moments of camaraderie and felt them essential for success. His philosophy was 'the group that plays together, stays together'.

Waugh was circumspect and wasn't going to panic over the defeat by New Zealand. He pointed out that the 'equation' to make the final six was simple. Australia had to win three games to get in. The Pakistan match at Headingley on Sunday, 23 May, now loomed as vital for Australia.

Waugh wanted ten per cent lifts from just about everyone, but in reality more was needed. The fielding had not been of the highest standard. The batting looked brittle and the bowling just above average by comparison with other teams.

As well, Waugh's captaincy was under fire. The ABC's Tim Lane suggested there was a rift between the skipper and Warne. He asked Waugh at a press conference before the Pakistan game if he and Warne were feuding. The two players hotly denied it. It was suggested there was some residual tension after Warne had been dropped from the Test side, and his success in leading the one-day side in the CUB tournament earlier in the year.

Waugh was said to be 'white hot' for some time over the inference of Lane's question. The journalist defended his remarks by saying that they came from a source 'close to the team'. The captain was concerned that there might just be something behind Lane's remarks. He brought the issue up at a team meeting, but apart from the odd minor grumble about other concerns, he found no dissent.

'I now feel totally reassured everyone is 100 per cent behind the team,' a relieved Waugh said. If there were any residual tension between him and Warne—and both players claimed there wasn't—it would now dissolve as they showed a unified front. Perhaps Lane's remarks had galvanised unity within the squad. It needed all the gains it could get.

One-day crunch

Pakistan presented a team for the Cup more fired-up and united than it had for some time, knowing that at the end of the tournament three players could be named and given cricket 'sentences' for their parts in the bribes scandal, where several Pakistanis were alleged to have been involved in match fixing over the past decade. Pakistani authorities would wait for any possible decision until after the Cup so as not to impede the side's chances.

Reiffel, a success at Headingley in a 1993 Ashes Test, was named in the team to play Pakistan, replacing the injured Shane Lee. Waugh won the toss and in good seaming, swing conditions, sent Pakistan in. The decision looked a good one at one stage when the Pakistanis were three for 46, but brilliant teenager Abdur Razzaq (60 off ninety-nine balls), Inzamam (run out for 81 off 104 balls) and Moin (31 off just twelve deliveries) raced the side up to eight for 275. Only Fleming could contain them, taking two for 37, but McGrath (one for 54), Warne (one for 50), Reiffel (one for 48), Steve Waugh (none for 37 off six overs), Martyn (none for 25 off two overs) and Lehmann (none for 17 off two overs) were treated severely.

Australia then had to bat against the best and fastest bowling attack in the competition. It started badly when Gilchrist was bowled third ball by Wasim. Shoaib Akhtar overplayed his role as a fiery verbaliser, giving plenty to Steve Waugh and Ponting, the two hardest nuts in the Australian team.

According to Waugh in his diary, at one point the speedster attempted to 'nudge' Waugh with his boot. The Australian captain said to him, 'Every dog has his day,' which implied that this match was his big moment. It generated more heat and ensured there would be tension between these sides in future encounters.

Mark Waugh (41 off forty-seven), Ponting (47 off sixty), Steve

Waugh (49 off sixty-six) and Bevan (61 off eighty) rose to the occasion, but the Australians fell just 10 runs short. It was a gallant effort. But such performances were forgotten quickly in this cut-throat form of the game. The truth was that no top order Australian batsman could stay around for a big hundred.

Three days later Steve Waugh received a lift watching Manchester United on television beat Germany's Bayern Munich in the Champions Leagues Soccer Final. United came back from nil–one down well into injury time and scored twice to win. It reminded the captain that anything was possible in sport.

Nevertheless, the loss to Pakistan left Australia in big trouble. To make the final six, it had to beat Bangladesh on 27 May at Chester-le-Street and the West Indies on 30 May at Old Trafford *and* with a better run rate than the West Indies and New Zealand. If it won both games it then had to defeat India, Zimbabwe and South Africa, the three qualifiers from group A. Its poor showing in the preliminary games, where points also counted, meant it had to win all three in the Super Six—in other words, win five successive games—to make the final four and the semi-finals. Even more against the odds was the chance of Australia winning the semi-final and then the final to take the Cup. Seven games in succession seemed a near-impossible target that even Bradman's Invincibles would have had difficulty managing.

Meanwhile the selectors' knives were being sharpened. If Australia didn't make the Super Six, Waugh might be dumped as one-day skipper.

Australia needed inspiration and India provided some. It had struggled early but Tendulkar returned from India and made 140 against Kenya—the first century of the tournament—which gave his team a decisive win.

In its next game against Sri Lanka India went a step further and whacked a record World Cup score of six for 373. Saurav Ganguly (183 from 158 balls) and Rahul Dravid (145 from 129 balls) put on a record 318 stand. These efforts demonstrated to the Australians that a team could make a big leap in form during the tournament.

Australia played Bangladesh on 27 May. Waugh won the toss and put the opposition in. Bangladesh managed seven for 178 (Minhajel Abedin 53 not out). Australia, forced to go for quick runs to improve its run rate, reached the target with seven wickets to spare. Gilchrist (63) was among the runs as was Moody (56 not out), whose effort pushed him in front of Shane Lee for the all-rounder's spot in the side. Brendon Julian's form allowed him to take Martyn's place.

On Saturday, 29 May, there was a shock in group A when Zimbabwe easily beat South Africa, putting pressure on the concurrent game between England and India. India won and this put England out of the competition, a major blow for the hosts, who had expected to go on. South Africa, Zimbabwe and India went through to the Super Six. Australia would face the West Indies for the right to go through from group B.

Waugh won the toss and sent the West Indies in under threatening skies at Old Trafford. Writing in the London *Sunday Times* on the morning of the match, Waugh 'believed' that Glenn McGrath 'would put his hand up' and 'be the man to do damage to the West Indies in the same manner as he did during the recent Test series in the Caribbean'. The Australian skipper favoured public comments for psychological reasons. This was followed by a piece by Warne in the Saturday *Times*, in which he focused on Lara and how McGrath had success in going round the wicket to him.

McGrath did as predicted and bowled superbly, taking five for 14 off 8.4 overs, the best performance of the entire tournament. He took Lara's wicket with the ball, to that point, of the World Cup. Pitching on leg stump, it clipped the top of the off to bowl the West Indian skipper for 9. Warne backed up McGrath, taking three for 11.

The West Indies made just 110 but Australia was in trouble early in reply, losing Mark Waugh (3) to Ambrose. At one stage it was four for 62 but a determined partnership between Steve Waugh and Michael Bevan made the game safe.

It was a 'must' effort from Waugh, who, like several other one-day captains such as Ranatunga, Alec Stewart and Azharuddin, was in trouble at home over their teams' performances. Waugh had been criticised for the way he was handling the team on and off the field. Some journalists suggested the team was not as harmonious as it was under Mark Taylor. There were calls from some quarters for Waugh to be relieved of the one-day captaincy at least, should Australia make an early exit from the Cup. Selectors' chairman Trevor Hohns and his co-selectors looked on with keen interest at Waugh's performance. But his 19 not out in the crisis would prevent critics from becoming too vociferous. Still, Waugh could not avoid minor criticism when the West Indies batted. He refused to bring the field up to save the single when Ridley Jacobs, who carried his bat with 49 not out, was shielding the West Indies tail. Lara too was less attacking than he should have been in Australia's innings. He could have gone all out to take wickets but held back. One slip was not enough when wickets had to be taken.

The game ended in a bizarre manner when Australia reached four for 90. The match was clearly in its grasp, but Waugh and Bevan began defending each ball, not trying to grab the runs to win. The reason was to do with the Cup rules. Australia's run rate would be superior to the West Indies' run rate if it made the runs in under 47 overs. But it wanted its opponent's bowling rate (run and bowling rates were counted in the Cup) to be superior to New Zealand's, so that the West Indies would go through to the Super Six in front of New Zealand. The reason? Australia carried two points through to the Super Six if a team it had beaten made it through with it. In this case it was the West Indies, which Australia beat on 30 May, and not New Zealand, which had beaten Australia. Points carried forward would play a part in deciding who went through to the semi-finals beyond the Super Six. Australia therefore had to help lift the West Indies' net run rate, which was calculated from the bowling and batting rate.

This questionable rule equation saw the game stopping almost dead at Old Trafford. The batsmen were booed by the crowd, many of whom were unaware of the rules and why the Australians were using such apparently odd, boring tactics. The win came in the forty-first over with a no ball, a fitting end to the farce, which was no fault of the batsmen, who were simply doing the best by their team.

As it turned out, at the end of 30 May, the West Indies' net run rate was 0.53 as opposed to New Zealand's 0.00. This meant that the final game of the early eliminations between New Zealand and Scotland at Edinburgh would see who would sneak through in group B out of the Kiwis and the Windies.

New Zealand made it, along with Pakistan, South Africa, Zimbabwe (the fluke of the tournament), India and Australia.

On 1 June, the Australian team's sports psychologist, Sandy Gordon, joined the team in his role as a 'confessor', and helped members of the squad unburden themselves to him about homesickness, staleness, personal problems, their form and so on. The man with the most on his mind was Shane Warne, who had not been himself for two weeks. He was coming in for heavy criticism, some of it gratuitous or vicious, in the media and from spectators during matches. To a degree, he had brought focus on himself by saying that Ranatunga was bad for Sri Lankan cricket and that he should not be playing the game. He was also off the boil in terms of his bowling. This was the most pertinent factor in Warne's demeanour. If he struck form he would change inside ten minutes. He was an individual who thrived on the spectacular. Anything short of this impinged on his mien.

Waugh was the other team psychologist. He was concerned about Warne personally and in terms of the team's slim chances of pulling off a near sporting miracle and taking the Cup. But he was concerned with the mental state and preparation of every player. He spoke with each man and the team at meetings that reviewed and previewed performances, strategies and tactics.

At a team meeting, before the Super Six games versus India, he urged the players to remember why their performance against the West Indies had been so good. He wanted a repeat of the urgency, aggression, hustle, determination and desire shown in the game, even if events were not going their way.

The Waugh twins were cheered by the opportunity to meet the Queen on 2 June, their thirty-fourth birthday. They joked in the team bus on the way to a function at Buckingham Palace that it was 'sporting' of her Majesty to remember them. In a tradition that went back to the beginning of the twentieth century the monarch chatted informally with the touring Australians. The chat centred on how outstanding their striped blazers were and they were unsure whether she liked their attire or not. After pondering this monumental triviality, Steve Waugh celebrated his birthday by going to the theatre with Shane Lee to see the musical *The Buddy Holly Story*. He enjoyed breaking the routine of restaurants and movies, and was seen smiling in the foyer signing autographs.

This relaxed day occurred in the lull before the Super Six finals. Waugh felt his team was on a winning roll after its encouraging performance against Pakistan and the two most recent wins.

Solid as a Super Six

Australia met India at The Oval on Friday, 4 June, and the line-up included Reiffel once more. Azharuddin won the toss in front of a noisy, Indian-supporting large crowd. He sent Australia in under 'overcast conditions', a weather description that had become a cliché during this tournament. Waugh and Gilchrist opened with a strong stand of 97. This put Australia on top from the beginning. Mark Waugh ended with 83, and looked to have found his best form. There were classic shots in his wide repertoire and a few improvisations that always marked him as a lateral-thinking champion. He was supported by every other batsman, who either scored in the twenties or thirties as Australia stroked up to six for 282.

It was a good score on this wicket and under conditions that would have left Steve Waugh satisfied with 225. Yet every Australian was on edge. India's fine batting line-up, led by Tendulkar, could make those runs if given half a chance. McGrath gave them none. Tendulkar opened. It took the rangy quick four balls to deliver a near-unplayable 'pearler'. It was a fraction outside off stump, forcing Tendulkar to push at it. Like Lara in the previous game, the great Indian batsman did not play a bad stroke. In fact, Tendulkar was good enough to get a snick to it and keeper Gilchrist took a sharp catch. McGrath then removed Dravid (2) with a similar ball that had to be played at. Gilchrist took a harder, higher chance. India was two for 10. Their two biggest scoring batsmen of the Cup were out of the contest.

Fleming—ever lurking in the shadow of McGrath—then struck, to force Ganguly (8) to play on. India was three for 12. Azharuddin on 3 received another unplayable ball from McGrath. It bounced off a good length, caught a leading edge and Steve Waugh took it easily. India was four for 17 in the seventh over. As pinball machines say, it was 'game over'.

Ajay Jadeja played a brilliant innings, scoring 100 not out off 138 balls, but not even he threatened Australia as India was dismissed in the forty-ninth over for 205.

Man of the Match Glenn McGrath took three for 34 off ten and Fleming two for 33 off nine. Reiffel took none for 30 off ten and was steady. Considering his few opportunities, he was running into form with the troublesome white ball. Under English conditions, he was the best fourth bowling option of the Cup, behind McGrath, Fleming and Warne and in front of Moody, who was proving useful with bat and ball.

Waugh looked a happy man after the game. His face was a permanent half-grin. He was relieved that Australia was still in the fight for the Cup. At one point it had had to win seven games to win. Now it was four, and the first of those would be Zimbabwe. Waugh, in the psychological stakes, had already branded them as the pretenders in the Super Six. He didn't expect them to win one of their three games. He was already leapfrogging over them. His mind was on Australia's final game in the Super Six, versus South Africa.

The Proteas were the heavyweight of the Cup to this point, along with Pakistan, and these two shaped up at Trent Bridge on 5 June. South Africa scraped in by three wickets, thanks to Lance Klusener's big hitting (46 from forty-one balls) at the finish of their innings. Steve Waugh watched the game on television and made notes. To win the Cup, Australia would have to get over both of these sides. It was a perfect opportunity to do some homework on them. Waugh and his bowlers had a specific game plan now for every South African and Pakistani batsman, right down to number nine. For instance, Klusener had been marked for attention by Fleming and Reiffel, who would be most likely bowling to him inside the last twenty overs. They were accurate and could move the ball away from the left-hander. Warne would be brought on to bowl the moment either Cronje or Cullinan arrived at the wicket. McGrath and Fleming could bottle up Saeed Anwar by bowling around the wicket. The fielders could put pressure on Inzamam-ul-Haq, who was a poor runner between the wickets— and so on.

Steve Waugh lost the toss at Lord's on 9 June and Zimbabwe sent Australia in to bat. The reasoning was that McGrath would be tough on the Lord's wicket. It seemed a little cock-eyed. McGrath would have to be faced at some point and the wicket looked fine.

Mark Waugh made a mockery of the decision, scoring 104 in 120 balls and leading Australia towards the good tally of four for 303. His brother Steve also batted well (62 off sixty-one balls) and Ponting sprinted to score 36 in thirty-five balls, as did Bevan (37 not out in thirty-five balls).

Zimbabwe's opening bat, Neil Johnson, with 132 not out from 144 balls, fought hard and at one stage seemed as if he could challenge Australia. However his team lost five wickets between 150 and 200, killing any chance of a serious fight. None of the Australian bowlers was overly impressive, although McGrath—one for 33 off ten—was tight. Reiffel, although expensive, snared three wickets at a critical time.

The highlight for Australia came not from its bowlers, but its captain, who rung changes and each time pulled off a wicket. He didn't panic but took risks and was inspired in the way he contained batsmen at critical times and forced errors.

After the game, Waugh counselled his star spinner Warne during a walk in the park near the team hotel in Kensington. A belting by Zimbabwe's Neil Johnson had been the last in a string of worries for Warne, which included personal pressures. Warne wanted to retire. He'd had enough after the long fight back from injury, the bribery affair, and a *News of the World* beat-up article about an alleged dalliance with a 'porn star', which was calculated to cause him off-field concern at a critical time in the World Cup. It was helping to put Warne off his game, even his career. Now a little stick here and there in the World Cup—and the criticism that followed—was proving too much.

Steve Waugh advised Warnie against quitting. He had confidence in his champion spinner. Waugh suggested he complete the tournament, go home, discuss it all with his family (his wife, Simone, father, Keith, and brother, Jason, were the key people involved) and then make a decision. The skipper reiterated that Australia needed Warne at his peak to win the contest. He reminded him of his fine form just a few weeks earlier during the one-day series in the West Indies, in which Warne was the best player.

Waugh's effort with Warne marked him as a different kind of skipper, one who was caring and who was prepared to nurse his talent and give them support both private and public. Waugh wasn't sure how his brilliant strike bowler would react to the advice, but it at least gave Warne a sense of being needed by the man he wanted to hear it from most. Whether this unconditional support would inspire him remained to be seen.

In the second-last game of the Super Six, New Zealand beat India, thus securing a place in the semi-finals. India was eliminated. The equation at the finish was simple. Australia had to tie or win in the final game of the Super Six against South Africa in order to make the semi-finals. If it lost, Zimbabwe would sneak into the semis without winning a game in the second round of matches (the super-sixers)—a stark weakness in the competition.

Waugh realised what a precarious life he was leading as captain when Trevor Hohns told him just before the South African sudden-death match that had Australia been eliminated early from the Cup, his tenure as captain might well have been over. Waugh again told him that if he wasn't wanted, then the selectors should make the change. But the captain knew that this would not happen now. For the moment, he could hold on to the job. Waugh felt that taking the team at least one step higher—with victory over South Africa and a place in the semi-finals—would probably see him skipper for at least the 1999–2000 season.

Sudden death

At the last team meeting before the Leeds game, Shane Warne prepared for a crisis game in terms of his career. He showed he was switched on by making the comment that any batsman caught by Herschelle Gibbs should not walk.

'He has a tendency to flick the ball away before accepting it properly,' Warne said.

This was met by the response, 'Get real, Warnie,' and a few derisive laughs from other team members.

'I'm fair dinkum,' Warne replied. 'Stand your ground if Herschelle catches you.'

South Africa, along with Pakistan and New Zealand, had qualified for the Super Six. Yet the Proteas were bursting to win against Australia. It would put this major rival out of contention. Nothing would give Cronje and his team more pleasure.

Australia was playing for its survival. It left out Lehmann, who had a split finger, and replaced him with Damien Martyn.

South Africa won the toss and batted. Gibbs and Cullinan were aided by luck as they began confidently. Waugh brought Warne on after spells from Reiffel (who removed Kirsten for 21), McGrath and Fleming. Cullinan had looked set, but Warne soon constipated him and the runs dried up. Warne beat him three times in one over. The batsman seemed to have learned nothing in how to tackle his nemesis. Gibbs looked less uncertain. Warne and Fleming had tough catches missed off them.

Waugh planned to bowl Warne out with his ten overs. The spin bowler conceded just 27 runs in his first eight overs. In his ninth, he struck twice, putting back Cullinan (bowled, 50) and Cronje (lbw,

0). South Africa was three for 141, and Australia was back in the game.

Gibbs went on to 101 in 134 balls before McGrath bowled him. It was an important, confident innings, despite the several lucky strokes he played. Jonty Rhodes was his jaunty self in conjuring 39 rather invisibly off thirty-six balls before Fleming removed him. Klusener, coming in at four for 219, bludgeoned his way to 36 in twenty-one balls.

The Proteas reached seven for 271, an excellent score on an uncertain wicket.

Only Warne had bowled well, taking two for 33. It wasn't enough to make him consider playing on after the Cup, but it meant he would not quit before Australia was eliminated or had won the tournament. Fleming took three for 57, and Reiffel one for 47 off nine. McGrath was out of sorts, bowling four full tosses in his final two overs when trying to spear in yorkers. Moody and Bevan had bad days with the ball.

Steve Waugh was not pleased and described the bowling effort in general as 'pretty ordinary'—an understatement, considering that only one of six bowlers used was not harshly treated. They would have to lift several notches. At least three bowlers would have to perform to Warne's standard if Australia was to have a chance of taking the Cup. The fielding was not as good as it could have been either. Fumbles in the outfield, dropped catches and poor returns marred the performance. Too often the South Africans had turned ones into twos, and their running between the wickets—and out-fielding—had been the best of the tournament.

Australia began batting as it had fielded. Gilchrist (5) was bowled by Elworthy and then Mark Waugh (5) was run out in a case of 'he who hesitates is lost'. Ponting had driven to midwicket and set off. Waugh waited to see if it was fielded and set off too late to beat the throw to the keeper. Had he answered the call he would have made it. Martyn came in, settled himself and then on 11 played a half-pull which dollied to mid-on. Australia was three for 48, and all but out of the tournament.

Steve Waugh would not go without a fight. His form had improved through the games. He received expected sledging from the South Africans, particularly Herschelle Gibbs. The Proteas wanted to let Waugh know they were aware of his remarks indicating that they were 'chokers'.

'Let's see how he takes the pressure now,' Gibbs called.

Waugh was undeterred. He was peaking in parallel with his team. At first he seemed to settle down Ponting, who was batting with control and purpose, and then excite his partner as their partnership steadied and built.

All the time, Waugh and Gibbs chipped away at each other. It was friendly enough 'banter' or sledging. Waugh was winning the battle. He was still at the wicket.

He and Ponting managed a 126-run stand before Ponting also mistimed a pull to be caught for a mature, top-class 69 in 110 balls. But it was Waugh's day. He kept giving himself room to swing through and over covers, and was bold in smashing balls on both sides of the wicket.

At 50 he was spurred on by the thought of all the criticism and adverse comments that had been aimed at him.

He had one let-off. On 56 he flicked Klusener to midwicket. Herschelle Gibbs took the catch, but in his eagerness to hoist the ball skyward, he fumbled it. Recalling Shane Warne's acute observation about Gibbs's catching technique, Waugh stood his ground. He was not out. 'I hope you realise you've just lost the game for your team,' Waugh remarked boldy (and, on his own later admission, 'stupidly') to a crestfallen Gibbs, who was quiet for the rest of his innings.

The Proteas looked to Allan Donald in the thirty-ninth over to stem the flow or take a wicket. Waugh greeted him by giving himself room to a short ball outside off stump, which he launched over cover for four. The ball had bounced back thirty metres from the advertising board with Donald barely finishing his follow through. He looked bemused. Like every other bowler in the tournament, he had suffered some stick. But not like this, not first ball of a spell.

Waugh improvised more than usual and was bolder than anyone

had seen him. The wicket was not good by afternoon and the South Africans were able to get balls to jump at the batsman's chest. Fingers were struck often. It was a hard day at the office. At 91, Waugh bent to one knee and literally swept himself off his feet in hitting Steve Elworthy for a mighty six over midwicket. His century took 91 balls.

Waugh scored 113 of the 199 that he put on with Ponting and Bevan. From the time he had arrived at the wicket, the other batsmen collected 90 between them. Waugh batted on to a magnificent 120 not out in 110 balls with 10 fours and two sixes. His effort, supported by Ponting, Bevan (27) and Moody (15 from sixteen balls), won the game with just two balls to spare.

The English writers liked the knock. David Hopps in *The Guardian* wrote, 'The discriminating stroke-play, the calculating mind, and more bottle than a morning milk float: these are all strengths that have made Waugh the most redoubtable of modern Test batsmen.'

'The strongest man in the game,' Mark Nicholas said in *The Daily Telegraph*, 'dug deeper still into the reserves which carry the cricketing circus around the world. The Australian balcony began to crunch on their gum, Waugh tightened his lips . . .'

This was just Waugh's second century in 266 one-day internationals, but had to be ranked as the best ever by an Australian, given the circumstances and the opposition.

Waugh would have had a whirl of emotions rushing through him when he had arrived at the wicket but on the surface he seemed immune to the tension surrounding the game and the plight of his side. Waugh had always said he loved performing in these moments, critical times when most would prefer not to be in the middle. He played 'beyond his means' in a desperate attempt to win and keep his place as one-day captain.

When pressed by journalists, Waugh conceded, 'I'd rate that as high as any innings I've ever played.'

In fact, it had been the equal to anything from Lara, Tendulkar or brother Mark.

Waugh brought a touch of dry humour to the press conference by saying, 'Thanks, guys,' to the Australian press for their criticism. It had drawn out his best. 'I hope we're regarded as ruthlessly professional now,' he said, 'because I've been on the other side of the fence in the mid-eighties when Australia were really copping it and, I tell you, it's no fun over there. People putting you down, getting on your back. I don't want to be subject to ridicule. To ensure it doesn't happen, you've got to be ruthless when you're on top to make sure those good times keep going.'

Hit head-on by a big semi

And they did roll on. Their amazing victory had put Australia into the semi-finals. Cronje suggested his team would be better with Kallis back after strained abdominals, giving it a fifth good bowler.

Waugh, however, was smiling more. He knew that the momentum and force were now with his team. 'I always knew we would fight back,' he said. 'Sometimes you can take games too much on face value rather than examining the karma or character of a side.'

The final teams in order of finishing were Pakistan, Australia, South Africa and New Zealand. Australia and South Africa, two extremely competitive rivals, were drawn to clash again in a semi-final four days later, on Thursday, 17 June, at Edgbaston, a day after the Pakistan–New Zealand match.

Waugh continued the psychological war against South Africa by suggesting again that it might fail under pressure in this critical game. But he was careful to correct a reporter who suggested Waugh had previously said South Africa were liable to 'choke'. Whatever the words, the meaning had been clear, and it was daring and provocative. Yet Waugh's previous comment demonstrated his willingness to put himself on the line and say what he thought, regardless of the repercussions. If Australia lost he would never be able to use the line again against South Africa, and he would look foolish if Australia 'choked'. Only Wasim Akram and Arjuna Ranatunga had as much gall among recent Test captains.

Hansie Cronje won the toss. The overcast skies influenced him to send Australia in. Waugh would have chosen to bat despite the cloud, so Australia would have been in first whichever way the coin had come down. It demonstrated a difference in attitude in terms of the confidence the two captains had in their batting line-ups. Waugh would back himself and his men and go for a score first most times, supporting the simple adage that it's better to have runs on the board and thus put the opposition under pressure.

Waugh's thinking was tested in the first over when his brother tried to avoid a lifter from Pollock and it feathered his glove on the way through to keeper Boucher. Ponting and Gilchrist restored order to a point before the latter was out caught, cutting over point for 20. Then Donald forced Lehmann (1) to play at a lifter that he nicked to slip. Australia was three for 58 and soon four for 68 when Ponting, who had looked in fine touch again, drove the first ball of Donald's spell straight to Kirsten at short cover and was out for 37.

Steve Waugh was in and while not in the touch of the previous game, he still seemed impregnable. He and Bevan fought back in a good partnership of 90. Waugh was not as in command as in his sensational 120 not out, as he sparred and lunged. The timing was not quite right, which was understandable. Very few players in history would be able to come up again, having played the innings of a lifetime. Yet he plugged on, talking to himself, urging more and admonishing the mis-strokes.

On 56, the score at which Gibbs dropped him the previous Sunday, he edged one behind off Pollock. The jubilant South Africans felt they had the game now. Moody came and went for a duck, lbw to the rampaging redhead Pollock. It was downhill from there and only Bevan (65 from 101 balls), aided by a brave cameo from Warne (18 from twenty-four balls), resisted as Australia crumbled to all out for 213.

It didn't seem enough considering the way the South African openers Gibbs and Kirsten, both in-form players, began. Waugh tried McGrath, Fleming, Reiffel and Moody to no avail. He was forced to bring Warne on earlier than planned—the hope being that three or four would be out and the spinner could come in for the kill. It wasn't to be. Warne had to try to break through. In just his second over he bowled a ball that drifted beautifully to the right-handed Gibbs on 30. His bat and pad followed it. The ball pitched well forward of the rough and Gibbs thought he had it covered. But it broke sharply and clipped the top of the off stump. This was vintage Warne. Waugh embraced him. There was no sign of the quitter now.

Cronje was beaten by the second delivery he faced from Warne as it curled past him and hit his foot or bat, or both. The ball was snaffled by Mark Waugh at slip. Everyone thought it was a catch, although the replays suggested he may have been not out. Cronje looked pained and his face compressed as umpire Shepherd ruled him out.

South Africa was three for 53. The game had swung—not Australia's way yet, but the fulcrum was now dead centre. Then Cullinan was run out. South Africa was four for 61 and, like the star bat that was wandering off the oval, in a mess.

Yet all was not lost. Warne continued to tie down and force errors and misses. But his overs crept on. After eight that conceded just twelve runs, Waugh took him off. He wanted something in his armoury for later. Australia now went into defensive mode as it was forced to use its weak link, Moody, the fifth bowler. For some reason, Waugh refused to use Bevan. Why? Perhaps he thought a few poor overs, as in the last game, would loosen Australia's hold. Whatever the reason, it allowed South Africa back into the contest. The fielders, performing much better than in previous matches, scraped, chased and prowled as Jonty Rhodes and Jacques Kallis fought to gain the ascendancy.

Rhodes clobbered Moody's military medium stuff for six over square leg. He was moving along well on 43 when he tried something similar against Reiffel. Bevan, feeling calm and confident after his fine innings, ran in and took the ball at knee height. He made a tough catch look easy. South Africa was five for 145. It was still in the box seat with barely a run a ball to get and just 68 short of the target with half the side intact.

Pollock began in fine style and was 19 in thirteen balls, mainly off Warne's last over. A single brought Kallis (53) on strike. He tried to emulate Pollock, misjudged a Warne dipper, and top-edged to Steve Waugh at short cover. South Africa was six for 175. But with Pollock and Klusener in, they looked home.

Warne finished with four for 29 off ten. Waugh's faith in him and Warne's innate drive and exceptional skills had won through. But the game was yet to be won.

Next over, Pollock (20) played on to a widish, yet good in-swinging yorker from Fleming. The Proteas were seven for 183. The clubbing Klusener was still at the wicket, and while he was alive South Africa was viable too. He produced a prodigious drive through midwicket for four and kept launching into everything. McGrath, obviously suffering from an injury (like Kallis, who had bowled and batted with a little restraint), came back and bowled Boucher (5). There were 24 to get off eighteen balls.

Reiffel missed a tough catch and conceded three runs in the missing. Then he made amends by brilliantly throwing out Elworthy. Dramatic events were coming every ball. Klusener slogged to Reiffel at long on. He jumped for the catch. Such was the force off Klusener's three-pound bat that the ball bounced off the fielder's hands and over the boundary for six. At a time when most fielders would be wishing that the ball didn't come to them, Reiffel was picked out three times in a few balls.

Klusener took a single and faced up for the last over—from Fleming. Waugh tossed the ball to the lean Victorian and said, 'This is what we play for.'

South Africa needed nine to win, eight to draw level. The batsman manufactured two terrific drives through the field on the off to the fence. The scores were level. Four balls could be bowled. Australia had to take a wicket, and thus tie the game, which would squeeze it through to the final on a superior run rate.

Klusener, on the other hand, had to score just one to get his team into the final and eliminate Australia. Waugh brought all fielders in, encircling the wicket. The batsman would have to go over the top. There would not be a quick single to be had. Fleming went around the wicket. He slogged at one well up, didn't connect properly and refused to take a single. Donald backed up too far and turned to see Lehmann run in and just miss the wicket with a throw from seven metres. Donald smiled at umpire Shepherd with relief.

Fleming charged in next ball and speared in a similar delivery. Again, Klusener couldn't strike it cleanly. The ball went down the wicket past the stumps. Mark Waugh collected it behind the stumps, flicked it at them and missed. At the same time, Klusener, who had yelled for the run, barged down the wicket and through. Donald, mindful of his near miss by backing up the ball before, rightly judged it a suicide run by his partner. But seeing him charging down the wicket, he had no choice. Donald panicked, dropped his bat and dashed towards the other end.

Fleming collected the ball from Mark Waugh mid-pitch after his follow through and underarmed it along the ground to keeper Gilchrist, who dislodged the bails.

Donald was hopelessly out of his ground and South Africa out of the competition. It was a tie. Australia had 'won'. The yellow shirts converged into a bulbous, dancing daffodil.

Everyone was stunned as poor Klusener and a shattered Donald trudged off, heads down. It would be cruel to say they had failed under pressure as Waugh had boldly predicted. It was just semantics. There were about five points of panic by each side, if anyone was counting.

Australia had fought hard and was lucky to win. South Africa was unlucky to lose. Damien Fleming brought back some perspective by joking, 'We've been doing a lot of ten-pin bowling in England. It was all worth it.'

Lance Klusener also remarked later that it was not a disaster. He couldn't recall anyone being killed on the pitch. This was so, but the South Africans, both players and public, took their performances very much to heart as they emerged into the world light again in the 1990s. There would be excuses forever. The reality was that since coming out of the wilderness South Africa had never beaten Australia in a Test or one-day series. Something in the psychology of the fierce competition between these two countries always favoured the Aussies. In the minds of the South African public they were the hated foe. But there were would be no gloating from the Aussie dressing room. Once in the confines of it, they burst into their theme song, adopted from Australian Rugby League: 'I get knocked down, but I get up again . . .'

How apt this was. There were no renditions of 'We are the Champions' here. Just a musical review of what more than a billion people had just witnessed. They had been down and out for the count, but had dragged themselves back into the fray each time.

In the after-match presentation, Waugh said, 'It was the great escape', and that he felt sorry for the South Africans. Later he amended his words, and said at the media conference, 'I *almost* felt sorry for the South Africans. It is a great shame somebody had to lose this game. They had been the number-one side in the world for a few years. But they can leave the World Cup with their heads held high. They gave 100 per cent and they could have had this game because we felt down and out four or five times. But to win a game like this no one can call us a disjointed or fragmented side . . .

'Warnie was the man. We desperately needed some wickets after they had made a good start and he came on and got them for us. He bowled a great spell.'

Warne sat next to his skipper at the media conference very much the loyal deputy. He was named Man of the Match. Waugh's faith in him and encouragement in the toughest moments on and off the field had been crucial to Australia's success.

'My eyes were spinning,' Warne said, 'and at one stage I had to calm myself down. I thought a tie was a fair result.'

And so the gallant South Africans were on their way home. Now the build-up to the big finale commenced.

Steve Waugh relaxed. He was a happy man, totally deserving of his success so far. He had been criticised by many. Scribes had been quick to find fault. He had made errors, but in his own way was as forceful and innovative as his predecessor Mark Taylor. Better still, he was learning and would adapt. His great strength, like Bradman and Ian Chappell before him, was a capacity to lead from the front.

As Geoff Marsh said, 'He is the man you want next to you in the trenches.'

If there were deficiencies in his strategic and tactical skills they were outweighed by the thought in the mind of every player that here was the toughest, best big-occasion batsman in the world today. Lara, Tendulkar and Steve's brother Mark had all failed under knockout pressure in this tournament. Steve, by contrast, had succeeded, with scores of 62, 120 not out and 56, and had played by far the finest innings of the tournament. He never stopped saving and winning for his side. He had now led them in six straight games without a defeat. At one point for Australia—the lowest—it faced having to win seven in a row to win the Cup. Waugh had never thought it impossible.

The team returned to London the next morning—18 June—as Pakistan had a solid net. Already scores of Pakistanis were trying to steal into the ground and hide out for the weekend so they would see the game on Sunday.

At 3 pm the pre-game competition began with a media conference at the Royal Garden Hotel in Kensington. Wasim faced about fifty media people first. One question was about the bribery affair. It was shut down by his manager, who claimed it wasn't relevant to the game. But it was. Any player in a winning team would be hard to punish after the High Court's finding, which was due to be made public. Public opinion wouldn't allow more than a slap on the wrist in a country with a history of corruption. All Pakistan would embrace them, but only if they were winners. If they lost, it would not be quite as palatable a situation for the guilty.

Wasim, like a schoolboy, told the predominantly Asian journalists that his team was the toughest. Australia didn't have a fifth bowler. Pakistan, he was certain, would win, because Australia had had two exhausting encounters.

Waugh came on after him at 4 pm and said, also like a schoolboy, that his team was the toughest. He discounted Wasim's remarks about a fifth bowler as pre-match propaganda and praised his bowling line-up. He felt Australia was more pumped than Pakistan because of the two close games. A journalist reminded Waugh that Australia had had that terrific fightback against the West Indies in the 1996 World Cup, only to go down against Sri Lanka. Waugh had an answer. He didn't blink when he said, 'We didn't realise the dew would be on the ground when we bowled second. This time we're better prepared. We've done our homework.'

You had to believe him. He seemed to have even done his homework on responding to every media question.

'The boys are pretty keen to win,' he said. Eight of them had played in the game lost to Sri Lanka in 1996 and they wanted to experience being the champions. It wasn't quite the same for Waugh. He'd been in the winning team in 1987.

Another reporter asked how the Australians were handling all the hype, including a message from the Prime Minister.

'And the Leader of the Opposition,' Labor Party supporter Waugh broke in before answering the question by affirming that the players appreciated the support. It was a long way from the cold, wet days of mid-May when the world had written off the Australians.

Both captains looked confident. But Waugh was the calmer, the more relaxed. Gone was the tension that had been etched into his expression for weeks.

The grand finale

Sunday, 20 June, was wet early and overcast. The game was delayed forty-five minutes.

Wasim got the first cheer for winning the toss. He decided to bat. Waugh, always the psychologist, said he was quite happy to bowl, and he meant it. There was much to be said for Australia being in the field again after its knife-edge performance and comeback from the dead against South Africa. It could pick up the same intensity quickly. On the other hand, Australia could, as Wasim suggested, be drained and flat.

Mark Waugh at slip soon showed what mode and mood Australia was in by taking a flying catch from Wasti (1) off Glenn McGrath. The bowler was getting plenty of lift from a fine batting pitch that might not have allowed any other in the tournament to extract as much.

After a few minutes play the sun was battling for ascendancy over the clouds and this didn't aid Fleming, who was getting too much swing. He bowled several wides, and was belted for two fours by Saeed Anwar in his second over. Yet he made up for everything with a prodigious in-swinger that bowled Saeed off an inside edge.

Saeed had made a century in his last outing and could lay claim to being the best opener in the world. He had been in fine form before his fall for just 15 off seventeen deliveries. Pakistan was two for 21 and in trouble.

Ijaz Ahmed and Abdur Razzaq steadied the ship. At 67, Razzaq was dropped by McGrath at long off. The drinks trolley came on. With two billion watching, McGrath wished the earth would swallow him. One run later, Razzaq drove Moody to Steve Waugh at mid-off and was out to another brilliant catch low to Waugh's right as he dived forward. The skipper was so agile that at first it appeared Ponting had taken the catch. It seemed that Waugh's hamstring and groin would last the tournament and the gruelling five months on the road after all.

Gilchrist ran out of his way to McGrath to tell him to forget his miss. It had only cost one run. It was a little thing, but showed the unity and concern that these well-bonded Aussies had for each other.

At three for 69, Steve Waugh turned to Shane Warne for a bowl. How different this was from the previous game. Then he came on when last rites were being contemplated for his country with South Africa none for 48. Now, at Lord's, the speedsters had opened up the Pakistani batting, giving Warne a chance to drive the knife right in.

At 77, Warne startled Ijaz first then bowled him with a fine leg break for 22. In came Moin Khan earlier than normal to keep the attack up to the Australians. Warne had him caught behind for 6, when he tried to defend a ball that jagged away from him. Pakistan was five for 91. A few Australian supporters in the Edrich Stand went to the hospitality tent to grab some free midday champagne. They missed Reiffel snaffling Inzamam (15), caught behind at 104. In truth they missed nothing. The big Pakistani was unlucky. Replays indicated his bat had slapped his pad and the ball had floated by. Umpire Shepherd could be forgiven. From front on it looked out. From behind it was in. Inzamam made one of the slowest exits from the historic arena in living memory, so retarded in fact that one or two members in the pavilion asked him to remove himself with alacrity. Poor Inzamam. He was crying as he dragged himself past more sympathetic members in the Long Room. The big, hard-hitting lad who had done most to beat Australia with 81 in the team's only other encounter in the Cup had been unlucky.

The two teams that Inzamam most liked to do well against were India and Australia. When asked why he said, 'Because India is India, and Australia are the toughest competitors in the world. A fifty against them is worth a hundred against anyone else.'

Warne then trapped Afridi, who was defeated in flight while attempting to sweep. His lbw left Pakistan on seven for 113 and in real trouble. Waugh brought back McGrath to finish off the innings. Next, Moody bent his near seven foot (205cm) frame low for a caught and bowled to remove Mahmood (8) making the score eight for 129. Mushtaq joined his skipper. Warne replaced Moody, and Akram hit him for six. Soon after he tried to repeat the shot. It only reached Steve Waugh at midwicket.

Pakistan was nine for 132 as Shoaib attempted to come out to bat. The nineteen-year-old was so nervous that he walked out the wrong door of the Long Room and stomped on seated members' toes in an effort to reach the players' gate. He need not have given himself the embarrassment. Ponting soon took a great one-hand catch at second slip off McGrath and Mushtaq was out for a duck. Pakistan was all out for 132, the lowest score in a World Cup final. No player had scored more than 22, except for the extravagant last man, extras, which added 25.

Warne's figures were four for 33 off nine overs. He had been confident enough to try bowling wrong 'uns, flippers and something that may even have been a new kind of delivery—one that deceived Ijaz Ahmed. The leggie had lifted and bowled magnificently, as had McGrath, who took two for 13 off nine. In his first spell off six overs, McGrath offered only three balls the batsmen could score off, and one of them was a long hop that Saeed smashed past point for four. He had produced excellent new ball bowling on an off-stump line that tied up the batsmen.

Every Australian player had contributed. The team had peaked at the perfect time. There had been a concern from some Australian supporters that the team might crumble facing a low total and the frightening speed of Shoaib Akhtar.

Before the Australian innings began, Wasim gathered his men in a circle in front of the members' stand. He gave them a 'cornered tiger' speech—similar to the one that inspired Pakistan's 1992 victory in the Cup in Melbourne. It would either see them claw their way back into the competition or leave them as pathetic pussies. The members doddered back to their seats in the hope of seeing a fightback. The impression in the Long Room was that most were pro-Pakistan.

Shoaib built up amazing pace and peaked at 152 km/h, so quick, one commentator observed, that he almost overtook himself walking back. But few people cared to watch the FedEx speed meter. They were too busy following the ball moving at even greater pace off the bat to the fence.

Gilchrist began with intent, smashing a fine, driving 54 off thirty-six deliveries, including an up-and-under six to third man, before being caught off Mushtaq's first ball. Australia was one for 75 in eleven overs—the fastest opening of the Cup. Shoaib was smashed out of the attack after four overs, in which he took none for 37. The youngster may have learned not to bellow before a big game again. He had told the world how he was going to destroy Australia, but his effort on a good wicket went flatter than the Gibson Desert. Wasim (one for 41 off eight overs) was also flayed with cool nonchalance.

Ponting put the game beyond doubt with a quick-fire 24. Mark Waugh hit 37 not out, giving him a tally of 375 for the Cup and the first Australian to pass 1000 runs in World Cup cricket. Lehmann, 13 not out, hit the winning four as Australia reached the target in just twenty overs (a rate of nearly 7 an over) with eight wickets to spare.

The match was all over at 4.30 pm after just 59.1 overs. The big crowd had been robbed of forty overs, mainly because of brilliant application by a mentally stronger combination. If Australia had been beaten, you couldn't imagine them going down without a terrific fight. Yet some had predicted Pakistan would be either magnificent or fall to pieces under pressure. The latter occurred. This had been the biggest win in World Cup history.

Against all odds Australia had been undefeated in its last seven games to take the World title. It could claim to have produced the best Test and now one-day side in the world at the end of the millennium. Steve Waugh was on top of the world in both forms of the game.

Wasim was at the opposite end of the spectrum. He was at pains after the match to acknowledge a superior side and to thank the fervent support both in England and in Pakistan for inspiring his side. Yet the next morning the papers had shots of fanatical, fickle supporters in Lahore burning photos of him.

Warne took the Man of the Match award, his second successive title in the two most important games of the tournament. His tally of twenty wickets (at 18.05) was equal to New Zealand's Geoff Allott as the World Cup's top wicket taker. He had come a long way in the last week of the Cup. Before it, he was so dispirited that retirement was on his mind. Now he was a hero, and feeling like one, once more.

Lance Klusener was given the Man of the Tournament award. He deserved it, but no more so than Steve Waugh.

When the Australians appeared on the main balcony for the ceremony, Ian Chappell was commentating. He was no doubt proud that the aggressive, positive cricket started by him nearly three decades ago was still paying huge dividends at the end of the century. Waugh had delivered with the bat: 398 runs at an average of 79.6 and had performed at his best when it counted. On top of this fine form, he had marshalled the troops superbly in the last three matches, again when it mattered. Yet if Waugh resented Chappell's previous criticisms it didn't show. Perhaps, like Bradman before him, Steve Waugh had learned to handle critics by giving great performances on the field. There could be no better response. Say nothing, do well and make fools of them, had been the Don's motto and Waugh seemed to have adopted it. It took another level of character to approach attacks on his performances and style this way.

At the post-match conference, Waugh searched for an answer to Australia's success. 'Mental toughness can be contagious,' he said. 'See someone in adversity winning a game from nowhere and all the other guys start thinking they can do the same.'

After much criticism, even abuse, the Australian selectors had proved correct in taking the hard road to success by choosing horses for courses for the Test and one-day sides. They could now take a bow. The squad was not infallible, but it was the best in the world, and that was all that mattered at the end of the World Cup tournament. Other nations would now consider this approach more seriously, given Australia's success. Dumping Mark Taylor and Ian Healy from the one-day squad late in 1997 had been the first step in the policy. Never again would even a great Test player be assured of a place in the one-day squad.

At 8.30 pm, four hours after the final had finished, light was fading fast at Lord's. No one was left except the Australians and a few patient officials. Ponting led the team onto the arena and to the wicket. He placed the cup in the middle of it and climbed onto Tom Moody's shoulders. He pulled a poem from his pocket, read it with feeling and then led the team in singing 'Under the Southern Cross I stand'.

They were so uplifted that they sang it twice more. Waugh was delighted to lead such a united squad, who he felt had won the Cup 'for each other'.

Geoff Marsh remarked that it didn't get any better than this.

Everyone, especially Steve Waugh, concurred. Waugh was entitled to bask in the satisfaction of collective achievement under his tight leadership. It was not perfect, he admitted, but as close as they had come. The ultimate question had been asked. Every player 'had put his hand up'.

Waugh's job was now secure for the time being. Given fitness and good form, how long would he hold it? Waugh had said that 1999 would probably be his last World Cup, which meant he was not counting on being captain or playing for Australia beyond 2002. Still, in the back of his mind, he must have been hoping that he would last that long, otherwise he would have been more definitive about not being there in 2003. It all depended on form and fitness. Waugh had carried groin and hamstring injuries for years and admitted during the tournament that he may not be able to bowl much any more. Yet you had the impression that Waugh would bowl himself if he felt right and the occasion demanded it. He would take it a Test series at a time and assess his progress.

13

MONSOONS AND MURALI

Meeting the Don

Early in August 1999, a rare quiet time for Australia's top cricketers, Steve Waugh found himself fulfilling a long-held dream to have an audience with one of his sporting heros, Sir Donald Bradman. Waugh flew to Adelaide and met the Don in the great cricketer's Kensington Park home of sixty-four years.

Waugh, like most top cricketers in the past seventy years, had been introduced before, but there had been no chance to chat. The Australian captain's desire for the rendezvous had been heightened when Bradman granted an audience to his favourite contemporary batsman, Sachin Tendulkar, and bowler, Shane Warne, on his ninetieth birthday in 1998. Waugh felt he had much to learn for his own edification.

Bradman's son, sixty-year-old John Bradman (until recently, Bradsen), stopped the meeting after just over an hour. Waugh would have preferred to have been part journalist–interrogator, part fellow-captain accepting intelligence, but was trapped for most of the time between these two conflicts of interest. The reporter in Waugh wanted to drag as much out of Bradman as possible without appearing to be the interrogator. But Bradman would not have appreciated this. Unless arranged through the Bradman Museum, he refused all interviews. So Waugh found himself treading warily and lacking the confidence to ask direct questions, as he would if researching for, say, future publication purposes.

At the end of the hour, Waugh told *The Australian*'s Mike Coward, 'I was just starting when it was time to go. It was great to talk to him; just be in his presence. There was so much more I would have liked to ask. But I didn't want him to think I was interrogating him. But I felt I just touched the tip of the iceberg and would love to have another meeting and to find out about so many people—Babe Ruth included.'

The iceberg metaphor was more suitable than Waugh intended. Bradman always guarded his privacy—and his thoughts—from media inquisition. He was cautious and could freeze out anyone—world sporting heroes and prime ministers included—who intruded. Bradman knew from decades of experience that his words could be misinterpreted or misconstrued. He also felt he had given enough to the media for more than seventy years. At the Waugh meeting he was nearly ninety-one. He wanted peace and privacy in his twilight time. He, more than any living Australian, had earned this. But the legend surrounding him prompted others to believe he somehow always owed something to the nation—an obligation to be 'available', like a national museum, open all hours. Often forgotten was the fact that Bradman had been most accessible via the mail. He once calculated he had replied to well over a million letters from all round the world over seven decades.

Waugh could only lament that Bradman had 'retired' from all public life. 'It would be wonderful if he was more accessible to players,' Waugh said. 'There is so much to learn from him. We talked about the players of his day and the pitch conditions and, of course, about captaincy. And he talked of his enjoyment of the one-day game and how he watches it on television.'

But when Waugh turned journalist, Bradman had clammed up.

'He was so humble he didn't give much away, really,' Waugh said, diplomatically.

Waugh demonstrated Australia's recent fixation with Tendulkar by asking Bradman if he had any tips on how to get him out. The Indian was due to tour Australia for a three-Test series—the Border–Gavaskar Trophy competition—late in 1999.

Bradman parried that one by saying he would need to see more of the Indian before making any judgments. (He had given broad hints on this by suggesting Tendulkar's bat was too heavy. If fast bowlers could get bounce and away swing outside off-stump the Indian might find himself edging the ball behind when trying to cut.) This was not much use to Waugh, given Tendulkar's imminent arrival. By the time Bradman had watched the Indian, the series would be over.

Waugh was on safer ground when discussing the game, its history, 'issues and personalities'. He was 'amazed' to learn that Bradman was never hit on the hands when batting, mainly because he missed hitting very little. He was, however, hit on the forearm by Larwood at The Oval in 1930 when Bradman dominated all bowlers, scoring 232, and again in the Fifth Test at Sydney in the infamous Bodyline series in 1932–33, when he made 71.

Waugh took pictures and asked for books to be signed. He gave Bradman a leather-bound copy of his photographic book, *Images of Waugh*. Bradman reciprocated by giving him an inscribed copy of *The Art of Cricket*.

Waugh was buoyed by the encounter, saying he would stay in touch. He was much the richer for the contact.

On the road again

Waugh's Australians arrived in Sri Lanka in mid-August refreshed from nearly two months break from cricket. The captain was talking up the need to focus the squad on international competition. Yet he seemed more relaxed than ever before in his illustrious, long career. And with good reason. He was captain of teams in both forms of the game. He had led Australia to a drawn series in the West Indies and then had captained the side to a World Cup victory. He, like most senior cricketers, regarded the Test arena as the superior competition, yet paradoxically his prestige for being the winning captain in the 1999 World Cup one-day competition was greater. If he had lost in the West Indies, he would have been criticised but forgiven. It was, after all, his first Test series as leader. If Australia had slid out of the World Cup without a whimper, Ian Chappell and others would have been vocal about Waugh's inability to lead. He might even have lost the one-day leadership to his deputy Shane Warne. His Test leadership would then have been in jeopardy.

For the time being, he could do little wrong. Commentators in Sri Lanka were praising him during the first two days of the triangular one-day series, India being the third team. Instead of the banal criticism he received in the West Indies he was receiving banal praise.

'The Australian batting was good, the bowling and fielding were good and Waugh [as captain] was good,' Jeff Thomson 'informed' cable television viewers after the second game against India at Galle.

Waugh was having the honeymoon he had been denied earlier, when critics such as Peter Roebuck in Fairfax papers and on the Internet had attacked him. Now the skipper's facial expression was not clouded or tight. He looked fitter and stronger, as if he had spent much of his two months break in a gymnasium. Yet if he appeared relaxed, he was not *relaxing* his efforts to keep Australia at number one in everything and improving all the time.

The one-day team was evolving under his leadership with 'phase two' being the attempt to consolidate at least two all-rounders in the team. (Phase one began in 1997–98 when the Test and one-day teams were split.) Queensland's Andrew Symonds, 24, a hard-hitting batsman who could bowl medium-pace and field brilliantly, joined Moody, who had been a fair contributor during the World Cup. Reiffel's retirement had given a chance to Symonds, an exceptional Birmingham-born athlete of part–West Indian descent. His parents moved to Australia when he was 18 months old. A few years previously, after two good seasons with Gloucestershire, he had been offered a place on tour with the England A squad—England's second XI. He had rejected the offer in favour of making the Australian team his aim. Symonds holds the world first-class six-hitting record, smashing twenty in a match for

Gloucestershire. Waugh and the selectors were hoping he would develop. The advantage of hard-hitting all-rounders became apparent with performances in the World Cup by South Africa's Klusener, Kallis and Pollock. If Symonds did perform well and Gillespie could stay fit, Australia would be a better one-day unit than at the Cup. There was also room for improvement with the openers, and with Lehmann and Ponting. If all these players could lift a notch in supporting the team's six one-day champions—Warne, Bevan, the Waughs, McGrath and Gilchrist—then Australian would maintain its number-one status.

McGrath had a minor leg injury, allowing Symonds to play in the first game of the AIWA Cup on a ground opposite a fort at Galle on 22 August. Waugh lost the toss and Australia was sent in. He would have batted in any case. On most occasions he preferred to set a score for the opposition, but he didn't care if Australia had to chase. By contrast, the Sri Lankans, without Ranatunga and with Dav Whatmore back as coach, liked to chase, being unsettled if they batted first. Waugh told his team members that he might send the Sri Lankans in one day, just to upset their rhythm.

Australia began well with a 60-run partnership in sixty-four balls before Perera had Mark Waugh caught for 28. Gilchrist then received the worst 'third umpire' decision yet to be given in international cricket. Ricky Ponting pushed to point. The batsmen hesitated before Gilchrist came through and was in by a metre before the wicket was broken. Keeper Romesh Kaluwitharana had dropped the ball before his gloves made contact with the wicket. On two counts, Gilchrist was in. But third umpire D.N. Pathirana pressed the red button. Gilchrist was on his way without dissent.

Steve Waugh failed when bowled by Sri Lankan captain Sanath Jayasuriya for 6, thus keeping the trend of slow beginnings in one-day series followed by a gradual crank up to the finals. Ponting (38), Lehmann (26) and Bevan (42 in forty-four balls) seemed in fair form considering the lay-off, while Symonds was unlucky to be run out for 8. Australia struggled in the rain-interrupted day to nine for 206 in forty-three overs.

Gillespie managed life from a dull track and won the game in half an hour by taking three wickets. Sri Lanka was four for 41 and never recovered. Gillespie's three for 26 earned him the Man of the Match award ahead of the unlucky Jayasuriya, who took an excellent five for 28.

Warne looked a little rusty, but not far off the pace in taking two for 31. He was assisted in the field when Lehmann took an outstanding running catch in the deep to dismiss Zoysa (4). This wicket gave Warne the record number of wickets for Australia in one-day cricket as he moved passed Craig McDermott (203).

The next day was a game against India, which batted first but was soon in trouble. Gillespie trapped Ganguly (10) lbw and Moody had Tendulkar caught by Lehmann. The champion bat looked scratchy, scoring 14 in just thirty-three balls. The euphoric Australians converged on Moody as if he had bowled a great ball. Instead, Tendulkar had misjudged a lofted pull off an ordinary delivery. India (seven for 151) never recovered and was hampered by more monsoonal rain, which limited the innings to thirty-eight overs. Warne bowled better, getting rid of the dangerous one-day champion Ajay Jadeja (30) when he was cornered into striking over the top and was caught by Fleming in the deep. Warne also bowled Prasad (4) with a flipper.

Waugh this time gave Symonds a chance with the ball ahead of Moody, and he moved one of his military-medium deliveries away from Rahul Dravid (5) just enough to gain an edge to the keeper. Sensing Symonds's confidence was up, Waugh allowed him to bat first wicket down after brother Mark (12) was caught behind. Symonds made a dashing 68 not out off sixty-eight balls. His partnership (134) with the in-form Gilchrist (68 from ninety-two balls) allowed Australia to win by eight wickets in just 29.1 overs.

Steve Waugh said after the game that Australia had begun this competition the way it had finished the World Cup. Given the ease of victory in both games, this was not propaganda. He had given both Moody and Symonds a chance to lay claims to the all-rounder's role, ensuring competition between them. Warne was keen to hit form early so that he would have the edge over MacGill for the spinner's spot in the Tests. Lehmann and Ponting needed to keep scoring runs. Their places were not secure. Gilchrist had something to prove after his ordinary World Cup. Fleming couldn't let his touch slip knowing that Dale was returning to form, at least judging from his efforts in the nets. The rivalry for places would be more helpful than hurtful to Australia's chances as long as the team kept united and interested. It was Waugh's job to maintain this. His quiet 'boosting' of each player through discussions about team and individual aims seemed to be working. There was little grumbling in the squad.

The tournament moved on to the Premadasa Stadium in Colombo. Waugh brought in McGrath, along with Dale and Martyn, in an attempt to give everyone in the squad at least one game. He liked to keep them inspired. Sri Lanka was confident, having beaten India in its previous game, but Australia's openers, Gilchrist (38) and Mark Waugh (84) looked like shutting them out of the game early with an 83-run partnership. Sri Lanka fought back and restricted Australia to nine for 241. Five different slow bowlers took nine Australian wickets.

Sharp fielding restricted Sri Lanka's batting. The bowling was not outstanding, although Dale and Damien Martyn were tight. After the Sri Lankans lost five for 87, Waugh shared the ball around, even giving himself a bowl.

Warne was expensive early, but came back to finish any thoughts of a Sri Lankan revival, having the adventurous twenty-year-old newcomer Chamara Silva (55) and Suresh Perera both stumped. Sri Lanka reached 214, giving Australia another comfortable win. Mark Waugh was named Man of the Match.

'We've just got to do better against this type of bowling,' Waugh said afterwards. 'We talked about it, but we played too many big shots again.' Then he added his usual psychological warfare statement. 'Both times against Sri Lanka we haven't batted that well, but expect an improved performance if we play against them in the final.'

Two days later, Australia went into the next game, against India, with what its captain hinted was its best line-up, leaving out the unlucky Fleming, Dale and Martyn. Symonds and Moody, both all-rounders, were selected, signalling Australia's intention to retain their wider skills in one-day cricket.

The out-of-sorts Tendulkar did not play because of a back injury and Jadeja captained in his stead. He won the toss and surprised by sending the Australians in. The openers put on forty, but Mark Waugh (18) seemed tired after his 84 in the hot playing conditions of the previous innings. Symonds (45) joined the rampaging Gilchrist (77) for a 110-run partnership that looked likely to push Australia's score to 270 plus, but India fought back to restrict the total to eight for 252.

Gillespie took two wickets in three balls in his third over, reducing India to five for 41. India was in a near-impossible situation. It recovered thanks to Sadogapan Ramesh (71) and Robin Singh (75) to reach 211—still 41 short. Gillespie returned his best one-day figures yet with four for 26 off 9.1 overs. Gilchrist was Man of the Match.

Australia had now gone through eleven games without a defeat— a record (allowing for the tie with South Africa in the '99 World Cup). Now the Aussies had made the final against Sri Lanka, which had sneaked ahead of India on run rate, despite a stunning 120 from Tendulkar in the previous game, which India had won. Sri Lanka had won only one of four games as opposed to Australia's clean sweep of the preliminary rounds.

Moody had an allergic reaction to medication on the morning of the final. Fleming took his place. Waugh won the toss and batted in his 273rd one-day international, equalling Allan Border's record. Gilchrist began with his usual flurry of fours but was out for 21 off sixteen balls. Muttiah Muralitharan spun a low off-break into the stumps of Mark Waugh (32). Muralitharan and Upul Chandana broke through the middle order. They extracted exceptional turn and made all batsmen cautious. Steve Waugh, right on cue, found form but was also bowled by a ball from Muralitharan, which was similar to the one that had dismissed his twin. It was a case of identical ball, different stroke. Waugh went to drive. The delivery went through between bat and pad. Steve's 43 from sixty-eight balls was top score, yet not enough. Australia reached 202 all out on the last ball of the allotted fifty overs. The captain's public concern about his team's handling of spin—a regular problem on the subcontinent—had been justified.

The dashing keeper, Romesh Kaluwitharana, opened and batted brilliantly, making 95 from 117 balls. Sri Lanka cruised to an eight-wicket victory in the AIWA Cup. It brought back unpalatable memories of the 1996 World Cup boil-over when Sri Lanka beat Australia in the final.

Only Gillespie (one for 37 off nine overs) and Fleming (one for 28 off seven) had bowled well. McGrath (none for 47 off seven) had had a shocker and Warne (none for 46 off eight) had had an off day as Australia capitulated, with a lot of snarls at the batsmen and little else. Man of the Series Adam Gilchrist said the team had to have one bad performance in such a successful run. This was fair comment and he could say that—he was going home. Captain Waugh, who was staying on for the three-Test series, put a different spin on events. He warned that Sri Lanka's one-day effort suggested they would be hard to beat in the Tests. Its spinners and rampant stroke makers would see to it.

Spin shocks

The loss, although in an insignificant series that Australia dominated, worried Waugh. He had wanted to win the three-Test series beginning on 9 September and get on a winning streak in Test cricket after the drawn series in the West Indies, which Australia should have won. Many critics felt Waugh's inexperience had contributed to the less-than-expected result in the Caribbean earlier in the year.

The tourists' XI for the game against the Sri Lankan Board XI was replete with competitive options. MacGill, Miller and Warne were pitted against each other, as were Blewett and Hayden for the opening spot next to Slater. Only two in each group would make it. Waugh and one of his fellow selectors, Marsh, would keep an open mind on the spinners, whereas the third selector, Warne, would not. He wanted his Test place back and would select himself.

The contest made Waugh's selection tasks easier. Miller shone in the Board's second innings, taking six for 57 in a fine display. He would take one of two spinners' positions. The 'two leg spinners' policy had been dumped. Only one would be selected, which made Miller a certainty on Sri Lankan wickets. Spin was likely to hold sway. Off- and leg-spin options gave Waugh more variety. Miller also provided another alternative—his medium-pacers would support McGrath and Gillespie. This gave Waugh five bowling alternatives rather than four. It left a MacGill versus Warne contest for the other position. MacGill was at a disadvantage. He had not bowled in first-class cricket since the West Indian Tests in March and April five months ago. He had to be content with net practice. Warne, on the other hand, had bowled in pressure one-day games in the West Indies in April and the World Cup in May and June. Then he had competed in the one-day AIWA Cup from 22 to 31 August. He was in fine form and acclimatised.

On all counts, Warne had the edge. He would be selected. MacGill's main hope to break back into the side now was if Warne were injured or if he bowled poorly. There was a slim chance that Waugh would choose to play all three spinners. But then who would miss out? Gillespie or McGrath, or one of the batsmen—Ponting or Blewett.

The batting in the Board game sorted itself out too. Blewett scored 23 and a terrific 148 to win the match for the tourists by four wickets, whereas Hayden only managed 24 and 11 not out. Thus the batting order for the Test was Slater (3 not out and 51 in the Board match); Blewett; Langer (4 and 52 in the Board match); Mark Waugh; Steve Waugh (42 and 21); Ponting (35 and 10); Healy (0 and 2); Warne (18 run out and 4 not out); Miller (15); Gillespie; and McGrath (1). Sri Lanka brought back Aravinda De Silva and Arjuna Ranatunga for the game to be played at the pollution-free, enchanting little city of Kandy, in view of the Knuckle mountain range, 2000 feet above sea level.

Steve Waugh played his psychological games with the opposition through the media by suggesting that if he won the toss he might bowl. The wicket looked conducive to speed. In the end he batted. He had not sat down to watch when the score was three for 9 and the skipper was in. It wasn't ideal. Then again, Waugh always thrived on this sort of backs-to-the-wall situation. He settled, although he lost his brother for 6, with the score at 16. After scoring 19 he was dismissed in a way that had troubled him a decade ago—slashing at a ball well up from the lean, left-arm opening bowler, Nuwan Zoysa and caught at first slip by Aravinda De Silva. The other left-arm speedster, Chaminda Vaas, was the early destroyer, with terrific inswingers that trapped Slater (0) lbw second ball and jagged away from Langer (7) for a slips catch. The score was five for 40. It was seven for 60 at lunch. This was without their great spinner Muralitharan warming up.

Ponting (96) and Gillespie (41) put on a century stand to drag Australia's score up to 188. Muralitharan took four of the last five wickets. He managed biting spin more like a leg spinner. His quicker balls, which caused some umpires to worry about their legitimacy, were difficult to keep out.

Waugh still had worries with his top order. Only he and Langer looked like solid characters, who sold their wickets dearly, similar to Border, Boon and Marsh in the preceding era of the late 1980s and early 1990s. The contemporary players—Slater, Blewett and Mark Waugh—had too many lapses in concentration, as did Lehmann. Ponting hovered somewhere in between the more permanent and the pretenders. His Test and one-day places were not secure, but he seemed to be maturing. His 96 in this game had been a good knock in a crisis. Ponting played the spinners better than before and showed restraint against the pacemen. He only lost his wicket when in with last man, McGrath, and approaching a century. He deserved those four extra runs.

Waugh casualty

Sri Lanka went to stumps on two for 69, Miller taking a wicket with the last ball of the day. He took another in the same over the next morning. Aravinda De Silva and Mahela Jayawardene then put on a big stand. In the middle of it Gillespie and Steve Waugh ran for a catch at deep backward square leg from different directions straight into each other. The crowd noise drowned out any calling. They collided. Gillespie's elbow hit Waugh's nose and smashed it. Waugh's hip collected Gillespie's lower leg and fractured his tibia. Sanath Jayasuriya organised a military helicopter to take the two casualties to a Colombo hospital. Gillespie was out of the tour and would miss three months. Waugh had a broken nose and was concussed. He was operated on at 5.30 pm on the day of the accident, which meant he was unlikely to be released inside seventy-two hours. By then the game could be over.

Warne took over as captain and brought himself on. Australia was a top bowler short and in trouble. Warne lifted. He broke the 107-run partnership when he had Jayawardene caught at midwicket, and later took the prize wicket off De Silva, caught off a top edge trying to sweep. Warne had satisfaction from also forcing left-hander Ranatunga (4) to cut against the spin and edge to Healy. Sri Lanka were all out for 234 with Warne taking five for 52, his first 'Michelle'—or 'five for'—since he had taken his 300th wicket against South Africa in Sydney in January 1998. It was a strong performance in keeping with his World Cup form, except that a Test was more demanding, and the Sri Lankans were fine players of spin. It had helped Australia fight back for the second time in the game.

Miller took four for 62, his best Test figures. Australia was 46 in arrears. They soon lost four for 49. Decisions against Langer (who hit the ball and was adjudged lbw) and Blewett (who didn't touch the ball and was given out caught) were woeful, and didn't help Australia's plight. It would be impossible for Steve Waugh to fly back that afternoon, which meant Australia was effectively six wickets down for three. With forty-five minutes or twelve overs until the end of day two, it was possible that Australia could be all out before stumps. Only Ponting, Healy, Warne, Miller and McGrath stood between Sri Lanka and victory in a little over two days. Muralitharan broke through to bowl Healy (3). Warne (7) was run out when Ponting called 'yes' then changed his mind. Miller had little idea how to play the off-spinner, when he should have had some clues. He was lucky to still be there at stumps with Ponting not out 22. Australia was six for 89; in reality eight for 43. Miller was soon out the next morning, but McGrath (10 not out from twenty-nine balls) stayed in a 41-run stand before Ponting (51) was caught off a fall toss from Chandana. Australia's lead was 94.

Warne led a spirited effort in the field. At one point Sri Lanka was three for 39. Soon after, Jayawardene was smartly caught and bowled by Miller at full stretch to his left. Local umpire Peter Samuel said not out, indicating it had been a 'bump ball'. Warne spoke quietly to Samuel at the bowler's end and suggested the umpire call for a video. By this time television coverage was showing that it had not been a bump ball. The batsman should have been out. Samuel, perhaps fearful he would be shown up for his umpiring howler, refused to change his decision. Warne calmed the disconsolate Miller and urged the players to put the incident behind them. At 60, Miller (who ended with three for 48 from thirteen overs in a row) had Jayawardene caught for 9, but it was no consolation, not in a tight contest where every run and every wicket was vital. Veteran Ranatunga joined De Silva and was dropped by McGrath at mid-off. Moments later the left-hander should have been given out lbw when he shouldered arms to Warne (none for 18 off 6.5 overs). Umpire Venkat ruled not out and with this decision went any real hope of a win for Australia. Sri Lanka ran out victors by six wickets—its first win ever against Australia in eleven starts.

The tourists had to regroup in time for the Second Test at Galle beginning on 22 September. Steve Waugh was advised by doctors not to play, but he was determined to lead Australia in the Second Test. It was a critical moment. If he let Warne take over and his deputy did a further good job, then the leadership issue could emerge again. This made it likely that Waugh would play even though he had suffered a compound nose fracture and would take more time to recover. Gillespie would be replaced by Scott Muller on tour.

Form worries

In the days after the First Test Geoff Marsh expressed his concern about the poor batting performances of Australia's top seven over the past twenty innings. Steve Waugh had scored 954, at an average of 63.6. This put him in the company of, if not above, his two main world rivals, Tendulkar and Lara, at least in statistical terms. But after the skipper the figures were ordinary. Slater, Langer and Ponting were all on about 38. Mark Waugh was averaging 35, Blewett 19.25 and Healy 17.8. Mark Waugh was the big disappointment. After running closer to Steve in the years 1993 to 1998, the younger twin was falling behind.

Slater and Steve Waugh had scored eight of thirteen centuries among those players. More than half Slater's 764 runs had come in four of his twenty innings. He was brilliant but not consistent. Blewett, a prolific scorer in first-class matches other than Tests, didn't seem to be able to make the step up. Langer, who always looked solid and in control early in an innings, was still being removed for low scores more often than not.

Healy, at thirty-five years, presented the biggest worry for Marsh and his co-selectors. His highest score in the past fourteen innings had been a paltry 16 runs. If this kept up in the next two Tests on the current tour he could lose his place to Gilchrist in the 1999–2000 summer.

The game against a President's XI at Colombo gave Simon Katich and Scott Muller a chance to impress selectors. They both did well. Muller took five for 64 and two for 24, while Katich scored 40 run out and 36 not out. Encouraging signs for Australia were a century by Slater and 43 by Mark Waugh. It was an improvement on Mark's string of ducks in Sri Lanka seven years earlier.

Steve was happy with his fitness, despite admitting to concussion for a week after the collision with Gillespie. He said he woke up feeling like journalists do every day. Waugh believed he had to play, considering Australia's recent brittle batting and the threat from Warne as his replacement, but his decision was a risk. He would have trouble breathing through his damaged nose when he had to push himself on the field. Yet Waugh had the mental strength to look beyond the risks. He judged that success and maintaining his leadership was worth it.

Waugh defended brother Mark when questioned about his form, saying that the first four ducks in Sri Lanka were 'years ago', which was true (1992). But Mark still needed to lift his rating.

Waugh expected the Galle wicket to be hard and fast. It might provide a chance for some form from his top order to come through. He blamed the lack of form on one-day cricket. 'I think all around the world Test cricketers have lost the knack of how to play five days,' Waugh said. 'Players have forgotten a Test match is five days and you can battle it out for a session without scoring a lot of runs. That element of the game has been lost in the last couple of years and that's what we'll be trying to get back in our batting. Tough Test-match batting.'

This was a calculated utterance. Waugh had three batsmen who tended to be dashers rather than defenders: Slater, Blewett and Mark Waugh. Langer, Steve Waugh and Ponting were more likely to mix defence with attack. Of the rest, Healy and Warne were dashers.

Sri Lanka won the toss, batted and reached a satisfactory six for 254 at stumps. Waugh, disregarding headaches and breathing problems with his reconstructed nose, marshalled his troops well. He fielded mainly at gully, without a helmet or nose guard. It may have been foolhardy, but it sent a strong signal to the opposition.

Warne bowled superbly, taking three for 29. His first victim was Marvan Atapattu caught behind. He first tied down Jayawardene and his old foe, Ranatunga, then had them caught trying to drive over the top. On day two McGrath and Fleming polished off the tail at 296. Fleming spoiled his performance by leaning close to Chaminda Vaas after dismissing him. The bowler first verballed his victim then made contact with his shoulder. It was yobbish behaviour and out of character: Fleming was a mild individual. Australian plans to intimidate the opposition had caused him to overreact. Fleming just wasn't a natural bad guy like McGrath or Merv Hughes. He was asked to see the match referee after stumps.

The Australians began well with a 138 opening stand between Blewett (62) and Slater (an excellent 96). Then Muralitharan struck, taking five wickets to reduce the Australians to five for 188. Muralitharan used his top spinner—or straight-on ball—to advantage, as no batsman seemed able to pick it. Steve Waugh remained 2 not out and Ponting 0 not out.

Ponting was out the next morning, while Waugh hung on. But wickets continued to fall. When last man McGrath came to the wicket, Waugh, on 19, lashed out and was caught. Australia had reached 228—68 behind. Monsoonal rain ruined the last three days, with Sri Lanka left on none for 55 in its second innings.

At the official end of the match, Waugh said the positives to come out of the game were the performances of Slater, Blewett and Warne, with McGrath showing patches of form. He defended his batsmen but conceded that batting failures and a loss in the Third Test at Colombo could put pressure on some careers. He didn't name them, but Langer, Mark Waugh and Blewett would be under scrutiny.

The Australians' main concern was Muttiah Muralitharan. He had taken twelve wickets in three innings in the first two Tests. Waugh addressed the problem in a media conference, as ever speaking his mind. 'It takes about half an hour to get used to him,' he said. '. . . He's hard to pick.'

Waugh's method of picking the off spinner's variations—especially his dangerous drifting straight ball—was to watch the seam. The straight one appeard to spin through the air running across the pitch. The batsman saw all leather.

Monsoonal rains in Colombo held up play for an hour on the first day of the Third Test but Waugh decided to bat in the sauna-like conditions. Blewett (70) and Slater (59) delivered their second successive century (126) opening stand. Mark Waugh received a terrible decision when a ball from Muralitharan missed his bat by about fifteen centimetres, hit his pad and flew to Ranatunga. Mark wished that local umpire K.T. Francis, in his last Test, had retired a game earlier.

Steve replaced his brother, as he had done more often than not, at three for 182. Langer (32) was again caught in slips, beaten by Muralitharan's sharp spin. Steve Waugh (10 not out) and Ponting (11 not out) took the score to four for 203 at stumps. There was little play on day two. Umpire Willey gave Waugh (14) out caught behind off spinner Rangana Herath. The replays showed that he had not touched the ball. Now both the Waugh brothers had been dismissed cheaply because of wrong decisions. It was time for replays to be used by the third umpire to adjudicate such decisions—for catches at least. It was absurd that millions of viewers around the world could see the action that umpires were not allowed to view in aiding their decision making.

Ponting saved the umpires from opprobrium by scoring 90 not out as Australia recovered to seven for 318. Ponting had developed on tour. He had always played speed well enough; now he was adept at handling spin. Ponting went on to 105 not out in Australia's total of 342, reached on day three. Rain again held up proceedings. On day four, Australia had Sri Lanka at four for 61, with Fleming taking three, but the weather intervened once more. Day five was washed out, leaving the game a soggy draw.

Sri Lanka won the series one–nil. Muralitharan was the difference. He had taken fifteen wickets at 23.27 in four innings. But his figures should be put in perspective. He had bowled 166.2 overs, three times as many as Warne, who was in good form, taking eight wickets at 14.38, more than 100 more overs than Vaas (ten wickets at 14.3), and Miller (eight wickets at 21.5). The stand-out batsmen were De Silva, who scored 192 at 96, and Ponting, whose aggregate was 253 with an average of 84.33. Blewett's 146 at 36.5, and the fact that he had had two good opening stands with Slater, secured him a place at the top of the order for the beginning of the Australian summer.

Waugh was yet to win a Test series as skipper. Pressure was now on him and his squad to lift their performances against Zimbabwe before the long hot summer of nine Tests.

Second chances in Zimbabwe

Steve Waugh led the way in warm, dry Bulawayo against a Zimbabwe President's XI by smashing 161 off 146 balls in a three-day game at the Queen's Sports Club Ground ending 11 October. This innings helped set up the tourists for a 244-run win. It was Waugh's fifty-fourth first-class hundred. He figured in a 254-run partnership with brother Mark, who also returned to form, scoring 116 (his seventy-second century) after 63 in the first innings. Justin Langer at last hit his straps too, scoring 148 runs in the first innings. McGrath, who had lost his rhythm in Sri Lanka with all the stop–starts, found it under cloudless Zimbabwean skies, taking five for 36 and two for 37. Fleming was as reliable as ever, taking three for 41 and three for 16, while Warne maintained his recovered touch with one for 51 and three for 50.

It was a near-perfect preparation after a tiring 37-hour flight to Zimbabwe that should have taken eight hours as the crow flies. The team's collective spirit was lifted. They carried that feeling into the Test at Harare and rolled Zimbabwe for 194. McGrath and Warne each took three wickets. Australia's response on day two was poor, losing both openers for 8. Langer and Mark Waugh steadied the side with some solid enterprise until Langer (44) ran himself out going for a second run to the speedy Henry Olonga at deep fine leg. He had been batting well and needed a big score to restore confidence.

Steve came to the wicket at 96. He wasn't in great form but, as ever, would not surrender easily. Meanwhile Mark Waugh treated the small crowd to a more controlled effort until he reached 90. Then he gave a lazy caught and bowled to Grant Flower, thus depriving himself of his seventeenth Test hundred. Steve ploughed on, giving a chance in his thirties and another on the third morning at 94. He made Zimbabwe pay for dropping him twice by moving to his twentieth Test hundred with a typical crunching square cut for 4. Waugh became the seventeenth player to reach twenty Test hundreds and this milestone gave him a sweet sense of satisfaction. His career so far had been a tale of two halves. From 1985 to 1992 he hit only three Test hundreds and averaged just 36.1 in forty-six Tests. From 1993 to 1999 in seventy-three Tests he had hit seventeen centuries at more than 60.

It was testament to his refined technique and high regard for the not out innings. Some still regarded this as selfish. But his approach often ensured Waugh batted from the fall of the third wicket to the end of an innings. His performances were for the good of the team. If selfishness meant not surrendering his wicket, then his country was benefiting in proportion to the boost in his average. It was approaching double what it was in his more cavalier days.

In this innings against Zimbabwe, Waugh improved and batted at his best in his third fifty. He let Fleming have his head and the tailender smashed 65, his second-highest score in Tests. Waugh entered his beloved 'zone' of high-score concentration. He sat back even when his batting pupil McGrath (13) was in and remained 151 not out in Australia's 422. It was his thirty-seventh not out.

Zimbabwe battled to one for 80 off forty-four overs by stumps on day three, despite lots of appealing by Warne, who petulantly bowled a bouncer in response to a series of rejections. Murray Goodwin (91) and Trevor Gripper took the score to 154 the next morning before Miller, bowling well, trapped Gripper lbw for 60. Zimbabwe lost its last eight wickets for 32 to be all out 232, Goodwin being last out after a fine fight. McGrath (three for 46) took the big early wickets, Miller (three for 66) broke up the middle and Warne (three for 68) took three for none in thirteen balls to wrap up the tail.

Australia polished off the five runs required, giving it a ten-wicket win in the inaugural Southern Cross Trophy match between the two nations.

Waugh took some satisfaction away from the game, knowing that the Test tour had brought a win, a loss and two draws. As ever, there was little time for reflection as the modified squad prepared for three one-dayers against Zimbabwe.

Australia accounted for Zimbabwe three–nil in the three one-dayers. In both the Bulawayo and the first Harare matches, the stars were Mark Waugh (106 in ninety-six balls and 54 not out in ninety-five balls) and Damien Fleming (three for 33 and three for 14). These two tourists were rested for the third game at Harare. Ponting (67, 31 not out and 87 not out) continued his good form, while Martyn (57 from 38 balls) made the most of his only batting chance in the first game. Bevan's 77 not out in the third game helped keep his one-day average just under 60.

Neil Johnson (110) in the first game and Andy Flower (99 not out) in the last did best for the home team, which was out-classed. Zimbabwe had some way to go to challenge the leading one-day sides.

Waugh felt more confortable going home with three more wins. Since the World Cup Australia had lost just one one-dayer in eight.

14

MILLENNIUM SUMMER PART ONE: PAKISTAN

No rest from the wicket

Steve Waugh was left as the second-oldest player in the Test squad behind Colin Miller with the retirement of Ian Healy. The keeper had called it a day after continued poor batting over three series, in which he could not lift his average into double figures. He went out after 119 Tests and 395 dismissals. Many thought Healy had been the finest keeper of the twentieth century: he had sustained a higher quality behind the stumps for a longer period than any other keeper. Adam Gilchrist was a readymade replacement. The 28-year-old Western Australian had played seventy-one one-day internationals and he could bat. He had every right to expect to achieve a better average than Healy's more than useful 27 plus. The new man would add spine to the batting at number seven, in the tradition Healy had created during his career, in which he had notched up four Test centuries. Healy had been attacking and a fighter with cool nerves. The same description could well apply to Gilchrist.

The other new man for the First Test against Pakistan at the Gabba was Scott Muller, who replaced Colin Miller.

Steve Waugh indulged in some mind games in the usual talk-up of the series. First Pakistan publicised Shoaib Akhtar and his speed. There were expectations that he would reach 160 km/h. Waugh noted that this would merely mean the ball would speed to the fence more quickly.

The Australian skipper yet again came in for more criticism about his leadership, especially from *The Age* newspaper's Peter MacFarline, who compared him unfavourably to Mark Taylor. Waugh hit back about that sort of 'crap', as he called it, and noted that MacFarline had not been seen at the cricket since 1990. (Waugh couldn't have known that MacFarline had a crippling illness that didn't allow him to go anywhere.)

Waugh noted that Taylor's reputation was growing the longer he was retired. And new captains were always compared to their predecessors. 'Taylor was compared to Border and Border to the skipper before him,' Waugh added. Apart from their abilities as leaders, they differed in style and demeanour. Border was laconic and could be grumpy. Taylor was amiable and diplomatic. Waugh was punchy and undiplomatic. He had also added a touch of audacity with his psychological warfare of comments off the field that sometimes bordered on folly. No skipper in the history of Australian cricket had been this confrontational in attempts to unsettle the opposition.

As the First Test approached, Steve Waugh was preoccupied with the imminent birth of his second child. He agreed with his wife Lynette that he would miss the birth if it occurred during the Gabba Test beginning 5 November. He surprised by winning the toss and sending Pakistan in. At the end of day one, the tourists were at a respectable six for 280. Only wickets to Fleming (four for 65) late in the day saved Waugh from embarrassment.

Big Inzamam (88) and Yousuf Youhana (95) caused the main problem. The next day Moin Khan (61 run out) led the Pakistanis on to all out 367.

The Australian openers Blewett and Slater weathered the early attack of Shoaib and Wasim and then capitalised, taking the score to none for 233 at stumps. Slater (134 not out) cracked his thirteenth

Test hundred in style, bringing up his 100 in 150 balls. He was equally adept against pace and the wily spin of Mushtaq Ahmed, as was Blewett (77 not out), who was content to play second fiddle.

On day three, they took the score on to 269 before Umpire Nicholls, who was having a bad Test, gave Blewett out lbw to Mushtaq. The ball was a top spinner going straight on and hit Blewett six inches outside off stump. The batsman's crime was to shoulder arms.

A succession of wickets then fell. Slater (169), Langer (1), Steve Waugh (1) and Ponting (his first Test duck) were removed, reducing Australia to five for 342 soon after lunch. This tested the new depth of the Australian order, with Gilchrist joining Mark Waugh. They combined for a century-plus stand, with first Waugh (100—his seventeenth Test hundred—from 148 balls), then Gilchrist (81 in just eighty-eight balls) dominating. It was judged as Waugh's most fluent innings, which was a high accolade—he was the smoothest functioning batsman in the game.

Gilchrist stole the afternoon with 5 fours in one six-ball over from Mushtaq. The Test debutant demonstrated his intention of slaughtering the opposition. His controlled, 'killer' approach would add punch to Australia's middle order. It took a 146.2 km/h round-the-wicket yorker from Shoaib to bowl him.

Australia reached nine for 499, giving it a lead of 132 before the rain arrived and delayed play. Warne then delivered his best and most ferocious Test innings, smashing 86 off ninety balls, which included 4 sixes in two overs off Mushtaq. The last-wicket stand between Warne and Muller realised 86 and took the Australian team to 575 and a lead of 208.

Twice the home team had been cut back by the tourists, but had recovered both times, demonstrating it had the qualities of the long-reigning West Indies team of the seventies, eighties and nineties. It more often than not could find something extra to stave off defeat or turn a potential loss into a victory. Australia's strike rate was more than 4 an over, showing that Test cricket could be exciting.

Pakistan's Saeed Anwar took advantage of a dropped slips catch by Mark Waugh, who was suffering from a virus. Warne also appeared to catch him at slip, but came up with the ball unsure whether he had taken it cleanly. When he indicated this to the third umpire, Saeed was given not out.

Saeed went on to his ninth Test hundred in fine style, unleashing a wide array of strokes. He was 118 not out at stumps and his team was four for 223—just 15 ahead. Typical Brisbane storms stopped play just after tea, but as usual the ground was ready for play the next morning.

The break and the night had given Waugh time to rethink his tactics with his key bowlers. John Buchanan came to the fore with video and statistical analysis, which showed where Anwar was plundering the bowlers. The plan was to cut off the Pakistani's run supply. He was to be restricted until he was forced into error. It worked. A lucky break gave Warne a wicket first ball when Abdur Razzaq hit a full-toss to Ponting at silly point. Then McGrath came round the wicket to left-hander Saeed and tied him up. This approach cramped the batsman and it took him several overs to score one run before the paceman had him caught behind. Two runs later, Warne looped one down the leg side passed Azhar Mahmood, who had advanced down the wicket. Gilchrist, having a good Test, effected the stumping. The new glove-man was finding it a challenging experience to keep to Warne, especially when balls were whizzed down outside the right-hander's leg stump, which blocked the view of the ball.

A little slather and whack from captain Wasim (28) held off the Australians until Fleming came back to wrap up the tail with three wickets, giving him five for 59 for the innings and nine wickets for the match.

Pakistan made 281—a lead of just 73. Blewett (40 not out) and Slater (32 not out) knocked off the runs to give Australia a crushing ten-wicket win. Yet it was only on day five that the locals took control. It had been a quality Test and was Waugh's fourth win as skipper from nine starts. But for his own failure with the bat, he couldn't have hoped for a better commencement to a long, demanding summer. He had four wins and three defeats as skipper, and it was a relief to be on the positive side of the ledger.

After the game, Waugh spoke about maintaining the high standard set in the Test. He acknowledged the role of Buchanan, who had had only two days to acquaint himself with the team. Buchanan had been appointed at the start of the 1999–2000 season to replace the retired Geoff Marsh. Waugh had opted for Buchanan because he represented a futuristic, dynamic approach to coaching. The new appointee took computer analysis into the twenty-first century and was adding a new dimension to being an assistant to the captain. The coach would stretch the boundaries of what was expected from players. For instance, he would ask them to work on the skills with the wrong hand. Left-handers would bat and bowl right-handed and vice versa. Fielders would be asked to attempt becoming proficient at picking up with the non-preferred hand. Buchanan would search for and implement any activity that would improve an individual or the team. He had made his presence felt at Brisbane.

'He gave us a little bit of extra focus', Waugh said, 'that maybe we didn't have in the past. He was very good for the side.'

Each morning, John Buchanan would assist Waugh in assessing the day before and where the team, and each individual, should head and what they should achieve that day. Buchanan had been Queensland's coach. He had improved that team's confidence and consistency, which had helped them to take the Shield. 'Buck' or 'Pluto', as he was nick-named, liked to analyse the opposition form, strengths and weaknesses in detail. Some players—such as Mark Waugh, Greg Blewett and Damien Fleming—in the national squad would be hard to convince about the need for 'homework'. Others, such as Steve Waugh, Warne, Gilchrist, McGrath and Langer, thrived on it.

Ian Healy, another who liked to profile opponents, admired Buch-anan and thought he had been a big plus for Queensland and that he would do a fine job with the national team. 'The power of positive doing,' the former keeper said, 'rather than the power of positive think-ing is his motto.'

Waugh took advantage of the early finish to the game and caught a flight to Sydney for 'the best delivery of all'. Lynette was in labour with their second child.

Baby Austin arrived between Tests and Waugh was able to relax before the Second Test, beginning on 18 November at Hobart. He could rest easy in the knowledge that his son, who would surely be known as 'Aussie', was a spectator when the game began. But would it be a Test to remember?

Waugh had former champion opening bat and member of Bradman's 1948 Invincibles, Bill Brown, address the players at a dinner before the game. The team was relaxed with Brown, who had presented Gilchrist and Muller with their baggy green caps before the Brisbane Test. Having him speak was an inspirational, bonding move—a link with the finest winning traditions of the past. Brown was his usual dry, amusing, self-deprecating self. But the speech had an underlying theme—the current team was there to achieve great things and make its own history.

Waugh was not limiting these addresses to former cricketers. Anyone who could inspire the team, such as the much-respected tennis champion Pat Rafter, would be invited. The skipper was capable of lifting the side himself, but he called on people from outside the squad, the era and even the sport. There would be times as captain when it would be nigh impossible to be inspirational, such as in a miniform slump as he was experiencing in the current series. And was it wise to be asking for more from players when you were going well and they were not? Waugh thought it better to have others, who were dispassionate, to deliver the words that might steel individuals for a lift.

At the start of the Second Test Waugh again sent the opposition in—this time on a dampish pitch, which in theory would give his bowlers an advantage on day one. McGrath took the opportunity and twice broke through. Mohammad Wasim (91) held up the advance by some adventurous batting, belting Warne for three lofted fours in one over and out of the attack before he could find a rhythm. Australia's fielding was typified by fine low catches to Mark Waugh and Gilchrist. This, plus steady bowling from McGrath, Warne in later spells, Fleming (three wickets each) and Muller, who was nervous in his early games, wrapped up Pakistan for 222.

Slater and Blewett weathered the blitz from the Pakistan attack of

Wasim, Shoaib and Waqar, who formed the best trio of speed men in world cricket. Australia was none for 29 at stumps and Slater and Blewett went on the next morning to a partnership of 76. Slater and Langer, on his last chance if you thought newspaper reporters were the country's selectors, took the score to 191 before Langer (59) was dismissed by Saqlain in a poor bat–pad decision. Slater, who had performed well and was in good touch against pace and spin, top-edged a full toss from Saqlain and was caught for 97, his seventh time out in the nineties.

Steve Waugh was in at three for 206, but soon lost Mark Waugh (5), who was trapped by a swinging Waqar yorker. The skipper had to look on as Saqlain (six for 46) ran through the Australians, his freakish off breaks studded with balls that came straight on and others that broke the other way, similar to a leg break.

Waugh was forced to go for runs when his batting pupil, McGrath, was in at eight for 246. He slashed at Akram and was caught by Ijaz for 24. Australia was all out for 246, having lost its last nine wickets for 55. It was a feeble capitulation. Pakistan's application had turned the game on its head. One moment the media and spectators were predicting an easy Australian victory, the next, Pakistan had taken control of the game.

The visitors didn't let go when they batted a second time, reaching one for 61 at the end of day two, giving them the lead by 37.

On day three, Pakistan consolidated until Warne trapped Saqlain, the nightwatchman, with the score at 100. At 121, with Saeed looking dangerous again, Warne delivered one of his greatest-ever deliveries to any left-hander. He ripped it hard from around the wicket into the rough well outside the off stump and some way short of the batsman. It spun so far and fast that it uprooted the leg stump, sending it cartwheeling. Ijaz (82) and Inzamam (116 not out) then restored Pakistan's ascendancy with a 137-run link, and this led to a stumps score of seven for 351.

On day four, Australia needed quick wickets. Warne obliged, forcing a cut from Inzamam, who was brilliantly caught one-handed by Mark Waugh at slip. Gilchrist soon afterwards ripped off a glove and threw out Waqar for a duck. Wasim held up Australia at the end of the innings and took the score to 392, giving the tourists a lead of 368.

Australia began well in the second innings, until Slater (27) cut Shoaib to second slip. With the score at 81, Blewett cut at Azhar Mahmood and seemed to be caught behind. Umpire Parker couldn't make a decision. He referred to Umpire Peter Willey, who put his finger up. Then Mark Waugh was lbw first ball. Australia went to tea at three for 98, with Steve Waugh batting with the redoubtable Langer.

Fightback of the century

Australia needed 271 with possibly four sessions left and seven wickets in hand. The odds were with Pakistan. Steve Waugh (28) was well caught and bowled by Saqlain. Then Ponting went for his third duck in succession. Before the series, Waugh had anointed him as the batsman to lead the next generation of Australian cricketers. He would overcome this hiccup. But for now he had helped put his country in a messy situation at five for 126.

Langer spoke to the incoming Gilchrist. 'You never know,' he said. 'We could still win this.'

They were still there at stumps with the score at five for 188.

On the morning of the fifth day, Gilchrist chatted to Bill Brown at breakfast. 'You should go on and make a century today,' Brown told him. It lifted Gilchrist. Brown had said it with expectation. The mere fact that the likeable legend would say this without ifs, buts or maybes, planted the seed in the new man's mind that he would indeed do it. He began thinking of how he would behave when he reached three figures, and even how he would handle the media conference afterwards. Such self-belief was worthy of success in itself.

Thus prepared, Gilchrist and his fellow left-handed Western Australian continued on their complementary partnership. Langer showed the grit for which he is respected and held up one end. Gilchrist, a one-day champion, was allowed, by Langer's sterling effort, to bat as if he was still in the short version of the game. He cut loose with hooks, drives and cuts. They ran well between the wickets. Langer may have been lucky to survive a catch off Wasim. Umpire Parker gave it not out—he simply didn't hear the nick, if there was one. Nor did Langer or Gilchrist. Wasim carried on a treat and Pakistani heads went down, demonstrating the problem of having a fast bowler as skipper. Wasim had bowled his heart out and lost his cool for several minutes in the crisis. Was Parker's decision a square-off for Langer's demise in the first innings? Most likely not. Parker was too professional.

A malaise overtook the tourists. Mistakes in the field were frequent as Gilchrist launched into all the bowlers. Saqlain, acting like a silly schoolboy, zigzagged in at mid-off as Shoaib ran in to bowl, which was not within the rules. A player could only move forward in a straight line to the batsman. The fielder was in Gilchrist's line of vision. He backed away. It happened again. Perhaps the spinner was reacting to the pasting he was receiving, but he was frustrated bowling to two astute left-handers, and being overused. His famed off spinner's wrong 'un was dangerous to right-handers, but innocuous to left-handers as it drifted into or past pads. They swept with impunity.

Saqlain's theatrics brought sharp rebuke from umpires and the batsmen. It didn't help the Pakistanis in such a delicate situation. They wanted wickets, not clowning or poor sportsmanship. When he came on again, Saqlain had lost his composure. He delivered one ball from well behind the stumps. The batsman hit him. At lunch Australia was 90 short. After the break, Langer stepped up and out-scored Gilchrist. They took the bowling apart.

Gilchrist played the innings of his life. He began defensively, if you call 50 in seventy-two balls cautious, but his second fifty took just thirty-eight balls. His century took 110 balls. His 149 not out came from 163 balls. It was a better knock than Botham's magnificent fight-back innings (also 149 not out) in the Third Test of the 1981 Ashes. Gilchrist's innings was chanceless. His stroke execution was cleaner and more controlled.

Langer was out five runs short of victory for 127. The sensational partnership had realised 238 runs. It was also Langer's fourth century and best knock, given the pressure and match situation. Langer won Man of the Match for his all-round performance of 59 and 127. He had more than justified his captain's faith in him. Waugh, who had had a lean match, could take some of the credit for expressing that belief in Langer publicly.

After the game, Langer said that only one thing counted. His skipper had complete faith in him. Steve Waugh had given Langer the confidence he needed by telling him and then the media before the game that he was the best number three in the country.

'Langer and Gilchrist's 238 was the best partnership I've seen in Test match cricket,' Waugh said, 'given the pressure and the state of the game.'

It could be considered the best effort of all the run chases in history, considering the standard of bowling they had to face. Shoaib was bowling at more than 151 km/h. He was also dangerous, with his short ball and swinging yorker. Next to Alan Davidson, Wasim was the best left-arm paceman in fifty years. He bowled superbly early and never let up the pressure. Waqar was always difficult with his reverse swing. Azhar was a strong back-up and bowled better than his more lauded teammates. Saqlain had taken six for 46 in the first innings and everyone had expected him to be a threat again. Yet the Australian counterattack rattled this brilliant line-up.

Australia's six for 369 win was the third-highest fourth innings in a run chase for victory in the history of Test cricket. Only Bradman's Invincibles, with three for 404 in 1948, and India in 1975–76 with four for 406 versus the West Indies, made more.

The win gave Australia the series two–nil. The Second Test had been a titanic contest between two well-matched squads. Waugh's confidence was high after his strong management of a team that had come back from the dead. It made a mockery of Australia's incapacity to chase low scores in the fourth innings in Tests and demonstrated how much the game was played in the head. 'It was the type of fourth innings chase we had wanted for some time,' he said.

Waugh seemed to be enjoying the captaincy. This series win was a huge relief. After a shaky two all start in the West Indies, a loss in

Sri Lanka and a one-off win in Zimbabwe, he had had the break-through he wished for. His win–loss–draw ratio of five wins, three losses and two draws was more than respectable. Waugh had brought his own style and sense of history to the top job. He had had four of Bradman's Invincibles at the Hobart Test. There was also the touch of the players wearing their baggy greens at media conferences. Off the field they looked like schoolboys, but the point was being made. There was a terrific pride in the honour of representing the nation; they were an unshakeable unit; they were never beaten. Waugh had introduced an extra element of resolve that had some influence over the way the team had put on its Lazarus act in the Second Test. It would never be known as the Invincibles, but a dimension of invin-cibility was being injected into the line-up, in much the same way it had with Bradman's team in 1948, and the long-reigning West Indies of the 1980s.

Waugh's choice of Buchanan as coach was wise. If the skipper ever tended to be slow in reacting to a change in a game, it was Buchanan's job to suggest tactical changes as exemplified when Australia pinned down Anwar in Brisbane. The coach had all the data and evidence at his fingertips for redirection of tactics. Before games too, he was assist-ing Waugh in strategies for Tests. Each player had a clearly defined role—a rough blueprint before a game—which would be modified as the game progressed. Much less was being left to whim or chance than with previous regimes. Would this limit Waugh's personal flair? Prob-ably not. He still had the option to pull a change in the field, the batting order or with his bowlers based on instinct. And Waugh has stated he was learning to trust his own instinct more. The combination of precision planning and the occasional flash of flair would be the hallmark of his captaincy.

It had surfaced in Hobart in November 1999. Perhaps one day young 'Aussie' Waugh would watch a replay of the game that followed his birth and be inspired by his father's development as captain of Australia. Steve had now led his team to three wins on the trot. He was hungry for more.

Burying the dead-rubber blues

The chance for four in a row presented itself in Perth in the Third Test, beginning just four days later on 26 November. Another good effort by the Australians would prepare it well for the challenge by India to follow. The selectors showed they were merciless in their striving for the best combination by dropping Muller and Miller. They were replaced by Kasprowicz and Brett Lee. Waugh announced who was in the side—Kasprowicz—early rather than subject the players to nervous nights and the in-form Kasprowicz could prepare himself mentally. Lee, as Waugh noted, could look and learn from the experienced speedmen—McGrath, Fleming and Kasprowicz.

The captain showed compassion for Scott Muller, who had been dumped after two Tests in which he had taken seven wickets. The media claimed that a member of the Australian team—if not Shane Warne, then someone else—had said of Muller: 'Can't bowl and can't throw,' during the Hobart Test. Channel Nine was forced to deny that their effects microphones had picked up the comment from a player. The gratuitous words had come not from a player but a cameraman, first known only as 'Joe' and then, when the issue blew up, 'Joe Previtera'. (Even a spectator received publicity when he owned up to the same remark, made to his son. This revelation only clouded things.) Waugh pointed out that Muller had taken 'important' wickets, made a telling contribution with the bat and had held an athletic catch.

Wasim won the toss for the first time and decided to bat. Australia would bowl first for the third successive time in the series. The bouncy Perth wicket suited McGrath (three wickets), Kasprowicz (four) and Fleming (three). All three managed plenty of outswing and the Pakistanis batted as if still dispirited by the Hobart demoralisation, making 155.

Yet for a flash, in Test terms, in the first ninety minutes of Australia's innings, this mercurial squad showed what it could do. They removed four for 54, including the struggling Steve Waugh, who couldn't quite control a lifting, midriff-high ball from Mohammad

Akram. It was popped to Yousuf Youhana at short leg for an easy catch. It was the sort of nothing dismissal that would always irritate a champion like Waugh, who would play a thousand tougher deliveries with ease. Yet batsmen often managed to get out to ordinary balls when their form was one good innings from their best.

Still, if Waugh was going to have a rotten trot, it was the right time to do it. Others in the team, such as Langer, were in touch. He and Ponting, who had scored three successive ducks, combined for a partnership of restoration. At stumps Australia was four for 171, a lead of 16 runs. Langer was 63 not out; Ponting 62 not out.

Day two saw these two go on and on. Langer was again the anchor as his more flamboyant partner flayed the attack and made up for his failure to score in the series so far. Their partnership of 327 was almost the difference between the two teams. Australia was dismissed for 451, a lead of 296. Langer was tired when he top-edged a hook from Shoaib and was caught for 144. Ponting was caught not long afterwards. He drove to reach his double century but was caught at point for 197.

The Langer–Ponting partnership was the highest ever between the two countries, surpassing the Langer–Mark Taylor link of 279 in Peshawar in 1998, when Taylor made his famous 334 not out. Langer's knock began four days after his mighty performance with Gilchrist at Hobart. His week had been a big one, a reward for persistence. Langer's career had begun in 1993 and this was his fifth century.

Mohammad Akram (five for 138) was the best of the Pakistani bowlers.

Pakistan fought back in its second innings but without much purpose, except perhaps to make Australia bat again. The batsmen flayed at the bowling and there was no application or planning in their method. They failed by twenty runs, with Ijaz making a brilliant 115, and Wasim 52. It was Ijaz's sixth century against Australia and his twelfth overall. Yet dazzling as he was, there was no one likely to provide the anchor that would allow the side to push for a lead of 100 or so and perhaps embarrass the home team.

McGrath took four for 49 and seven for the match, his best effort for the series, in which he took fourteen at 28.07. Fleming took eighteen wickets at 22.28 and was the stand-out bowler, ably supported by Warne, twelve wickets at 30.83. Ponting took Man of the Match. Langer, with consecutive centuries, was Man of the Series with 331 runs at 82.75. Two other batsmen—Gilchrist with 264 at 88.00 and Slater 325 at 81.25—made up the trio with averages in the eighties, which was an unusually high return. No Pakistani averaged 50 against Australia's sometimes brilliant, yet nearly always steady, bowling. Only Saqlain returned wickets in the double figures, with ten at 25.10.

Waugh could be well pleased with the final innings win and three-nil result, giving him six wins as skipper with three losses and two draws, and lifting him to a better than fifty per cent ratio in his first eleven Tests at the helm. He was also buoyed by the four-in-a-row winning streak. He would use this as a platform for more victories against India.

Waugh's own form—just 58 runs at 14.50—would play on his mind. He did not wish to fall into the rut that dogged Mark Taylor, who only maintained his place in the team for several seasons because Australia kept winning.

15

MILLENNIUM SUMMER
PART TWO: INDIA

Tendulkar's greater Test

Waugh was thankful for the two extra days to prepare for the biggest challenge so far in his captaincy against Sachin Tendulkar and his Indian team. The Third Test against Pakistan finished on 28 November, giving the Australians twelve days to clarify their strategy and tactics. Last time these two teams had met for a Test series in early 1998—nearly two years earlier—Taylor's Australians were underprepared. They had not seen many of the Indians play whereas the Indians had done their homework, having watched the Tests and one-dayers Australia played against South Africa in Australia in 1997–98. They had the knowledge needed to take charge in the First Test and win the series, which they did. Even in the trial game against Bombay (Mumbai) the Indians had looked well set. Tendulkar got his initial double century in first-class cricket and then dominated the Test series. Taylor and his squad had limitations. Warne's painful shoulder was hanging by a thread. He was long overdue for surgery. McGrath was absent, injured.

This time, in the millennium Tests, Warne was back to somewhere near his best and itching for the contest. McGrath, after an indifferent series against Pakistan, ended at Perth close to his most lethal. They would be Waugh's main weapons in tandem against Tendulkar and Rahul Dravid, who was not far out of his skipper's batting class. The two of them had belted a world-record one-day stand of 331 (Tendulkar 186 from 151 balls and Dravid 153) against New Zealand in Hyderabad just before their Australian tour. They were in form. Tendulkar secured his first double century in Tests versus New Zealand. It had taken the master batsman seventy-one Tests to make it. But it was a bit like murder. Once a killer had the taste, he was often keen to do it all again. And murdering bowlers had been Tendulkar's way of life since he first played a competitive game for his school in the mid-1980s. Despite being low key in his media utterances, nothing would give him greater satisfaction than belting the strong Australian attack for his second and even a third double century in the series. His form in Australia was good. He had hit a stylish 80 in the preliminary game against Queensland, which the tourists lost by ten wickets. He and Dravid were expected to be well supported by the talented Saurav Ganguly and Vangipurappu Laxman.

Waugh, Buchanan and the Australian bowlers would be searching for the knock-out punch for Tendulkar. He was India's miniature Goliath. The Indian team had a tendency to fold if he were dismissed cheaply in either form of the game. Should Tendulkar come in early, he would be the target for McGrath and the under-rated Fleming, who was at the peak of his considerable powers, with line, length, swing and guile. If that failed, or if Tendulkar emerged from the pavilion at three for plenty, he could run straight into a Warne–McGrath combination. McGrath had dismissed him cheaply in their only Test encounter—in India in 1996—and again in the '99 World Cup. The paceman had just won the balance of their battles in one-day cricket. On the other hand, Tendulkar had won most of his encounters with Warne. Yet they were unfair contests. In their first Test encounters, way back in 1992, Warne was a tyro leggie, who was belted by the teenage champion en route to two centuries in Australia. Six years later in India, Warne had been at a genuine disadvantage with his shoulder injury. Tendulkar again smashed two centuries and Warne once more took a deal of 'stick'.

This time round in Australia, the champion spinner would have no excuse. The wickets would give them an even playing field, with Warne being able to turn the ball late in some games. Tendulkar would be able to play his shots, particularly his drives, on all wickets. His record in nine Tests against Australia was 824 runs at 58.86 with a highest score of 177. Very few batsmen in history had a similar record.

India's bowlers, too, were not to be undervalued. The tourists rested their three best bowlers, Javagal Srinath, Venkatesh Prasad and Anil Kumble for the one-day series versus New Zealand. They also had a sensible lead-up of three weeks before the First Test in Adelaide, which would begin on 10 December 1999.

Waugh began the psychological warfare early by reminding the media of India's poor record away from home. He added that he believed 'that they're a bit more hard-nosed than they were in the past touring Australia. If we relax and get too carried away about how we played against Pakistan we'll certainly get into trouble against India.'

Waugh was distracted by the ongoing 'can't throw, can't bowl' saga, which the media was mainly running with. The ABC, which would have loved to expose a Channel Nine conspiracy to protect Warne, said that the ABC's effects microphone didn't pick up the remark, thus vindicating Warne's claim that he did not say it.

Waugh tried to do the normal family things during his break such as fixing the roof, picking up Rosalie after school and changing his son's nappies, but the media queries were relentless. His pre-match conferences in Adelaide reflected his feelings. He suggested the media should focus on the achievements of Australia as the top cricketing nation, and not be sidetracked into trivial issues such as alleged sledging. He claimed that there was less sledging in the last Pakistan Test than he could recall in recent seasons. But Ponting's 'chatting' of Indian batsmen after an umpiring decision had gone against Australia hadn't seemed trivial. It was an unnecessary outburst.

It was clear that Buchanan and the skipper had again set goals for every player selected (the Australian team remained unchanged).

Whenever a player was interviewed, he would talk about his 'aims', without specifics. But Waugh's targets leaked out. He wanted to reach 8000 runs in Tests and score a century. The latter would make him the only player in history to score a Test century against each of the eight other Test-playing nations. Ironically, it was his brother Mark who had failed to do this when he scored 90 against Zimbabwe three months earlier. Now it was Steve's chance. He had only missed out against India. His average in Tests against India was 33.

The game plan centred on the three Ps—patience, pressure and partnerships—which were impressed upon the Australians. They had paid off against Pakistan, especially with three fine partnerships of 200 or more, but the alliteration referred also to bowlers working in tandem to dismiss opposing batsmen.

The Indians, for their part, seemed to be trying to emulate the Australians' aggressive, sledging ways. In lead-up games they upset umpires and batsmen alike. It was out of character.

Waugh won the toss and batted on the true Adelaide wicket in the First Test in the Border–Gavaskar Trophy series. He was in at three for 45 when Blewett (4), Langer (11, from a poor lbw decision when he struck the ball into his pad from well outside the line of off stump), and Slater (28) were removed. He soon lost brother Mark (5)—a score that would see another round of media baying for his dumping. Ponting joined Waugh and they took the score to four for 76 at lunch.

Venkatesh Prasad had done the damage in the first session, but for some reason Tendulkar ignored him straight after lunch and opened with Ganguly in support of Srinath. This helped Ponting and Waugh get on top. They both moved easily on the good pitch to their fifties. Waugh said he 'sort of went along for the ride' provided by the dashing Ponting, who was batting with the same flair as his previous knock of 197 versus Pakistan. Waugh was more circumspect, happy to have a first fiddle of such character. Anil Kumble, bowling his fast leg breaks, didn't turn the ball much on the true wicket. While economical, he was not penetrating.

Waugh's batting, as ever in Tests, was an understatement. He was methodically working within his self-imposed parameters, concerned with building a score. He had been Tendulkar-conscious before the game, seeking advice from anyone with a cricket brain on how to reduce this champion. It was an obsession that at times seemed Jardine-like in its proportion. Yet Waugh refused to attempt to match him with, say, an innings similar to the one he produced in the World Cup against South Africa, when he belted 120 not out off 110 balls. He could have tried it, but odds were in a Test he would be removed for a bright 40. Instead, Waugh was out to show the Indians and a billion of their supporters that he hadn't stayed on top of world batting for the better part of seven years for nothing. His average (just over 50) was 6 runs below Tendulkar's. They had arrived at them by different routes. In effectiveness for their respective teams, they were about equal. Now in this innings, Waugh—en route to 100 and beyond—was attempting to dictate terms to Tendulkar. He had done this with Lara in the Third Test in the West Indies earlier in the year when he rose to the occasion and scored a magnificent 199. But the West Indian had outdone him with a last innings 153 not out that had won the game—by a solitary wicket. Waugh's innings had been technically better. But Lara's, while flawed, created victory. Waugh was now, in this innings, working towards another big score and throwing down the gauntlet to Tendulkar.

Waugh was lucky not to be run out at 67, and Ponting was dropped at slip on 90. But they were all the chances as first Ponting, then Waugh reached a century in the last session. Waugh now had the first of his personal goals to be achieved in this game—a century against every other of the eight Test sides. It was his twenty-first Test century, and it drew him level with Tendulkar, who had managed his in fifty-one fewer Tests. Waugh had scored twenty more fifties, including nine nineties, which indicated a distinct difference between the two. Tendulkar had converted half his fifties to centuries, compared to Waugh, who had a conversion rate of a third.

Soon after reaching his century, Waugh began cramping in the lower leg. Ponting urged him on, but then suffered from his skipper's lack of long-innings fitness. Waugh drove deep into the offside. There was a fumble. Ponting came back for two after a mix-up of verbal signals, but his captain was not prepared to run, even though the mis-field justified a second for younger, fitter legs. Ponting was run out for 125. He was to remark generously after the game that perhaps 'you should never run on a mis-field'. Their partnership of 239—the fourth 200 plus of the summer—was a record-breaking link, surpassing a Bradman–Morris link for the fifth wicket of 223 (unbroken) against India in 1947–48.

Waugh went to 117 not out and Australia was five for 298. The skipper's score placed him neatly on 8000 runs in Test cricket. His full stats at that moment read 194 innings, thirty-seven not outs, twenty-one centuries, 41 fifties and an average of 50.95. He now had 891 runs in 1999 at 55.68.

The innings gave Waugh relief. He needed a score and he set his considerable mind-force for a big one. He was concerned by his fitness. Despite hot baths, rub-downs and tablets to combat his condition, he had just a 'couple of hours' sleep because of the pain. Another hot bath the next morning, Waugh joked, didn't help. But his capacity to laugh at his own plight was instructive. He could handle the pain. He was in charge of himself and his game. He would go on to acquire more runs on day two.

Once more another batsman stole the show. After Gilchrist hit back a caught and bowled first ball of the morning, Warne came in and blasted his way to 86 in a hundred balls, losing Steve Waugh caught at 150. Waugh's performance had been a silent challenge to his Indian counterpart, with whom he appeared not to make any contact at all on the field during his entire innings. Australia reached 441—an expected score on the Adelaide wicket.

Blewett, who had failed with the bat, almost justified his position with a sensational throw from the deep to run out Indian opener Ramesh. Soon afterwards, McGrath troubled Gandhi with a sharp lifter at his throat. He fended off an easy catch to square leg. Later McGrath had Laxman (41) caught, leaving India three for 90. In came Tendulkar to a big reception. There was significance in his emergence at Adelaide—it was Bradman's home. And the Indian held an audience like no other when he came to the wicket. Many fans wanted to see him hit a hundred. But the Australian team was alerted and electrified by another motivation. It wanted him out before he did damage for perhaps the entire series. Everyone was brought to the brink. Expectations ran high.

This was the moment the Australian public had waited nearly eight years for. The home team had its game plan with this player, who had been anointed by Don Bradman as his modern incarnation: bowl tight and put as much pressure on him as possible and be patient in doing it.

Waugh stood at midwicket, his face granite. He was all concentration. He produced very little 'verbal', leaving that to his chirpy vice-captain and the ever-encouraging keeper Gilchrist. The only time Steve spoke was to deliver a tactic or some broader strategy between overs. In this respect he was a contrast to Tendulkar in the field, who was all chat and less tactical.

The Australian captain prepared to use his two big guns, McGrath and Warne, in tandem. McGrath was accurate at one end, bowling in the well-known corridor just outside off stump, up enough to entice a stroke, short enough to induce bounce. At the other end, Warne was in at him six times inside two minutes, thus multiplying the pressure. There would be no let-up from a second speedster but, instead, Warne, the crisis manager, doing his job.

Waugh's plan worked. Tendulkar looked uncertain. His toes didn't twinkle as they can. His mind had seized up and with it, his feet. He was inhibited, as if in awe of the task ahead. He hardly dared to attack. Dravid seemed less tense, but there was a running mix-up engendered by this aggressive strategy. Apart from the odd scoring shot, Warne and McGrath bottled up the Indians, who went defensive. In the end it undid Dravid, who edged Warne to Langer at short leg. India was four for 107. Left-hander Ganguly joined Tendulkar. The slow trend continued, with them both 12 not out at stumps. The score was four for 123.

McGrath took one for 1 in his last eight overs. Warne's one for 43 didn't reflect his superb effort. Waugh's keys had performed at their peak. It took the calibre of Tendulkar to remain at the crease. He faced sixty-nine balls for his dozen, an atypical return for the world champion. Both the Australians troubled him, but to the joy of 500 million Indians, many of whom would switch on their radios at about six o'clock (Australia was five hours ahead) the next morning, their hero was 'alive'.

Cloud cover on the morning of day two caused Waugh to open with McGrath and Fleming, rather than Warne. It didn't work. Tendulkar and Ganguly were in a different frame of mind facing the speedsters, who were not on line and kept drifting into the batsmen's pads, allowing runs on the leg side. Tendulkar was the star everyone expected. He also became chatty. Last night he had not uttered a word to his partner. Today he was full of encouragement up the wicket. Waugh was forced to bring back Warne. The spinner added another dimension. This was the most challenged he had been since the World Cup, and perhaps in his career. For the first time in approaching a decade he felt that the contest between himself, the greatest leg spinner of all, and the Indians, the best players of spinners in contemporary cricket, was even.

He began the morning with intensity. Any loose ball—about one every second over—was clouted. At the other end, McGrath, not at his peak, was taken off and replaced by Fleming. He speared in at Tendulkar's pads, the wrong line once more. After a maiden from Kasprowicz, Tendulkar emerged magically as the master. He crashed the first three balls of Kasprowicz's second over for four. Sixteen came off the over. Warne, at slip, was Kasprowicz's most vocal supporter. The spinner had suffered like this. He knew how tough it was.

Both batsmen sailed to fifty. Tendulkar looked set, the only chink in his armour being a touch of uncertainty against Warne. He decided to stay at home and stretch for him from the crease. He was in a defensive mode only against spin. He was working on the theory that he could turn over the strike, wear Warne down, see him off and then demolish the others. Waugh was onto this. He kept Warne on, sensing the spinner was his best hope. It was instinct and experience, which was all the skipper was left with. Kasprowicz had to be replaced after two overs went for 24. That left Waugh with diminishing options. The new ball wasn't far away. Did he bring back McGrath or Fleming, or should he try Blewett?

Fleming got the nod. Warne stayed on, placing the ball on a perfect length. He seemed to err by bowling round the wicket to the left-hander, which kept the ball coming helpfully in to the batsman. Yet still, Warne was bowling a good wrong 'un. Ganguly had trouble picking it.

Warne began delivering more to Tendulkar and the spinner was getting four or five balls in at him. Would a mistake come?

The Indian stretched to push one round the corner for a single, something he had been doing all innings to get off strike. The ball spun more and rebounded off his pad to Langer at short leg for a sharp catch. Did he hit it? It was one of those dismissals made questionable by replays. Were there three noises (bat, bat scraping on ground and pad) or two (bat scraping on ground and pad)? The slow-motion, front-on view gave the impression that the ball came off the pad only.

Whatever the facts, Tendulkar (61) was out at a critical moment. India was five for 215. Warne could employ his favourite tactic of 'swarming' the new batsman.

After lunch, Ganguly ran at Warne before he had let go of the ball. The bowler saw him coming and dropped his shoulder a fraction, changing his delivery from a leg break to a wrong 'un. It skidded low past Ganguly's swatting attempt to defend. Gilchrist took it brilliantly and stumped him. Ganguly walked. Warne had now removed India's three best bats—Dravid, Tendulkar and Ganguly, among the top half-dozen players of spin in the world. Warne's long wait for revenge against India—or at least a record to be satisfied with—was now more than a possibility.

Taking these three would rank in his mind as a most satisfying big performance. He had taken Tendulkar, Azharuddin and Dravid in the Test at Chennai in 1998, but the effort had been swamped by defeat for Australia and the knowledge that his shoulder was spent. He bowled then on memory and guts.

The Adelaide crowd was reacting to vintage Warne. The only factor stopping him causing a rout was fatigue. He had bowled almost all the morning and was now well into the post-lunch session. Waugh, following his instinct further, kept him on. Warne delivered one of his specials. Mannaua Prasad, a right-hander, received several wrong 'uns that spun away to leg. He probed or let them go. Then Warne, over the wicket, let go a ripping leg break, 10 km/h faster. It still swerved, hit near the rough, bit and spun behind the batsman, taking his leg stump. The Australians embraced. Prasad, bemused in a way reminiscent of Mike Gatting in 1993, could not believe he had been bowled. He looked around at the umpires, not accepting that the ball could bite that sharply from that far out. The umpire's nod confirmed he had been bowled. Warne ranked it in his best dozen deliveries.

Waugh kept his faith in the flagging spinner and let him have the new ball. But after a couple of overs he had had enough. His shoulder had stood the test. It was perfect. His pride had been restored. It was now salved in Tests against India—at least for the moment. There was still a maximum of five innings in which to bowl against these well-drilled combatants of spin.

Fleming removed the tail and India was all out for 285—156 short. Warne was the pick of the bowlers, with four for 92 off forty-two overs with twelve maidens. McGrath took two for 49. He and Warne had now taken more than 500 wickets bowling in the same side, often in tandem, making them one of the best wicket-taking combinations in cricket history. Fleming, the consistent one, took three for 70.

Australia went to stumps two for 71. Blewett (88) dropped anchor into the fourth day as Australia plodded and pushed to a lead approaching 400.

A quickfire 43 (off forty-six balls) from Gilchrist, who had an excellent game behind the stumps, took the score to eight for 239. It was enough for Waugh, who declared. It left India 396 to win. A score of fewer than 400, with about 116 overs in which to get them, on paper would have appeared a fair 'sale' to the Indians. They needed 3.4 runs an over. If their talented line-up got going that would be possible. The Indian dressing room was atwitter with possibilities. They were going for a win.

McGrath changed the equation in a flash. He bowled a sensational opening over to the hapless opener Gandhi and snared him caught behind. Fleming then bowled Laxman, getting under his big back-swing. Waugh followed instinct again. Even though he had his two opening bowlers taking wickets, he brought on Warne after a few overs, replacing Fleming.

The spinner removed Dravid, who tried to avoid playing one that spun and jumped. It deflected off his gloves to the keeper. India was three for 24. Three runs later, Tendulkar ducked a short ball from McGrath. It didn't get up. The ball collected his forearm below the level of the stumps. Umpire Parker gave him out. Side-on replays suggest it was a brave and accurate decision. The ball's trajectory had levelled and was dropping. It would have hit the top of the stumps two ball widths below the bails. Tendulkar, unlucky in the first innings, was out in a most unusual way in the second—for a duck in two senses. It demonstrated that even someone with his great skills could err, particularly when first at the wicket.

Warne then trapped Ramesh (28) lbw not playing a shot. The next morning Fleming was on a hat trick, but his good Victorian mate Warne missed a hot head-high chance. Warne was devastated, but Fleming and McGrath consoled him. Once again the players showed their unity. India was all out for 110, giving Australia a win by 285 runs. Fleming was the pick of the bowlers, taking five for 30, giving him eight for 100 for the game.

Warne had taken two for 21 off ten overs with six maidens—six for 113 for the match. He now had 349 wickets. Six would equal Lillee's 355 record for Australia; seven would break it.

Waugh had now led his team to five successive Test wins, ranking him with Bill Woodfull (twice), Don Bradman and Lindsay Hassett. Bob Simpson (two Tests) and Lawry (three) made up five wins in 1967 and 1968. Only the 'Big Ship' Warwick Armstrong with eight Tests wins in a row had a better record for Australia.

The media asked Waugh about brother Mark's form. He answered shrewdly, asking why a team with five successive wins should change. The skipper would not be able to influence the selectors, but he would put a case for his twin's retention. Mark, he said, was a 'proven match winner'. No one could argue with that.

The only flaw in Waugh's post-match remarks was his comment about India 'carrying scars into the next Test' because of the impact of the Adelaide loss. The captain was building a unique reputation for using his tongue in pre- and post-match psychological warfare. It was all part of Australia's 'in-your-face' style on, and now off, the field. But it sounded gratuitous compared to the quiet dignity of Sachin Tendulkar. He remarked that the umpiring decisions that went against him in Adelaide were history. He would leave the future to the 'Almighty'. He spoke of 'his job' in four innings to come. There was no menace in his voice, but a professional and calm outlook. Some in the Indian squad would try to meet fire with fire, which would be against Indian style and flamboyance. But Tendulkar would move on in his own way. His demeanour was reminiscent of Bradman in a tight spot. The Don always spoke of 'putting things behind him' and not dwelling on the past. Not even bodyline could stop him. He had marched forward to bigger and better performances. One sensed the pressure on Tendulkar was similar to that which Bradman had experienced. An 'enemy' nation feared him like no other. Its representatives plotted against him with unmatched intensity. The fact that these two got on so well with a deep mutual respect and liking after one short meeting was no coincidence.

Waugh as Midas

Steve Waugh had pushed for the inclusion of Brett Lee in the twelve for Melbourne, saying that he 'would have to come into calculations' considering his form in the New South Wales state game against Western Australia played before the Test. The skipper would deny he had lobbied for Lee. He didn't wish to be seen exceeding his brief as skipper. Officially he had no say in selection when the team was playing at home. (Abroad, it was different. The skipper could choose whom he wished from within the squad and even call for a replacement from home.) Unofficially he could privately ask the chairman of selectors, Trevor Hohns, for a particular player, but it would cause friction if he were seen to be lobbying publicly. In this case there was no doubting his strong preference, however he put his nomination.

Other Australian players, such as Gilchrist and Slater, mentioned Lee's lethal speed. Words such as 'scary' and 'frightening' daubed the airwaves. Waugh happened to mention he didn't care to face Lee in the nets. It was cunning pressure on the Indians, who were already feeling under siege from the opposition, Waugh's comments and the weight of the media coverage, which seemed to them to be heavily pro Australia.

Waugh, demonstrating his building power and influence in Australian cricket, got his way. Lee was selected in the twelve and was chosen in the eleven, leaving the unlucky Kasprowicz in the character-building job of carrying the drinks.

Tendulkar won the toss on a rain-delayed Boxing Day and sent the Australians in. Blewett (2) played on to Srinath and Langer (8) received a problematic lbw decision, the ball hitting him well above the knee, suggesting it may have gone over the stumps. He took it badly, remonstrating his way to the dressing room and making way for the nervous Mark Waugh. He and Slater, in good touch, took the score to 123, before Mark fell lbw to Ajit Agarkar. His score of 41 was his Test average and he had battled hard to find touch, but it would not be enough to keep the media hounds quiet.

Steve almost ran to the wicket, such was his keenness to get to the middle, which was a good sign. You wondered if it were another ploy, such were the mind games that this Australian captain was playing. He looked in touch as he and Slater took the score to three for 138 before bad light stopped play. The Indians would not agree to switch the lights on. Like the England team a year earlier, they were keeping cricket in the dark ages when the game was finding competition tough and growing. Test matches of five days were not as attractive to the paying public as one-dayers or other sports that lasted only hours rather than days. The ICC would consider this issue in 2001 but it would be too late to save games and help Test cricket.

On day two, Waugh and Slater stepped up the action in search of quick runs until Waugh (32) edged to M. Prasad off V. Prasad. The skipper was not happy, although he had contributed his ten per cent to the team objective of 300 on this wicket. Slater did three times more than his share, reaching 91 before he had a rush of blood and was caught hooking Srinath. It was his eighth time out in the nineties, on top of thirteen centuries.

Ponting and Gilchrist then put on an unbeaten 135, leaving Australia on a commanding five for 332. A storm hit and flooded the MCG, but the drainage system had the field dry by the next morning.

Within minutes of play beginning, Gilchrist (78) pulled high to mid-wicket and was caught off Agarkar; Ponting (67) was lbw to Srinath. Then Warne (2) snicked one off Agarkar and walked when he was caught behind. The score was seven for 345. New man Lee (27) joined Fleming (31 not out) and they formed a useful later-order link to add 59 runs, taking Australia past the landmark of 400. Lee's 77-minute stay helped him lose his first-Test nerves. He literally ran them out.

McGrath was the last man dismissed. Tendulkar was at the stumps when he dislodged the bails before the ball hit the wicket. McGrath was not out. A referral to the third umpire would have shown this on video. The Indian champion claimed he did not realise he had broken the wicket with his hand before the ball did. Someone of his integrity couldn't be doubted. But as media commentators noted, if it had been an Australian in the wrong technically, there would have been a hue and cry. This was because the Australians' aggressive style, which included intimidation and sledging in their written game plans, put their sportsmanship under the microscope. The incident passed without further investigation.

India batted before lunch, and Waugh brought Lee on for the last over. He bowled Ramesh, beating him with sheer pace with a ball measured at 154 km/h—faster than anything delivered by Shoaib Akhtar. He was bowling better too. After lunch, McGrath removed Laxman (5), and Lee had the dangerous Dravid caught behind. Tendulkar settled in for a salvage operation as wickets continued to fall. Lee sent back two in two balls, and a third in the same over.

Steve Waugh's faith in the young 'Demon' (as the press dubbed him) Lee was justified. Once more, the skipper's judgment seemed sharp. His unauthorised push for the new player would be hard to challenge, whether or not any of the selectors felt miffed by any perceived pressure they may have been put under via the media's reporting of Waugh's comments. Waugh was becoming the skipper who could do no wrong. Any incertitude displayed in the West Indies had evaporated as he had grown in the job.

His opposite number, however, was now having a big say in the unfolding dramas in Melbourne. Tendulkar was subdued. He couldn't afford to lose his wicket. Yet he was still in command. The pride of India batted with a presence only matched by Lara among contemporaries. Even in this comparison, the Indian seemed to have a sounder defence. He was unassailable. Lara's adventure seemed always to give opponents a chance. Such generosity was not evident with Tendulkar.

Fleming had him caught hooking to Langer at deep backward square leg for 116. It was his fifth century in eleven Tests against Australia. He was averaging a century about every three innings in this international contest. This was Bradman's rate through his entire career against all comers. The Melbourne crowd appreciated not only the Indian's genius but also his humility. They rose to applaud an outstanding ambassador and champion of the modern era.

India finished the long day—beginning at 10.30 am and ending at 7.11 pm—at nine for 235. The next morning McGrath (three for 39) finished India at 238, giving Australia a strong lead of 167.

Waugh could be well pleased and was expected to push for a lead of 400. Rain shortened the day again. Slater (3) was out lbw to Agarkar when he left a ball he should have played. Langer was caught behind for nine off Agarkar. Waugh then pulled another move, putting Gilchrist in at number four. The captain had promoted him to open the one-day side during the finals versus South Africa in the 1997–98 season, but this was different and more daring. There were immediate grumbles among members of the media, lounging in judgment, aloof from proceedings and out of touch with Waugh's unconventional thinking and his willingness to test his own instinct. Some observers made the unlikely, even silly suggestion that Steve was somehow 'protecting' his out-of-form brother Mark and his own average. But so much for some experts. Waugh, even when he could hear or read them, was now immune to such criticism.

All the Australian players concerned accepted the simple motivating fact: Gilchrist was the form attacking player of the 1999–2000 series. He could be tried as a pinch-hitter in circumstances where the run tempo needed lifting. 'Midas' Waugh's touch was in. Gilchrist delivered a spanking 55 off seventy-three balls.

He and Mark Waugh spoke later at the media conference about a new catchword in the Aussie camp: 'flexibility'. Any player had to be ready to bat or bowl anywhere at any time. Waugh was looking to it as another distinguishing feature of his time as captain. In Tests he would pull more such batting switches, which were more usual in one-day cricket.

Blewett the anchor made 32. Mark Waugh partnered Steve (32 again) until he was lbw to Agarkar, and then 'Junior' went on to a bright 51 not out, another memorable matinee knock. After a streaky start, the innings was marked by artistic flashes to the midwicket fence. Once more the captain's faith in a player was vindicated. It was Steve who said his brother was a match winner in a side that had won five in a row. Why, the captain asked, should he or Ponting (after three ducks) or Langer (after a poor tour of Sri Lanka and Zimbabwe) be dropped after a mini-slump? The captain had been correct each time. His public support for all three had been repaid with huge dividends for the team and the skipper's prestige. His reputation as a leader who supported his troops was now on the record and successful. Waugh was no diplomat delivering lip service. He was direct, but he was still mindful of his players' occasional predicaments.

Waugh's declaration at six for 208 left India 376 to win from 123 overs—around three runs an over. The tourists lost one for 40 by the end of another elongated fourth day. The equation now saw India chasing 336 to win from 105 overs on the final day. The runs per over needed had crept to more than 3.3. India had nine wickets left. The odds were for an Australian victory, with only Tendulkar offering any real chance of an Indian win or a draw.

Encounter of the summer

On the morning of day five, in another gloomy atmosphere that threatened rain, Fleming put the tourists on the back foot with a spearing yorker first ball to Sadagoppan Ramesh, who had a broken thumb. It caused him pain to dig the ball out. At the end of the over, the opener hesitated, then, with Umpire David Shepherd's encouragement, he left the field, retired hurt. This brought Tendulkar to the wicket early, which was no bad thing for India. The growing 16,000-plus crowd gave him another adoring reception.

Warne's early overs were all variation as he tempted Tendulkar with slower, floating deliveries. The bowler was having an unlucky day with tough dropped chances and lbw shouts turned down. Umpire Shepherd was not giving anything away. In Warne's second over of the day, Tendulkar (then 16) was trapped in front when he padded up. The decision was not out. It could have been given in favour of the bowler and no neutral observer would have complained.

Tendulkar was less certain on Australian wickets with their greater bounce and potential for more turn, depending on the bowler. Kumble, with his finger spin masquerading as wrist spin, had been innocuous so far. Warne, with his greater 'bite', was always capable of the unplayable ball that defied the laws of physics.

Tendulkar ignored Warne's illusion of delicious offerings, especially with a long-on placed for the big hit. This placement too was illusory. It stopped the Indian champion from having a go, thus bottling him up, which was playing into Warne's hands. The bowler as ever was prepared for a long war of attrition. When Tendulkar took no notice of his floaters, the spinner switched his attack to around leg stump. Warne, with his pinpoint accuracy and control, would often test a batsman's technique by starting outside leg stump and moving right across to outside off, probing for weaknesses to exploit. But this was

Tendulkar and the spinner had had plenty of time to study his technique in several big hundreds against him. Warne could only work hard to force him into error or create the break with a ripping ball that somehow got through his mighty defence.

The just-outside-leg-stump line received all Warne's loving attention. Besides, there were footmarks to exploit. He had noticed Tendulkar was paddle-sweep happy. It was at times an arrogant shot played more to upset an opponent and to prove who was on top, rather than for any aesthetic or major run-gathering purpose.

Tendulkar defended or tucked Warne round the corner for the too-easy single that he jogged. Again the world champion bat, while not this day the master in control, was still at the wicket. The danger for Australia was the knowledge that he could wear the bowlers down and then let loose. Warne, who characterised his life as a soap opera, was going through an epic episode, the subtlest of thrillers that perhaps only the serious cricket fans could fully appreciate. They were either glued to their seats at the ground or similarly stuck to their television sets. It was the contest of the summer, and no one could predict the end. Would Tendulkar come out of his shell and give Warne a shel-lacking as he had often done before? Or would Warne slip in the leg spinner's equivalent of the Muhammad Ali-type jab that would catch the world champ off guard?

Neither of these scenarios was played out before lunch.

Lee had the resolute Rahul Dravid caught behind, making India effectively three for 72. After ten consecutive overs from Warne, Tendulkar sighed as he saw the leg spinner was to be replaced by Blewett for the last over before lunch. It was one of those lateral-thinking moves meant to lull the batsmen. Tendulkar celebrated his survival against Warne by leaning into Blewett's less alarming deliveries for easy pickings—two fours and a single. Ganguly faced the last ball before lunch. Blewett caused him to play on. The batsman lingered at the wicket either stunned or to watch the replay. Waugh was demonstrating his touch again. India was reduced to three for 110 at lunch. Tendulkar stood between Australia and victory.

After lunch, Waugh soon had Warne on again. The Australian

skipper saw him as his best bet to snuff out the Indian star. After the early sparring, Warne was manoeuvring for that knockout blow as their encounter hotted up. The spinner settled again on that outside leg stump line. But in this spell there was a well-studied change in Warne's plan. He was edging the ball closer and closer to the leg stump. Tendulkar's intransigence gave the bowler twelve deliveries in a row at him. One ball spun round his legs, shaving his stumps. Then he jammed down on one in a botched effort to paddle-sweep fine. The ball squeezed out and again missed the stumps by a coat of varnish. There was a pattern in Tendulkar's batting that suggested he was vulnerable, as if the weight of saving India for the second time in the series was too much to bear. His run scoring had evaporated despite the encouraging enterprise from first-gamer Kanitkar at the other end.

After eleven successive deliveries of intriguing uncertainty, in which Tendulkar abandoned the idea of turning over the strike, Warne had spun his web. He tied his opponent up, all the while marginally changing that line to a point where the batsman was in lbw territory—especially if he padded up.

Tendulkar chose to use his pad to a ball on leg stump that spun only a fraction. Umpire Shepherd was in no doubt he was plumb in front, despite being reluctant to give lbw for a shotless effort.

Warne threw his arms heavenwards, thrilled to have won this greatest of all pure cricket battles. He would take bags of sensational wickets, but very few in his entire brilliant career would give him as much satisfaction. He had worked intently, dictating to this opponent for the first time in his career of about twenty encounters. If the spinner had been asked to choose between taking another six wickets and Lillee's record on the MCG or dismissing Tendulkar, the odds are he would have settled for the champion's solitary wicket. In the end that was all he took, returning figures of one for 63 off twenty-six overs with seven maidens. But it was the match ender, if not the match winner. It was also a moment for Warne to savour for another reason. India and its fine players of spin were the last frontier for the leggie. He had conquered every other nation in his career except this one, against which he had started his Test cricket life so ineptly.

Warne had come full circle in almost eight years. If he retired tomorrow he had done it all with the ball. It had begun with one wicket—Ravi Shastri's—for 150. This period had ended by pure chance with one wicket but, with no disrespect to Warne's first victim, the most prized wicket in the twentieth century behind that of Bradman.

Tendulkar's demise on 52 meant the Indians would fall, especially as Ramesh would not bat again. India had half its team left. Waugh rang the changes. He tossed the ball to brother Mark. His form in the nets had impressed Steve. Mark didn't let him down, taking two wickets to build the sudden myth about his older brother's golden sixth sense. ('Was it ESP?' Steve asked tongue-in-cheek after the game.) Mark reached a milestone of fifty wickets and 5000 runs. The only other Australian with this record was brother Stephen.

When the new ball came he ignored McGrath. Was he injured? Waugh denied it at the media conference. Observers thought it odd that he left his number-one striker out of the wicket-taking action.

'We're getting rid of stereotypes,' Waugh explained. 'Just because [McGrath] is a quick bowler doesn't mean he gets the ball first.'

In short, he preferred Lee, who was 'hot' and willing to charge in and upset the tail. India collapsed and was all out when Fleming ran out Kumble (13) with a direct hit. This fine piece of fielding gave Australia a win by 180 runs, and the series two–nil.

This was its sixth successive win. Of all Australian teams, only Warwick Armstrong's 1920–21 sides had strung together more wins—eight in a row. Clive Lloyd's West Indies of the mid-1980s had the world record of eleven straight wins.

'The cricket we've played this summer,' Waugh said, 'I'd back against any side in just about any era.'

When challenged on this he avoided the issue, saying it was hard to compare teams of different eras. He didn't think it mattered that Australia had won at home. This was in direct contrast to Tendulkar's comments. He said the different wickets helped the home side, whether it be in India or Australia.

The Indian's response did not explain the difference in the efforts of the two teams. There was a palpable contrast in the way they went about their work, especially in the field. The Australians seemed more unified as they hurried between overs early in an innings. They handled the big field with ease. Their throwing arms were better. They were quicker and more desperate. More generally, given an equal standard of players spread throughout the squads, it would probably be easier to unify the Australians, with their mono-culture, than the Indians, who were from a much bigger nation with far greater diversity of culture and background.

At the post-match media conference, Waugh said, 'We're playing really good cricket and we're getting out of tough situations. If the situation demands, we're digging in and fighting hard. It is tough Test match cricket and if you're found wanting mentally, I think we're going to find that in an opposing player.'

The captain warmed to the task of articulating how his team had developed. He added that in fifteen years as an international player he had competed alongside various players who would command a place in the current team (you think of Border, but who else? Perhaps Boon and McDermott?). But this, he felt, was the strongest, tightest unit Australia had had on the field.

'When I retire I'll probably say who's the best team I've played with,' he added, 'but at this stage it's certainly up there ... If we're going to lose a Test, someone's going to have to play really well to beat us. That's our goal, to put ourselves on the line every time, be disciplined and be patient, which we have been. We put the pressure on the opposition and we don't play many bad sessions, which is another goal of ours.'

Waugh was ebullient. Despite these determined pronouncements, he was not the dour fellow he had appeared in the past or on the field. His relaxed other side—the amusing one that his teammates knew well—was emerging. And it could afford to. Australia had now won eight Tests under him. His record included three losses and two draws, giving him nearly a 61.53 per cent win ratio in thirteen Tests, which in ten months had placed him with the most successful Australian skippers of all time. Steve Waugh at the end of 1999 was third only to Warwick Armstrong (80 per cent, with eight wins from ten starts with two draws and no losses) and Don Bradman (62.5 per cent, with fifteen wins from twenty-four starts with three losses and six draws).

Indian journalists queried the strength of their own team, suggesting that they were not as good as Waugh was claiming. He didn't agree, saying again that his team was so unified that it could play this way against any opposition.

Was he overconfident? Not really. The record was on the board. Waugh kept zinging in the sound bites that would make news and headlines for twenty-four hours. Of Brett Lee he said, 'I think he will do for pace bowling what Warnie did for leg spin bowling. Kids will get out there and take up quick bowling because he's exciting and good to watch.' He said Warne's dismissal of Tendulkar was the match-winning wicket. 'He got the crucial wicket, which is what great bowlers do for their team.'

Steve Waugh had led Australia clear of all other nations in Test and one-day cricket right at the end of the century. It was satisfying to the skipper. Now observers seemed to think that Australia would go on to a clean sweep for the entire home summer. This was already a definitive 'line in the sand', a key difference between the teams of Border and Taylor. A two–one series win was not enough. Waugh saw the chance to make an issue of avoiding the dead-rubber blues. The second opportunity would come in Sydney in just three days' time.

The date would be 2 January 2000.

The capping of history

Steve Waugh wanted to mark the new century with a gesture that would become a tradition. It was the wearing of replicas of the skull-caps that adorned the 1901–02 side led by Joe Darling. His team played the First Test of the 1900s at Sydney in December 1901. Waugh, with his strong sense of the game's history, wanted that unifying link with the past and the symbolic importance of the Australian cap. Bradman had begun it in the post-war era in the First Test of the

1948 Ashes series at Trent Bridge. He directed his team to wear the caps into the field to present a unified front to the English team and the watching nation. It became a tradition, which was not adhered to with the same dedication in the 1960s, 1970s and 1980s.

In the 1990s, the teams began wearing the baggy green in the first session of each day. When appointed captain, Waugh began donning it to media conferences.

The twelve velvet caps for the first day of the SCG Test, with their reduced peaks, changed the look of the players. The skipper thought they gave his men more 'character' straight away.

'I think you've got to know where you've come from,' he said, 'to know where you're going.'

The day began with a presentation of the caps to the Australians and a small ceremony to congratulate Mark Waugh for playing his 100th Test. He was just the sixth player in Australian history to achieve this. The others were Allan Border, Steve Waugh, Ian Healy, David Boon and Mark Taylor.

Tendulkar won the toss and batted under gloomy skies. India promoted keeper M.S.K. Prasad to open. McGrath dismissed him caught by game-centurion Mark Waugh early before a rain break. About an hour was lost. When the game resumed, Lee removed the other opener, Laxman, with sheer pace. He fended off a short one. Slater ran in from point to take an easy catch. Tendulkar joined Dravid and was troubled by the pace of Lee, who beat him three times but failed to take the edge.

After tea, Tendulkar took to McGrath, who had just one man out behind square leg. The Indian relished the chance to hook the paceman to the boundary twice and hit another straight four. McGrath had the last laugh, capturing Tendulkar (45) lbw.

Waugh threw the ball to Blewett for the last over before tea, and he again removed Ganguly (1) first ball. The captain with the golden touch took the catch. After tea, India went from bad to worse as Lee removed three more, including Ajit Agarkar, who was caught in slips for his fourth first-ball duck. Bad light stopped play with still another 100 minutes scheduled. India was on eight for 121.

McGrath finished the tail at 150, after a fightback from Anil Kumble. The paceman took five for 48, his sixteenth five-wicket haul. Lee took four for 39. Warne, in pursuit of Lillee's record, only had twelve overs (four maidens) for none for 22. The pacemen had cut him out of the wickets and it was unlikely that he would pick up five in the second innings. Warne would have to wait for the New Zealand Tests in March to reach 356.

Australia soon lost Slater (1), then Blewett (19). Langer came in and scratched around, looking anything but secure. He lost Mark Waugh, who played on to Ganguly, just as Australia's prime minister, John Howard, told ABC radio listeners how good the batsman was looking. In came Steve at three for 146. Australia was four runs short of India with seven wickets in hand. It was the most interesting time in the game, but no one would call it critical, considering the tourists' lacklustre form. They already had a hangdog look in the field. Waugh seemed positive and set for something big as he and Langer cruised to a 121-run partnership. The lead was 117 when India took the new ball. Srinath had Waugh (57) lbw first ball with the new red cherry, but unless there was a collapse, the match already appeared to be heading Australia's way. Waugh was not happy after being stopped from going on to a century. Yet he would settle for a score several points over his average. Only one player (Allan Border) in Australian cricket history had sustained such an average and played more Tests than Steve Waugh. Waugh was in Test number 125 and enjoying it.

Ponting, now the best number six in the world, and Langer, playing beautifully after a fitful first fifty, put the issue beyond doubt by stumps on day two. Australia was four for 331—181 in the lead with two of the hardest-headed players ever to represent the country in command. Ponting, textbook in his stroke execution, was on 34 not out. Langer, all grit and endeavour, was well over the 'scratchies' and into big hundred country. He had a capacity to roam this territory more than any other contemporary Australian player except for Waugh. His approach was straightforward. If you reached a hundred, it was the perfect time to go on for a lot more. This concept flowed from him easily. Yet it didn't allow for a few characteristics he possessed that others didn't. A batsman had to have serious stamina and powers of concentration beyond even the average Test player. Langer's background in the martial arts had helped him in the terrain of the mammoth score. He was 167 not out.

The next day he reached 223, the highest score ever by an Australian against India ahead of other double centurions Kim Hughes (213), Dean Jones (210), Greg Chappell (204) and Don Bradman (201).

Langer was to tell the media afterwards that he put a lot of his success down to the confidence instilled in him by his captain. He spoke of the goals set and the planning under Waugh and coach Buchanan. Langer felt this had helped each individual and the team overcome the dead-rubber blues that had plagued Australian teams after they had won series under Border and Taylor. Langer's complete Test season had been strong. He scored the most runs—620—at 68.89 with three centuries.

The Indians' shoulders sank as they watched Gilchrist stride out at five for 457 before lunch on day three. He and Ponting flayed the bowling until a mid-afternoon declaration by Waugh at five for 552. Australia was 402 ahead. The runs represented a quaint piece of numeracy from Waugh. India had a lead of 400 in the Second Test at Calcutta early in 1998. The tourists would have to go beyond 400 to make the home team bat again. Ponting remained on 141 not out in a near flawless display of batsmanship. After starting the season with three ducks, he had amassed 572 in just six innings. His average was 81.71. The season marked the consolidation and maturing of the gifted, tough Tasmanian. He should have won the Man of the Series, with three good Tests against India and two centuries. Instead it was to go to Tendulkar, who topped India's batting averages with a modest—for him—278 at 46.33. The Indian captain was bemused by his award win.

Gilchrist's 45 not out lifted his final 1999–2000 Test aggregate to 485 at an average of 69.29, an exceptional performance for a number seven. Once more the selectors' decision to replace a great player, Ian Healy, with a successor had paid off. Gilchrist added an average of another 50 or 60 runs per innings to the team's scoring capacity, compared to a year ago.

Australia rolled India in its second innings for 261 in a hard, concentrated 260 minutes in the field. Only V. Laxman, with a terrific knock of 167 from 198 balls with 27 fours, stood between Australia and a thrashing for the tourists well before stumps on day three. This innings ranked as perhaps the second-best of the summer behind Gilchrist's 149 not out at Hobart. The rest of India minus the injured V. Bharadwaj added just 94. Four of those came from Tendulkar, whom Fleming caused to miscue for an easy catch to Langer at short cover. McGrath took five for 55, making it ten for 103 for the match and thirty-two at 20.03 for the six Tests. He was more than well supported by Fleming (thirty wickets at 22.67), Shane Warne (twenty at 35.25) and Brett Lee (thirteen wickets at 14.15). Waugh predicted after the game that McGrath would end up one of Australia's great bowlers. He already was in that class. Statistically, he was even more effective than Shane Warne had been through most of the 1990s. McGrath was averaging 4.68 wickets a Test compared with Warne's 4.33.

Warne failed to take a wicket, returning none for 60 and none for 82 for the match. The wicket had been a batsman's paradise and more conducive to speed than spin. Yet it was still a big disappointment for him and his fans. Warne was now likely to break Lillee's record in New Zealand, away from the adoring home crowds. It was very un-Warnie and an anticlimax. The television soapie script of his life would have seen him take the five wickets required on the last afternoon. Waugh had given him every chance, but it wasn't to be. Instead of the blond's beaming grin at the media conference for the Australians, there were the steely-eyed smiles of Waugh, Ponting, Langer and McGrath.

Waugh had the drained look of a happy, satisfied leader in need of several cold beers. He had now led a team through an extraordinary six–nil summer of Test wins. He told the conference it was in his team planning notes that had been read out before the First Test against Pakistan at Brisbane.

If it had been reported then, a few cynics among the now rapt gathering of impressed scribes in the museum under the SCG grandstand would have said, 'Tell him he's dreaming.' It would have angered the Asian media, who would have taken Waugh's enormous willpower as arrogant and bombastic propaganda. Yet few if any among his loyal band of merry men would have doubted the possibility. In the end, not even the weather, variable in some games and rotten in Melbourne, had stopped the rampage.

Waugh said the turning point from hopeful goal to a possibility came in Hobart when Langer and Gilchrist staged that fightback. Self-confidence in the squad had changed to serious unified team belief. 'Once we won that,' he said, 'we knew we could win any match.' That performance would give every team under Waugh a sense that they were never beaten, no matter what the scorecard said. Waugh said India was too negative and that he 'almost felt sorry for them'. Australia gave them no respite.

Waugh now had won nine Tests as skipper from fourteen encounters. The last seven wins on end made Armstrong's eight in a row a challenge that would provide enormous incentive to the team for the First Test in New Zealand in two months' time.

On top of that, Waugh could now claim a 64.29 per cent win ratio with nine wins from fourteen matches. The fact that he was now ahead of Bradman in the win ratio would no doubt cause Waugh another minor glimmer of satisfaction as he reflected—briefly—on his dream summer as skipper. Only Armstrong's eight wins from ten matches was better. To equal this 80 per cent win-ratio Waugh would have to win the next eleven games on end—making a record of twenty wins from twenty-five matches. That would not be likely. But at the current rate, if he captained the team for two more years, he would rank as the most successful captain in eighty years. Given that Armstrong won his games against a depleted England after World War I, it was within the realms of possibility that Stephen Waugh would rank as the most successful skipper, at least in terms of leading a winning side, of all time.

The clean sweep of six–nil for the 1999–2000 Australian summer—

the first time it had ever been done—brought on a rash of comparisons as to which was the best side of all time.

Neil Harvey, a star of Bradman's 1948 Invincibles, which was generally regarded as the best post-war team, suggested that only Warne would make that side. When comparing these two teams that had played more than half a century apart, more objective reviews had trouble deciding two of the openers from Slater, Arthur Morris and Sid Barnes. There were no arguments about who was number three and the captain. Bradman had both roles. Number four had to go to Neil Harvey and five to Lindsay Hassett. Ricky Ponting would challenge for number five, but not yet. Steve Waugh would take six and vice captain and Keith Miller would secure number seven and the all-rounder's spot. Eight had to be taken by Don Tallon, who was a great keeper and an accomplished bat. Gilchrist could challenge for that spot in a few years but not in 2000. Nine was Ray Lindwall's place. Not only was he rated as one of the best fast bowlers of all time, he had also notched two Test hundreds. Ten was Warne's place and eleven McGrath's. After this 'paper' speculation, players from the Richie Benaud and Ian Chappell eras suggested their teams were better than Waugh's squad.

Waugh was thrilled with his leadership success but was not satisfied with his batting over the summer. His 334 aggregate and an average of 37.11 (sixth on the Australia list) took him back to those statistics when he was dropped from the Test side in 1991, although a more realistic analysis would consider his figures for all of 1999, the first year of his captaincy. He had hit 993 runs at 49.65, which indicates that the responsibility of leadership had not diminished his scoring capacity.

Waugh would be wanting to make sure that his dropping back under 40 per innings for the six Tests in 1999–2000 was not the price he had paid for the demands of captaincy. He, more than anyone, would be aware that if he continued at this lower level he would come under pressure from the media concerning his place in the side in a similar way to Mark Taylor. It would be increased by his own utterances on the subject of 'passengers'. There wouldn't be any while he was captain. Already one or two Indian journalists wanted to know when he was planning to retire. When asked this after the Melbourne Test against India he politely replied that he had no intention to stand down at this time. He didn't deem it necessary to tell the questioner that his overall average was still just over 50. Waugh was not about to make serious plans for the after-cricket life when he was leading a champion team.

16

MILLENNIUM SUMMER PART THREE: ONE-DAY THRILLS AND SPILLS

Pakistan's ruse

Waugh received a surprise when he looked at the Pakistani team sheet for the first match in the CUB one-day tournament on 9 January 2000 and saw the name Shoaib Akhtar. He checked if it was correct. It was. The Pakistanis had rushed Shoaib back into the side after engineering a reverse of the ICC advisory panel's ruling that the fast bowler had to stay out until his alleged suspect action (when bowling extra fast or a bouncer) was rectified. The Pakistanis argued that because the bouncer was illegal in one-day cricket, Shoaib should be able to play. That ball, thrown, ripped, lollied or otherwise, was illegal. The ICC caved in. But it was only papering over the cracks. The problem would have to be faced again after the Australian summer. The shock inclusion rocked the Australians when set just 186 to win after Symonds had taken three for 34.

Waugh came in at three for 72, and was trapped lbw first ball playing back to a big in-swinger. Despite Bevan (31 not out) holding up one end, Australia collapsed for 139, giving Pakistan a 45-run win. It gave the Pakistanis a psychological advantage over the Australians,

302

especially with Shoaib taking three for 31. They carried on their good form in a titanic struggle against India in the second game, which they won on the last ball. Tendulkar was again removed cheaply. His form was a disappointment for the Australian crowds, himself and his team.

In the third game, Australia versus India at Melbourne, a 73,000-plus house saw Australia mount a fair score of seven for 269 on a first-class batting wicket. Steve Waugh came to the wicket at three for 118 and looked in good touch until run out by Ponting on 23 (in thirty-one balls). The Tasmanian put the mistake behind him and went on to a powerful 115 off 121 balls. Approaching his century, he didn't worry about three figures but kept playing for the team. This was in contrast to Saurav Ganguly, who seemed to relax on 100 and was run out when he didn't ground his bat. The incident caused mayhem in the outer, with the Indian fans throwing plastic bottles onto the arena. The problem was caused by a green light on the scoreboard that indicated Ganguly was not out. This was corrected but the damage was done. Play was held up for fifteen minutes when several players, including Steve Waugh and the two Indian batsmen, went to the fence and tried to reason with the rubbish throwers. India was then four for 177 and never recovered. It reached six for 241, giving Australia a 28-run win.

Tendulkar was run out for just 12. His confidence was down. In the after-match media conference he complained about the tight travel arrangements, saying there was too much cricket being played. It was symptomatic of India's lack of spirit on the whole tour.

In the fourth game on 14 January at the SCG, Tendulkar at last opened. It was the position from which he had scored most of his twenty-four one-day hundreds. But McGrath, who was fast becoming his nemesis, had him caught behind for 1. The canny paceman troubled all the batsmen and his match-winning opening spell saw him remove three. He ended with the amazing figures of four for 8 off ten overs. The Indians had no one to counter him. Symonds was twice on a hat trick. He took four for 11 off 3.3 overs. India made 100. Top score was extras, 32.

Australia found the going tough on a difficult wicket, which was made a fraction worse by a small rain interruption. Gilchrist played his usual smash and grab game for 37, but Srinath, bowling with intelligence and accuracy, proved effective in taking four for 30, including Steve Waugh (4), whom he trapped lbw, playing back. It was a decision that could have gone either way. Waugh would work on a problem with the in-cutting ball on a good length, which had now trapped him several times this summer. Symonds came in at five for 59 and he and Martyn played their way out of trouble. Symonds (28 not out from thirty-two balls) hit Kumble for three fours in an over to take the score to 96 and Martyn (13 not out from thirty-three balls) had the pleasure of hitting a four and the winning run to give Australia a five-wicket win. Martyn's steadiness in the crisis would have given him perhaps his greatest satisfaction in cricket. It was here at the SCG six years earlier that he had been caught for 6 in a tight Test against South Africa that Australia had lost by just 5 runs. He had paid dearly for that innings and was dropped from Test calculations thereafter. Symonds's fine double saw him receive the Man of the Match award.

It now seemed likely that India would drop out of the tournament, leaving the best of three finals to Pakistan and Australia. Waugh, Buchanan and the team had a chance to focus on the Pakistanis and how to combat this mercurial team.

Waugh was conscious of his lack of one-day runs and knew that he needed a good score to take the pressure off. He had not made a fifty in the last seven innings since his fine 56 against South Africa in Australia's second-last game of the World Cup at Birmingham in June 1999.

His chance came on a wet 16 January at the MCG in a day game reduced to forty-one overs each. Pakistan batted first at Waugh's invitation and recovered after being seven for 106, reaching nine for 166 (Shane Lee, three for 24; Abdur Razzaq 51 not out from fifty-four balls). Steve Waugh came in with the score at three for 42 after Shoaib Akhtar had taken two wickets (Gilchrist 21 in thirteen balls and Ponting 0). He saw off the speedster with a watchful defence and embarked on a mini partnership of 50 with Bevan

(15 run out), which put Australia in the game. Then Waugh (81 from 92 balls) and Martyn (39 from 61 balls) combined to take Australia home easily by six wickets with 13 balls to spare. It wasn't Waugh's most polished knock, but it was chanceless and gained him the Man of the Match award. More importantly, he had contributed to a win.

The twentieth century's best

Two days later on 18 January, the ACB arranged a luncheon at Darling Harbour, Sydney, to announce its Australian team of the century. Waugh was one of a panel of Australians and former opposition players—Lord Cowdrey, Sir Alec Bedser, Sir Garfield Sobers and Sunil Gavaskar—who made the selection.

On the morning of the announcement, Waugh published his own team. In batting order it read Ponsford, Morris, Bradman, Trumper, Greg Chappell, Border, Miller, Healy, Lillee, McGrath and Warne. Waugh thought McGrath, at the end of his career, would be ranked with Lillee. He chose Trumper ahead of a host of other great batsmen, including Neil Harvey, Charlie Macartney, Stan McCabe, Clem Hill, Michael Slater and Bob Simpson.

'Trumper's average [in Tests of 39.04] was not great,' Waugh said, 'but in his era [he played first-class 1894–1914] he was a lot better than anyone else and the next best player averaged below 30.'

He had forgotten about Clem Hill, who averaged 39.21, and Warwick Armstrong, 38.68.

Waugh said he would like to have met Trumper. When interviewed by the luncheon compere, Andrew Denton, he said he wished he had seen Trumper and Bradman bat. He would like to have played as an amateur in the 1930s, when cricketers performed for the honour of representing their country, and for enjoyment. Denton asked ACB chairman Denis Rogers to take note. Steve Waugh would prefer to play for nothing!

Waugh had always been a big fan of Trumper's. He had once bid more than $10,000 for Trumper's Test cap, but was pipped by a Sydney barrister.

The team chosen by the panel was different. Trumper, McGrath and Border didn't make it. Neil Harvey, Lindwall and Bill O'Reilly did. Border was made twelfth man, a selection that caused the most public reaction. Protesters, like Steve Waugh, wanted Border in because he had played so well in the 1980s when Australia was its weakest and he was facing the brilliant, dangerous West Indian speedsters.

The team in batting order was Bill Ponsford, Arthur Morris, Don Bradman (captain), Neil Harvey, Greg Chappell, Keith Miller (vice captain), Ian Healy, Ray Lindwall, Shane Warne, Dennis Lillee and Bill O'Reilly, with Allan Border as twelfth man.

Keith Miller, who captained New South Wales, was selected as Bradman's deputy, despite never having led a Test team. Miller was highly regarded as a leader by those who played under him in state cricket. Yet the choice was surprising, considering that Border captained Australia ninety-three times, Greg Chappell forty-eight, Morris twice, and Lindwall and Harvey once each.

Neil Harvey said the selection of five of Bradman's 1948 Invincibles—himself, Bradman, Morris, Miller and Lindwall—as opposed to just Warne from Waugh's current team, confirmed that the 1948 side was better and the best Australian team ever. A few weeks earlier, Harvey had responded to Waugh's comment that his team could beat any other side in history by saying that only Warne from the current team would make the 1948 side. Clearly a majority of the twenty experienced judges agreed with Harvey.

The next day Waugh was back to reality and happy to lead his world-champion one-day side against Pakistan in Sydney in a day–nighter. He had the advantage over the other nineteen judges of actually playing. He was running champion teams that were attempting to set world-winning records over several series, which was different from teams of champions that dominated individual series. There was an opportunity for Waugh to defy history and create records that might in the future, perhaps long before the end of the twenty-first century, see another panel judge his team the best ever.

The SCG wicket was far better than in the last encounter and Waugh was content to bat on it first. Akram struck early this time, removing Gilchrist for 13 and Ponting for a duck. Waugh came to the wicket at a more comfortable three for 113, but was bowled by Shoaib for 6, after the paceman had forced brother Mark (43) to play on. This time it was the steady Bevan (77 from ninety-seven balls) and Martyn (50 from fifty-six) who stroked Australia out of trouble and built a platform for the scintillating Symonds (47 from just twenty-six balls) and Shane Lee (23 from thirteen). Australia reached 286, its third-highest one-day score at the SCG.

Waugh was well-pleased with his batting line-up. He now had two devastating hitters—Gilchrist at one and Symonds at seven—as well as four other powerful stroke makers in Mark Waugh, Ponting, himself, and Martyn. Then there was the phenomenal Bevan, with his consistent run of fifties. All of these factors contributed to a perfect balance of blistering attack and fine strokeplay. No other nation could match this first seven. Especially satisfying for the Australian camp was the development of Damien Martyn, and the sudden burst of brilliance from Symonds, who was also proving reliable with the ball, not to mention his athleticism in the field. Symonds, Waugh said, reminded him of the heavy hitter Simon O'Donnell a decade earlier. Symonds was making it possible for Australia to think in terms of 100 in the last ten overs—something that Pakistan had been working on. Australia was aiming at building a steady base with wickets in hand and then finishing with a rush.

This time Pakistan fooled the opposition by starting with the problematic weather in mind. It blazed towards 100 as storms threatened. McGrath copped an unusual belting as 50 was reached in 5.2 overs and 100 in just twelve overs. At this point it would have been good for Pakistan if the game had been rained off. It was ahead in the new Duckworth–Lewis scoring system. But the storm didn't come. Instead, there was Stuart MacGill, the finest leg spinner in the world over the past year, in place of the injured Warne, the finest in the world over the past decade. MacGill spun the ball prodigiously. He not only stopped the run-scoring stone dead, he took wickets. MacGill finished with four for 19 off his allotted ten overs and won Man of the Match. Pakistan was soon eight for 143 and reached 205 in 45.2 overs.

A tired but pleased Waugh faced the media with MacGill afterwards and said he was looking forward to time off. He made it sound like a couple of weeks. He had just two days before flying to Melbourne to prepare for another game against Pakistan. The heavy schedule that had taken toll of Tendulkar had also touched the Australian skipper. He didn't know what day it was.

In the meantime, Pakistan beat India in Hobart despite a return to form by Tendulkar (93). India now had to win its last four games to make the finals. Australia kept India's hopes alive by beating Pakistan by 15 runs at the MCG on 24 January in front of 56,815 spectators in a close game. Waugh called it Australia's best win because of the match's closeness. Man of the Match Bevan hit 83 in 101 balls. Ponting recovered after his three ducks (to match his three in the Tests) to make 53, while Symonds was promoted to number five where he scored 35 in thirty-six balls, which Waugh noted was the aim of the move. Shahid Afridi ran himself out for 45 off forty-eight balls, while Ijaz, with 85 off 104 balls, nearly stole the show.

Steve Waugh led the team proudly on Australia Day at Adelaide but didn't have much to do on the field. An early exertion was to toss the coin correctly and send his team in on a good second-day track (after India had beaten Pakistan comfortably the day before, thanks to a great 141 from 144 balls by Ganguly). The start could not have been better. Gilchrist (92 from 102 balls) and Mark Waugh (116 from 131) put on 163. Man of the Match Mark found his true form and took the pressure off himself after a mediocre season. The rest of the bats rattled on runs at better than a run a ball each. Steve Waugh sent in Symonds, Shane Lee and Harvey (unlucky to be run out for a duck) before him and in the end wasn't needed. Australia piled up its second-best one-day score, five for 329 (three for 332 versus Sri Lanka a decade earlier was the best) and appeared awesome. Most impressive was the application of all batsmen in a game that in other years the Australians would have lost. It was a dead match for the home squad, but they batted then bowled as if it were a final. Brett Lee did the damage, taking five for 27 including Tendulkar (18), caught slicing down to square third man, where MacGill took a fine running catch. India was never in the hunt. It made 177 (Dravid 63 from eighty-two balls), and lost by 152 runs.

Waugh seemed to be presiding over a team with a new authority. In recent tournaments, Sri Lanka in September 1999 excepted, it had struggled to come from behind to win the big matches at the crunch. Now there was no build to a peak. There was a permanent peak, or higher level of performance, that was superior to the opposition. It wasn't as if India and Pakistan were weak sides. Australia had gone up a notch since the World Cup.

Pakistan beat India comfortably on 28 January and Australia completed the Indians' summer of humiliation with a four-wicket win two days later. Waugh's lean trot with the bat continued. He was bowled for just 19 from forty-eight balls, while Bevan, now slotting in at number four, continued on his one-day run accumulation with 71. Mark Waugh's 40 confirmed his return to form in time for the finals. The win for Australia was its seventh in succession. Ten successive wins would equal the previous Australian record. Eleven would draw level with the world record created by the West Indies. Waugh's team had now lost just two matches in the last twenty-three encounters, thus confirming it as the best one-day exponent in the world. More pertinent was the sense that this squad was evolving as a better combination with every series. This fickle game had once been considered a 'giggle and hit' affair with victories about as meaningful as the outcome of a dice roll. Now the Australians were turning it into something more scientific and exciting. There were no boundaries to their improvement in all aspects of the sport.

Waugh looked forward to a night at the Crown Casino on 31 January for the inaugural Allan Border Medal night—a chance for the players to enjoy a break from cricket. It proved to be simply a change of venue to choose the best cricketers from 1 February 1999 to the end of January 2000. Yet it was an evening of inspiration.

Votes were cast 3, 2 and 1 by all players, umpires and selected members of the media. Votes were weighed 2.38:1 in favour of Tests to one-dayers in determining the medallist.

Glenn McGrath surprised no one by winning with ninety-seven votes ahead of Steve Waugh, eighty-seven, Ricky Ponting, seventy-seven and Shane Warne, seventy-five. McGrath was also adjudged Best Test Player. Shane Warne surprised by winning the Best One-day Player award by one vote over Mark Waugh, despite missing most of the January 2000 CUB series. His excellent form in the West Indies, the World Cup, Sri Lanka and Zimbabwe were enough to give him the title.

Brett Lee won the Sir Donald Bradman best young player award, and Darren Lehmann won the Best State Player medal.

The night was the original idea of Shane Warne, who thought cricket should have an award ceremony similar to the most prestigious one in football, the Brownlow Medal. He put it to Tim May and the Australian Cricketers' Association, the ACB and Channel Nine, who broadcast it. Another special feature was the addition of three inductees to the Australian cricketers' hall of fame—Allan Border, Neil Harvey and Warwick Armstrong. The original ten inductees were Fred Spofforth, Jack Blackham, Victor Trumper, Clarrie Grimmett, Bill Ponsford, Don Bradman, Bill O'Reilly, Keith Miller, Ray Lindwall and Dennis Lillee.

The Border Medal night was sure to become cricket's biggest annual occasion.

As if to confirm his status as the first medallist and a good bet for the second, McGrath finished the first CUB final at the MCG on 2 February within minutes of the game's beginning with three wickets—Shahid Afridi, Ijaz Ahmed and Inzamam-ul-Haq. They all departed in his first three overs. Pakistan never recovered and was all out for 154. McGrath kept the pressure on for nine overs, finishing with three for 17. Brett Lee backed him up with three for 18 off 8.2.

Australia won easily by six wickets, with Ponting (50) and Bevan (54) batting steadily to wrap up the game in 42.4 overs.

Waugh was 19 not out from thirty-one balls. He came in when

Shoaib was having his second spell in a desperate attempt to collapse Australia. Shoaib had been a problem for Waugh in earlier games, but not this time. The skipper saw it through and looked forward to a two–nil series win.

The second final, at Sydney on 4 February, in front of 38,173 people, saw Waugh win the toss and bat—and bat and bat. All batsmen except for Bevan, who had a rare failure (3), contributed. Mark Waugh, back to fine form, scored 53 off seventy-three balls, while Gilchrist, dropped on 7, went on to 51 in forty-two balls. The 74-run start set the pattern. Ponting (78 from eighty) and Symonds (45 from forty-five) capitalised and were backed up by Steve Waugh (37 run out from thirty). Australia scored 7 for 337, the best total ever by an Australian team after 453 games, and the highest on Australian soil.

Pakistan came out of the blocks as expected. But the rush was halted by McGrath (five for 49) and Brett Lee (three for 51). The challengers were dismissed for 185, giving Australia a massive 152-run win, and the CUB series two–nil.

More Waugh attacks

The victory in the CUB series final made it nine in a row, leaving Australia one game short of a national record and two games short of the world record.

Waugh ended with 195 runs at 27 for the tournament, following his moderate 334 at 37 in the Tests. Several journalists, including Martin Blake in the *Age–Sydney Morning Herald* and Robert Craddock in the *Herald Sun–Daily Telegraph*, pondered the captain's future as soon as the Australian 1999–2000 international season finished.

Blake said Waugh should retire or be dropped from the one-day game. 'He's not the commanding presence he once was in the abridged game. While it is true that he helped his team win the World Cup, it's also true that he does not move in the field as he once did, rarely hits cleanly as he once did and that he breaks down if he bowls too much.

With Australia's growing list of all-rounders, Waugh would be close to the last man picked at the moment.'

Craddock, who had editorialised for the dumping of Mark Waugh, noted that 'the day was looming when Steve's one-day career will glide to a halt. He has done an exceptional job as captain but there is nothing more for him to achieve and planning will soon start for the next World Cup [in South Africa in 2003].'

It was unlikely that these opinions would have had any impact on Steve Waugh. He fell back on his 'reinventions' as first a batsman, and later a leader, after critics had written him off. He saw attacks on his capacities in these two areas as wrong-headed. They acted as a spur. He would be determined to prove the commentators wrong. Now, when he had established himself as one of the best and most reliable bats in Australian history and with a stunning first year as captain behind him, there would be a drive to go on—in the dwindling time he had remaining—to more goals, especially as captain. To remain leader he would have to pull his weight with scores, which made it unlikely that his batting would fall away. At the end of his first year as captain, Waugh was faced with leadership opportunities, not the least being his chance to break winning Test and one-day records. These, if attained, would go some way towards immortalising him as a leader.

The critics spoke of the tough grind and that Waugh had no time of his own. Pressures were building on his mental and physical limits along with his family and business interests. Yet leading such a winning combination would push him on. He would take his precious extra two days after the two–nil CUB victory and move with the one-day caravan to New Zealand on 14 February, barely ten days after crushing Pakistan. In front of him was a blur of more one-day cricket—six games—and then three Tests, all over another two months of hard labour. And when he came up for air, there would be a flight to South Africa in mid-April for another one-day competition. By then Waugh would not look at them as a separate tournament. They would be just three more one-dayers he would have to drag his dodgy groin and hamstrings through.

Whether he would succeed without breaking down was anybody's guess. But one thing was certain. He would give everything in trying. Steve Waugh's sense of history and the chance to make it in an extraordinary way would be an even greater incentive than answering commentators calling for his end.

MILLENNIUM SUMMER PART FOUR: NEW ZEALAND, NEW TARGETS

Off-field follies

Distractions off the field took attention from New Zealand's poor form and weather at the start of Steve Waugh's campaign when Australia's game plan was slipped under the wrong door in their Wellington hotel room. The recipient, instead of handing in the Australians' property, passed it on to a radio station. Or did she? The 'revelations' gave the one-day series a publicity injection. The Australians were billed as the 'baddies' for their words. Could it have been a ploy similar to ones used to stimulate interest in wrestling or boxing?

'Let's keep everything under control; sledging, body language,' the plan advised. The 'sledging' directive only confirmed what every cricket follower knew. This unfortunate activity was institutionalised. In the analysis of players, Chris Cairns was said to be a 'a little fragile'. The Australians were advised to 'intimidate' Roger Twose early in his innings. 'He does not quite believe in his ability.' The New Zealand captain, Stephen Fleming, was described as being 'a bit lazy' in relation to his stroke play. Nathan Astle was 'a bad runner'. Craig McMillan was said to be 'very impatient' and 'prone to silly mistakes'. Chris

Harris's body language was highlighted. It 'can effect others' so the tourists should 'keep him down ... When he is bowling be mentally aggressive to him.' Simon Doull would always deliver a 'four ball'— something that could be smashed away.

It caused the Australians to be booed onto the field in the first game at Wellington. The match was washed out with Australia in command on one for 119 (Mark Waugh 45 not out, Matthew Hayden 64 not out) after just 23 overs. Chris Cairns was not so much fragile as ineffective after dismissing Gilchrist for a duck. Chris Harris did his best not to present his usual facial contortions and hands-on-hips, hangdog look.

During the game, Shane Warne compounded Australia's bad-boy image in an altercation with teenage boys. One of them had photographed him smoking and he wanted the film. The boys said he swore at them and snatched a bag from them. Warne denied it. Police were called. The matter was smoothed over and no charges were laid. But the spinner was left with a further tarnished image after his remark on landing that New Zealanders were 'frustrated Australians'. He probably meant that Kiwis wanted to be Australians, which was a bit sweeping and only meant as a jestful gibe. He tried to avoid the usual platitudes on arrival on the neverending cricket circuit and didn't think it would be taken seriously. Warne, normally diplomatic and a good media performer, had a few repairs to do after another unfortunate start to a series, which brought back memories of the beginning of the 1994 South African tour. But to suggest that he had a poor attitude to young fans in general was wrong.

Warne suffered more than any modern player apart from Tendulkar from attention from fans. He craved privacy, which he hadn't had for approaching a decade. The smoke was one of his tiny, usually private, luxuries. He didn't want the extra publicity of him photographed dragging on a cigarette. It was not good for his image and that of the team, which was recognised as a fit unit. He admitted he had taken it up again after being dropped from the Test team and he was having trouble with the addiction.

At a time when bad publicity was good for business the team moved to Auckland for the second game. A sell-out 33,050 spectators assembled in the hope of seeing the bad guys—particularly Warnie—from across the Tasman Sea get their comeuppance. He came in for juvenile, unfunny abuse from spectators and puerile banners were displayed depicting him as fat and questioning his sexuality.

New Zealand won the toss and batted but it had no answer to Australia's strikers—McGrath (three for 33), Brett Lee (three for 21), Warne (two for 35) and Shane Lee (two for 27)—and stumbled to 122. Mark Waugh took a freakish slips catch off Warne, diving to his left and unsighted. In the middle of the mayhem a section of the crowd behaved boorishly and threw fruit at the Australian fielders. Brett Lee, who took a sensational catch on the run at third man to dismiss Cairns, received a plum on the neck for his brilliance. Later he was given a more fitting Man of the Match award.

Waugh dropped himself down to number seven and sent Symonds (33) in at number three after Mark Waugh (2) was out early. Hayden (50) batted well again and did most to ensure a five-wicket win. Two weeks earlier he would have been reflecting on another fine season without international recognition. Now, with Ponting injured, he had been Australia's best bat in two successive games.

These one and a quarter performances demonstrated how much Australia had improved since being beaten by New Zealand in the World Cup. It had now lost just two games in twenty-six and was aiming at equalling England's 1991–92 record of not losing in twelve matches on end.

Waugh lost the toss in the third game at Carisbrook, Dunedin, and Australia was sent in, to make four for 310. Gilchrist regained touch with 77 from eighty-five balls; Mark Waugh played like Geoff Marsh a decade earlier by dropping anchor for 75 off 142 balls; Bevan contributed yet another fifty (52 from seventy); and Symonds slammed 34 from just thirteen.

Steve Waugh looked in touch in his first real outing in New Zealand, making 43 from forty-two balls before Chris Cairns let go a high full-toss by mistake. In taking evasive action, Waugh twisted his ankle and had to retire hurt. He made it out onto the field for a few overs but had to retire, leaving the experienced Warne in charge. New Zealand replied bravely with Nathan Astle (81 from eighty-three) on fire and Roger Twose (62 from sixty-one) in dynamic form. Warne delayed his own introduction to the bowling crease. After nineteen overs, New Zealand was bolting along at seven an over and seemed to be making the first serious challenge to the Australians all summer. Then part-timer Damien Martyn, bowling his accurate medium-pacers, trapped Twose lbw. Warne soon after bowled Astle. The acting skipper performed well, taking two for 50 in the middle of the near-rampage.

Wickets began to fall and the run rate slowed. At seven for 246, Australia was on top. Adam Parore was hit by a short one from Brett Lee. It clipped his forearm (which was not raised above shoulder height), snapped his helmet strap and sent his headgear crashing into the batsman's stumps. The umpires didn't call no ball. Parore was on his way, leaving New Zealand eight for 246 and with no hope of victory. The crowd erupted, throwing bottles and cans onto the arena. Play was halted for twelve minutes. New Zealand was all out 260— 50 runs short—giving Australia a two–nil lead in the series, with three to play. The tourists had now gone twelve games without a loss, equalling England's record.

After the game, Steve Waugh expressed his displeasure at yet another interruption to a one-day contest. Australia, it seemed, was always competing with the opposition *and* the crowd. In the West Indies a year earlier two games had been ruined by an unruly, dangerous mob. In Melbourne in January 2000, the Indian section of the crowd had held up play. Now, in another pathetic display, New Zealand spectators had interfered again. Kiwi competitiveness towards the Australians had boiled over, perhaps fuelled by stirring publicity over the Warne incidents. The visitors had their bad-guy image boosted, although the incident had been triggered by a New Zealand umpiring decision that was correct anyway. It was a bit rich to blame the tourists, who had had several poor decisions—particularly caught behind—go against them in two completed contests.

New Zealand won the toss at Christchurch in the fourth game, and Stephen Fleming again sent Australia in. Gilchrist, in murderous form, crashed a century in seventy-eight balls and was out at 128 in ninety-eight balls. He and Mark Waugh (70 in eighty-eight balls) put on 189 for the opening stand. Steve Waugh came in at four after Symonds was run out for a duck. While he had passed a fitness test on his ankle in the morning, he was not in the mood to run. Instead, he took on the ordinary New Zealand attack and slammed five sixes in 54 from forty-four balls. He was back in good one-day form and justifying his place. Australia went on to a record six for 349, the fourth occasion it had passed 300 in 1999–2000. This included a world record of 15 sixes in a one-day international, and on a medium-sized ground.

Chris Cairns, the best New Zealand paceman, returned none for 76 off ten—one of the worst returns ever by a Kiwi.

New Zealand had another task of scoring seven runs an over. It did well at that rate for about twenty overs, but again Shane Warne (three for 50 off nine overs) came on, took wickets and reduced the rate. Nathan Astle (45 from forty-five) was trapped lbw by Warne. Stephen Fleming (82 from eighty-eight) was brilliant until Warne first retarded then dismissed him, caught at wide mid-on by Steve Waugh. New Zealand was nine for 301 at the close. Damien Fleming (three for 58) had also been effective.

This gave Australia its thirteenth successive game without a loss—a world record. At the media conference Waugh said that this was just the beginning. It was a signal to New Zealand that there would be no slackening off by the Australians in the final two one-day games.

Waugh also said Adam Gilchrist would be the first batsman to reach 200 in a one-day game. This was definitive and designed not to put pressure on his star opener–keeper, but to sew a positive seed of expectation and inevitability. Waugh, a psychologist's dream, was stretching the boundaries of sporting mind-games. His ebullience, though, was understandable. He would not beat his chest and say 'we're terrific'. Instead, he uttered comments that made everyone consider the dimensions of how far this team could go. Waugh did say his side now had to be compared with the West Indies unit of the mid-1980s that had racked up eleven wins in a row from June 1984 to February 1985, and South Africa from 1996 to 1998. But even this remark invited scrutiny that weighed in Australia's favour. In that 1996 to 1998 period, South Africa won ten on the trot in two months early in 1996 but did not beat Australia in an official series. If Waugh's team continued to win then it would further distance itself from these other sides. Commentators could draw their own conclusions. Another telling comment was that the 'bulk' of this team would compete at the next World Cup in 2003. This was telegraphing that he intended to be there as player and captain. He would be 37 going on 38. It was the broadest hint yet that Waugh intended to stay as skipper.

As ever, the Australian captain's utterances made excellent copy.

There had been a lot of 'jaw-jaw' about Australia not dropping a game in this series, but you wondered if it would collapse at Napier. New Zealand seemed to have improved every game. It was bound to drive home one win, wasn't it? Waugh won the toss and sent New Zealand in—perhaps just to have a go at chasing. Nathan Astle, after being dropped on 0 by Bevan in the covers, went on to a fine century (104 in 128) and New Zealand reached nine for 243. Australia fielded at its worst since early in the World Cup, but it was bound to happen at some point. Still, the bowling was top rate. Damien Fleming put in as usual, taking four for 41. Ian Harvey took one for 35 off ten. Harvey's variety of slower balls were the best ever seen in one-day cricket and he was hard to get away, making him economical, and brilliant for a tight finish. Warne (one for 34 off ten) was superb. His accuracy was pin-point, as ever. He delivered about three loose deliveries in sixty and was unlucky not to take three wickets.

In response Waugh juggled the batting order. With Symonds rested, he brought Warne into the number five spot. Hayden succeeded again, making a strong 57 from 61. Warne made 12 from ten balls at number five, not really a winning move, but there was more behind it than making runs. Warne hadn't had much exposure at the top of the order and more would give him confidence so he would respond well more often than not when called on for quick runs. Warne had been used as a 'pinch-hitter' before, but this baseball terminology in itself was self-defeating by implying that the player had no right to be at number three or four. Warne was a big hitter being used for a bit of slather and whack to upset the opposition. Such delineation and categorising would now be redundant.

Steve Waugh continued his own good form, scoring 43 from thirty-four balls. His favourite shot, the heave over wide mid-on for six while down on one knee, was executed twice. Bevan was the star with 107 from 141. After knuckling down, Australia won comfortably, losing just five wickets and with twenty-six balls to spare.

It was Australia's fourteenth game without a loss (one game washed out) and its fourth win in a row in New Zealand. Fourteen was to be the new world record. Australia lost the last game. Waugh won the toss and juggled the batting order, putting Martyn in to open with Hayden, himself at number three, Bevan at four, Mark Waugh at five, Gilchrist at six and Symonds at seven. Martyn (116 not out from 135) became the fifth player to carry his bat as his teammates had a day they would rather forget. Two run-outs could have been avoided. The Lee brothers received poor umpiring decisions. The upshot was a score of 191. New Zealand, led by its classy left-handed skipper, Fleming, polished off the runs with more trouble from the lights, some of which went off temporarily, than the Australian bowlers. The tourists lost by seven wickets. The run had ended.

Australia won the series four–one. New Zealand hoped that its win would send it into the Tests with a greater chance of winning.

Steve Waugh and John Buchanan began plotting Australia's eighth successive Test win. At the media conference, even Damien Martyn was surprised to hear that he was in the team at number six.

Flexibility force

The catch-cry of 'flexibility', heard throughout the summer, was paying off. Every team member—particularly the fringe players—was developing well. It was a reason for the strong team performance every game and the winning streak. Each player in the squad was made to feel 'part of the team' and individuals were being rotated to give everyone more than one game. No one could feel left out. Rotation had been a quasi-practice on other tours, but it was something new to be part of team policy.

The results for the individuals and the team were tangible.

Ian Harvey was coming on fast at this level. Waugh was using him to bowl at the end to give him 'pressure' experience that Fleming, McGrath and Warne were used to. Harvey's capacity for variety was unique. He had made it a speciality. He had so many different types of delivery that a batsman could never be sure which ball was coming. There were an exceptional number of plays and misses when he delivered. Thanks to Waugh's policy, Harvey was already comfortable at the highest level. He had a good temperament to begin with, and this experience lifted him further.

Bevan had slotted in at number four. The reticent left-hander was even happy to talk it up, encouraged by his captain and coach. He told a media conference he was inspired at four to make hundreds. That's what he wanted to do. Waugh intervened when Bevan was asked if he saw himself as purely a one-day player.

'The selectors see Bev as a Test player,' Waugh said, 'not as a one-day player. He was very close to selection for the [Test] team.'

Bevan had been overlooked in favour of Damien Martyn for the Test squad. Once more, Waugh's direct public support for a player in front of the media contingent was magnificent for Bevan's continuing confidence build. An example was Bevan's behaviour after dropping Nathan Astle in the one-dayer at Napier. It steeled him to make amends and he went on to win Man of the Match.

Others such as Gilchrist and Symonds had benefited. Gilchrist had become a Test player under Waugh, making the transition with ease and outstanding results. Symonds had emerged to be a formidable all-round force with bat, ball and fielding. His bowling was his weak link. But even when he was being belted Waugh didn't panic and take him off. The captain had sent him in to bat at three and he had performed well. Waugh was demystifying tough positions by giving players opportunities.

Martyn above all had come through under the Waugh–Buchanan

policy. His one-day form had been superb, especially under pressure. It had destroyed the myth about his temperament after his one Test indiscretion six years ago. Now he was in the Test team again. Waugh had signalled this at the beginning of the New Zealand tour. It had become a self-fulfilling prophecy. Martyn had played accordingly, and capped off his comeback with a fine century in the last one-dayer.

Aiming at Armstrong

Steve Waugh decided to rest his ankle and let Warne captain the tourists in the four-day tour match at Hamilton against Northern Districts. The batting form in that game was a good pointer to the Test. After the home team was dismissed for 300, Slater and Blewett were out cheaply, then Langer (155) and Martyn (109) got runs, with Hayden on 67 not out when Warne declared at four for 383. Northern Districts made 280 in its second innings. Warne let the normal openers start the innings and then put in the tail, which had missed out on a hit in the first. It was a most democratic—dare it be said, socialist—move as Australia lost five for 198 to win by five wickets. Slater missed out again, making just 9. Blewett made 83 not out.

On form, Matthew Hayden, in a truly democratic group, would be given the nod to open. But cricket was just as much about loyalty and what had gone before. Slater was sorely out of touch, but could not be dropped. If he were, there was a case for every batsman being in and out of the team since Sri Lanka in August 1999. The hope, as ever, was that he would come good. He was a proven champion. It was a case of 'form is variable, class is permanent'.

Slater had his chance early when Waugh won the toss and batted in the First Test at Eden Park, Auckland. Slater went for 5, a little unluckily. A ball brushed his pad and then the off bail. Still, he was beaten. Cairns would have been unlucky not to get the wicket. Blewett stayed for ninety-eight minutes for 17. He seemed to have lost his capacity to play run-scoring strokes. Yet the wicket was not easy. It spun early. Daniel Vettori, the left-arm finger spinner, and Paul Wiseman, the right-arm off spinner, were in their element on day one. Langer belted Vettori out of the attack, taking 25 off him in three overs. He used the smack over midwicket. But on 46 off forty-seven balls of excellent batting under the conditions, he left his crease to hit Wiseman and was stumped. Steve Waugh joined his brother, who was sedate but in touch. Steve had reached 17 when Vettori induced an edge for a slips catch. The rest of the team fumbled and slipped about the pitch until Australia was all out for 214. Mark Waugh remained 72 not out. He faced 144 balls in 197 minutes. It was a rare knock for this fine stroke player, who curtailed his game here and there in the interests of the team. His class on a perceived poor wicket came through. Vettori took five for 62. He was closing on 100 wickets.

By stumps the game had swung Australia's way. New Zealand was four for 26. Brett Lee (two wickets), Warne (one) and McGrath (one) had all taken part. Warne's wicket was the most telling. Mathew Sinclair, who scored 214 in his first (and most recent) innings, was uncomfortable against Warne, who trapped him lbw with a top spinner, to which the batsman did 'the leave'.

Fleming (21) and Astle (31) put up resistance on day two before Warne found an edge to Astle's bat for a slips catch. Then Gilchrist stumped Fleming beautifully off Miller, when the batsman lifted his toe for half a second. Warne trapped McMillan (another 'leave') lbw, giving him 354 wickets. But that's where he remained as McGrath, held back by Waugh for reasons known only to the skipper, returned like the Terminator to finish off the innings. He took four for 33, Warne three for 68. The leg spinner needed just two wickets to break Lillee's record. New Zealand was all out for 163.

The Australians led by 51 when they commenced their second innings. Slater was out for 6 from an unnecessary shot. Blewett hung for more than an hour and made 8 before Vettori had him caught at slip. Langer was in the same belligerent mood as in the first innings. He crunched 47 in sixty-four balls, including two sixes off the spinners, before Vettori had him mis-hitting to midwicket, going for one too many. Mark Waugh was in touch again, but succumbed on 25 to Vettori, who had him caught behind. Steve (10) played a nothing shot to be caught and bowled by Wiseman. It could have been catching practice, so easily did it return to the surprised bowler.

Australia was five for 114 at stumps on day two. The wicket was for a three-day game, rather than five. The next morning Martyn and Gilchrist played positively. Both got away with their favourite shots. Martyn had the breathtaking audacity to cut and back-cut Vettori's arm-ball right off his stumps. It worked a few times but eventually he was bowled. His 36 had been well made. There was no questioning his temperament, but his shot selection could have been a fraction better. Gilchrist, with more sweeps than a chimney cleaner, backed his judgment and risked an lbw decision or mis-hit. He hit almost everything truly.

When rain stopped play for the second time just before lunch, Gilchrist had reached 50 and Australia was seven for 206—a lead of 257. After a hundred-minute break, Gilchrist (59) was out trying to hit Vettori for six and Australia was removed for 229, giving it a 280 lead. The late order played as if the game had to finish that night or at lunch on day four. Waugh had taken the attitude that they should hit out rather than stay around. Perhaps a mix of sound defence and hitting the loose one would have been more in order. Vettori had been brilliant. He had taken seven for 87, giving him twelve for 149 for the match. He had passed 100 wickets at twenty-one years and forty-six days, the youngest spinner ever to do so, ahead of Pakistan's Saqlain Mushtaq (twenty-two years and 324 days). Paceman Kapil Dev of India and Pakistan's Waqar Younis were the only two bowlers to reach that milestone earlier in their lives than Vettori.

New Zealand was set 281 to win in two and a half days.

Waugh pepped his players up for a win. 'Goals' and 'aims' were so much part of team planning that much focus was put on Shane Warne going for the Australian wicket-taking record. Perhaps too much. When he came on to bowl, he was tense. He went for 31 off five overs before Waugh took him off. It took Miller to do damage. He took three wickets and at one point New Zealand was four for 43.

McMillan and Astle fought back. Their link looked dangerous. Waugh brought Warne back. He looked better in this spell. When the partnership was 78, he bowled Astle (35) round his legs. This drew him level with Lillee at 355 wickets.

At stumps, New Zealand was five for 151—130 runs short.

Day four was washed out. The game began about an hour late on day five. Waugh used Miller and Cairns hit an above-the-head catch to Waugh at midwicket. New Zealand was six for 151. Parore came in and took to Miller. Waugh replaced him with Warne, while McGrath plugged up one end by bowling in the 'corridor'. He could just about claim it as his own. Seven runs came from nine overs. Warne bowled well, but without luck until lunch. After the break, Waugh used Lee. He induced a cover drive from Parore. Waugh took a terrific catch falling forward, making New Zealand seven for 195. McMillan survived a strong lbw appeal, then slapped Warne for two fours. Blewett at backward point dropped him—all in the one over.

Lee bowled with hostility. He had McMillan, after a gallant struggle, caught by Warne at slip for 78. New Zealand was eight for 204. Waugh, showing the correct sentiment, did not leave Warne on in the hope that he would take his 356th wicket. Miller replaced him in order to bowl to the left-handed Vettori, to whom he could spin the ball away towards slips. This he did and an edge was snaffled well by Warne again at slip, his second catch in four balls. New Zealand was nine for 204. Miller, five for 55, had his first 'Michelle' ('five for') in Test cricket.

Waugh then brought Warne on for one last final fling and he had Wiseman sweeping for a popped-up catch behind with the score at 218. Warne had 2 for 80. The spinner had his Australian Test cricket record. His 356 wickets were at 25.54 each in eighty-two games.

Waugh had juggled his bowlers well in a tight situation that looked threatening for Australia. It was the toughest Test of the extended 1999–2000 summer next to the sensational comeback at Hobart against Pakistan. These bowling changes had all been part of the strategy prepared with Buchanan before the team entered the field on the last morning. The fourth day washout had given the coach and captain extra time to think through their actions. A lot depended on the bowlers delivering at their best. McGrath, gifted for his ability to deliver accuracy, movement and bounce, had come through with top marks. Miller, always ready to be popped back into the attack for a left-hander, had delivered with more than journeyman application. His cool temperament and sheer delight at being in this great company were evident in equal measure as he bagged five and was the most potent bowler.

Lee, held back for an aftershock effect, had been excellent as well. Just when the batsmen thought they had seen off the menacing McGrath, who forced the batsmen to concentrate at their sweating maximum, on came the fastest bowler on earth. It was too much even for the gritty McMillan. How right had Steve Waugh been in pushing for the fast-tracking of Lee into Test cricket!

Then there was Shane Warne. He had been too tense about the record, and his form had dropped. Yet the sheer intensity of his efforts and the mental fatigue for the New Zealand batsmen in facing his relentless 'in your face' bowling added to the Australian breakthrough. Even though he had taken just two wickets in the second innings, it could easily have been five. Warne had taken five for the match, just above his average in Tests over nearly a decade.

The catching by Warne and Steve Waugh—two sound grabs each—had also impacted on the result. Had the two tougher chances been spilled it might have been a different finish.

Australia had a 62-run win, its eighth in a row. This equalled the record set by Warwick Armstrong in two Ashes series in 1920–21 in Australia (five–nil) and 1921 (three–nil).

This achievement—the best run of successive wins in eighty years—could be added to the new one-day world record of fourteen games without loss. The Test wins had been made in three different countries—Zimbabwe, Australia and New Zealand—against four different Test teams—Zimbabwe (one), Pakistan (three), India (three) and New Zealand (one).

The winning streak had begun in Africa in October 1999 and continued to March 2000 making it nine wins in a row. This put Steve

Waugh and his team level with Armstrong's Australians, and ahead of England (seven games 1884–85 to 1887–88, and also from 1928 to 1928-29), and the West Indies (seven games from 1984–85 to 1985–86, and also from 1988 to 1988–89).

The world record stands at eleven wins by the West Indies from 1983–84 to 1984–85.

Waugh could relax a little. He now had ten wins from fifteen starts as skipper, a 66.67 per cent win ratio ahead of seven other exceptional Australian captains—Don Bradman, Lindsay Hassett, Bill Woodfull, Mark Taylor, Ian Chappell, Richie Benaud and Greg Chappell.

The tour match at Napier versus Central Districts provided nothing startling for the tourists and confirmed most existing form or lack of it. Hayden and Blewett opened and were on trial for a spot next to Slater in the Second Test. Both failed. Steve Waugh failed twice when he needed a big score. Langer (79), Martyn (61 not out) and Mark Waugh (93 not out) got scores. Fleming confirmed his class with five for 21 and three for 55, but Waugh opted for the retention of Miller. There was no change for the game at Wellington.

The Test at Wellington was to be a huge challenge for Australia. It hadn't won there since March 1946, which had been the first ever 'recognised' Test between the two countries. Then again, New Zealand had only won once, in 1989–90, while the other four games had been drawn.

The tourists were aiming now at nine successive wins, an Australian record. The weather was expected to be cold and with gale force winds, but the temperature on the first day, 24 March, was about 17 degrees. Fleming won the toss and batted on a yellow strip. Lee took two early wickets and Miller proved a marvel by bowling five balls of off spin to left-handed Fleming, before switching to his long run and medium pace to the right-handed Sinclair, whom he trapped lbw.

Warne came on and had Fleming caught in his first over. New Zealand went to lunch at five for 69. After the break Cairns was dropped by Mark Waugh and went on to a smashing century. Astle hit 61 before Warne had him caught in slip and Adam Parore stayed with the tail for 46. New Zealand reached 298, fighting back after a poor start. Warne had the figures of four for 68, taking his tally to 360. Lee, with three for 49, continued his dream start to Test cricket.

New Zealand won the day by removing out-of-sorts Blewett for a duck and nightwatchman Warne (7) on the last delivery—lbw to an arm-ball.

On day two, which was bitterly cold engendered by an Antarctic gale, Langer and Mark Waugh went cheaply. Then Slater (143, his fourteenth century) and Steve Waugh, both in need of big scores, put on 199 for the fifth wicket. Slater found his form with cuts and pulls. Waugh eschewed the hook and pull, but made the territory behind point his own with powerful cutting. He also worked the ball off his toes forward of square leg in trademark fashion. Waugh was 109 not out at stumps with Martyn, also in touch on 40 not out. Australia was five for 318 when offered the light forty-five minutes before stumps.

Waugh's twenty-second century was his first in New Zealand. Once more he had delivered in a tight situation and when critics were demanding a score. On day three, Martyn reached 78 after a 114-run link with Waugh. Australia lost quick wickets, but Waugh was in his 'zone' mode and not going to surrender his wicket by going for quick runs. He continued his policy of letting the tail have its head (if that were physically possible). It didn't quite work, although Glenn McGrath stayed thirty-two minutes for his 14 runs in a last-wicket stand of 33. It wriggled the score up to 419. Waugh remained not out on 151. He had now scored 150 against every nation. His average, which had slipped under 50, was back over the mark yet again. Waugh reached 8352 runs in his two innings in this game, which placed him sixth on the all-time run-makers' list behind Allan Border (11,174 for 156 Tests), Sunil Gavaskar (10,122 from 125 Tests), Graham Gooch (8900 from 118 Tests), Javed Miandad (8832 from 124 Tests) and Viv Richards (8540 from 121 Tests). Waugh had passed Geoff Boycott and David Gower.

Once more, the Waugh policy with the tail was contentious. If he had farmed the strike with McGrath, who was batting well, and the others (Lee and Miller), Australia could have reached 450. Nevertheless, a lead of 121 was solid.

New Zealand opened well, with Matthew Horne and Craig Spearman putting on 48. Then Lee broke through, bowling Horne with a swinging full toss. A few balls later he did the same to Sinclair (0) with a brilliant swinging yorker. Miller had Spearman (38) caught bat–pad. Then it was Warne's turn. He bowled Astle with a flipper and next ball had McMillan caught when he popped a ball up attempting to sweep. New Zealand was five for 88 and tottering. Then Cairns joined Fleming and 'did a Botham,' by slapping 6 sixes in 61 not out. He turned the game in a brilliant display of controlled big hitting. It was not slather and whack. His strokes were precise. He was more than lucky to be in after being run out. Replays referred to the third umpire showed from side on that his toe was not over the line when the bails lifted. Cairns foolishly had not grounded his bat. The third umpire, in a decision that spoiled the good work of the on-field umpires, gave Cairns the green light. The Australians felt cheated.

When bad light stopped play early again, New Zealand was five for 189, a lead of 78, with Fleming on 53 not out and looking in command.

On the fourth morning, Cairns received a poor lbw decision and was on his way for 69. Fleming (60) then pushed uppishly to Miller. Doull belted 40, and New Zealand was all out for 294, giving Australia a target of 174 to win. Warne (three for 92) and Lee (three for 87) had been the better bowlers.

It was one of those in-between scores that had given Australia trouble in the last twenty years. Slater bounced out to Vettori's first ball and was stumped for 12. The spinner was suffering with a back injury.

Blewett hung on grimly, fighting for his Test spot, but if he were to be in the side, opening didn't seem the place for him. He lasted a couple of hours for 25 before chopping on. Langer, set and on 57, slashed at a poor wide delivery and was caught in the covers. A fourth bad shot selection was made by Steve Waugh (15), who tried to a run a ball away through point. Australia was four for 144. Supporters chewed their nails. It was the sort of position that had seen the collywobbles set in before.

But this time there was no cause for alarm as Mark Waugh (45 not out) and Martyn (17 not out) stroked their way home for a six-wicket win at four for 177.

The victory gave Australia the series and the Australian record of nine successive victories, surpassing Warwick Armstrong's side. Waugh could feel well pleased with the achievement. He had captained a history-making side again.

The last Test of the New Zealand series at Hamilton (and ninth of a long summer for the Australians) was not the usual dead rubber for the Australian team. If it were victorious, it would have won three dead rubbers in three successive series, a clean sweep of all the 1999–2000 millennium summer games, its tenth Test win in succession, and now the biggest incentive of all—a crack at the world record of eleven Tests in succession that the West Indies had set in 1983–84 to 1984–85 under Clive Lloyd.

There was much to play for and this, the Australian camp hoped, would keep the fatigue of a long season at bay.

Australia dropped Greg Blewett and brought in Matthew Hayden. New Zealand brought in pace bowler Daryl Tuffey for his first Test. Simon Doull was dropped and Wiseman replaced Vettori.

Waugh won the toss and sent New Zealand in under sunny skies. The move was justified as the home team made a typical score for the series, 232, with the usual early collapse then recovery. McMillan fought back with 79 and Cairns, in a less aggressive mood, collected 37. They both fell to Lee, who took five for 77. He and McGrath (four for 58) did the damage.

Australia lost one (Hayden) for 4 by stumps and sent in Warne as nightwatchman. It slumped next morning to be five for 29 (Steve Waugh being caught Fleming off Cairns for 3). Yet even at this critical moment, the captain felt confident.

'I was not worried,' he said later. 'I knew someone would play well. I had a feeling we would get out of it, somehow.'

More than 'someone' fulfilled Waugh's prophecy. Mark Waugh (28) staged a mini recovery with Martyn to make it six for 104, then Martyn (89 not out) and Gilchrist (a dashing 75 in eighty balls) blasted a revival, only to see it frittered away by the tail. Australia's 252 left it just 20 in front. New Zealand then batted true to its series form by losing three for 58 by stumps. On day three Cairns was peppered with bouncers as he attempted to attack in the way of the previous two Tests. Lee eventually bowled him for 71 in 104 balls. New Zealand fell for 229, its sixth score under 300 in the series, which underscored Australia's strong attack more than New Zealand's mediocrity with the blade. Gilchrist completed ten dismissals for the match, falling just one short of Jack Russell's world record of eleven. Lee took another three for 46, while Warne (two for 61) chipped in to remove Astle, whom he controlled in the series, and the dangerous McMillan, whom the leggie also had the better of. McGrath and Miller took two wickets apiece.

Australia's reply chasing 210 for victory was three for 137 by stumps. Langer, on 71 not out, smashed the fastest 50 ever recorded by an Australian. It took him forty-two balls. He went on the next day to 100 in 102 balls, with flowing cover drives and fierce pulls. It was the third-quickest century by an Australian after Ray Lindwall and Jack Gregory and it was Langer's seventh Test century. It included 16 fours and took 147 minutes. He went on to 122 not out in 122 balls as Australia cruised to a six-wicket win. Steve Waugh (on 18) was hit on the wrist by a steepling delivery from new man Tuffey. He retired hurt near the end, but despite the blow was more than happy with the result.

In this game, Australia had wiped away both the dead rubber blues and the concern that it had trouble in chasing low fourth-innings totals.

Waugh had high praise for Langer after the game, dubbing him the best bat in the world 'at the moment'. On form, few could disagree. Gilchrist also came in for accolades. He created an Australian record in the match, taking ten wickets—all catches—which was one more dismissal than achieved in one game by Gil Langley versus England at

Lord's in 1956, Rod March versus England at Brisbane in 1982–83 and Ian Healy versus England in 1994–95. This, plus Gilchrist's dashing 75 at a critical moment in the game, was enough to just pip Langer for Man of the Match.

Waugh's one big innings of 151 not out gave him a series average of 53.5 from an aggregate of 214. Langer (288 at 57.6) and Martyn (241 at 60.25) were the others to average 50 or more. Mark Waugh, with 190 at 47.5, also had a strong impact. Lee with 18 wickets at 17.5, Warne 15 at 27.6, McGrath 12 at 22.42 and Miller, 12 at 25.92, all contributed to the series victory.

The skipper hardly had time to recover from the celebrations and see his family before he was repacking his suitcase and 'coffin' for a series of three one-day games in South Africa. These games had been conceived after the World Cup in 1999. The Australian and South African cricket boards seized the chance to capitalise on the interest generated by the rivalry between the two countries. The result was three one-dayers in April in South Africa and three more in Australia in August to be played under the roofed-in, new Colonial football stadium in Melbourne.

When these games were announced in 1999, the three in August seemed fine. The ACB would be breaking new ground by playing games during Australian Rules football finals—an aggressive marketing coup—and in the AFL's own stadium. But the three in South Africa appeared a mini-series of inconsequential games too far, at least to Australian cricket followers, especially after an extended millennium summer in Australia and New Zealand.

It wasn't surprising that Waugh and his men could not sustain their winning form. They lost the first game at Durban, scoring nine for 240 (Gilchrist 51, Martyn 74, Steve Waugh 2), while South Africa notched four for 241 in 48 overs, (Gary Kirsten 97, Jacques Kallis 61) and won by six wickets. Australia won the second at Cape Town by five wickets when the miserly McGrath with two for 13 off ten overs and Brett Lee, two for 33, reduced South Africa to nine for 144. Gilchrist made a world one-day record of six dismissals (all caught), which came quickly on top of his ten dismissals in the last Test in New Zealand. He was showing that his efforts behind the stumps were strong enough to justify his place even if he failed with the bat.

Australia replied with five for 145. Martyn maintained his summer-long form with 50. Steve Waugh didn't bat, preferring to use Shane Lee (8) at number three, Bevan (39), Symonds (19 not out) and Harvey (11 not out). The third game swung this way and that in much the manner of the World Cup games between these two even sides. Australia batted first and looked beaten at six for 114. Steve Waugh made a fighting 51 and was aided by Harvey (38) and Shane Warne (32). Australia made 205. South Africa replied with six for 209, the clubbing Klusener 52 not out, making up for his error in the World Cup when he ran out Donald and pushed Australia into the final.

This gave the Proteas a two–one win. It was South Africa's first-ever victory in an official ICC series in either Tests or one-day internationals against Australia since South Africa returned to international cricket in the early 1990s.

Waugh's final half-century for the millennium super-summer meant that, from Sri Lanka in August 1999 to South Africa in April 2000, he had done 'enough' with the bat in the thirteen Test and twenty-seven one-day games to justify his spot as a batsman. His team had lost two one-day tournaments in this period to Sri Lanka and South Africa and had won three, versus Zimbabwe, India and Pakistan, and New Zealand. It had lost one Test series versus Sri Lanka, and won the next three, versus Pakistan, India and New Zealand, as well as winning the one-off Test versus Zimbabwe.

It was a fine result—the best in Australian cricket history. As long as Waugh kept doing 'enough' and his team kept winning, he would retain the captaincy. He now had the best record of any captain in Test history who had led in fifteen Tests or more. His win ratio of 70.59 per cent (twelve wins from seventeen games) put him ahead of Don Bradman 62.5 per cent (fifteen wins from twenty-four games); Douglas Jardine, England, 60 per cent (nine from fifteen); Frank Worrell, West Indies, 60 per cent (nine from fifteen); Lindsay Hassett, Australia, 58.33

per cent (fourteen from twenty-four); Mike Brearley, England, 58.06 per cent (eighteen from thirty-one); Bill Woodfull, Australia, 56 per cent (fourteen from twenty-five); Viv Richards, West Indies (twenty-seven from fifty); Monty Noble, Australia (eight from fifteen); Percy Chapman, England, 52.94 (nine from seventeen); Mark Taylor, Australia 52 per cent (twenty-six from fifty); Hansie Cronje, South Africa, 50.94 per cent (twenty-seven from fifty-three); and Ian Chappell, Australia, 50 per cent (fifteen from thirty).

If Waugh sustained such a record, he would be able to dictate when he retired.

The loss of the minor one-day series in South Africa caused Waugh to re-emphasise to his players that they should never take winning for granted. It also highlighted a problem that had much wider implications than the problem of Waugh and his squad playing too much cricket without a breather. The one-day games, and to a lesser extent the Tests, had been devalued to a point where corruption through bookmakers had become a major crisis for the game. Players in some teams had been compromised and matches were alleged to have been 'thrown'.

Just before the South African series, Hansie Cronje was accused of taking money from bookmakers. He was alleged to have organised the outcome of games in a one-day series in India in March 2000. Cronje at first feebly denied he had taken money (saying, 'Look at my bank account') and then later admitted it. He was fired as captain of South Africa, which was led in the one-dayers by Shaun Pollock. A furore broke out. A tape, if authentic, seemed to condemn Cronje of asking for 75,000 pounds to throw a one-day game. The media began asking questions about the outcome of Tests, especially at Centurion in the 1999–2000 South Africa versus England series. In that game, Cronje created a Test precedent when he forfeited an innings in order to provide England with a one-day style run chase. England made the runs and won the Test. As more allegations leaked out, South African players broke ranks and made telling statements to the media. Cronje's teammate, Daryll Cullinan, said the Centurion innings forfeit by his captain—a unilateral decision by Cronje—was out of character. 'In fifteen years he never gave anything away,' Cullinan claimed.

Other accusations emerged concerning almost all cricket nations. One by former England all-rounder Chris Lewis was that some English players had taken bribes. In early May, an ICC meeting in London resolved to take tough action against match-fixers. In late May, Pakistani judge Malik Mohammad Qayyum released his long awaited investigative report into bribery and corruption in cricket and the Pakistani board banned former captain Salim Malik and fast bowler Ataur Rehman for life. Another former captain, Wasim Akram, was recommended for investigation. The finding against Salim Malik vindicated the brave stand taken by Shane Warne and Mark Waugh, who had originally named Malik as trying to bribe them in Pakistan in 1994.

In India, a crisis loomed when former player Manoj Prabhakar alleged that national icon and current coach Kapil Dev offered him a bribe to throw a match, also in 1994.

In Australia, former off-spinner Ashley Mallett, threw doubt on the Second Test in Australia in 1997–98 against South Africa. Mallett was assisting the South African team in that game in Sydney, which Australia won. He suggested that the South African team morale, selection and bowling tactics were suspicious. Steve Waugh contradicted this allegation, saying it was a tough, hard-fought game. Mallett's view seemed a stretch, but with so many accusations flying it would be a while before headline grabbers and those with genuine claims would be sorted out. To help this, the ACB appointed its own investigator, Sydney barrister and former National Crime Authority member, Greg Melick.

The broader corruption issue looked likely to engulf cricket in every major playing nation through the rest of 2000.

Steve Waugh was ubiquitous during this hectic non-playing period, even bobbing up in the papers in response to a Melbourne footballer's request for advice. He made a quick trip back to South Africa for an award. The ACB required him for certain duties. Advertising agencies and promoters chased him. Waugh returned to India for the opening of the girls' wing for the children of lepers at Barrackpore near Calcutta. He was also preparing for mid-August one-day games versus South Africa at the Colonial Stadium in Melbourne. After that there would be non-stop action, beginning with the 2000–2001 season when the West Indians would be in Australia for five Tests, a three Test series versus India in early 2001, followed by another Ashes contest in England.

During the mighty 1999–2000 millennium summer Australia had won twenty-seven matches and lost just five. It had won all Tests played. Steve Waugh had succeeded beyond even his imagination of building a team in his own tough image. Yet still he was not satisfied. There were challenges ahead, such as the world record of eleven Test wins in a row.

'We can play better cricket,' Waugh said, looking forward to the West Indies series of five Tests in 2000–01. 'We dropped catches in New Zealand and our batting could be a lot more consistent.

'I believe this [the ten successive Test wins] is only the beginning,' he said. 'We'll be fired up for the first Test against the West Indies at Brisbane [on 24–28 November]. You'll see us play some exciting cricket next summer.'

Stephen Waugh's penchant for aiming high and succeeding made it easy to believe him.

STEPHEN RODGER WAUGH

Career Statistics

Compiled by Ross Dundas

Born: 2 June 1965 Canterbury (New South Wales)
Right hand batsman—Right arm medium bowler
Test Career Debut: v India, Melbourne, 1985–86

Batting

Season	Opponent	Venue	M	Inn	NO	Runs	HS	50	100	Avrge
1985–86	India	Australia	2	4	–	26	13	–	–	6.50
1985–86	New Zealand	New Zealand	3	5	–	87	74	1	–	17.40
1986–87	India	India	3	4	3	59	39*	–	–	59.00
1986–87	England	Australia	5	8	1	310	79*	3	–	44.29
1987–88	New Zealand	Australia	3	4	–	147	61	2	–	36.75
1987–88	England	Australia	1	1	–	27	27	–	–	27.00
1987–88	Sri Lanka	Australia	1	1	–	20	20	–	–	20.00
1988–89	Pakistan	Pakistan	3	5	–	92	59	1	–	18.40
1988–89	West Indies	Australia	5	9	1	331	91	3	–	41.38
1989	England	England	6	8	4	506	177*	1	2	126.50
1989–90	New Zealand	Australia	1	1	–	17	17	–	–	17.00
1989–90	Sri Lanka	Australia	2	4	1	267	134*	2	1	89.00
1989–90	Pakistan	Australia	3	4	–	44	20	–	–	11.00
1989–90	New Zealand	New Zealand	1	2	–	50	25	–	–	25.00
1990–91	England	Australia	3	4	–	82	48	–	–	20.50
1990–91	West Indies	West Indies	2	3	1	32	26	–	–	16.00
1992–93	West Indies	Australia	5	9	–	228	100	–	1	25.33
1992–93	New Zealand	New Zealand	3	4	–	178	75	2	–	44.50
1993	England	England	6	9	4	416	157*	2	1	83.20
1993–94	New Zealand	Australia	3	3	2	216	147*	–	1	216.00
1993–94	South Africa	Australia	1	2	–	165	164	–	1	82.50
1993–94	South Africa	South Africa	3	4	1	195	86	2	–	65.00
1994–95	Pakistan	Pakistan	2	3	–	171	98	2	–	57.00
1994–95	England	Australia	5	10	3	345	99*	3	–	49.29
1994–95	West Indies	West Indies	4	6	2	429	200	3	1	107.25
1995–96	Pakistan	Australia	3	5	1	200	112*	–	1	50.00
1995–96	Sri Lanka	Australia	2	3	2	362	170	1	2	362.00
1996–97	India	India	1	2	1	67	67*	1	–	67.00
1996–97	West Indies	Australia	4	6	–	188	66	2	–	31.33
1996–97	South Africa	South Africa	3	5	1	313	160	2	1	78.25
1997	England	England	6	10	–	390	116	1	2	39.00

Season	Opponent	Venue	M	Inn	NO	Runs	HS	50	100	Avrge
1997–98	New Zealand	Australia	3	5	1	130	96	1	–	32.50
1997–98	South Africa	Australia	3	5	–	238	96	2	–	47.60
1997–98	India	India	2	4	–	152	80	1	–	38.00
1998–99	Pakistan	Pakistan	3	5	1	235	157	–	1	58.75
1998–99	England	Australia	5	10	4	498	122*	2	2	83.00
1998–99	West Indies	West Indies	4	8	1	409	199	1	2	58.43
1999–00	Sri Lanka	Sri Lanka	3	3	–	52	19	–	–	17.33
1999–00	Zimbabwe	Zimbabwe	1	1	1	151	151*	–	1	–
1999–00	Pakistan	Australia	3	4	–	58	28	–	–	14.50
1999–00	India	Australia	3	5	–	276	150	1	1	55.20
1999–00	New Zealand	New Zealand	3	6	2	214	151*	–	1	53.50
Total			**128**	**204**	**38**	**8373**	**200**	**42**	**22**	**50.44**

Captaincy	M	Inn	NO	Runs	HS	50	100	Avrge
As Non Captain	111	177	34	7213	200	40	17	50.44
As Captain	17	27	4	1160	199	2	5	50.43

Opponents	M	Inn	NO	Runs	HS	50	100	Avrge
England	37	60	16	2574	177*	12	7	58.50
India	11	19	4	580	150	3	1	38.67
New Zealand	20	30	5	1039	151*	6	2	41.56
Pakistan	17	26	2	800	157	3	2	33.33
Sri Lanka	8	11	3	701	170	3	3	87.63
South Africa	10	16	2	911	164	6	2	65.07
West Indies	24	41	5	1617	200	9	4	44.92
Zimbabwe	1	1	1	151	151*	–	1	–

	Inn	NO	Runs	HS	50	100	Avrge
First Innings	75	13	3858	199	20	12	62.23
Second Innings	52	7	2667	200	13	8	59.27
Third Innings	54	12	1479	134*	9	2	35.21
Fourth Innings	23	6	369	47*	–	–	21.71

Venues in Australia	M	Inn	NO	Runs	HS	50	100	Avrge
Adelaide	12	21	2	929	170	4	3	48.89
Brisbane	13	20	3	796	147*	4	3	46.82
Hobart	5	9	3	272	134*	–	1	45.33
Melbourne	13	24	5	943	131*	4	2	49.63
Perth	11	16	2	611	99*	5	–	43.64
Sydney	12	17	1	624	100	5	1	39.00
Total	**66**	**107**	**16**	**4175**	**170**	**22**	**10**	**45.88**

Venues in England	M	Inn	NO	Runs	HS	50	100	Avrge
Birmingham	3	4	–	147	59	1	–	36.75
Leeds	3	3	2	338	177*	–	2	338.00
Lord's	3	4	3	186	152*	–	1	186.00
Manchester	3	5	1	397	116	2	2	99.25
Nottingham	3	5	1	149	75	1	–	37.25
The Oval	3	6	1	95	26	–	–	19.00
Total	**18**	**27**	**8**	**1312**	**177***	**4**	**5**	**69.05**

Venues in India	M	Inn	NO	Runs	HS	50	100	Avrge
Calcutta	1	2	–	113	80	1	–	56.50
Chennai	2	4	2	53	27	–	–	26.50
Delhi	2	3	2	106	67*	1	–	106.00
Mumbai	1	1	–	6	6	–	–	6.00
Total	**6**	**10**	**4**	**278**	**80**	**2**	**–**	**46.33**

Venues in New Zealand	M	Inn	NO	Runs	HS	50	100	Avrge
Auckland	3	6	–	69	41	–	–	11.50
Christchurch	2	3	–	137	74	2	–	45.67
Hamilton	1	2	1	21	18+	–	–	21.00
Wellington	4	6	1	302	151*	1	1	60.40
Total	**10**	**17**	**2**	**529**	**151***	**3**	**1**	**35.27**

Venues in Pakistan	M	Inn	NO	Runs	HS	50	100	Avrge
Faisalabad	1	2	–	20	19	–	–	10.00
Karachi	3	6	–	114	73	1	–	19.00
Lahore	1	1	–	59	59	1	–	59.00
Peshawar	1	2	1	50	49*	–	–	50.00
Rawalpindi	2	2	–	255	157	1	1	127.50
Total	**8**	**13**	**1**	**498**	**157**	**3**	**1**	**41.50**

Venues in South Africa	M	Inn	NO	Runs	HS	50	100	Avrge
Cape Town	1	1	–	86	86	1	–	86.00
Centurion	1	2	1	127	67	2	–	127.00
Durban	1	1	–	64	64	1	–	64.00
Johannesburg	2	3	1	205	160	–	1	102.50
Port Elizabeth	1	2	–	26	18	–	–	13.00
Total	**6**	**9**	**2**	**508**	**160**	**4**	**1**	**72.57**

Venues in Sri Lanka	M	Inn	NO	Runs	HS	50	100	Avrge
Colombo	1	1	–	14	14	–	–	14.00
Galle	1	1	–	19	19	–	–	19.00
Kandy	1	1	–	19	19	–	–	19.00
Total	**3**	**3**	**–**	**52**	**19**	**–**	**–**	**17.33**

Venues in West Indies	M	Inn	NO	Runs	HS	50	100	Avrge
Bridgetown	3	5	1	281	199	1	1	70.25
Kingston	2	3	–	309	200	–	2	103.00
Port–of–Spain	3	5	1	124	63*	1	–	31.00
St John's	2	4	2	156	72*	2	–	78.00
Total	**10**	**17**	**4**	**870**	**200**	**4**	**3**	**66.92**

Venues in Zimbabwe	M	Inn	NO	Runs	HS	50	100	Avrge
Harare	1	1	1	151	151*	–	1	–
Total	**1**	**1**	**1**	**151**	**151***	**–**	**1**	

Batting Position	Inn	NO	Runs	HS	50	100	Avrge
3	7	–	252	100	1	1	36.00
4	8	2	196	90	1	–	32.67
5	96	16	4529	200	23	14	56.61
6	69	15	2836	177*	14	6	52.52
7	19	3	543	134*	3	1	33.94
8	5	2	17	12*	–	–	5.67

Bowling

Season	Opponent	Venue	Ct	Balls	Mdns	Runs	Wkts	Avrge	5w/i	10w/m	Best
1985–86	India	Australia	–	108	5	69	2	34.50	–	–	2/36
1985–86	New Zealand	New Zealand	2	216	9	83	5	16.60	–	–	4/56
1986–87	India	India	2	210	5	130	2	65.00	–	–	1/29
1986–87	England	Australia	8	651	26	336	10	33.60	1	–	5/69
1987–88	New Zealand	Australia	3	450	26	169	2	84.50	–	–	1/2
1987–88	England	Australia	–	137	5	51	3	17.00	–	–	3/51
1987–88	Sri Lanka	Australia	3	168	11	47	4	11.75	–	–	4/33
1988–89	Pakistan	Pakistan	2	468	17	216	2	108.00	–	–	1/44
1988–89	West Indies	Australia	3	834	17	472	10	47.20	1	–	5/92
1989	England	England	4	342	15	208	2	104.00	–	–	1/38
1989–90	New Zealand	Australia	–	–	–	–	–	–	–	–	–
1989–90	Sri Lanka	Australia	2	36	3	6	–	–	–	–	–
1989–90	Pakistan	Australia	1	18	–	13	1	13.00	–	–	1/13
1989–90	New Zealand	New Zealand	–	–	–	–	–	–	–	–	–
1990–91	England	Australia	1	228	15	90	1	90.00	–	–	1/7
1990–91	West Indies	West Indies	1	210	6	90	–	–	–	–	–
1992–93	West Indies	Australia	5	348	14	162	3	54.00	–	–	1/14
1992–93	New Zealand	New Zealand	1	246	18	71	2	35.50	–	–	1/15
1993	England	England	5	192	9	82	2	41.00	–	–	2/45
1993–94	New Zealand	Australia	1	108	3	41	1	41.00	–	–	1/10
1993–94	South Africa	Australia	1	144	10	30	4	7.50	–	–	4/26
1993–94	South Africa	South Africa	3	467	29	130	10	13.00	1	–	5/28
1994–95	Pakistan	Pakistan	2	180	5	78	1	78.00	–	–	1/28
1994–95	England	Australia	3	–	–	–	–	–	–	–	–
1994–95	West Indies	West Indies	6	144	7	62	5	12.40	–	–	2/14
1995–96	Pakistan	Australia	1	96	2	40	1	40.00	–	–	1/18
1995–96	Sri Lanka	Australia	1	114	8	34	4	8.50	–	–	4/34
1996–97	India	India	–	78	5	25	1	25.00	–	–	1/25
1996–97	West Indies	Australia	2	151	7	63	1	63.00	–	–	1/15
1996–97	South Africa	South Africa	3	51	1	20	1	20.00	–	–	1/4
1997	England	England	4	120	3	76	–	–	–	–	–
1997–98	New Zealand	Australia	4	90	6	30	4	7.50	–	–	3/20
1997–98	South Africa	Australia	1	186	10	74	2	37.00	–	–	1/12
1997–98	India	India	2	72	1	38	–	–	–	–	–
1998–99	Pakistan	Pakistan	1	120	6	41	1	41.00	–	–	1/19
1998–99	England	Australia	–	66	3	28	2	14.00	–	–	2/8
1998–99	West Indies	West Indies	1	30	–	19	–	–	–	–	–
1999–00	Sri Lanka	Sri Lanka	1	–	–	–	–	–	–	–	–
1999–00	Zimbabwe	Zimbabwe	1	24	1	17	–	–	–	–	–
1999–00	Pakistan	Australia	3	30	1	20	–	–	–	–	–
1999–00	India	Australia	4	–	–	–	–	–	–	–	–
1999–00	New Zealand	New Zealand	4	42	–	20	–	–	–	–	–
Total			**92**	**7175**	**309**	**3181**	**89**	**35.74**	**3**	**–**	**5/28**

Captaincy	Ct	Balls	Mdns	Runs	Wkts	Avrge	5	10	Best
As Non Captain	78	7049	307	3105	89	34.89	–	–	5/28
As Captain	14	126	2	76	–	–	–	–	–

Opponents	Ct	Balls	Mdns	Runs	Wkts	Avrge	5	10	Best
England	25	1736	76	871	20	43.55	I	–	5/69
India	8	468	16	262	5	52.40	–	–	2/36
New Zealand	15	1152	62	414	14	29.57	–	–	4/56
Pakistan	10	912	31	408	6	68.00	–	–	1/13
Sri Lanka	7	318	22	87	8	10.88	–	–	4/33
South Africa	8	848	50	254	17	14.94	I	–	5/28
West Indies	18	1717	51	868	19	45.68	I	–	5/92
Zimbabwe	I	24	I	17	–	–	–	–	–

	Ct	Balls	Mdns	Runs	Wkts	Avrge	5	10	Best
First Innings	28	2541	112	1108	37	29.95	–	–	4/26
Second Innings	27	2291	93	1106	21	52.67	–	–	3/51
Third Innings	13	804	41	271	11	24.64	–	–	4/34
Fourth Innings	24	1539	63	696	20	34.80	3	–	5/28

Venues in Australia	Ct	Balls	Mdns	Runs	Wkts	Avrge	5	10	Best
Adelaide	13	912	51	346	11	31.45	–	–	4/26
Brisbane	8	697	25	316	10	31.60	–	–	3/76
Hobart	2	258	12	100	5	20.00	–	–	3/20
Melbourne	3	714	36	369	15	24.60	I	–	5/92
Perth	16	891	29	420	10	42.00	I	–	5/69
Sydney	5	491	19	224	4	56.00	–	–	3/51
Total	**47**	**3963**	**172**	**1775**	**55**	**32.27**	**2**	**–**	**5/69**

Venues in England	Ct	Balls	Mdns	Runs	Wkts	Avrge	5	10	Best
Birmingham	3	168	7	87	I	87.00	–	–	1/38
Leeds	I	60	3	38	–	–	–	–	–
Lord's	–	156	6	107	I	107.00	–	–	1/49
Manchester	I	60	I	40	–	–	–	–	–
Nottingham	4	120	8	38	–	–	–	–	–
The Oval	4	90	2	56	2	28.00	–	–	2/45
Total	**13**	**654**	**27**	**366**	**4**	**91.50**	**–**	**–**	**2/45**

Venues in India	Ct	Balls	Mdns	Runs	Wkts	Avrge	5	10	Best
Calcutta	–	–	–	–	–	–	–	–	–
Chennai	4	162	4	98	I	98.00	–	–	1/44
Delhi	–	114	5	54	2	27.00	–	–	1/25
Mumbai	–	84	2	41	–	–	–	–	–
Total	**4**	**360**	**11**	**193**	**3**	**64.33**	**–**	**–**	**1/25**

Venues in New Zealand	Ct	Balls	Mdns	Runs	Wkts	Avrge	5	10	Best
Auckland	3	174	9	52	3	17.33	–	–	1/14
Christchurch	I	174	10	65	4	16.25	–	–	4/56
Hamilton	–	18	–	10	–	–	–	–	–
Wellington	3	138	8	47	–	–	–	–	–
Total	**7**	**504**	**27**	**174**	**7**	**24.86**	**–**	**–**	**4/56**

Venues in Pakistan	Ct	Balls	Mdns	Runs	Wkts	Avrge	5	10	Best
Faisalabad	I	174	9	80	I	80.00	–	–	1/44
Karachi	–	318	11	147	2	73.50	–	–	1/28
Lahore	I	138	5	42	–	–	–	–	–
Peshawar	I	48	I	19	I	19.00	–	–	1/19
Rawalpindi	2	2	47	–	–	–	–	–	–
Total	**5**	**768**	**28**	**335**	**4**	**83.75**	**–**	**–**	**1/19**

Venues in South Africa	Ct	Balls	Mdns	Runs	Wkts	Avrge	5	10	Best
Cape Town	1	189	12	48	5	9.60	1	–	5/28
Centurion	1	–	–	–	–	–	–	–	–
Durban	1	164	12	40	3	13.33	–	–	3/40
Johannesburg	2	138	6	46	3	15.33	–	–	1/4
Port Elizabeth	1	27	–	16	–	–	–	–	–
Total	**6**	**518**	**30**	**150**	**11**	**13.64**	**1**	**–**	**5/28**

Venues in Sri Lanka	Ct	Balls	Mdns	Runs	Wkts	Avrge	5	10	Best
Colombo	–	–	–	–	–	–	–	–	–
Galle	1	–	–	–	–	–	–	–	–
Kandy	–	–	–	–	–	–	–	–	–
Total	**1**	**–**	**–**	**–**	**–**	**–**	**–**	**–**	**–**

Venues in West Indies	Ct	Balls	Mdns	Runs	Wkts	Avrge	5	10	Best
Bridgetown	5	210	6	99	–	–	–	–	–
Kingston	1	90	5	23	2	11.50	–	–	2/14
Port-of-Spain	1	48	1	29	1	29.00	–	–	1/19
St John's	1	36	1	20	2	10.00	–	–	2/20
Total	**8**	**384**	**13**	**171**	**5**	**34.20**	**–**	**–**	**2/14**

Venues in Zimbabwe	Ct	Balls	Mdns	Runs	Wkts	Avrge	5	10	Best
Harare	1	24	1	17	–	–	–	–	–
Total	**1**	**24**	**1**	**17**	**–**	**–**	**–**	**–**	**–**

Best Bowling in an Innings

1	5/69	v England, Perth, 1986–87
2	5/92	v West Indies, Melbourne, 1988–89
3	5/28	v South Africa, Cape Town, 1993–94

Best Bowling: —5/28 v South Africa, Cape Town, 1993–94

How Dismissed

Dismissal	Dismissed	Percentage
Bowled	31	15.20
Caught Wicket–Keeper	51	25.00
Caught Fieldsman	60	29.41
Leg Before Wicket	19	9.31
Stumped	3	1.47
Run Out	2	0.98
Not Out	38	18.63
Total	**204**	

Wickets Taken

Dismissal	Dismissed	Percentage
Bowled	12	13.48
Caught Wicket–Keeper	24	26.97
Caught Fieldsman	32	35.96
Leg Before Wicket	21	23.60
Total	**89**	

Batsmen Dismissed

Position	Dismissed	Percentage
Openers	12	13.48
No 3	9	10.11
No 4	9	10.11
No 5	17	19.10
No 6	12	13.48
No 7	6	6.74
No 8	9	10.11
No 9	6	6.74
No 10	5	5.62
No 11	4	4.49

Batsman dismissed the most

Carl Hooper	South Africa	6
'Hansie' Cronje	South Africa	4
Chris Broad	England	3
Mike Gatting	England	3
Brian McMillan	South Africa	3
Jonty Rhodes	South Africa	3

Centuries

1	177*	v England, Leeds, 1989
2	152*	v England, Lord's, 1989
3	134*	v Sri Lanka, Hobart, 1989–90
4	100	v West Indies, Sydney, 1992–93
5	157*	v England, Leeds, 1993
6	147*	v New Zealand, Brisbane, 1993–94
7	164	v South Africa, Adelaide, 1993–94
8	200	v West Indies, Kingston, 1994–95
9	112*	v Pakistan, Brisbane, 1995–96
10	131*	v Sri Lanka, Melbourne, 1995–96
11	170	v Sri Lanka, Adelaide, 1995–96
12	160	v South Africa, Johannesburg, 1996–97
13	108	v England, Manchester, 1997
14	116	v England, Manchester, 1997
15	157	v Pakistan, Rawalpindi, 1998–99
16	112	v England, Brisbane, 1998–99
17	122*	v England, Melbourne, 1998–99
18	100	v West Indies, Kingston, 1998–99
19	199	v West Indies, Bridgetown, 1998–99
20	151*	v Zimbabwe, Harare, 1999–00
21	150	v India, Adelaide, 1999–00
22	151*	v New Zealand, Wellington, 1999–00

Highest Score: 200 v West Indies, Kingston, 1994–95

Captaincy

Opponent	Captain	Won	Lost	Drawn	Tied	% Won
India	3	3	–	–	–	100.00
New Zealand	3	3	–	–	–	100.00
Pakistan	3	3	–	–	–	100.00
Sri Lanka	3	–	1	2	–	0.00
West Indies	4	2	2	–	–	50.00
Zimbabwe	1	1	–	–	–	100.00
Total	**17**	**12**	**3**	**2**	**–**	**70.59**

Dismissed in the nineties

8	Michael Slater	Australia
7	Alvin Kallicharan	West Indies
7	Steve Waugh	Australia
6	Rohan Kanhai	West Indies
6	Gordon Greenidge	West Indies
5	Clem Hill	Australia
5	Ken Barrington	England
5	Geoff Boycott	England
5	Sunil Gavaskar	India

Most Test Appearances

Player	M	Aust	Eng	SAf	WI	NZ	Ind	Pak	SL	Zim
Allan Border	156	–	47	6	31	23	20	22	7	–
Kapil Dev	131	20	27	4	25	10	–	29	14	2
Steve Waugh	128	–	37	10	24	20	10	17	8	1
Sunil Gavaskar	125	20	38	–	27	9	–	24	7	–
Javed Miandad	124	25	22	–	16	18	28	–	12	3
Viv Richards	121	34	36	–	–	7	28	16	–	–
Ian Healy	115	–	33	12	28	11	9	14	11	1
Graham Gooch	118	42	–	3	26	15	19	10	3	–
David Gower	117	42	–	–	19	13	24	17	2	–
Dilip Vengsarkar	116	24	26	–	25	11	–	22	8	–
Desmond Haynes	116	33	36	1	–	10	19	16	1	–
Colin Cowdrey	115	44	–	14	21	18	8	10	–	–
Courtney Walsh	114	33	31	5	–	10	15	15	3	2
Clive Lloyd	110	29	34	–	–	8	28	11	–	–
Geoff Boycott	109	39	–	7	29	15	13	6	–	–
Gordon Greenidge	108	29	32	–	–	10	23	14	–	–
David Boon	107	–	31	6	22	17	11	11	9	–
Mark Taylor	104	–	33	11	20	11	9	12	8	–
Salim Malik	103	15	19	1	7	18	22	–	15	6
Mark Waugh	103	–	24	12	23	11	11	12	9	1
Ian Botham	102	36	–	–	20	15	14	14	3	–

Leading run scorers

Batsman	Country	M	Inn	NO	Runs	H.S	50	100	Avrge
Allan Border	Australia	156	265	44	11174	205	63	27	50.56
Sunil Gavaskar	India	125	214	16	10122	236*	45	34	51.12
Graham Gooch	England	118	215	6	8900	333	46	20	42.58
Javed Miandad	Pakistan	124	189	21	8832	280*	43	23	52.57
Viv Richards	West Indies	121	182	12	8540	291	45	24	50.24
Steve Waugh	Australia	128	204	38	8373	200	42	22	50.44
David Gower	England	117	204	18	8231	215	39	18	44.25
Geoff Boycott	England	109	193	23	8114	246*	42	22	47.73
Gary Sobers	West Indies	93	160	21	8032	365*	30	26	57.78
Colin Cowdrey	England	115	188	15	7624	182	38	22	44.07
Gordon Greenidge	West Indies	108	185	16	7558	226	34	19	44.72
Mark Taylor	Australia	104	186	13	7525	334*	40	19	43.50
Clive Lloyd	West Indies	110	175	14	7515	242*	39	19	46.68
Desmond Haynes	West Indies	116	202	25	7487	184	39	18	42.30
David Boon	Australia	107	190	20	7422	200	32	21	43.66
Wally Hammond	England	85	140	16	7249	336*	24	22	58.46
Greg Chappell	Australia	88	151	19	7110	247*	31	24	53.86

Test Career

Test	Date	Opp	Venue	Inn	Pos	How Out	Runs	Balls faced	O	M	R	W	Ct	Res
1	26/12/85	IND	Melbourne	1	6	c Kapil Dev b Sivaramakrishnan	13	32	11.0	5	36	2	—	D
				3	5	b Shastri	5	31	—	—	—	—	—	
2	02/01/86	IND	Sydney	2	7	c Sivaramakrishnan b Yadav	8	37	7.0	0	33	0	—	D
				3	4	lbw b Shastri	0	21	—	—	—	—	—	
3	21/02/86	N.Z	Wellington	1	7	cwk Smith b Coney	11	48	4.0	1	9	0	—	D
4	28/02/86	N.Z	Christchurch	1	7	lbw b Hadlee	74	172	23.0	6	56	4	—	D
				3	7	cwk Smith b Bracewell	1	10	—	—	—	—	—	
5	13/03/86	N.Z	Auckland	1	8	c Reid b Bracewell	0	4	5.0	1	14	0	—	L
				3	8	b Bracewell	0	3	4.0	1	4	1	—	
6	18/09/86	IND	Chennai	1	8	not out	12	48	11.0	2	44	0	—	T
				3	7	not out	2	8	4.0	0	16	0	—	
7	26/09/86	IND	Delhi	1	4	not out	39	78	6.0	2	29	0	—	D
8	15/10/86	IND	Mumbai	3	7	b Yadav	6	12	14.0	2	41	0	—	D
9	14/11/86	ENG	Brisbane	2	8	cwk Richards b Dilley	0	5	21.0	3	76	3	—	L
				3	7	b Emburey	28	41	—	—	—	—	—	
10	28/11/86	ENG	Perth	2	3	c Botham b Emburey	71	111	24.0	4	90	0	3	D
				4	—	—	—	—	21.3	4	69	0	—	
11	12/12/86	ENG	Adelaide	1	7	not out	79	107	19.0	4	56	0	—	D
12	26/12/86	ENG	Melbourne	1	7	c Botham b Small	10	30	3.0	1	10	0	—	L
				3	5	b Edmonds	49	103	8.0	4	16	0	—	
13	10/01/87	ENG	Sydney	2	5	cwk Richards b Small	0	1	6.0	2	6	0	2	W
				4	6	c Athey b Emburey	73	172	6.0	2	13	0	—	
14	04/12/87	N.Z	Brisbane	2	6	c Jones b Morrison	21	83	22.0	9	35	2	2	W
15	11/12/87	N.Z	Adelaide	2	5	lbw b Snedden	61	174	2.0	1	2	0	—	D
16	26/12/87	N.Z	Melbourne	2	6	c Jones b Bracewell	55	92	31.0	11	71	0	—	D
				4	6	c Patel b Chatfield	10	30	10.0	4	17	0	—	
17	29/01/88	ENG	Sydney	2	6	cwk French b Dilley	27	85	10.0	1	44	0	—	D
				3	—	—	—	—	22.5	5	51	3	—	

No.	Date	Opp.	Venue	How Out (1st inns / 2nd inns)	Runs	Balls	Result
18	12/02/88	S.L	Perth	c Labrooy b Amalean	20	54	W
19	15/09/88	PAK	Karachi	lbw b Iqbal Qasim / st Salim Yousuf b Iqbal Qasim	0 / 13	9 / 67	L
20	23/09/88	PAK	Faisalabad	st Salim Yousuf b Tauseef Ahmed / c and b Shoaib Mohammad	1 / 19	8 / 32	D
21	07/10/88	PAK	Lahore	c Ijaz Ahmed b Iqbal Qasim	59	121	D
22	18/11/88	W.I	Brisbane	lbw b Marshall / c Haynes b Marshall	4 / 90	23 / 167	L
23	02/12/88	W.I	Perth	cwk Dujon b Ambrose / c Hooper b Patterson	91 / 26	142 / 48	L
24	24/12/88	W.I	Melbourne	c Greenidge b Ambrose / c (sub)Harper b Ambrose	42 / 3	105 / 14	L
25	26/01/89	W.I	Sydney	not out	55	120	W
26	03/02/89	W.I	Adelaide	cwk Dujon b Walsh / run out	12 / 8	42 / 28	D
27	08/06/89	ENG	Leeds	not out	177	242	W
28	22/06/89	ENG	Lord's	not out	152	249	W
29	06/07/89	ENG	Birmingham	not out / b Fraser	21 / 43	40 / 54	D
30	27/07/89	ENG	Manchester	c Curtis b Fraser	92	174	W
31	10/08/89	ENG	Nottingham	c Gower b Malcolm	0	8	W
32	24/08/89	ENG	The Oval	b Igglesden / not out	14 / 7	28 / 12	D
33	24/11/89	N.Z	Perth	c Greatbatch b Snedden	17	48	D
34	08/12/89	S.L	Brisbane	c Ranatunga b Ramanayake / b Gurusinha	60 / 57	99 / 147	D
35	16/12/89	S.L	Hobart	cwk Tillakaratne b Labrooy / not out	16 / 134	24 / 177	W

Test	Date	Opp	Venue	Inn	Pos	How Out	Runs	Balls faced	O	M	R	W	Ct	Res
36	12/01/90	PAK	Melbourne	1	6	cwk Salim Yousuf b Aaqib Javed	20	35	–	–	–	–	–	W
37	19/01/90	PAK	Adelaide	3	6	cwk Salim Yousuf b Wasim Akram	3	3	3.0	0	13	–	–	D
				2	5	lbw b Wasim Akram	17	47	–	–	–	–	–	
38	03/02/90	PAK	Sydney	4	6	b Tauseef Ahmed	4	38	–	–	–	–	1	D
39	15/03/90	N.Z	Wellington	2	6	b Hadlee	25	75	–	–	–	–	–	L
				3	7	c Greatbatch b Hadlee	25	62	–	–	–	–	–	
40	23/11/90	ENG	Brisbane	2	6	c Smith b Small	1	4	7.0	2	20	0	–	W
41	26/12/90	ENG	Melbourne	4	6	b Fraser	19	47	4.0	2	7	0	–	W
42	04/01/91	ENG	Sydney	2	6	c Stewart b Malcolm	48	61	6.0	2	19	0	–	D
				4	7	cwk Russell b Hemmings	14	28	7.0	6	4	–	–	
43	05/04/91	W.I	Port-of-Spain	1	7	cwk Dujon b Walsh	26	54	14.0	3	40	0	–	D
44	19/04/91	W.I	Bridgetown	3	7	cwk Dujon b Patterson	2	5	5.0	0	10	0	–	L
				2	8	not out	4	11	2.0	0	3	0	–	
45	27/11/92	W.I	Brisbane	4	3	cwk Williams b Ambrose	10	19	28.0	6	77	0	–	D
46	26/12/92	W.I	Melbourne	3	3	cwk Williams b Ambrose	20	68	14.0	2	46	0	–	W
				3	3	c Lara b Ambrose	38	77	5.0	2	6	–	–	
47	02/01/93	W.I	Sydney	3	4	c Simmons b Bishop	1	4	4.0	1	14	0	–	D
				3	3	c Simmons b Ambrose	100	207	11.0	1	43	0	–	
48	23/01/93	W.I	Adelaide	2	5	cwk Murray b Ambrose	42	78	13.0	4	37	0	–	L
				4	5	c Arthurton b Ambrose	4	11	5.0	1	8	0	–	
49	30/01/93	W.I	Perth	3	3	cwk Murray b Bishop	13	32	6.0	3	8	0	2	L
				3	5	c(sub)Logie b Bishop	0	8	–	–	–	–	–	
50	25/02/93	N.Z	Christchurch	3	5	lbw b Owens	62	125	4.0	2	9	0	–	W
51	04/03/93	N.Z	Wellington	2	5	cwk Blain b Morrison	75	149	2.0	2	28	0	–	D
52	12/03/93	N.Z	Auckland	4	5	c Jones b Watson	41	77	15.0	7	19	0	–	L
				3	5	lbw b Patel	0	6	14.0	6	15	–	–	
53	03/06/93	ENG	Manchester	1	6	b Such	3	19	–	–	–	–	–	W
				3	6	not out	78	134	–	–	–	–	–	

No.	Date	Opp	Venue			Dismissal	R	B	O	M	R	W			Res
54	17/06/93	ENG	Lord's	1	6	not out	13	32	4.0	1	5	—	—	0	W
55	01/07/93	ENG	Nottingham	4	6	cwk Stewart b McCague	13	26	2.0	0	13	0	—	0	D
56	22/07/93	ENG	Leeds	2	5	not out	47	145	8.0	4	12	0	—	0	W
57	05/08/93	ENG	Birmingham	4	6	not out	157	305	1.0	0	3	—	—	—	W
58	19/08/93	ENG	The Oval	2	6	cwk Stewart b Bicknell	59	175	5.0	2	4	2	—	0	L
59	12/11/93	N.Z	Perth	4	6	b Fraser	20	36	12.0	2	45	2	2	2	D
				2	6	lbw b Malcolm	26	81							
60	26/11/93	N.Z	Hobart	4	6	cwk Blain b Patel	44	100	4.0	0	10	0	—	0	W
				3	6	not out	25	49	7.0	2	10	1	—	—	
61	03/12/93	N.Z	Brisbane	4	6	not out	147	281	4.0	0	8	—	—	0	W
62	28/01/94	SAF	Adelaide	2	6	cwk Richardson b Donald	164	276	3.0	0	13	—	—	0	W
63	04/03/94	SAF	Johannesburg	3	6	cwk Richardson b Snell	45	82	18.0	7	26	7	4	4	L
				2	6	not out	0	—	6.0	3	4	—			
64	17/03/94	SAF	Cape Town	4	6	cwk Richardson b Matthews	86	164	9.0	3	14	2	—	0	W
				2	6	b Matthews			10.0	3	28	3			
65	25/03/94	SAF	Durban	3	7	c Wessels b Matthews	64	150	9.0	3	20	3	—	5	D
				3					22.3	9	28	9		3	
66	28/09/94	PAK	Karachi	1	6	b Waqar Younis	73	85	27.2	12	40	12	—	0	L
				3	6	lbw b Wasim Akram	0	—							
67	05/10/94	PAK	Rawalpindi	1	6	b Waqar Younis	98	188	2.0	0	9	0	—	0	D
				4	6				15.0	3	28	3			
68	25/11/94	ENG	Brisbane	4	7	c Hick b DeFreitas	19	30	13.0	2	41	—	—	—	W
69	24/12/94	ENG	Melbourne	3	6	c (sub)White b Tufnell	7	21	—	—	—	—	—	—	W
				6		not out	94	191							
70	01/01/95	ENG	Sydney	3	6	not out	26	73	—	—	—	—	—	—	D
				2	6	b Gough	—	8							
71	26/01/95	ENG	Adelaide	4	6	cwk Rhodes b Fraser	0	8	—	—	—	—	—	—	L
				2	5	c Atherton b Lewis	19	33							
				4	5	b Malcolm	0	1							

Test	Date	Opp	Venue	Inn	Pos	How Out	Runs	Balls faced	O	M	R	W	Ct	Res
72	03/02/95	ENG	Perth	1	5	not out	99	183	—	—	—	—	—	W
73	31/03/95	W.I	Bridgetown	3	6	c Ramprakash b Lewis	80	141	—	—	—	—	2	W
				2	5	cwk Murray b Benjamin	65	81	—	—	—	—	2	
74	08/04/95	W.I	St John's	4	5		—		6.0	—	20	2	—	D
				1	5	b Benjamin	15	28	3.0	—	19	2	—	
75	21/04/95	W.I	Port-of-Spain	3	5	not out	65	159	—	—	—	—	—	L
				1	5	not out	63	101	—	—	—	—	—	
76	29/04/95	W.I	Kingston	2	5	c Hooper b Benjamin	21	19	—	—	—	—	—	W
				4	5	c Lara b Benjamin	200	425	11.0	5	14	2	—	
77	09/11/95	PAK	Brisbane	1	5		—		4.0	0	9	0	—	W
				4	5	not out	112	275	—	—	—	—	—	
78	17/11/95	PAK	Hobart	3	5	cwk Moin Khan b Mushtaq Ahmed	7	25	2.0	—	3	0	—	W
				2	5	cwk Moin Khan b Mohammad Akram	29	94	6.0	—	18	3	—	
79	30/11/95	PAK	Sydney	4	5	st Rashid Latif b Mushtaq Ahmed	38	104	8.0	—	19	0	—	L
				1	6	b Mushtaq Ahmed	14	26	—	—	—	—	—	
80	26/12/95	S.L	Melbourne	4	5	not out	131	252	—	—	—	—	—	W
81	25/01/96	S.L	Adelaide	3	5	b Pushpakumara	170	316	—	—	—	—	—	W
				1	5	not out	61	129	19.0	8	34	4	—	
82	10/10/96	IND	Delhi	3	5	cwk Mongia b Kapoor	0	5	13.0	5	25	1	—	L
				3	5	not out	67	221	—	—	—	—	—	
83	22/11/96	W.I	Brisbane	3	8	c Lara b Bishop	66	184	8.1	—	15	—	—	W
84	26/12/96	W.I	Melbourne	3	5	cwk Murray b Bishop	58	131	—	—	—	—	—	L
				1	5	b Benjamin	37	87	10.0	5	22	0	—	
85	25/01/97	W.I	Adelaide	2	5	c Hooper b Chanderpaul	26	62	—	—	—	—	2	W
86	01/02/97	W.I	Perth	3	5	cwk Browne b Ambrose	1	20	7.0	—	26	0	—	W
				3	5	c Hooper b Walsh	0	6	—	—	—	—	—	
87	28/02/97	SAF	Johannesburg	2	4	cwk Richardson b Kallis	160	366	—	—	—	—	—	L
88	14/03/97	SAF	Port Elizabeth	1	5		—		4.0	0	4	1	—	W
				2	5	cwk Richardson b McMillan	8	49	—	—	—	—	—	
				4	5	c Cronje b Kallis	18	55	4.3	0	16	0	—	
89	21/03/97	SAF	Centurion	1	5	cwk Richardson b Schultz	67	132	—	—	—	—	—	W
				3	5	not out	60	179	—	—	—	—	—	L

No.	Date	Country	Venue	Inns	How Out	R	B	O	M	R	W	Ct	Res
90	05/06/97	ENG	Birmingham	1	cwk Stewart b Caddick	12	20	12.0	2	45	0		L
				3	lbw b Gough	33	101						
91	19/06/97	ENG	Lord's	2	lbw b Caddick	0	1						D
92	03/07/97	ENG	Manchester	1	b Gough	108	174	4.0	0	20	0		W
				3	cwk Stewart b Headley	116	270						
93	24/07/97	ENG	Leeds	2	c Crawley b Headley	4	12						W
94	07/08/97	ENG	Nottingham	1	b Malcolm	75	102	4.0	1	11	0		W
				3	c Hollioake b Caddick	14	25						
95	21/08/97	ENG	The Oval	2	lbw b Caddick	22	34						L
				4	c Thorpe b Caddick	6	19						
96	07/11/97	N.Z	Brisbane	1	lbw b Cairns	2	6						W
				3	cwk Parore b Cairns	23	61						
97	20/11/97	N.Z	Perth	2	b O'Connor	96	161					2	W
98	27/11/97	N.Z	Hobart	1	c McMillan b Doull	7	11	9.0	2	20	3		D
				3	not out	2	18						
99	26/12/97	SAF	Melbourne	1	c Cullinan b Donald	96	188	6.0	4	10	0		D
				3	cwk Richardson b Pollock	17	27						
100	02/01/98	SAF	Sydney	2	b Donald	85	199	2.0	0	12	0		W
101	30/01/98	SAF	Adelaide	2	cwk Richardson b Pollock	6	8	7.0	2	12	0		D
				4	cwk Richardson b Klusener	34	93						
102	06/03/98	IND	Chennai	2	b Kumble	12	17	8.0	4	10	0		L
103	18/03/98	IND	Calcutta	2	c Dravid b Venkatapathy Raju	27	71						L
				4	(run out)	80	175						
104	01/10/98	PAK	Rawalpindi	1	lbw b Kumble	33	138	10.0	3	27	0		W
				3	c Saqlain Mushtaq b Aamir Sohail	157	326						
105	15/10/98	PAK	Peshawar	1	cwk Moin Khan b Shoaib Akhtar	1	3						D
				3	not out	49	122						
106	22/10/98	PAK	Karachi	1	lbw b Shahid Afridi	0	2						D
				3	cwk Moin Khan b Shakeel Ahmed	28	60						
107	20/11/98	ENG	Brisbane	1	cwk Stewart b Mullally	112	282						D
				3	not out	16	30						

Test	Date	Opp	Venue	Inn	Pos	How Out	Runs	Balls faced	O	M	R	W	Ct	Res
108	28/11/98	ENG	Perth	2	6	b Tudor	33	61	–	–	–	–	–	W
				4	5	not out	15	29	–	–	–	–	–	
109	11/12/98	ENG	Adelaide	1	5	c Hick b Gough	59	109	–	–	–	–	–	W
				3	5	c Hick b Headley	7	22	2.0	1	3	0	–	
110	26/12/98	ENG	Melbourne	2	5	not out	122	198	6.0	2	8	2	–	L
				4	5	not out	30	49	–	–	–	–	–	
111	02/01/99	ENG	Sydney	1	5	b Such	96	171	–	–	–	–	–	W
				3	7	b Headley	8	29	–	–	–	–	–	
112	05/03/99	W.I	Port-of-Spain	1	5	cwk Jacobs b Dillon	14	43	–	–	–	–	–	W
				3	5	cwk Jacobs b Collins	0	5	–	–	–	–	–	
113	13/03/99	W.I	Kingston	1	5	c Joseph b Collins	100	165	–	–	–	–	–	L
				3	5	cwk Jacobs b Perry	9	8	–	–	–	–	–	
114	26/03/99	W.I	Bridgetown	1	5	lbw b Perry	199	377	–	–	–	–	–	L
				3	6	b Collins	11	32	–	–	–	–	–	
115	03/04/99	W.I	St John's	3	5	not out	72	166	5.0	0	19	0	–	W
				2	5	cwk Jacobs b Ambrose	4	27	–	–	–	–	–	
116	09/09/99	S.L	Kandy	3	10	c De Silva b Zoysa	19	35	–	–	–	–	–	L
117	22/09/99	S.L	Galle	1	5		–		4.0	1	17	0	–	D
				2	5	cwk Kaluwitharana b Herath	19	49	–	–	–	–	–	
118	30/09/99	S.L	Colombo	4	5	cwk Kaluwitharana b Herath	14	69	1.0	0	1	0	–	D
119	14/10/99	ZIM	Harare	2	5	not out	151	352	–	–	–	–	–	W
120	05/11/99	PAK	Brisbane	4	5	cwk Moin Khan b Shoaib Akhtar	1	13	4.0	1	19	0	–	W
121	18/11/99	PAK	Hobart	2	5	c Ijaz Ahmed b Wasim Akram	24	45	–	–	–	–	–	W
				4	5	c and b Saqlain Mushtaq	28	69	–	–	–	–	–	
122	26/11/99	PAK	Perth	2	5	c Yousuf Youhana b Mohammad Akram	5	8	–	–	–	–	–	W
				4	5		–		–	–	–	–	–	
123	10/12/99	IND	Adelaide	4	5	c Prasad b Agarkar	150	323	–	–	–	–	2	W
				3	5	c Prasad b Agarkar	5	23	–	–	–	–	–	
124	26/12/99	IND	Melbourne	1	5	cwk Prasad b Venkatesh Prasad	32	68	–	–	–	–	1	W
				3	6	lbw b Agarkar	32	41	–	–	–	–	–	

No	Date	Opp	Venue			How Out	R	Min	O	M	R	W	Ct	Res
125	02/01/00	IND	Sydney	2	5	lbw b Srinath	57	124	–	–	–	–	1	W
126	11/03/00	N.Z	Auckland	4	5	c Spearman b Vettori	–	34	–	–	–	–	–	W
				1	5	c and b Wiseman	17	16						
127	24/03/00	N.Z	Wellington	3	6	not out	151	312	4.0	0	10	0	2	W
				2	5	c Fleming b O'Connor	15	22						
128	31/03/00	N.Z	Hamilton	4	6	c Fleming b Cairns	3	5	–	–	–	–	2	W
				4	5	retired hurt	18+	32	3.0	0	10	0		

INDEX

Photo Credits

Cover
John Daniels/ALLSPORT

Inside pages
Don't cuss me man: Botterill/ALLSPORT
Chin music: Jason Childs/The Age
Waugh appeals: Darrin Braybrook/The Age
Family man: Tim Clayton/The Age
Waugh's duck: Joe Armao/The Age
Waugh attacks: Ray Kennedy/The Age
No flies on him: Rodger Cummins/The Age
Mobile power: Jack Atley/ALLSPORT
Waugh room: Wayne Taylor/The Age
Portrait of a champion (civvies): Heath Missen/The Age
A rare grin: Max Nash/AP Photo
One-day wonders: Joe Armao/The Age
The brains trust: Hamish Blair/ALLSPORT
Full face of a champion: Wayne Taylor/The Age
The capping of history (skull cap—blakc): Dallas Kilponen/The Age
The cutting edge: The Age

Every effort has been made to identify individual photographers and permission holders. The publishers would be pleased to hear from any copyright holders who have not been acknowledged.